D1377828

The Role and Impact of the Internet on Library and Information Services

Recent Titles in
Contributions in Librarianship and Information Science

Barriers to Information: How Formal Help Systems Fail Battered Women
Roma M. Harris and Patricia Dewdney

The Myth of the Electronic Library: Librarianship and Social Change in America
William F. Birdsall

Academic Libraries: Their Rationale and Role in American Higher Education
Gerard B. McCabe and Ruth J. Person, editors

The Closing of American Library Schools: Problems and Opportunities
Larry J. Ostler, Therrin C. Dahlin, and J.D. Willardson

Innovation and the Library: The Adoption of New Ideas in Public Libraries
Verna L. Pungitore

The Impact of Emerging Technologies on Reference Service and Bibliographic Instruction
Gary M. Pitkin, editor

Brief Tests of Collection Strength: A Methodology for All Types of Libraries
Howard D. White

Censorship and the American Library: The American Library Association's Response to Threats to Intellectual Freedom, 1939–1969
Louise S. Robbins

Librarianship and Legitimacy: The Ideology of the Public Library Inquiry
Douglas Raber

Scholarly Book Reviewing in the Social Sciences and Humanities: The Flow of Ideas Within and Among Disciplines
Ylva Lindholm-Romantschuk

Libraries, Immigrants, and the American Experience
Plummer Alston Jones, Jr.

Preparing the Information Professional: An Agenda for the Future
Sajjad ur Rehman

The Role and Impact of the Internet on Library and Information Services

---

Edited by Lewis-Guodo Liu

Contributions in Librarianship and Information Science, Number 96

GREENWOOD PRESS
Westport, Connecticut • London

Library of Congress Cataloging-in-Publication Data

The role and impact of the Internet on library and information services / edited by Lewis-Guodo Liu.

p. cm.—(Contributions in librarianship and information science, ISSN 0084–9243 ; no. 96)

Includes bibliographical references and index.

ISBN 0-313-30920-5 (alk. paper)

1. Library information networks. 2. Internet. I. Liu, Lewis-Guodo. II. Series.

Z674.75.I58R65 2001

025.04—dc21 2001023873

British Library Cataloguing in Publication Data is available.

Library of Congress Catalog Card Number: 2001023873
ISBN: 0-313-30920-5
ISSN: 0084-9243

First published in 2001

Greenwood Press, 88 Post Road West, Westport, CT 06881
An imprint of Greenwood Publishing Group, Inc.
www.greenwood.com

Printed in the United States of America

The paper used in this book complies with the Permanent Paper Standard issued by the National Information Standards Organization (Z39.48–1984).

10 9 8 7 6 5 4 3 2 1

Copyright Acknowledgments

The editor and publisher gratefully acknowledge permission to reprint the following:

Chapter One "A Brief History of the Internet" by Barry M. Leiner, Vinton G. Cerf, David D. Clark, Robert E. Kahn, Leonard Kleinrock, Daniel C. Lynch, Jon Postel, Larry G. Roberts, and Stephen Wolff appears on the website http://www.isoc.org/internet/history/brief.html and is reprinted with permission of its authors and the Internet Society in its form as of 2000.

Chapter Three "The Internet and Collection Management in Academic Libraries: Opportunities and Challenges" by Thomas E. Nisonger appeared in a similar form in *Collection Management for the 21st Century*, ed. G.E. Gorman and Ruth Miller, published by Greenwood, an imprint of Greenwood Publishing Group, Inc., Westport, CT.

Chapter Eight "The Emergence of Business Information Resources and Services on the Internet and Its Impact on Business Librarianship" by Lewis-Guodo Liu from *Online Information Review* 24(6): 234–254. Copyright © 2000. With permission from MCB University Press.

CONTENTS

INTRODUCTION

Lewis-Guodo Liu

The development of the Internet has been evolving for almost four decades since its inception in concept and continues to grow rapidly. It has had a profound impact on society in general and on the field of library and information science in particular. In the past decade, scholars and librarians made tremendous efforts in researching better ways of utilizing various Internet technologies to improve library and information services. But the research efforts by library science scholars and librarians did not start until 1990. The research literature on the effect of the Internet on libraries and information services before 1990 was scarce.[1] Since 1990, the literature has been flourishing. By 1994, articles and books on the Internet and libraries were counted in hundreds and covered a great variety of topics including the Internet and

- academic libraries and scholarly research and communication
- bibliographies, directories, guides, and glossaries
- business resources
- collection development and resources sharing
- community networking and services
- community colleges
- electronic publishing, document delivery, and interlibrary loan
- global and international networking
- government information, policies, and role in the national information infrastructure
- Internet resources and tools
- Internet training and education
- law libraries
- legal, ethical, and security issues
- library science education

- medical and health science libraries
- online public access catalogs, indexing, cataloging, and organization of information
- privatization and commercialization
- public libraries
- reference services
- school libraries and school media specialists
- special libraries
- standards and protocols
- users' needs and human cognition
- women, minorities, the disabled, and equality[2]

While these topical categories are by no means exhaustive, they cover major areas of library and information services. This body of literature is mostly descriptive and lacks in-depth analysis. A large number of the articles and books describe Internet tools, such as email, bulletin boards, and File Transfer Protocol, due to the fact that libraries and librarians had recently started learning and using the Internet.[3]

Between 1994 and 1995, the literature on the Internet and library information services grew at a rapid rate. Over 1,000 articles and books were published in this period.[4] While the literature continued to cover the topics it had covered before, a new trend emerged: a large number of articles and books started covering information resources and services on the Internet, including those related to accounting, archives, arts, charity, communication, economics, education, employment, engineering, entertainment, environment, the humanities, languages, law, the social sciences, mathematics and the sciences, business, government, medical health sciences, and so forth.[5] The literature not only began to expand its coverage but also became more analytical.

Today, the literature on the Internet and libraries has grown so large that it cannot be easily organized due to the rapid development of various Internet technologies and efforts made to apply these technologies in library operations. A simple keyword search in *Library Literature and Information Index*, a primary electronic index of library and information science research literature, retrieved over 6,500 items related to the Internet. The emergence of the Internet not only provides great opportunities for libraries to provide better services but also poses tremendous challenges to librarians and library and information science scholars. The chapters in this volume provide discussions on current issues and trends in how library and information science scholars and practicing professionals take advantage of the Internet and make efforts to meet new challenges. This book is a continuous effort in researching the role and impact of the Internet on library and information services. It is written by scholars and practitioners in the fields of library and information science, computer science, and computer engineering. The important feature of this book is that almost all the contributors are both scholars and practitioners. They do research, publish, and work in their professional fields. They have not only witnessed and observed but also experienced and participated in the development of the Internet and used the Internet in a professional way.

This volume consists of four parts and 13 chapters. Part I deals with the history and development of the Internet. The purpose of Chapter One is to inform the reader how the Internet evolved over the past four decades or so. While there are a large number of books and articles describing the history of the Internet, this chapter is written by a number of scholars and researchers who are actual developers of the Internet themselves. The firsthand story is always worth reading. Part II examines the Internet impact on some of the major functional areas of library operations, including library administration, collection development, cataloging, interlibrary loan and document delivery, reference service, and bibliographic instruction. Part III looks at the impact of the Internet on various library and information services, including business, government, archive, media information services, and information services for the sciences. Part IV discusses Internet training in libraries. The Internet has become an indispensable source of information in recent years since many information sources are made available only on the Internet. Internet training has become increasingly important for students, faculty members, librarians, and the general public to effectively access and retrieve information on the Internet.

The Internet is in essence a means of long-distance communication in the modern time. For the first time in human history, people can access and retrieve information from the whole world in multimedia format at their fingertips. In fact, human long-distance communication has a long history. It has been evolving from the use of pigeons in Egypt (2900 BC), human runners in Egypt (1928 BC), beacons/torches in Troy (1184 BC), calling posts in Persia (400 BC), heliographs and flags in Greece (400 BC), couriers on horseback in China's Chou Dynasty (1122-256 BC), the relay system by Kublai Khan (1215-1294),[6] and kites for military communication in China (1500).[7]

Modern telecommunications were developed only in the past 200 years or so. The first electric telegraph was used in England in 1838, and the first long-distance electric telegraph was invented by Samuel F. B. Morse, covering a distance of 40 miles.[8] The pioneers of telephone started the experiment on transmitting sound mechanically using a wire over a short distance (Robert Hooke of England in 1667), a diaphragm vibrated by sound waves using electrical contacts (Bourseul of France in 1854), and a collodion membrane using a battery circuit (Johann Philipp Reis of Germany).[9] But the telephone that is capable of transmitting the human voice did not come into existence until 1876, when Alexander Graham Bell of the United States invented it.[10]

The evolution process from the earliest human long-distance communication to today's Internet has taken almost 5,000 years! The authors of Chapter One are the pioneers of the Internet. They developed packet-switching technologies, Internet protocols, and other Internet technologies that have laid the foundations for the later development of the Internet. They discuss how the Internet has evolved from the initial concepts to the application of packet-switching technology, to protocol development, to the formation of the Internet community, to the commercialization of the Internet, and to the future of the Internet. The reader will learn more about the evolution of the Internet by reading this chapter.

Library directors, like managers in other professions, are responsible for planning, organizing, directing, and controlling physical, financial, and human resources in their libraries. Their domain typically covers a number of functional areas, including library collection and technical services, reference services, interlibrary loan and document delivery, library computer system and automation, fund-raising for their libraries, and so on. The wide use of the Internet in libraries has had a huge effect on library administrators. In Chapter Two, Arthur Downing observes that the Internet has an impact on many aspects of library administration, including the management of facilities, the mission of the library, the image of the library, the internal organization of the library, staff recruitment and development, budgeting, fund-raising, and interlibrary cooperation. He also discusses legal issues related to the use of the Internet in libraries.

The Internet affects the collection development policies and practices. The emergence of the Internet provides more access to information than ever before. Library users can access various kinds of information in a variety of formats via the Internet. The library collection manager is increasingly faced with the challenge of allocating limited financial resources between traditional library materials and access services. The traditional "information warehouse" model has been challenged by the recent "information access" model. The advantages of using the Internet to access information have generated heated debates over "access versus ownership" among library directors, collection managers, and scholars. Many support the "information access" model. Some still hold onto the "information warehouse" model. Others propose an "access *and* ownership" model. An extreme example of the "information access" model is Stevens Institute of Technology. This institute has eliminated all of its print journal subscriptions. All the requested articles are obtained through interlibrary loan service, and much of the workload is done via the Internet.[11] While the "information access" model seems to gain momentum, a recent study by this author shows that there is a strong relationship between library print volumes and serials and prestige of academic programs in Carnegie Research I, II, Doctoral I and II universities.[12] The findings are astounding: the more print volumes and serials a library owns, the higher an academic program is ranked. And prestige, according to the economic theory of universities, is the only way that universities can successfully compete for research grants, tuition revenues from students, and donations from various institutions and individuals. Given the increasing costs of library materials and decreasing budgets, library directors have to make decisions regarding the optimal way to meet the information needs of their patrons.

In Chapter Three, Thomas E. Nisonger examines the effect of the Internet on collection management. He specifically discusses issues on how the

Internet has been used to facilitate traditional collection management functions; collection management of traditional and Internet resources; how the Internet affects management of the core collection, acquisitions, cooperative collection development, and staffing; and how the Internet will affect collection management in the future.

The explosion of information on the Internet has created a great challenge for cataloging professionals. There is no question that Internet information resources and services should be cataloged. As more and more information is provided on the Internet by legitimate institutions, such as government agencies, scholarly communities, and well-established businesses, people increasingly seek information on the Internet. The Internet has become an important source of information. There is also little doubt that it is impossible and as well as unnecessary to catalog the whole Internet. The debates among catalogers are on the extent to which the Internet information resources should be cataloged and how they should be cataloged. William J. Wheeler and Matthew Beacom highlight how the Internet has affected cataloging theory and practice and discuss the efforts made by cataloging practitioners and scholars to organize information on the Internet.

One of important library services is interlibrary loan and document delivery. No library, regardless of its size, can own everything given limited financial resources. An alternative is to obtain needed items through borrowing from other institutions. The traditional way of document delivery is through mail, which can take days and weeks. Interlibrary loan scholars and librarians have long been concerned about improving the speed of delivery since "access delayed is access denied." The speed of document delivery is critical for scholarly productivity. The emergence of the Internet enables many libraries to deliver requested items in a timely manner. Ariel has been widely used to deliver interlibrary loan items. Recently, many libraries set up websites where requested items can be scanned and uploaded by sending libraries and downloaded by requesting libraries. The delivery speed is greatly improved. In Chapter Five, Cindy Kristof discusses the impact of the Internet on interlibrary loan and document delivery services in detail.

Reference service is an essential part of information services in libraries of all kinds. The Internet affects reference service in many ways. The emergence of information resources and services in virtually every subject area certainly provides a tremendous amount of information that can be used to answer reference questions in a timely manner. Reference librarians can help library users find information related to government, business, education, technologies, arts, history, culture, literature, sports, travel, and weather on the Internet. The use of the Internet has also created electronic user communities. In Chapter Six, Bryce Allen discusses how the Internet has changed the mechanisms used for reference service and the emergence of electronic user communities.

Library instruction activities consist of library orientation and library instruction. Traditional library orientation can be performed in many ways including face-to-face presentation (a librarian talks to a group of users and shows them around the library in person); audio tour (users listen to a recorded tape); and video tour (users watch a videotape). While these traditional ways of library orientation are still in existence, the Internet adds a new dimension. Many libraries provide library orientation on their home pages. The library orientation page can show the physical layout of library buildings, library collections, and locations of services, such as reference desk, circulation desk, and interlibrary loan department. It can be accessed not only in the library but also outside the library from a long distance at any time. Virtual tours on websites tend to be multimedia with animations to attract and serve potential customers. The highly animated virtual library tour at Baruch College of the City University of New York, for example, contains more than nine languages to serve the culturally and ethnically diverse student body.

Traditionally, library instruction is provided by librarians using a variety of instructional tools and formats, such as lectures, discussions, video and audio aids, slides, computer-assisted instruction, and handouts. Instruction librarians have now taken advantage of the Web. Multimedia files can be created on a web page. Instruction librarians can integrate multimedia features and texts into one file. A large body of research literature in educational psychology has revealed that more effective learning takes place when more senses of a human body are utilized. Conventional wisdom, such as "Seeing is believing" or "One picture is worth a thousand words" refers to the effectiveness of the use of visual and graphic presentations for learning. In Chapter Seven, Gillian Allen discusses how the Internet can be used for bibliographic instruction and covers instructional design, writing instruction, and evaluation in the context of both academic libraries and public libraries. She also includes various samples of instructional sites in her discussions.

The Internet has been playing an increasing role in information provision. Various information services, such as government, business, the sciences, archive, medical, and media information services have benefited greatly from the growth of information resources and services on the Internet.

Business information on the Internet, driven by e-commerce, has exploded and continues to grow at a rapid pace. In Chapter Eight, Lewis-Guodo Liu discusses the emergence of business information resources and services on the Internet and its impact on business librarianship. He identifies important resources in some major business areas, such as economics, finance, marketing, international business, and real estate and argues that business information on the Internet has become a very important part of business information services and that it poses great challenges to business librarianship. Subject knowledge in business has become increasingly crucial for business librarians to effectively identify, evaluate, select, and organize business information on the Internet. Without subject knowledge in business, business librarians will not be able to maintain the quality of business information services. He further argues that given the fact that a large percentage of business librarians in the United States do not have formal training in business, it is time for library and information science schools and libraries to address this issue by setting high standards for both recruiting instructors in business information and employing business librarians.

Federal, state, and local government agencies have set up websites to provide information for and disseminate information to corporations, small businesses, nonprofit organizations, and individuals. The communication between governments at all levels and people is greatly strengthened by the use of the Internet. It is increasingly easier to obtain a wide range of information produced by governments and information about governments through websites for free. In Chapter Nine, Sherry Engel provides an extensive review of how the Internet has influenced production, organization, access, provision, and dissemination of government information.

In Chapter Ten, Carolyn Mills and Jonathan Nabe investigate the way in which the Internet affects information services for the sciences. They present a convincing case that the Internet affects almost every aspect of information service for the sciences.

In Chapter Eleven, Mary S. Laskowski provides comprehensive discussions on the evolution of media centers in the context of academic libraries and the influence of the Internet on various operations of media centers.

The effect of the Internet on archives is reviewed by Sandra Roff and Anthony M. Cucchiara in Chapter Twelve. They discuss how national, local, and university archival libraries have been gradually applying Internet technologies to preserving, organizing, presenting, and maintaining archival materials and problems faced by archivists today.

The fast growth of the Internet and Internet related technologies has posed challenges to many Internet users. While the Internet provides a vast amount of information, Internet users need to develop the skills necessary to effectively access and retrieve information on the Internet. In Chapter Thirteen, D. Scott Brandt covers the conceptual model and rationale for Internet training. He also discusses various approaches to Internet training. Internet trainers may find this chapter useful and apply some of the concepts in their Internet training practices.

In the past 10 years, the Internet has had a profound impact on library and information services. Topics covered in this volume are by no means exhaustive. Hopefully we will be able to continue to address emerging issues in future volumes.

It is the hope of the editor and all the contributors that this volume can be used by students of library and information science schools to learn how the Internet is used by library professionals and how it affects library operations. Researchers who are interested in issues related to the Internet and libraries can also find this volume useful since the chapters not only offer current discussions on the Internet and libraries but also provide a large body of literature on each topic discussed. Library practitioners can use this book to learn about current issues in their profession.

NOTES

1. Lewis-Guodo Liu, "The Internet and Library and Information Services: A Review, Analysis, and Annotated Bibliography," *Occasional Papers. No. 202* (Graduate School of Library and Information Science, University of Illinois at Urbana-Champaign, December 1995), p. 1.
2. Ibid., p. 4.
3. Ibid., p. 14.
4. Lewis-Guodo Liu, *The Internet and Library and Information Services: Issues, Trends, and Annotated Bibliography* (Westport, CT: Greenwood Press, 1996), p. ix.
5. Ibid., p. vii.
6. Gerard J. Holzmann and Bjorn Pehrson, *The Early History of Data Networks* (Los Alamitos, CA: IEEE Computer Society Press, 1995), pp. 43-44.
7. Joseph Needham and Ling Wang, *Science and Civilization in China: Volume 4. Physics and Physical Technology* (Cambridge and London: Cambridge University Press, 1965), p. 576.
8. *Encyclopedia Americana. International Edition.* Vol. 26 (Danbury, CT: Grolier Incorporated, 1993), p. 391.
9. Douglas M. Considine and Glenn D. Considine, eds., *Van Nostrand's Scientific Encyclopedia* 8th ed. (New York: 1995), p. 3035.
10. Ibid.
11. Richard P. Widdicombe, "Eliminating All Journal Subscriptions Has Freed Our Customers to Seek the Information They Really Want and Need: The Result More Access, Not Less," *Science and Technology Libraries* 14 (Fall, 1993): 3-13.
12. Lewis-Guodo Liu, "The Contribution of Library Collections to Prestige of Academic Programs of Universities: A Quantitative Analysis," *Library Collections, Acquisitions, and Technical Services* 25, no.1 (Spring, 2001): 49-65.

PART I

THE DEVELOPMENT OF THE INTERNET

CHAPTER ONE

A BRIEF HISTORY OF THE INTERNET

Barry M. Leiner, Vinton G. Cerf, David D. Clark, Robert E. Kahn, Leonard Kleinrock, Daniel C. Lynch, Jon Postel, Larry G. Roberts, and Stephen Wolff

INTRODUCTION

The Internet has revolutionized the computer and communications world like nothing before. The invention of the telegraph, telephone, radio, and computer set the stage for this unprecedented integration of capabilities. The Internet is at once a worldwide broadcasting capability, a mechanism for information dissemination, and a medium for collaboration and interaction between individuals and their computers without regard for geographic location.

The Internet represents one of the most successful examples of the benefits of sustained investment and commitment to research and development of information infrastructure. Beginning with the early research in packet-switching, the government, industry and academia have been partners in evolving and deploying this exciting new technology. Today, terms like "bleiner@computer.org" and "http://www.acm.org" trip lightly off the tongue of the random person on the street.[1]

This is intended to be a brief, necessarily cursory and incomplete history. Much material currently exists about the Internet, covering history, technology, and usage. A trip to almost any bookstore will find shelves of material written about the Internet.[2]

In this chapter,[3] several of us involved in the development and evolution of the Internet share our views of its origins and history. This history revolves around four distinct aspects. There is the technological evolution that began with early research on packet-switching and the ARPANET (and related technologies), and where current research continues to expand the horizons of the infrastructure along several dimensions, such as scale, performance, and higher-level functionality. There is the operations and management aspect of a global and complex operational infrastructure. There is the social aspect, which resulted in a broad community of Internauts working together to create and evolve the technology. And there is the commercialization aspect, resulting in an extremely effective transition of research results into a broadly deployed and available information infrastructure.

The Internet today is a widespread information infrastructure, the initial prototype of what is often called the National (or Global or Galactic) Information Infrastructure. Its history is complex and involves many aspects: technological, organizational, and community. And its influence reaches not only to the technical fields of computer communications but also throughout society as we move toward increasing use of online tools to accomplish electronic commerce, information acquisition, and community operations.

ORIGINS OF THE INTERNET

The first recorded description of the social interactions that could be enabled through networking was a series of memos written by J.C.R. Licklider of MIT in August 1962 discussing his "Galactic Network" concept. He envisioned a globally interconnected set of computers through which everyone could quickly access data and programs from any site. In spirit, the concept was very much like the Internet of today. Licklider was the first head of the computer research program at DARPA,[4] starting in October 1962. While at DARPA he convinced his successors at DARPA, Ivan Sutherland, Bob Taylor, and MIT researcher Lawrence G. Roberts, of the importance of this networking concept.

Leonard Kleinrock at MIT published the first paper on packet-switching theory in July 1961 and the first book on the subject in 1964. Kleinrock convinced Roberts of the theoretical feasibility of communications using packets rather than circuits, which was a major step along the path toward computer networking. The other key step was to make the computers talk together. To explore this, in 1965 working with Thomas Merrill, Roberts connected the TX-2 computer in Massachusetts to the Q-32 in California with a low speed dial-up telephone line creating the first (however small) wide-area computer network ever built. The result of this experiment was the realization that the time-shared computers could work well together, running programs and retrieving data as necessary on the remote machine, but the circuit switched telephone system was totally inadequate for the job. Kleinrock's conviction of the need for packet-switching was confirmed.

In late 1966 Roberts went to DARPA to develop the computer network concept and quickly put together his plan for the "ARPANET," publishing it in 1967. At the conference where he presented the paper, there was also a paper on a packet network concept from the U.K. by Donald Davies and Roger

Scantlebury of NPL. Scantlebury told Roberts about the NPL work as well as that of Paul Baran and others at RAND. The RAND group had written a paper on packet-switching networks for secure voice in the military in 1964. It happened that the work at MIT (1961-1967), at RAND (1962-1965), and at NPL (1964-1967) had all proceeded in parallel without any of the researchers knowing about the other work. The word "packet" was adopted from the work at NPL, and the proposed line speed to be used in the ARPANET design was upgraded from 2.4 kbps to 50 kbps.[5]

In August 1968, after Roberts and the DARPA-funded community had refined the overall structure and specifications for the ARPANET, an RFQ was released by DARPA for the development of one of the key components, the packet switches called Interface Message Processors (IMPs). The RFQ was won in December 1968 by a group headed by Frank Heart at Bolt Beranek and Newman (BBN). As the BBN team worked on the IMPs with Bob Kahn playing a major role in the overall ARPANET architectural design, the network topology and economics were designed and optimized by Roberts working with Howard Frank and his team at Network Analysis Corporation, and the network measurement system was prepared by Kleinrock's team at UCLA. [6]

Kleinrock's early development of packet-switching theory and his focus on analysis, design, and measurement, his Network Measurement Center at UCLA was selected to be the first node on the ARPANET. All this came together in September 1969 when BBN installed the first IMP at UCLA and the first host computer was connected. Doug Engelbart's project on "Augmentation of Human Intellect" (which included NLS, an early hypertext system) at Stanford Research Institute (SRI) provided a second node. SRI supported the Network Information Center, led by Elizabeth (Jake) Feinler and included functions such as maintaining tables of host name to address mapping as well as a directory of the RFCs. One month later, when SRI was connected to the ARPANET, the first host-to-host message was sent from Kleinrock's laboratory to SRI. Two more nodes were added at UC Santa Barbara and University of Utah. These last two nodes incorporated application visualization projects, with Glen Culler and Burton Fried at UCSB investigating methods for display of mathematical functions using storage displays to deal with the problem of refresh over the Net, and Robert Taylor and Ivan Sutherland at Utah investigating methods of 3-D representations over the Net. Thus, by the end of 1969, four host computers were connected together into the initial ARPANET, and the budding Internet was off the ground. Even at this early stage, it should be noted that the networking research incorporated both work on the underlying network and work on how to utilize the network. This tradition continues to this day.

Computers were added quickly to the ARPANET during the following years, and work proceeded on completing a functionally complete host-to-host protocol and other network software. In December 1970 the Network Working Group (NWG) working under S. Crocker finished the initial ARPANET host-to-host protocol, called the Network Control Protocol (NCP). As the ARPANET sites completed implementing NCP during the period 1971-1972, the network users finally could begin to develop applications.

In October 1972 Kahn organized a large, very successful demonstration of the ARPANET at the International Computer Communication Conference (ICCC). This was the first public demonstration of this new network technology to the public. It was also in 1972 that the initial "hot" application, electronic mail, was introduced. In March, Ray Tomlinson at BBN wrote the basic email message send and read software, motivated by the need of the ARPANET developers for an easy coordination mechanism. In July, Roberts expanded its utility by writing the first email utility program to list, selectively read, file, forward, and respond to messages. From there email took off as the largest network application for over a decade. This was a harbinger of the kind of activity we see on the World Wide Web today, namely, the enormous growth of all kinds of "people-to-people" traffic.

THE INITIAL INTERNETTING CONCEPTS

The original ARPANET grew into the Internet. The Internet was based on the idea that there would be multiple independent networks of rather arbitrary design, beginning with the ARPANET as the pioneering packet-switching network, but soon to include packet satellite networks, ground-based packet radio networks and other networks. The Internet as we now know it embodies a key underlying technical idea, namely that of open- architecture networking. In this approach, the choice of any individual network technology is not dictated by a particular network architecture but rather could be selected freely by a provider and made to interwork with the other networks through a meta-level "Internetworking Architecture." Up until that time there was only one general method for federating networks. This was the traditional circuit switching method where networks would interconnect at the circuit level, passing individual bits on a synchronous basis along a portion of an end-to-end circuit between a pair of end locations. Recall that Kleinrock had shown in 1961 that packet-switching was a more efficient switching method. Along with packet-switching, special purpose interconnection arrangements between networks were another possibility. While there were other limited ways to interconnect different networks, they required that one be used as a component of the other, rather than acting as a peer of the other in offering end-to-end service.

In an open-architecture network, the individual networks may be separately designed and developed, and each may have its own unique interface which it may offer to users and/or other providers, including other Internet providers. Each network can be designed in accordance with the specific environment and user requirements of that network. There are generally no constraints on the types of network that can be included or on their geographic scope, although certain pragmatic considerations will dictate what makes sense to offer.

The idea of open-architecture networking was first introduced by Kahn shortly after having arrived at DARPA in 1972. This work was originally part of the packet radio program, but subsequently became a separate program in its own right. At the time, the program was called "Internetting." Key to making the packet radio system work was a reliable end-end protocol that could maintain effective communication in the face of jamming and other radio interference or withstand intermittent blackout such as caused by being in a tunnel or blocked by the local terrain. Kahn first contemplated developing a protocol local only to the packet radio network, since that would avoid having to deal with the multitude of different operating systems, and continuing to use NCP.

However, NCP did not have the ability to address networks (and machines) further downstream than a destination IMP on the ARPANET and thus some change to NCP would also be required (The assumption was that the ARPANET was not changeable in this regard). NCP relied on the ARPANET to provide end-to-end reliability. If any packets were lost, the protocol (and presumably any applications it supported) would come to a grinding halt. In this model NCP had no end-end host error control, since the ARPANET was to be the only network in existence and it would be so reliable that no error control would be required on the part of the hosts.

Thus, Kahn decided to develop a new version of the protocol which could meet the needs of an open-architecture network environment. This protocol would eventually be called the Transmission Control Protocol/Internet Protocol (TCP/IP). While NCP tended to act like a device driver, the new protocol would be more like a communications protocol. Four ground rules were critical to Kahn's early thinking:

- Each distinct network would have to stand on its own and no internal changes could be required to any such network to connect it to the Internet;
- Communications would be on a best-effort basis. If a packet didn't make it to the final destination, it would shortly be retransmitted from the source;
- Black boxes would be used to connect the networks; these would later be called gateways and routers; and
- There would be no information retained by the gateways about the individual flows of packets passing through them, thereby keeping them simple and avoiding complicated adaptation and recovery from various failure modes. There would be no global control at the operations level.

Other key issues that needed to be addressed were:

- Algorithms to prevent lost packets from permanently disabling communications and enabling them to be successfully retransmitted from the source;
- Providing for host-to-host "pipelining" so that multiple packets could be enroute from source to destination at the discretion of the participating hosts, if the intermediate networks allowed it;

- Gateway functions to allow it to forward packets appropriately. This included interpreting IP headers for routing, handling interfaces, breaking packets into smaller pieces if necessary, and so on.
- The need for end-end checksums, reassembly of packets from fragments, and detection of duplicates, if any;
- The need for global addressing techniques for host-to-host flow control
- Interfacing with the various operating systems; and
- There were also other concerns, such as implementation efficiency, and internetwork performance, but these were secondary considerations at first.

Kahn began work on a communications-oriented set of operating system principles while at BBN and documented some of his early thoughts in an internal BBN memorandum entitled "Communications Principles for Operating Systems." At this point, he realized it would be necessary to learn the implementation details of each operating system to have a chance to embed any new protocols in an efficient way. Thus, in the spring of 1973, after starting the Internetting effort, he asked Vint Cerf (then at Stanford) to work with him on the detailed design of the protocol. Cerf had been intimately involved in the original NCP design and development and already had the knowledge about interfacing to existing operating systems. So armed with Kahn's architectural approach to the communications side and with Cerf's NCP experience, they teamed up to spell out the details of what became TCP/IP.

The give-and -take was highly productive, and the first written version[7] of the resulting approach was distributed at a special meeting of the International Network Working Group (INWG), which had been set up at a conference at Sussex University in September 1973. Cerf had been invited to chair this group and used the occasion to hold a meeting of INWG members who were heavily represented at the Sussex Conference.

Some basic approaches emerged from this collaboration between Kahn and Cerf:

- Communication between two processes would logically consist of a very long stream of bytes (they called them octets). The position of any octet in the stream would be used to identify it. Flow control would be done using sliding windows and acknowledgments (acks). The destination could select when to acknowledge, and each ack returned would be cumulative for all packets received to that point.
- It was left open as to exactly how the source and destination would agree on the parameters of the windowing to be used. Defaults were used initially.
- Although Ethernet was under development at Xerox PARC at that time, the proliferation of LANs were not envisioned at the time, much less PCs and workstations. The original model was national level networks like ARPANET of which only a relatively small number were expected to exist. Thus a 32 bit IP address was used of which the first 8 bits signified the network and the remaining 24 bits designated the host on that network. This assumption, that 256 networks would be sufficient for the foreseeable

future, was clearly in need of reconsideration when LANs began to appear in the late 1970s.

The original Cerf/Kahn paper on the Internet described one protocol, called TCP, which provided all the transport and forwarding services in the Internet. Kahn had intended that the TCP protocol support a range of transport services, from the totally reliable sequenced delivery of data (virtual circuit model) to a datagram service in which the application made direct use of the underlying network service, which might imply occasional lost, corrupted or reordered packets.

However, the initial effort to implement TCP resulted in a version that allowed for only virtual circuits. This model worked fine for file transfer and remote login applications, but some of the early work on advanced network applications, in particular packet voice in the 1970s, made clear that in some cases packet losses should not be corrected by TCP but should be left to the application to deal with. This led to a reorganization of the original TCP into two protocols, the simple IP, which provided only for addressing and forwarding of individual packets, and the separate TCP, which was concerned with service features such as flow control and recovery from lost packets. For those applications that did not want the services of TCP, an alternative called the User Datagram Protocol (UDP) was added in order to provide direct access to the basic service of IP.

A major initial motivation for both the ARPANET and the Internet was resource sharing. For example, allowing users on the packet radio networks to access the time sharing systems attached to the ARPANET. Connecting the two together was far more economical that duplicating these very expensive computers. However, while file transfer and remote login (Telnet) were very important applications, electronic mail has probably had the most significant impact of the innovations from that era. Email provided a new model of how people could communicate with each other and changed the nature of collaboration, first in the building of the Internet itself (as is discussed below) and later for much of society.

There were other applications proposed in the early days of the Internet, including packet-based voice communication (the precursor of Internet telephony), various models of file and disk sharing, and early "worm" programs that showed the concept of agents (and, of course, viruses). A key concept of the Internet is that it was not designed for just one application, but as a general infrastructure on which new applications could be conceived, as illustrated later by the emergence of the World Wide Web. It is the general purpose nature of the service provided by TCP and IP that makes this possible.

PROVING THE IDEAS

DARPA let three contracts to Stanford (Cerf), BBN (Ray Tomlinson), and UCL (Peter Kirstein) to implement TCP/IP (it was simply called TCP in the Cerf/Kahn paper but contained both components). The Stanford team, led by

Cerf, produced the detailed specification, and within about a year there were three independent implementations of TCP that could interoperate.

This was the beginning of long-term experimentation and development to evolve and mature the Internet concepts and technology. Beginning with the first three networks (ARPANET, Packet Radio, and Packet Satellite) and their initial research communities, the experimental environment has grown to incorporate essentially every form of network and a very broad-based research and development community. With each expansion have come new challenges.

The early implementations of TCP were done for large time-sharing systems such as Tenex and TOPS 20. When desktop computers first appeared, it was thought by some that TCP was too big and complex to run on a personal computer. David Clark and his research group at MIT set out to show that a compact and simple implementation of TCP was possible. They produced an implementation, first for the Xerox Alto (the early personal workstation developed at Xerox PARC) and then for the IBM PC. That implementation was fully interoperable with other TCPs but was tailored to the application suite and performance objectives of the personal computer and showed that workstations, as well as large time-sharing systems, could be a part of the Internet. In 1976, Kleinrock published the first book on the ARPANET. It included an emphasis on the complexity of protocols and the pitfalls they often introduce. This book was influential in spreading the lore of packet-switching networks to a very wide community.

Widespread development of LANS, PCs, and workstations in the 1980s allowed the nascent Internet to flourish. Ethernet technology, developed by Bob Metcalfe at Xerox PARC in 1973, is now probably the dominant network technology in the Internet, and PCs and workstations the dominant computers. This change from having a few networks with a modest number of time-shared hosts (the original ARPANET model) to having many networks has resulted in a number of new concepts and changes to the underlying technology. First, it resulted in the definition of three network classes (A, B, and C) to accommodate the range of networks. Class A represented large national-scale networks (small number of networks with large numbers of hosts); Class B represented regional scale networks; and Class C represented local-area networks (large number of networks with relatively few hosts).

A major shift occurred as a result of the increase in scale of the Internet and its associated management issues. To make it easy for people to use the network, hosts were assigned names, so that it was not necessary to remember the numeric addresses. Originally, there were a fairly limited number of hosts, so it was feasible to maintain a single table of all the hosts and their associated names and addresses. The shift to having a large number of independently managed networks (e.g., LANs) meant that having a single table of hosts was no longer feasible, and the Domain Name System (DNS) was invented by Paul Mockapetris of USC/ISI. The DNS permitted a scalable distributed mechanism for resolving hierarchical host names (e.g. www.acm.org) into an Internet address.

The increase in the size of the Internet also challenged the capabilities of the routers. Originally, there was a single distributed algorithm for routing that was implemented uniformly by all the routers in the Internet. As the number of networks in the Internet exploded, this initial design could not expand as necessary, so it was replaced by a hierarchical model of routing, with an Interior Gateway Protocol (IGP) used inside each region of the Internet and an Exterior Gateway Protocol (EGP) used to tie the regions together. This design permitted different regions to use a different IGP, so that different requirements for cost, rapid reconfiguration, robustness, and scale could be accommodated. Not only the routing algorithm but the size of the addressing tables, stressed the capacity of the routers. New approaches for address aggregation, in particular classless interdomain routing (CIDR), have recently been introduced to control the size of router tables.

As the Internet evolved, one of the major challenges was how to propagate the changes to the software, particularly the host software. DARPA supported UC Berkeley to investigate modifications to the Unix operating system, including incorporating TCP/IP developed at BBN. Although Berkeley later rewrote the BBN code to fit more efficiently into the Unix system and kernel, the incorporation of TCP/IP into the Unix BSD system releases proved to be a critical element in dispersion of the protocols to the research community. Much of the CS research community began to use Unix BSD for their day-to-day computing environment. Looking back, the strategy of incorporating Internet protocols into a supported operating system for the research community was one of the key elements in the successful, widespread adoption of the Internet.

One of the more interesting challenges was the transition of the ARPANET host protocol from NCP to TCP/IP as of January 1, 1983. This was a "flag-day" style transition, requiring all hosts to convert simultaneously or be left having to communicate via rather ad hoc mechanisms. This transition was carefully planned within the community over several years before it actually took place and went surprisingly smoothly (but resulted in a distribution of buttons saying "I survived the TCP/IP transition").

TCP/IP was adopted as a defense standard three years earlier in 1980. This enabled defense to begin sharing in the DARPA Internet technology base and led directly to the eventual partitioning of the military and nonmilitary communities. By 1983, ARPANET was being used by a significant number of defense R&D and operational organizations. The transition of ARPANET from NCP to TCP/IP permitted it to be split into a MILNET, supporting operational requirements, and an ARPANET, supporting research needs.

Thus, by 1985, the Internet was already well established as a technology supporting a broad community of researchers and developers and was beginning to be used by other communities for daily computer communications. Electronic mail was being used broadly across several communities, often with different systems, but interconnection between different mail systems was demonstrating the utility of broad-based electronic communications between people.

TRANSITION TO WIDESPREAD INFRASTRUCTURE

At the same time that the Internet technology was being experimentally validated and widely used among a subset of computer science researchers, other networks and networking technologies were being pursued. The usefulness of computer networking - especially electronic mail - demonstrated by DARPA and Department of Defense contractors on the ARPANET was not lost on other communities and disciplines, so that by the mid-1970s computer networks had begun to spring up wherever funding could be found for the purpose. The U.S. Department of Energy (DoE) established MFENet for its researchers in Magnetic Fusion Energy, whereupon DoE's high energy physicists responded by building HEPNet. NASA space physicists followed with SPAN, and Rick Adrion, David Farber, and Larry Landweber established CSNET for the (academic and industrial) computer science community with an initial grant from the U.S. National Science Foundation (NSF). AT&T's freewheeling dissemination of the UNIX computer operating system spawned USENET, based on UNIX's built-in UUCP communication protocols, and in 1981 Ira Fuchs and Greydon Freeman devised BITNET, which linked academic mainframe computers in an "email as card images" paradigm.

With the exception of BITNET and USENET, these early networks (including ARPANET) were purpose-built, that is, they were intended for, and largely restricted to, closed communities of scholars; there was hence little pressure for the individual networks to be compatible and, indeed, they largely were not. In addition, alternate technologies were being pursued in the commercial sector, including XNS from Xerox, DECNet, and IBM's SNA.[8] It remained for the British JANET (1984) and U.S. NSFNET (1985) programs to explicitly announce their intent to serve the entire higher education community, regardless of discipline. Indeed, a condition for a U.S. university to receive NSF funding for an Internet connection was that "the connection must be made available to ALL qualified users on campus."

In 1985, Dennis Jennings came from Ireland to spend a year at NSF leading the NSFNET program. He worked with the community to help NSF make a critical decision - that TCP/IP would be mandatory for the NSFNET program. When Steve Wolff took over the NSFNET program in 1986, he recognized the need for a wide-area networking infrastructure to support the general academic and research community, along with the need to develop a strategy for establishing such infrastructure on a basis ultimately independent of direct federal funding. Policies and strategies were adopted (see below) to achieve that end.

NSF also elected to support DARPA's existing Internet organizational infrastructure, hierarchically arranged under the (then) Internet Activities Board (IAB). The public declaration of this choice was the joint authorship by the

IAB's Internet Engineering and Architecture Task Forces and by NSF's Network Technical Advisory Group of RFC 985 (Requirements for Internet Gateways), which formally ensured interoperability of DARPA's and NSF's pieces of the Internet.

In addition to the selection of TCP/IP for the NSFNET program, federal agencies made and implemented several other policy decisions which shaped the Internet of today.

- Federal agencies shared the cost of common infrastructure, such as trans-oceanic circuits. They also jointly supported "managed interconnection points" for interagency traffic; the Federal Internet Exchanges (FIX-E and FIX-W) built for this purpose served as models for the Network Access Points and "*IX" facilities that are prominent features of today's Internet architecture.
- To coordinate this sharing, the Federal Networking Council[9] was formed. The FNC also cooperated with other international organizations, such as RARE in Europe, through the Coordinating Committee on Intercontinental Research Networking, CCIRN, to coordinate Internet support of the research community worldwide.
- This sharing and cooperation between agencies on Internet-related issues had a long history. An unprecedented 1981 agreement between Farber, acting for CSNET and the NSF, and DARPA's Kahn permitted CSNET traffic to share ARPANET infrastructure on a statistical and no-metered-settlements basis.
- Subsequently, in a similar mode, the NSF encouraged its regional (initially academic) networks of the NSFNET to seek commercial, non-academic customers, expand their facilities to serve them, and exploit the resulting economies of scale to lower subscription costs for all.
- On the NSFNET Backbone, the national-scale segment of the NSFNET - NSF enforced an "Acceptable Use Policy" (AUP) which prohibited Backbone usage for purposes "not in support of Research and Education." The predictable (and intended) result of encouraging commercial network traffic at the local and regional level, while denying its access to national-scale transport, was to stimulate the emergence and/or growth of "private," competitive, long-haul networks such as PSI, UUNET, ANS CO+RE, and (later) others. This process of privately-financed augmentation for commercial uses was thrashed out starting in 1988 in a series of NSF-initiated conferences at Harvard's Kennedy School of Government on "The Commercialization and Privatization of the Internet" and on the "com-priv" list on the net itself.
- In 1988, a National Research Council committee, chaired by Kleinrock and with Kahn and Clark as members, produced a report commissioned by NSF titled "Towards a National Research Network." This report was influential on then Senator Al Gore and ushered in high-speed networks that laid the networking foundation for the future information superhighway.

- In 1994, a National Research Council report, again chaired by Kleinrock (and with Kahn and Clark as members again), entitled "Realizing the Information Future: The Internet and Beyond," was released. This report, commissioned by NSF, was the document in which a blueprint for the evolution of the information superhighway was articulated and which has had a lasting effect on the way to think about its evolution. It anticipated the critical issues of intellectual property rights, ethics, pricing, education, architecture and regulation for the Internet.
- NSF's privatization policy culminated in April 1995, with the defunding of the NSFNET Backbone. The funds thereby recovered were (competitively) redistributed to regional networks to buy national-scale Internet connectivity from the now numerous, private, long-haul networks.

The backbone had made the transition from a network built from routers out of the research community (the "Fuzzball" routers from David Mills) to commercial equipment. In its 8 ½-year lifetime, the Backbone had grown from six nodes with 56 kbps links to 21 nodes with multiple 45 Mbps links. It had seen the Internet grow to over 50,000 networks on all seven continents and outer space, with approximately 29,000 networks in the United States.

Such was the weight of the NSFNET program's ecumenism and funding ($200 million from 1986 to 1995) and the quality of the protocols themselves, that by 1990 when the ARPANET itself was finally decommissioned,[10] TCP/IP had supplanted or marginalized most other wide-area computer network protocols worldwide, and IP was well on its way to becoming the bearer service for the Global Information Infrastructure.

THE ROLE OF DOCUMENTATION

A key to the rapid growth of the Internet has been the free and open access to the basic documents, especially the specifications of the protocols. The beginnings of the ARPANET and the Internet in the university research community promoted the academic tradition of open publication of ideas and results. However, the normal cycle of traditional academic publication was too formal and too slow for the dynamic exchange of ideas essential to creating networks.

In 1969, a key step was taken by S. Crocker (then at UCLA) in establishing the Request for Comments (or RFC) series of notes. These memos were intended to be an informal, fast distribution way to share ideas with other network researchers. At first the RFCs were printed on paper and distributed via snail mail. As the File Transfer Protocol (FTP) came into use, the RFCs were prepared as online files and accessed via FTP. Now, of course, the RFCs are easily accessed via the World Wide Web at dozens of sites around the world. SRI, in its role as Network Information Center, maintained the online directories. Jon Postel acted as RFC editor as well as managing the centralized administration of required protocol number assignments, roles that he continues to this day.

The effect of the RFCs was to create a positive feedback loop, with ideas or proposals presented in one RFC triggering another RFC with additional ideas, and so on. When some consensus (or a least a consistent set of ideas) had come together, a specification document would be prepared. Such a specification would then be used as the base for implementations by the various research teams.

Over time, the RFCs have become more focused on protocol standards (the "official" specifications), though there are still informational RFCs that describe alternative approaches or provide background information on protocols and engineering issues. The RFCs are now viewed as the "documents of record" in the Internet engineering and standards community.

The open access to the RFCs (for free, if you have any kind of a connection to the Internet) promotes the growth of the Internet because it allows the actual specifications to be used for examples in college classes and by entrepreneurs developing new systems.

Email has been a significant factor in all areas of the Internet, and that is certainly true in the development of protocol specifications, technical standards, and Internet engineering. The very early RFCs often presented a set of ideas developed by the researchers at one location to the rest of the community. After email came into use, the authorship pattern changed RFCs were presented by joint authors with a common view independent of their locations.

The use of specialized email mailing lists has long been used in the development of protocol specifications and continues to be an important tool. The IETF now has in excess of 75 working groups, each working on a different aspect of Internet engineering. Each of these working groups has a mailing list to discuss one or more draft documents under development. When consensus is reached on a draft document, it may be distributed as an RFC.

As the current rapid expansion of the Internet is fueled by the realization of its capability to promote information sharing, we should understand that the network's first role in information sharing was sharing the information about its own design and operation through the RFC documents. This unique method for evolving new capabilities in the network will continue to be critical to future evolution of the Internet.

FORMATION OF THE BROAD COMMUNITY

The Internet is as much a collection of communities as a collection of technologies, and its success is largely attributable to both satisfying basic community needs as well as utilizing the community in an effective way to push the infrastructure forward. This community spirit has a long history beginning with the early ARPANET. The early ARPANET researchers worked as a close-knit community to accomplish the initial demonstrations of packet-switching technology described earlier. Likewise, the Packet Satellite, Packet Radio, and several other DARPA computer science research programs were multicontractor collaborative activities that heavily used whatever available mechanisms there were to coordinate their efforts, starting with electronic mail and adding file sharing, remote access, and eventually World Wide Web capabilities. Each of these programs formed a working group, starting with the ARPANET Network Working Group. Because of the unique role that the ARPANET played as an infrastructure supporting the various research programs, as the Internet started to evolve, the Network Working Group evolved into Internet Working Group.

In the late 1970s, recognizing that the growth of the Internet was accompanied by a growth in the size of the interested research community and therefore an increased need for coordination mechanisms, Vint Cerf, then manager of the Internet Program at DARPA, formed several coordination bodies, an International Cooperation Board (ICB), chaired by Peter Kirstein of UCL, to coordinate activities with some cooperating European countries centered on Packet Satellite research, an Internet Research Group, which was an inclusive group providing an environment for general exchange of information, and an Internet Configuration Control Board (ICCB), chaired by Clark. The ICCB was an invitational body to assist Cerf in managing the burgeoning Internet activity.

In 1983, when Barry Leiner took over management of the Internet research program at DARPA, he and Clark recognized that the continuing growth of the Internet community demanded a restructuring of the coordination mechanisms. The ICCB was disbanded, and in its place a structure of task forces was formed, each focused on a particular area of the technology (e.g. routers, end-to-end protocols, etc.). The Internet Activities Board (IAB) was formed from the chairs of the Task Forces. It of course was only a coincidence that the chairs of the task forces were the same people as the members of the old ICCB, and Dave Clark continued to act as chair.

After some changing membership on the IAB, Phill Gross became chair of a revitalized Internet Engineering Task Force (IETF), at the time merely one of the IAB Task Forces. As we saw above, by 1985 there was a tremendous growth in the more practical/engineering side of the Internet. This growth resulted in an explosion in the attendance at the IETF meetings, and Gross was compelled to create substructure to the IETF in the form of working groups.

This growth was complemented by a major expansion in the community. No longer was DARPA the only major player in the funding of the Internet. In addition to NSFNet and the various U.S. and international government-funded activities, interest in the commercial sector was beginning to grow. Also in 1985, both Kahn and Leiner left DARPA, and there was a significant decrease in Internet activity at DARPA. As a result, the IAB was left without a primary sponsor and increasingly assumed the mantle of leadership.

The growth continued, resulting in even further substructure within both the IAB and IETF. The IETF combined working groups into areas, and designated area directors. An Internet Engineering Steering Group (IESG) was formed of the Area Directors. The IAB recognized the increasing importance of the IETF and restructured the standards process to explicitly recognize the IESG as the major review body for standards. The IAB was also restructured so that the rest of the task forces (other than the IETF) were combined into an Internet Research Task Force (IRTF), chaired by Postel, with the old task forces renamed as research groups.

The growth in the commercial sector brought with it increased concern regarding the standards process itself. Starting in the early 1980s and continuing to this day, the Internet grew beyond its primarily research roots to include both a broad user community and increased commercial activity. Increased attention was paid to making the process open and fair. This, coupled with a recognized need for community support of the Internet, eventually led to the formation of the Internet Society in 1991, under the auspices of Kahn's Corporation for National Research Initiatives (CNRI) and the leadership of Cerf, then with CNRI.

In 1992, yet another reorganization took place. In 1992, the Internet Activities Board was reorganized and renamed the Internet Architecture Board operating under the auspices of the Internet Society. A more "peer" relationship was defined between the new IAB and IESG, with the IETF and IESG taking a larger responsibility for the approval of standards. Ultimately, a cooperative and mutually supportive relationship was formed between the IAB, IETF, and Internet Society, with the Internet Society taking on as a goal the provision of service and other measures which would facilitate the work of the IETF.

The recent development and widespread deployment of the World Wide Web has brought with it a new community, as many of the people working on the WWW have not thought of themselves as primarily network researchers and developers. A new coordination organization was formed, the World Wide Web Consortium (W3C). Initially led from MIT's Laboratory for Computer Science by Tim Berners-Lee (the inventor of the WWW) and Al Vezza, W3C has taken on the responsibility for evolving the various protocols and standards associated with the Web.

Thus, through the over two decades of Internet activity, we have seen a steady evolution of organizational structures designed to support and facilitate an ever-increasing community working collaboratively on Internet issues.

COMMERCIALIZATION OF THE TECHNOLOGY

Commercialization of the Internet involved not only the development of competitive, private network services but also the development of commercial products implementing the Internet technology. In the early 1980s, dozens of vendors were incorporating TCP/IP into their products because they saw buyers for that approach to networking. Unfortunately they lacked both real information about how the technology was supposed to work and how the customers planned on using this approach to networking. Many saw it as a nuisance add-on that had to be glued onto their own proprietary networking solutions: SNA, DECNet, Netware, NetBios. The DoD had mandated the use of TCP/IP in many of its purchases but gave little help to the vendors regarding how to build useful TCP/IP products.

In 1985, recognizing this lack of information availability and appropriate training, Dan Lynch in cooperation with the IAB arranged to hold a three-day workshop for all vendors to come learn about how TCP/IP worked and what it still could not do well. The speakers came mostly from the DARPA research community who had both developed these protocols and used them in day-to-day work. About 250 vendor personnel came to listen to 50 inventors and experimenters. The results were surprises on both sides: the vendors were amazed to find that the inventors were so open about the way things worked (and what still did not work), and the inventors were pleased to listen to new problems they had not considered but were being discovered by the vendors in the field. Thus a two-way discussion was formed that has lasted for over a decade.

After two years of conferences, tutorials, design meetings, and workshops, a special event was organized that invited those vendors whose products ran TCP/IP well enough to come together in one room for three days to show off how well they all worked together and also ran over the Internet. In September 1988 the first Interop trade show was born. Fifty companies made the cut, and 5,000 engineers from potential customer organizations came to see if it all did work as was promised. It did. Why? Because the vendors worked extremely hard to ensure that everyone's products interoperated with all of the other products, even with those of their competitors. The Interop trade show has grown immensely since then, and today it is held in seven locations around the world each year to an audience of over 250,000 people who come to learn which products work with each other in a seamless manner, learn about the latest products, and discuss the latest technology.

In parallel with the commercialization efforts that were highlighted by the Interop activities, the vendors began to attend the IETF meetings that were held three or four times a year to discuss new ideas for extensions of the TCP/IP protocol suite. Starting with a few hundred attendees mostly from academia and paid for by the government, these meetings now often exceed 1,000 attendees, mostly from the vendor community and paid for by the attendees themselves. This self-selected group evolves the TCP/IP suite in a mutually cooperative manner. The reason it is so useful is that it comprises all stakeholders: researchers, end users, and vendors.

Network management provides an example of the interplay between the research and commercial communities. In the beginning of the Internet, the emphasis was on defining and implementing protocols that achieved interoperation. As the network grew larger, it became clear that the sometimes ad hoc procedures used to manage the network would not scale. Manual configuration of tables was replaced by distributed automated algorithms and better tools were devised to isolate faults. In 1987 it became clear that a protocol was needed that would permit the elements of the network, such as the routers, to be remotely managed in a uniform way. Several protocols for this purpose were proposed, including Simple Network Management Protocol or SNMP (designed, as its name would suggest, for simplicity and derived from an earlier proposal called SGMP), HEMS (a more complex design from the research community), and CMIP (from the OSI community). A series of meetings led to the decisions that HEMS would be withdrawn as a candidate for standardization, in order to help resolve the contention, but that work on both SNMP and CMIP would go forward, with the idea that the SNMP could be a more near-term solution and CMIP a longer-term approach. The market could choose the one it found more suitable. SNMP is now used almost universally for network-based management.

In the last few years, we have seen a new phase of commercialization. Originally, commercial efforts comprised mainly vendors providing the basic networking products and service providers offering the connectivity and basic Internet services. The Internet has now become almost a "commodity" service, and much of the latest attention has been on the use of this global information infrastructure for support of other commercial services. This has been tremendously accelerated by the widespread and rapid adoption of browsers and the World Wide Web technology, allowing users easy access to information linked throughout the globe. Products are available to facilitate the provisioning of that information and many of the latest developments in technology have been aimed at providing increasingly sophisticated information services on top of the basic Internet data communications.

HISTORY OF THE FUTURE

On October 24, 1995, the FNC unanimously passed a resolution defining the term Internet. This definition was developed in consultation with members of the Internet and intellectual property rights communities. RESOLUTION: The Federal Networking Council (FNC) agrees that the following language reflects our definition of the term "Internet." "Internet" refers to the global information system that -- (i) is logically linked together by a globally unique address space based on the Internet Protocol (IP) or its subsequent extensions/follow-ons; (ii) is able to support communications using the Transmission Control Protocol/Internet Protocol (TCP/IP) suite or its subsequent extensions/follow-ons, and/or other IP-compatible protocols; and (iii) provides, uses or makes accessible, either publicly or privately, high level services layered on the communications and related infrastructure described herein.

The Internet has changed much in the two decades since it came into existence. It was conceived in the era of time-sharing but has survived into the era of personal computers, client-server and peer-to-peer computing, and the network computer. It was designed before LANs existed but has accommodated that new network technology, as well as the more recent ATM and frame switched services. It was envisioned as supporting a range of functions from file sharing and remote login to resource sharing and collaboration and has spawned electronic mail and more recently the World Wide Web. But most important, it started as the creation of a small band of dedicated researchers and has grown to be a commercial success with billions of dollars of annual investment.

One should not conclude that the Internet has now finished changing. The Internet, although a network in name and geography, is a creature of the computer, not the traditional network of the telephone or television industry. It will, indeed it must, continue to change and evolve at the speed of the computer industry if it is to remain relevant. It is now changing to provide such new services as real time transport, in order to support, for example, audio and video streams. The availability of pervasive networking (i.e., the Internet) along with powerful affordable computing and communications in portable form (i.e., laptop computers, two-way pagers, PDAs, cellular phones), is making possible a new paradigm of nomadic computing and communications.

This evolution will bring us new applications: Internet telephone and, slightly further out, Internet television. It is evolving to permit more sophisticated forms of pricing and cost recovery, a perhaps painful requirement in this commercial world. It is changing to accommodate yet another generation of underlying network technologies with different characteristics and requirements, from broadband residential access to satellites. New modes of access and new forms of service will spawn new applications, which in turn will drive further evolution of the Net itself.

The most pressing question for the future of the Internet is not how the technology will change but how the process of change and evolution itself will be managed. As this Chapter describes, the architecture of the Internet has always been driven by a core group of designers, but the form of that group has changed as the number of interested parties has grown. With the success of the Internet has come a proliferation of stakeholders: stakeholders now with an economic as well as an intellectual investment in the network. We now see, in the debates over control of the domain name space and the form of the next generation IP addresses, a struggle to find the next social structure that will guide the Internet in the future. The form of that structure will be harder to find, given the large number of concerned stakeholders. At the same time, the industry struggles to find the economic rationale for the large investment needed for the future growth. For example, to upgrade residential access to a more suitable technology. If the Internet stumbles, it will not be because we lack for technology, vision, or motivation. It will be because we cannot set a direction and march collectively into the future.

NOTES

1. Perhaps this is an exaggeration based on the lead author's residence in Silicon Valley.

2. On a recent trip to a Tokyo bookstore, one of the authors counted 14 English-language magazines devoted to the Internet.
3. An abbreviated version of this article appears in the 50th anniversary issue of the *CACM*, February 1997. The authors would like to express their appreciation to Andy Rosenbloom, CACM senior editor, for both instigating the writing of this article and his invaluable assistance in editing both this and the abbreviated version.
4. The Advanced Research Projects Agency (ARPA) changed its name to Defense Advanced Research Projects Agency (DARPA) in 1971, then back to ARPA in 1993, and back to DARPA in 1996. We refer throughout to DARPA, the current name.
5. It was from the RAND study that the false rumor started claiming that the ARPANET was somehow related to building a network resistant to nuclear war. This was never true of the ARPANET; only the unrelated RAND study on secure voice considered nuclear war. However, the later work on Internetting did emphasize robustness and survivability, including the capability to withstand losses of large portions of the underlying networks.
6. Including among others Vint Cerf, Steve Crocker, and Jon Postel. Joining them later were David Crocker, who was to play an important role in documentation of electronic mail protocols, and Robert Braden, who developed the first NCP and then TCP for IBM mainframes and also was to play a long term role in the ICCB and IAB.
7. This was subsequently published as V. G. Cerf and R. E. Kahn, "A proto-col for packet network interconnection," *IEEE Trans. Comm. Tech. COM*-22, 5 (May 1974): 627-641.
8. The desirability of email interchange, however, led to one of the first "Internet books": !%@:: *A Directory of Electronic Mail Addressing and Networks* by Frey and Adams, on email address translation and forwarding.
9. Originally named Federal Research Internet Coordinating Committee, FRICC. The FRICC was originally formed to coordinate U.S. research network activities in support of the international coordination provided by the CCIRN.
10. The decommissioning of the ARPANET was commemorated on its 20th anniversary by a UCLA symposium in 1989.

REFERENCES

Baran, P. "On Distributed Communications Networks." *IEEE Trans. Comm. Systems* (March 1964).

Cerf, Vinton G. and Robert E. Kahn. "A Protocol for Packet Network Interconnection." *IEEE Trans. Comm. Tech.* COM-22, 5 (May 1974): 627-641.

Crocker, S. RFC001 Host software (April 7 1969).

Kahn, Robert. Communications Principles for Operating Systems. Internal BBN memorandum, January 1972. *Proceedings of the IEEE, Special Issue on Packet Communication Network* 66, no. 11 (November 1978). (Guest editor: Robert Kahn, associate guest editors: Keith Uncapher and Harry van Trees).

Kleinrock, Leonard. "Information Flow in Large Communication Nets." *RLE Quarterly Progress Report* (July 1961).

Kleinrock, Leonard. *Communication Nets: Stochastic Message Flow and Delay*. New York: McGraw-Hill, 1964.

Kleinrock, Leonard. *Queueing Systems: Vol. II, Computer Applications*. New York: John Wiley and Sons, 1976.

Roberts, Larry. "Multiple Computer Networks and Intercomputer Communication." *ACM* Gatlinburg Conference, October 1967.

Roberts, Larry and T. Merrill. "Toward a Cooperative Network of Time-Shared Computers." Fall AFIPS Conference, October, 1966.

PART II

THE IMPACT OF THE INTERNET ON LIBRARY OPERATIONS

CHAPTER TWO

THE IMPACT OF THE INTERNET ON THE ADMINISTRATION OF LIBRARIES

Arthur Downing

INTRODUCTION

As a library administrator, it is tempting to use the language of technological utopianism to describe the impact of the Internet on libraries. Digital collections, common communication protocols, wireless networks, gigabit-per-second data transmission, handheld computers, the astounding growth of the World Wide Web, and other technological advances, especially those related to the Internet, seem to offer libraries boundless opportunities to reach a level of service that was once considered an unattainable ideal. The ethos of the Internet, unrestricted universal access to information, seems closely akin to the Library Bill of Rights and the democratic principles of public education commonly attributed to the development of public libraries in the United States. The future of libraries as guided by the Internet and its associated technologies may appear to represent a path toward perfection, a future that holds the promise of barrier-free information access. Although library administrators may draw on such rhetoric to inspire staff (or themselves), persuade funders to support technology, and shape an ideal to aspire toward, nonetheless they are aware that in practice the Internet presents libraries with as many challenges to fulfilling their missions as it offers them opportunities to excel.

This chapter reviews how the Internet has already influenced the core areas of responsibility associated with library administration, considers the future directions of these areas, and identifies questions surrounding the relationship between the Internet and libraries that need to be addressed by library administrators. The discussion is organized around the following topics:

the management of facilities, the mission of the library, the presentation of the image of the library, the internal organization of the library, staff recruitment and development, budgeting, fund-raising, interlibrary cooperation, and legal issues. This analysis does not treat the impact of the Internet on the management of operations at the department level of a library.

Several cross-cutting themes are evident in the impact of the Internet on the aspects of library administration addressed below. (1) Globalization. The globalizing influences of the Internet have altered libraries in a variety of ways. The geographic limitations on a library's user community have been reduced substantially. As Simcox predicted, "It is likely that all libraries will find themselves a part of a world-wide community, in other words, the world will come to our doors via the Web."[1] The range of materials and the ideas represented in them that libraries had been able to offer their users have been increased and diversified. (2) Rising Expectations of Library Users. The immediacy of the Internet has increased demands to respond rapidly to information requests 24 hours per day, seven days per week. The delivery of information on demand is a growing expectation among users who are less understanding of why libraries cannot match the response times and services of commercial Internet content providers and service organizations. There is also an attitude that whatever is possible to accomplish using Internet technology should be available to library users without limits. (3) Open Access to Resources. The Internet has always operated from an extraordinary presumption of resource sharing, whether based on remote login to another institution's computer network or access to multimedia files on someone else's Web server. As participants in the Internet, libraries are expected to contribute as much information as possible to the public domain. Information seekers are encouraged by the mass media to believe that the information they need must certainly be available on the Internet, because everyone shares his or her information and everyone has expended the resources to convert data to digital format. (4) Computer-Mediated Communication. Relationships between libraries and their users are increasingly developed online. Organizational communication in the library is also being transformed by the growing use of electronic mail, groupware, and Internet conferencing. Research suggests that strong differences exist between face-to-face communication and computer-mediated communication with respect to the accomplishment of collaborative problem solving (e.g., reference) and the development of interpersonal relationships, but the methodological and theoretical limitations of this work to date prevent the adoption of universals.[2, 3]

LIBRARY BUILDINGS

One of the primary responsibilities of a library administrator is the maintenance of physical library facilities, including ultimate responsibility for routine upkeep and repairs, disaster recovery, space planning and utilization, and new construction. The growth of Internet-based information services in libraries has led to new requirements for library buildings.[4] Building infrastructure must now include sufficient data cabling and ports, high-speed telecommunication lines, and uninterruptible power supplies. Space allocation must take into account wiring closets, servers, routers, and other computer equipment. Public spaces and staff work areas may need to be retrofitted or redesigned to meet the hardware and infrastructure requirements related to Internet connectivity. Rapid changes in technology have made it difficult for library administrators to plan facilities that will be effective and economic in the delivery of electronic information services by the time a major construction project has been completed, let alone remain technologically relevant several years hence.

Library administrators are trying to understand the role of the physical library building within a vision of the library as an increasingly "virtual" institution.[5] Most administrators have had at least one experience dissuading someone (perhaps a legislator, library board member, or an executive in the parent organization) who has concluded that libraries are obsolete because "everything is now on the Web." The overestimation of the resources available on the Internet and the undervaluing of library services have led to the closing of physical libraries as an effort to trim costs by substituting digital collections and online services. To help counter these moves, the Trends Awareness Committee of the Public Relations Section of the American Library Association issued a list of advantages and disadvantages of virtual libraries as a tool for defending the allocation of resources to support physical libraries.[6] The growth of transregional and virtual universities has led higher education administrators and accreditation agencies to reconsider the necessity of physical libraries in the digital information age. Recently, the Middle States Commission on Higher Education surveyed academic library directors in its region regarding questions such as, "Is a library an absolute prerequisite for a degree-granting institution of higher education, or is it instead an indicator of some increasing level of quality above an acceptable minimum? If a physical library is not a prerequisite, what types or combinations of electronic resources could be considered acceptable substitutes?"[7] The commission concluded that for the moment, traditional libraries are still necessary to support an entire curriculum of study, although digital collections may be sufficient for certain majors or introductory courses.[8]

Rather than focusing on the attainment of an idealized concept of totally digital collections, it may be wiser for library administrators to work within a hybrid model that assumes the heterogeneity of collections, including both print and electronic formats for quite a while into the future.[9] Richard E. Lucier describes libraries developing digital collections as being in a transitional phase in which "information space" complements "information place."[10] The challenge for library administrators lies in the effective integration of these two dimensions of library service while working toward a digital future.

Although the extension of libraries into cyberspace has the potential for freeing administrators and library users from many limitations associated with operating in a physical facility, it has been common for the navigation of virtual libraries to be designed around metaphors based on traditional library buildings.

For example, the Internet Public Library, a library "created on and for the Internet community,"[11] is structured around the service points common in a physical library. Thus, the Internet Public Library Website has a reference center allowing for questions to be submitted and answered by e-mail, a reading room containing links to thousands of full-text digital publications, an exhibit hall for curated multimedia exhibits, as well as separate young adult and children's areas. As Ann Peterson Bishop and Susan Leigh Star point out, the use of a digital library interface that mimics a physical library is problematic.[12] On the one hand, it offers a navigational framework that is familiar to many users, which may ease and quicken the transition to use of digital resources. Nonetheless, mimicry may represent a lack of creative vision and be founded on an erroneous assumption that physical surroundings provide the most salient cues for orienting oneself in cyberspace. This assumption is certainly less likely to apply to a generation of Internet users who are more familiar with the conventions of the World Wide Web than with the organization of library buildings or library catalogs.

As we anticipate the shift of library-user contact from a face-to-face encounter to an Internet-mediated one, we should keep in mind the role that library architecture plays in creating social environments that reflect and reproduce social and political values.[13] In addition, elements of library architecture reinforce discourse rules that govern social interaction between librarians and users in the library setting. For example, the arrangement of the reference desk helps determine the nature of the service transactions between reference librarians and information seekers, particularly with respect to defining relative status and interpersonal distance. Despite the tendency to design virtual libraries to resemble physical libraries, it is unlikely that libraries will be able to maintain the type of social interactions that are enforced through architectural design of library buildings. Communication over the Internet fosters features of social interaction that are not generally promoted in physical libraries such as malleable identities, group collaboration in information seeking, and the rapid development of communities around common interests.

Rob Kling reminds us that the way in which an institution pursues computerization reflects the social values it prioritizes.[14] Will digital libraries be designed so that the library "doors" are open to all potential users, or will economic, educational, and linguistic barriers restrict access? The critical decisions that library administrators will reach regarding system design and content will determine the fundamental nature of what it means to "use a library" and recast the relationship between individuals and the library as an institution. Fortunately, Web technology already allows individuals to customize their online work environments. As a result, library users increasingly will be able to design an interface with their library that is consistent with their personal preferences and information needs. The development of MyLibrary at North Carolina State University represents a promising step toward integration of library services and Internet resources through an individualized interface.[15]

THE MISSION OF THE LIBRARY

As part of their long-range planning responsibilities, library administrators monitor institutional priorities as well as environments that are external and internal to the library to determine when the mission of the library needs revision. The Internet has required library administrators to reinterpret the roles of the library as information provider, producer, gatekeeper, and repository. The Internet has also presented libraries with opportunities to expand the scope of their responsibilities. As a result, library administrators have had to make strategic decisions that redefine the relationship of the library to its users and the position of the library within a larger organization or community.

The effect of the Internet on a library administrator's perception of his or her institution is frequently evident in the official mission statement of the library. In many cases the Internet is specified as a resource provided by the library,[16] but more often the reference is indirect. For example, in their mission statements, small public libraries may assign themselves the responsibility to provide local users with access to "worldwide" or "global" information resources. Prior to the World Wide Web, this charge would have been beyond the capability of libraries without a research focus. While technology has been an increasingly visible aspect of library operations since the early 1970s, library mission statements generally did not mention providing access to information technology or maintaining levels of technology until Internet access became available to library users. Similarly, the inclusion of language declaring a commitment to intellectual freedom was always important for libraries that feared attempts to ban books. However, the range of materials available over the Internet has made the necessity to defend intellectual freedom more widespread, as discussed in greater detail in the section on legal issues below. The effects of the Internet on the mission of the library are also reflected in the textual references and Web links to Internet use policies that are embedded in the mission statements posted on library websites.

The Internet has helped reshape the mission of libraries by offering library administrators new roles for their institutions. Although Internet connectivity was available originally in the computing departments of organizations, the library was often the first department to offer other staff access to the Internet along with training. Forward-thinking library administrators were able to parlay this service into more prominent roles in technology management within their organizations. One of the standard organizational models of technology management in colleges and universities now involves academic computing operations reporting to the library administration. Public libraries have established themselves as key sources of Internet access for the general population. A survey conducted in 1998 by the National Commission on Libraries and Information Science (NCLIS) revealed that 73.3% of all public library outlets, including main libraries and branches provided public Internet access.[17] The latest Library Link survey by MCI identifies public libraries as the primary location for Internet access among the 16% of respondents who use the Internet from places other than home, work, or school in the United States.[18] In Canada, public libraries also rank first among public points of access to the Internet, and they have overwhelming support among Canadians to serve in this role.[19]

Library administrators have had to reach critical decisions regarding the place of their libraries in the information environment emerging around the Internet. By taking the approach that the traditional mission of the library may be extended seamlessly to cover information services related to the Internet, the profession has staked out a prominent place in the digital age. The commitment of public library administrators to offer Internet access has helped bridge the demographic discrepancies known as the "Digital Divide." Some library administrators have acted to extend library responsibilities to areas such as electronic publishing and distance education. This is a rapidly changing scenario that requires vigilance, responsiveness, creativity, and leadership from library administrators if the relevance of libraries is to be maintained.

LIBRARY IMAGE

Once the mission of a library has been established and the preferred roles of the library vis-à-vis its users, its larger community, and the profession have been identified, the library administration must present a consistent image of the library that advances these goals. In the past, librarians managed public relations primarily through face-to-face presentations, in-house publications, and print media, although occasionally libraries have had the opportunity to take advantage of broadcast media to reach a larger or geographically remote audience. Generally, libraries concentrated on encouraging use among their primary clientele and were limited to the institutional image projected through public relations activities controlled by their parent organizations. The Internet has radically altered the nature of public relations management by libraries by creating new forums in which libraries must be prepared to advance an image; enabling immediate contact with a global audience; and offering powerful new forms of media to convey messages.

Libraries tend to undertake the development of their websites as a routine task with the primary objective being information retrieval by users, rather than message transmission by the library. It is important that library administrators understand the role a website may play in advancing the strategic goals of the library through image presentation and management. It is not uncommon for a library website to be visited tens of thousands of times per month. This audience includes potential funders, prospective employees, external evaluators, and other decision makers whose opinions of the library will be shaped by the messages they receive about the organization, including its priorities and capabilities as represented on the website. Research suggests that image creation and maintenance are the major functions of corporate home pages across countries as culturally diverse as the United States, Germany, and

Japan.[20] The Web is considered by corporate managers to be an effective means of promoting both short-term and long-term promotional objectives, the latter being effective for creating corporate awareness, "branding," and communicating corporate image.[21] One study indicates that the great majority of Fortune 500 companies use their websites to address issues of corporate social responsibility issues, although few engage in interactive dialogue with the public over their websites.[22]

Three aspects of a library website represent the most basic level of concern for image presentation. (1) Design of the website. The style and organization of a library website may create impressions of the library as research-oriented, conservative, inviting, innovative, relaxed, serious, service-oriented, culturally-diverse, and so on. (2) Technical features of the website. Libraries that would like to convey the message that they have a high degree of expertise with information technology may opt to include more advanced Internet applications on their sites. If the use of these sophisticated applications requires later versions of browsers, special plug-ins, higher bandwidth, or other features that would disfranchise users, it may be necessary to offer the same content in several formats. (3) Content of the website. Does the content of the website convey the impression that the library concentrates on the information needs of researchers or the general public? Does original content posted to the site suggest a subject specialization for the library? It is possible to represent multiple missions online, but the integration of these messages is more difficult to accomplish. One of the advantages of the Web as an information medium is that it allows organizations to serve a variety of publics more easily than traditional media.[23] A standard method of addressing multiple audiences is to provide a special portal for each potential user group (e.g., alumni, staff, guests, children, Spanish-speakers). Thus, a library may tailor a user's experience of the website and an intended impression of the library to a group affiliation.

One of the features of image management offered by the Internet is the gatekeeping role that organizational home pages may play.[24] In addition to setting an image through the general design and content choices described above, library administrators may take an active role in directing users toward conclusions about their libraries. Library websites frequently include newsletters or press releases that chronicle staff recruitment, library acquisitions, technological developments, special events, gifts, and other accomplishments. A library administrator may use these publications to depict the library in terms consistent with its mission and strategic goals.

Not only does the Web enable administrators to circulate the news to a much larger, potentially global audience, but some features of the Internet allow libraries to attract readers who otherwise might not have learned of the library. By registering with Internet search engines, libraries will receive visits from individuals searching for information on certain topics that are represented by material on the library's website. The visitor then establishes a cognitive association between the library and that subject area. For this reason, it is especially important for libraries that wish to take advantage of the Web to establish a global reputation for expertise in a particular subject area to contribute original content to the Web. For example, libraries with small, specialized collections need only digitize and share images, manuscripts, or finding aids to special collections in order to acquire a degree of notoriety that they could not have otherwise afforded through traditional methods of publicity. The Web is especially effective in establishing the reputation of a library, because the association is made to the user at the moment when the information is needed; it is not a link between an institution and a subject that must be remembered in case it is needed at some future time. The same approach may be used to establish a connection between a library and areas of specialization in librarianship. Through the materials they have posted on their websites and the Web organizational tools they have created, libraries have used the Internet to create reputations for themselves in areas such as government documents, intellectual property, and database licensing.

The Internet also helps organizations respond to the presentation of information about them by others. One of the characteristics of the Internet is its ability to amplify both positive and negative images of an organization through rapid dissemination of information via newsgroups, chat rooms, e-mail lists, and critical websites.[25] Corporations increasingly monitor the posting of information about their organizations on the Internet and respond accordingly, whether by engaging in a dialogue regarding the issue or presenting evidence to counter a negative impression. Opinions about libraries abound on the Internet in Usenet discussion groups, listservs, and website message boards. At the very least library administrators need to monitor these opinions to understand how their libraries are being perceived by the public. A further step would involve the development of an organizational strategy to correct inaccurate information or to publicize remedies that have been taken to solve legitimate problems previously announced on the Web.

The Internet offers an attractive and effective forum for individuals and groups to air their criticisms. Consequently, new "gripe sites" appear on the Web daily. One of the services of several commercial websites directed to job seekers is to provide insider information on companies and colleges through message boards containing postings from employees, students, and alumni. In some cases large corporations and government agencies have had websites dedicated solely to posting information, usually complaints, about the company and its practices. Although reports from the mainstream press may be posted to these sites, the items may also be the unsubstantiated opinions of individuals.

Although the creation of gripe sites has concentrated on commercial organizations and government agencies, libraries are equally open to criticism via the Web, as the following case demonstrates. In 1997 in response to requests from students, faculty, and library staff, the Newman Library of Baruch College designated 12 computer workstations near the reference desk for research purposes only. General surfing of the Internet was still available on the other 80 workstations available throughout the library and an additional 300 workstations located one floor above the library in a student computing laboratory. Given this ready availability of computers, the library did not expect a significant negative reaction, especially since library users had repeatedly complained that they could not access subscription full-text databases, because all workstations were occupied by students who were chatting online, reading email, or playing games. The browsers on the restricted workstations were modified to operate in kiosk mode in order to discourage users from violating the posted policy. Within a few days a group of students created a website to protest the use of kiosk mode in the library and offer tips for circumventing the browser restrictions. The protest website issued a call for all students to "unite against kiosk mode!", incorporating images of Mao Tse-Tung and Vladimir Lenin that resonated with the large international student population at the college. The protest group argued that the browser restrictions represented a form of censorship and violated the rights of users to freely surf the Internet. Following negotiations with the student leadership, the protest ended with a commitment from the library administration that restrictions would not expand to other areas of the library. The student protest web page was immediately modified to show the dove carrying an olive branch from the Picasso painting Peace with the declaration that "Student protest is suspended to demonstrate good will."[26] The organizers of this grassroots campaign demonstrated a keen understanding of how a website can rapidly mobilize political support through persuasive use of multimedia.

Libraries accustomed to responding to criticism in a printed school newspaper or a letter of complaint to an elected official will have to adjust their strategies for the Web. Dissatisfied library users may now take their grievances to a global public arena. In addition to responding to negative images, libraries must also use the Internet to shape public discourse around issues of importance to the library community. Library administrators must become adept at using the Web to move to a more active presentation of the image of their institutions and the setting of public agendas with respect to issues such as funding, intellectual freedom, and fair use of intellectual property.

INTERNAL ORGANIZATION

As noted in the previous section, a library website may serve as a tool for projecting an image of the institution to achieve its strategic goals. Toward this end, a particular professional perspective may serve as the dominant voice of the library website. For example, a website may take an orientation toward "instruction," "collections," or "reference" depending on whether the primary aim is respectively to teach, deliver collections in digital format, or answer users' questions. As Jay L. Lemke notes, organizations may be regarded as ecosocial systems in which meaning is constructed through interaction with a larger dynamic system, and a library's website may reflect competing discursively framed viewpoints operating in the organization. In addition to reflecting the internal structure of a library, a website also bears traces of the heteroglossic forces rooted in differing views of the role of the library vis-à-vis its users.[27]

One of the areas of library administration deserving greater attention is the degree to which library administrators will devise new forms of organization by drawing on the communicative relationships promoted through the Internet. Bob Travica has undertaken the most thorough consideration of organizational issues linked to the development of virtual libraries, offering four organizational models that may characterize virtual libraries.[28] (1) Subsystem model: The virtual library may be treated as a subsystem of the library organization, crossing the boundaries of departments but anchored to a set of technologies. (2) Inter-organizational model: The virtual library may serve as the focal point around which new networks of libraries emerge. (3) System model: The virtual library may transcend its associated technologies and represent a new form of virtual organization that redefines the relationship between the library and its users, as well as relationships within the organization itself. (4) Disintermediation model: As the Internet enables publishers to communicate directly with information seekers and provides everyone with the potential to become a global information provider, the virtual library may reflect the elimination of the role of the library as intermediary in the traditional chain of information delivery.

Travica's research on academic libraries showed an affirmative value orientation toward the concept of the virtual library among library administrators. However, he concluded that administrators tend to take a reductionistic view of virtual libraries that focuses on the technology. With respect to the four organizational models he proposed, he found that the virtual library is regarded as a technology-bound subsystem of the library. Travica suggests that this narrow view of virtual library is due in part to the nature of the professional discourse surrounding the virtual library, which has concentrated on technological issues. He states that this conceptualization of the virtual library also allows administrators to manage change more easily than the initiation of radical transformations of the library organization. Travica notes that the library administrators' adherence to traditional principles of management such as unity of command and scalar chain of command impedes the development of a virtual organization which includes various organizations, erases physical distance among organizational parts, and delivers service to the customer. A true virtual library organization will not be attainable until library administrators develop a stronger inclination to distributed work responsibilities, delivery of information on user premises, performance measures concerned with value-added to users' work, and expanded digital collections.

STAFF RECRUITMENT AND DEVELOPMENT

The need to maintain and develop Internet-based library services has led library administrators to incorporate new requirements in the job responsibilities of existing staff positions. Among the skills that employers expect to find in library school graduates are basic Internet competencies, which range from searching to building websites.[29] A survey of employers of librarians by Sara Nesbeitt found that 91% of the respondents expected job applicants to have Internet experience, even when this requirement was not stated in a position description.[30] Library schools have responded to the demands of the marketplace by introducing Internet-related courses into their curricula. With foundation support, several library schools have completely redesigned their curricula to prepare students for the emerging roles of information professionals in an information environment shaped by the Internet.[31]

Directors have also had to create new staff positions to support Internet-based services, usually without additional funds, or enter into partnerships with the information technology divisions of their organizations. Prior to the Internet, libraries already faced an increasing need to employ their own technical expertise to manage library systems and online services. The appearance of microcomputers in libraries added requirements for network management, hardware maintenance, and support of software applications. Due to the Internet, responsibility for database searching has become more prevalent among library staff, and elementary Web development skills have become common outside of library systems departments. In addition, projects involving digital media and advanced database management have led to more specialized technical positions. The expansion of library responsibilities into areas driven by the Internet, such as online publishing and distance learning, has also created new staffing needs.

The Internet itself is an increasingly important means of recruiting staff, especially in the field of technology. One industry analyst has forecast that by the end of the year 2000, 96% of all companies in the United States will use the Internet in their hiring practices. Print classified advertising for job openings is expected to decline beginning in 2002, with recruiters spending a total of $1.7 billion online by the following year.[32] Using the Internet for recruitment can involve activities as simple as posting vacancy announcements to an Internet discussion group or the employment opportunities section of the website of a professional association. Many publications will now include posting a job announcement on their website as part of the cost of running a print advertisement, or they will add a Web posting for a nominal charge. As part of their placement role, library schools now maintain websites that post position announcements and provide links to employment resources offered on the Web by other organizations. At the higher end of staff recruitment over the Internet, employers may choose to list positions for a fee with companies that operate recruiting websites. At this time over 60% of the business generated by Web-based recruiting firms is directed toward computer-related industries.[33] One issue of concern for librarians lies in the fact that there has not been sufficient experience with Internet recruitment to determine its impact on staff diversity and increasing minority representation in professions.

A 1997 survey of academic, public, and special libraries provides some insight into how the Internet has influenced the recruitment of librarians by employers.[34] Among the respondents, Internet-based email lists were the most common forum for library job advertisement, as well as the source of the candidates who were considered to be the best qualified. Consequently, there was almost unanimous agreement among the survey respondents who advertised over the Internet that they would do so again. One-third reported planning to reduce advertising in print resources in favor of Internet posting. Only 7% of the respondents reported searching online resume banks. Roy Tennant recommended that the library administrators concentrate on personality traits rather than technical skills when hiring staffing for digital libraries.[35] His approach emphasizes the ability of staff to evolve to changing organizational needs that are associated with high technology environments. Specifically, he suggested that recruiters look for flexibility in work assignments, innate skepticism, a capacity to learn constantly, a propensity to take risks, a public service perspective, an appreciation of the contributions of other staff, skill at enabling and fostering change, and the capacity and desire to work independently.

In addition to recruiting staff with the necessary skills in Internet technologies, library administrators face the challenge of ensuring that staff maintain and advance their skills in a rapidly changing area of technology. The substantial investment of capital that libraries make in technology must be accompanied by a similar commitment to continuing education, if this investment is not to be squandered.[36] As discussed in the section on Interlibrary Cooperation, library consortia and networks have become a major source of technology training.

The Internet has also enabled library administrators to adapt work requirements to the needs of employees, thereby making jobs more attractive for recruiting and retaining talent. For example, the Internet has greatly facilitated the growth of telecommuting across many industries. In 1999 more than 19 million Americans worked from home at least one day per month during regular business hours.[37] It has been forecast that the number of telecommuters will increase to almost 25 million by 2003.[38] The conventional wisdom is that administrators benefit from employees' telecommuting through improvements in employee retention, morale, productivity, savings on office space, and reduced absenteeism. In the field of librarianship, telecommuting started earliest in cataloging due to the nature of the work and the technological developments in this subspecialty.[39] Reference librarianship will also be transformed through telecommuting and outsourcing options made possible by the Internet. It is already common for libraries to offer some degree of electronic reference service. Even at libraries lacking a formal electronic reference program reference librarians are inclined to answer requests directed to them via email. Within the framework of electronic reference service in the foreseeable future library administrators will be able to employ reference librarians who work off-site at a great geographic distance from the employing physical library and the patrons being served. In this way libraries will be able to take advantage of lower costs of living in other areas of the world when hiring staff. Libraries will also use staff stationed in different time zones to support distance-learning programs and offer 24 hour service.

BUDGETING

The costs of acquiring and maintaining technology have become a substantial burden for libraries. Capital budgets that had been sufficient to support traditional facilities will not cover the replacement of expensive equipment on cycles that match user expectations or take maximum advantage of technological developments. As an increasing portion of the library budget is directed toward the support of technology, libraries are forced to defer other purchases, seek additional funding, and partner with other entities, such as the information technology divisions of their own organization. Through the Internet, libraries have acquired access to a new public domain of digital intellectual property,[40] but in order to take advantage of these resources libraries must invest in technology that diverts funds from collection development. In addition to hardware and infrastructure costs, libraries have had to contend with the costs of commercially produced electronic collections. With electronic publishing still in its infancy, there are not yet sufficient electronic resources to allow libraries to reduce the costs associated with maintaining print-based collections to an extent that sufficiently offsets the costs of online subscriptions. As discussed in the section below, library administrators frequently have to rely on consortium licensing agreements and fund-raising in order to acquire commercial Internet-based resources.

Electronic publishing has affected budgeting in ways other than contributing to the need for additional funds. Although the allocation of funds among formats of materials is generally determined by managers of acquisitions departments, the degree of investment in electronic formats has strategic importance for a library. There are implications for technological infrastructure, staffing, distance programs, and remote access by the public. Library administrators must decide the degree to which electronic versions duplicate print equivalents, as well as how much and what type of duplication are necessary. Consideration must be given to how the cancellation of a print source affects the ability of the library to support historical research. One of the benchmarks that have emerged for libraries is the percentage of the materials budget allocated to electronic resources, which intrinsically places print and electronic formats in opposition just as the library literature tends to speak of print "versus" electronic resources. With respect to budgeting, the building of digital collections has been accomplished too often at the expense of print collections.

The extensive amount of information that may be gathered about the use of library resources over the Internet has the potential for making budgeting decisions more informed and the use of library funds more effective. With standard report generating software for website logs, library administrators can monitor the frequency of use of particular web pages and databases, the type and version of the Web browser and operating system used by visitors, the geographic area and domain of users, entering and exiting pages, and referral sites. The types of data collected and the level of specificity regarding individual use are determined by the interest, technical expertise, and comfort levels of individual libraries. For registered users libraries are able to collect data at greater degrees of detail that may be matched with other variables for special analyses. These data may be applied by library administrators to understand how resources are being used, weigh use against organizational priorities, and adjust budget allocations accordingly. Improvements in services, collections, and systems design are possible from a library's improved understanding of the information-seeking behavior of its users. Consequently, the Internet may help library administrators spend scarce funds more wisely and ensure that library collections receive greater use. For example, push technology will deliver information directly to users based on profiles of information need. This proactive approach to information delivery stands in contrast to the traditional collection-building activities of libraries in which information purchased by a library awaits discovery by users, which is an outcome that may never occur.

As technology extends the information-gathering ability of libraries over the Web, library administrators will need to decide how much information they are willing to collect about their users and how they intend to use this information. Fortunately, previous experience with online library systems has provided libraries with models of practice regarding confidentiality/privacy and acceptable use of patron information which may serve as guides.

FUND-RAISING

Increasingly, the funding provided to libraries by their parent institutions or government agencies is not sufficient to support core library services, let alone satisfy the growing user expectations and financial demands posed by technology. Until the last two decades fund-raising had been a "long-neglected aspect of librarianship,"[41] undertaken by libraries only when the operations budget had to be supplemented to permit building construction or the introduction of a special service. Fund-raising and development are now regarded as central activities of library administration. The Certified Public Library Administrator Program of the American Library Association (ALA) requires a 2 ½-day course in fund-raising. The Fund-raising and Financial Development Section of the ALA's Library Administration and Management Association has 1,348 members. In 1992 the Association of Research Libraries conducted a survey to determine the extent of development and fund-raising activities in its member institutions. Of the 87 responding libraries, only 5% indicated that they had no development programs. Most institutions reported spending between $40,000 and $90,000 annually to support development activities. The majority of the responding institutions reported a staff of 1 to 1.5 FTE.[42]

Although the costs associated with technology have become a prime contributor to the economic burden on libraries, technology in the form of the Internet also offers new opportunities for libraries to expand their sources of revenue. Libraries have not utilized the Internet for fund-raising as early or as intensively as other not-for-profit organizations. Nonetheless, many libraries have already taken advantage of the World Wide Web to promote fund-raising activities that span annual giving campaigns, major gifts, and Friends of the Library programs.

Libraries commonly engage in giving campaigns that direct funds toward general operating expenses, capital funds, challenge grants, or special endowments, such as restricted funds for acquisitions. The source of these funds is predominantly direct-mail campaigns or telephone solicitations. However, the technological innovations that are driving the development of e-commerce, such as the use of secure servers for online shopping, also enable libraries to engage in ongoing fund-raising activities through web pages that solicit and process contributions. For example, the website of the New York Public Library provides a secure form for making cash donations using a credit card.[43]

Among the advantages of accepting donations over the Internet is the low cost compared to running a direct-mail campaign. By using a Web page for contributions, libraries can expand their donor base at a lower incremental cost than through more active methods of donor identification. The donor information from online contributions may be added immediately to a database to ensure ongoing contact and encourage future gifts. In contrast, the potential donors contacted during traditional fund-raising campaigns tend to be derived from lists of previous donors, registered library users, visitors to library events, or mailing lists purchased or exchanged with other institutions. These lists are labor-intensive to maintain as compared with website databases that are updated electronically. In addition, on the average, the amount of individual online donations to not-for-profit organizations doubles those generated via direct mail campaigns, due to the use of credit cards by online donors.[44] The Internet offers immediacy in responding to a donor's gift, as each donor can be thanked as soon as the gift is received.

The Internet presents libraries with a new arena for pursuing major gifts that has only been partially explored. Libraries such as the University of Pennsylvania system have already begun to use web pages to acknowledge major gifts and present case statements for gift opportunities.[45] Through "cyber-plaquing"[46] libraries may take advantage of the Web to acknowledge a major gift to an audience of millions more than would view a traditional physical plaque that is resident in a library. Using the Web to acknowledge major gifts allows library development officers to maintain a link between the library and a donor who is geographically distant. In the case of special exhibitions, lectures, author readings, and other cultural events permanent recognition to financial underwriters has been provided primarily through print materials with limited distribution and high production costs such as catalogs. The Web allows for more elaborate, multimedia documentation of these events with the opportunity for ongoing recognition of donors. Development officers may use Web-based materials online or offline, as downloaded files, for impressive donor presentations anytime and anywhere.

Cyberspace offers naming opportunities that are no longer bounded by the physical restrictions of a library building. Traditional naming opportunities in libraries have included rooms, pieces of furniture, and entire buildings. By using the Web, libraries are able to create virtual spaces that can bear the name of a major donor. As more institutions pursue the idea of completely virtual collections and remote services as a substitute for physical libraries, it is reasonable to expect that in the not-too-distant future donors will contribute in order to name libraries that have no corresponding physical buildings.

Friends of the library programs have become standard means of generating additional revenue for all types of libraries. According to Adam Corson-Finnerty and Laura Blanchard, the Web can play an important role in the expansion of a Friends program especially with regard to three particular tasks: (1) Keeping Friends informed of library news; (2) Recognizing and celebrating the contributions of the Friends; and (3) Attracting new Friends. Hundreds of public and academic libraries have developed web pages that aim to accomplish these three goals for their Friends of the library groups.[47] Library news items on Friends pages include announcements of upcoming events along with an indication of discounts for members. Friends' contributions are acknowledged through individual donor lists or descriptions of how aggregated contributions have been applied. Calls for membership usually indicate the range of contributions that Friends may make, such as money, time, expertise, collections, or other goods and services. Friends of the library pages generally include a membership application form, although few libraries allow for online payment of dues at this time.

In addition to using the Internet as a means of acquiring additional funds through donor contributions and fund-raising campaigns, libraries may rely on the Internet for generating revenue through the sale of goods and services. Although e-commerce is in its infancy, in 1999, online business-to-consumer transactions in America amounted to $20 billion. It is estimated that by 2004, this will increase to $184 billion. In 1999, 39 million Americans, comprising 17% of all American households, shopped online, with one-half spending $500 or more. Goldman Sachs estimates that by 2010, online commerce will account for 15 to 20% of all retail sales in the United States.[48] Libraries already sell merchandise such as tote bags, posters, books, and mugs through shops or Friends' groups. With a secure server the same transactions may be handled via the Internet. In this case, the market is not limited to the local community but extends to anyone who may have benefited from the use of the library's resources or services online or anyone who is attracted to the merchandise. This approach has already been adopted by a wide range of not-for-profit organizations including museums, social advocacy groups, and educational organizations.

Along with fund-raising activities based on donor contributions, libraries have increasingly turned to fee-based services as a means of generating additional revenue. The Web now allows libraries access to a global market for their fee-based services. Although the established, high-profile providers with large research collections, such as the library of the Canada Institute for Scientific and Technical Information, hold an advantage in the marketplace, there are still opportunities for small libraries on the Web, especially libraries with modest income goals. In the same way that specialty stores find expanded markets on the Web, small libraries with specialized collections and/or staff expertise in focused subject areas may use the Web to develop a client base that would not have been attainable before.

Library websites that promote fee-based services tend to provide forms for document delivery and research services but may also include other services such as resume assistance. The use of the Web permits a level of detail and currency in the description of services that cannot be matched by a printed brochure. In addition, libraries without budgets for publicity may now avoid the costs associated with mass mailings and advertisements by taking advantage of indexing by Web search engines and listserv discussion groups to gain attention. One example of a well-established service that has made effective use of the Web is FYI, the fee-based research service of the County of Los Angeles Public Library. The FYI Website supplies detailed information regarding available services and allows for the submission of requests electronically.[49] The ease and speed of communication via the Internet have enabled FYI to increase the breadth of its research services through partnerships with other institutions, including libraries in other states. Participating in the highly competitive, global marketplace of e-commerce is, of course, risky. Libraries that decide to become involved must scale their operations to match their abilities in terms of volume of sales, expected turn-around time, foreign language/inter-cultural facility, and payment/currency options.

The Internet has allowed libraries to extend the geographic boundaries and the portfolio of their fee-based services. Using virtual collections, online catalogs, and electronic reference services, libraries can provide a seemingly full range of services to a set of otherwise unaffiliated users who are geographically distant and dispersed. Several pioneering efforts to test the possibilities for fee-based library services using the Internet involve distance-learning programs. In 1998, the University of New Mexico General Library was awarded a contract to create and operate the Central Library of the Western Governor's University, a virtual university that uses shared distance-learning resources to offer accredited degree programs across 15 states. In this role, the library provides electronic course reserves, reference services, and access to commercial full-text electronic collections, along with traditional document delivery of books and photocopies of journal articles. While the contract was competed to generate income, the service also aims to "find out what works in creating a time and location independent virtual academic library-a library free from the costs of tradition."[50] This model of outsourcing is likely to become common not only among virtual and transregional universities but also for corporations seeking an alternative to maintaining their costly in-house special libraries.

Libraries that wish to earn income from e-commerce without becoming an online retailer may choose to establish an affiliation with an online vendor. Roper surveys done for Cone Communications in 1997 and 1999 indicated that 76% of American consumers would be likely to switch brands or retailers to those who are associated with a reputable charitable cause.[51] Consequently, commercial vendors have reached out to not-for-profit organizations to establish affiliations on the Internet. Nonprofit organizations have teamed with for-profit online vendors who attract shoppers to their websites by donating a portion of their sales income to charities. Both large national organizations and small community-based organizations are experimenting with this type of partnership.[52] In a variation on this approach, libraries have begun to link their websites to commercial websites as a source of income. For example, the City College of New York Library[53] provides a link from its website to a major online book vendor, with a percentage of each purchase made from the library's website resulting in revenue that is directed to the library's materials budget.

INTERLIBRARY COOPERATION

The advantages of resource sharing among libraries have been recognized formally since the early part of the 20th century through the development of library consortia that have facilitated reciprocal borrowing, interlibrary loan, coordinated collection development, storage facilities, training programs, and shared management and delivery of all varieties of public and technical services. At this writing, there are almost 500 consortia and networks operating in the United States alone.[54] Developments in networking technologies of the 1970s promoted the expansion of regional networks that increasingly focused their services on the development of union catalogs, automated interlibrary loan, and shared library management systems. In the 1990s networking activities among libraries became dominated by the use of the Internet to provide library services.[55] The general business meetings of the International Coalition of Library Consortia now concentrate on discussions with vendors of Web-based resources regarding licensing terms and fees and consortium strategies for the development of shared electronic collections.[56]

Library networks and consortia have been instrumental in the adoption and use of the Internet by their member institutions. One form of support has been the channeling of collective effort to obtain funding from government agencies and foundations for telecommunications, networking infrastructure, and hardware that would have been beyond the financial means of member institutions. Consortia also have served as the source of ongoing training and support for libraries that have had to develop local technical expertise in Internet technologies. On a national scale, Internet connectivity among health sciences libraries, especially hospital libraries, has been accelerated through Internet connection grants and initiatives of the National Network of Libraries of Medicine funded by the National Library of Medicine.

As the Internet has permeated all aspects of the practice of librarianship, it has also influenced the services supported by consortia. The use of Internet telecommunication protocols has advanced the sharing of print resources in stages from remote login to online catalogs, to virtual union catalogs, to Web-based interfaces that allow for patron-initiated interlibrary loans. Internet protocols have enabled the rapid delivery of print materials converted to digital format, whether via FTP, as an email attachment, or using library-specific software such as Ariel®.

A recent survey of individuals in leadership positions in library consortia in the United States indicated that licensing support for obtaining access to electronic information resources is regarded as the highest priority for service development.[57] Thus, existing consortia have expanded their traditional group purchasing programs to include the negotiation of consortium-based site licenses on behalf of their members. The advantages are clear: substantial discounts from vendors are attainable through aggregating buying power; the centralized management of vendor contracts by a consortium saves the resources of member libraries; consortia have a delivery system in place to provide support services such as training and user help. In addition to expanding the roles of existing consortia, the Internet has shifted the fundamental reason for the creation of new consortia toward the need to combine purchasing and negotiation power for the licensing of electronic resources over the Web.[58, 59]

One of the unfortunate consequences of the focus of consortia on the licensing of electronic information resources is the common instance of consortia competing against one another in the negotiation of licenses with vendors. Library directors are frequently able to compare the deals offered by a variety of consortia and choose the most favorable. This duplication of effort represents wasted time and resources on the part of many consortia. One potential solution lies in the trend toward national site licensing of electronic resources, where the goals of uniformity of access by users, cost savings, and simplicity in contract management are brought to a higher degree of realization. The Canadian National Site Licensing Project and the National Electronic Site License Initiative in the United Kingdom represent two advanced initiatives in this area. In both cases, the licenses are negotiated on behalf of institutions of higher learning.

As Rollo Turner warns, there may be unintended negative effects associated with national site licenses.[60] First, given the early stage in the development of electronic publishing, excluding the negotiation of more favorable pricing of print subscriptions from electronic subscriptions is a disservice to library users. Second, a national site license establishes a monopoly that requires a system for carefully monitoring the performance of the managing agent, which could stray from representing interests of the libraries to becoming an agent of the publishers. The reluctance to change a system that is used "universally" could place libraries ultimately at a negotiating disadvantage with respect to commercial vendors. Awarding such a large share of the market to a single vendor may curtail competition that would favor libraries in pricing, as well as ongoing development of both content and systems. The need for introducing a new system and training users could serve as a strong disincentive for nonrenewal of a license that vendors could exploit to achieve a stronger bargaining position.

Consortia may be regarded as strategic partners in libraries' attempts to apply the Internet to meet library users' rising expectations for service.[61] Consortia may serve as outsourcing agents for website development and management. Additionally, through economies of scale consortia enable smaller libraries to accomplish digital imaging projects that they could not afford to undertake locally. As part of its long-range plan OCLC has announced a wide array of Internet-based support services spanning the globe, including centralized electronic reference service for member libraries.[62]

With the arrival of the Internet, statewide consortia such as GALILEO in Georgia and VIVA, the Virtual Library of Virginia, have been established primarily to support the development of electronic libraries, although they are also involved in the provision of traditional services to support the sharing of print collections.[63] The future appears to lie in the creation of library consortia solely for development of digital collections and the services to support their use. In this respect the Internet Public Library (IPL), with its goal of establishing a true Internet Library Consortium, is a groundbreaking step. In its pursuit of this goal the IPL is seeking to develop a model for dues-paying members who would share distributed virtual library operations, such as online reference and electronic collections, through pooled expertise and funds.[64]

LEGAL ISSUES

As the Internet alters the information environment in which libraries operate, library administrators are faced with legal issues that resemble traditional problems, such as censorship, but require new approaches. The fear of incurring legal fees has already prompted one public library to reduce its use of the Internet to accessing the library OPAC, an online encyclopedia, and a few commercial databases.[65]

The new legal dilemmas confronting library administrators are partly due to the fact that libraries have become a primary source of Internet access for the public. As noted above, the 1998 NCLIS survey indicated that almost three-quarters of all public libraries in the United States provided public Internet access.[66] The library is the most popular location for accessing the Internet from places other than home, work or school.[67] Consequently, the manner in which libraries choose to manage on-site use of the Internet has become a controversial, high-profile issue.

A common approach to managing the use of the Internet in libraries has been to develop formal guidelines, such as acceptable-use policies. Academic and special libraries had a head start in this regard, because for many years universities and corporations had policies in place that governed the use of their computer networks and could be adapted to handle Internet use. Nonetheless, acceptable-use policies have become prevalent in public libraries as well. According to the 1998 NCLIS survey, approximately 85% of public library outlets have adopted an acceptable-use policy for the Internet.[68] These policies usually begin with a general statement declaring the scope of appropriate use of Internet resources consistent with the mission of the library. For example, depending on the type of library, use may be restricted to educational purposes, work-related activities, or research. Commercial and recreational use may be specifically prohibited or severely restricted. Frequently, access to the Internet is regarded by libraries as a service or privilege that may be suspended or revoked if the acceptable use policy is violated. In addition, users may be warned that certain violations may lead to disciplinary action and/or criminal charges. The specific prohibitions addressed in acceptable use policies tend to fall into three categories. (1) Unlawful activities such as copyright infringement, computer fraud, hacking into other systems, child pornography, and the sending of messages that contain harassment, threats, or abusive language. (2) Threats to computer system integrity including unauthorized use of accounts, altering computer or system configurations, connecting unauthorized devices to a network, deliberately spreading computer viruses, local hacking, or engaging in activities that degrade system performance. (3) Nuisance activities such as spamming, sending chain letters, congregating in groups around a workstation, or exceeding the permissible amount of time online.

The American Library Association recommends that libraries write Internet use policies and clearly set forth restrictions that specify time, manner, and place limitations.[69] Policies should expressly prohibit the use of the Internet for materials that are obscene or harmful to minors or represent child pornography as defined by applicable laws. Policies should be widely communicated through visible postings and educational forums.

In practice, many Internet use policies now include statements that forbid the viewing or transmission of material that is not only termed "obscene", but also "lewd," "sexually explicit," or considered to be a form of harassment by others. Some policies make a distinction between the private viewing of such materials and their display on monitors that may be viewed by other library users. In order to allow library users to view material on the Internet without the risk of offending other patrons, many libraries have installed privacy screens at computer workstations, situated monitors so as to block the direct view of passersby, or located Internet workstations in special areas of the library. Some libraries have chosen to include in their acceptable-use policies statements affirming the unrestricted right of library users to access all material available on the Internet as a principle of intellectual freedom. These statements may be accompanied by a disclaimer that the library does not endorse or sanction the views represented by sites that are accessible on the Internet from library computers and that the library cannot protect individuals from controversial materials that one may find offensive or disturbing.

The enforcement of acceptable use policies poses a particular difficulty for libraries that include vague prohibitions against accessing "offensive" material via the Internet without specifying the criteria to be applied in judging such material. Enforcement requires librarians to monitor users or rely on complaints from other users. Librarians may apply a tap-on-the-shoulder approach to enforcement, hoping that embarrassment or awareness of the sensitivities of others will deter Internet users from violating the policy. Due to the lack of clear definitions of prohibited materials and differences of opinion, users may be surprised to discover that they have crossed the boundaries of acceptability. The adoption of acceptable use policies that prohibit access to constitutionally protected materials may also be considered a violation of the Library Bill of Rights.[70]

Libraries whose users include children face special challenges in managing Internet access. There are greater pressures to apply narrow interpretations of "offensive" material and stricter enforcement of policies when children share Internet-accessible computers with adults. Libraries have been forced to reconcile their duty to protect the limited and variable First Amendment rights of children, alongside their responsibility to protect minors from materials on the Internet that are not suitable for children. Some libraries incorporate in their acceptable-use policies a declaration that the responsibility for restricting the use of the Internet lies with parents, not the library staff. Some libraries attempt to limit their legal exposure by stipulating that children may not use the Internet unless accompanied by an adult.

One of the solutions available for managing Internet use in libraries is the installation of commercial filtering software on public workstations that are connected to the Internet. According to the NCLIS survey almost 15% of the public library outlets in the United States use filtering software.[71] A survey of public libraries in California conducted in 2000 indicated that 28% are using Internet filters, with half using them only on children's workstations.[72] Most filters currently in use work by blocking access to Internet sites based on predetermined criteria, although some software operates affirmatively by allowing access only to sites that meet library or vendor-determined criteria for acceptability. Filters of the former type may check the URLs requested by library Internet users against a database of "blacklisted" sites or block access to Internet sites that contain words included in a list of prohibited terms.

The use of filters has sparked a heated debate within the library profession and led to several high-profile legal decisions. In July 1997 the American Library Association adopted a resolution declaring that the use of Internet filtering software violates the Library Bill of Rights when it blocks access to constitutionally protected speech.[73] In a separate statement on Internet filtering, ALA cites several key factors in support of its position on Internet filters.[74] First, the current software is deemed faulty in that it blocks access to sites that would be relevant and acceptable to users and it cannot take into account varying ages and maturity levels of library users. Second, ALA rejects the notion that librarians serve in loco parentis. The role of the librarian is limited to advising and assisting users in the location of information. Only parents have the right and responsibility to restrict their children's access to information. Third, ALA warns of the legal liability to which the use of filters exposes libraries. ALA argues that the use of filters represents an implied contract with parents that their children will not be exposed to certain types of material available on the Internet—a promise that the limitations of the current software prevent libraries from fulfilling. Fourth, without the use of filters libraries and library users are sufficiently protected by existing laws on child pornography and obscenity. Fifth, the use of filters violates a fundamental principle of librarianship. "Blocking Internet sites is antithetical to library missions because it requires the library to limit information access."[75]

The ALA position on the use of Internet filters by libraries draws on the opinion issued by the U.S. Supreme Court when it struck down as unconstitutional certain provisions of the Communications Decency Act (CDA) of 1996 which were intended to protect minors from exposure to "harmful material" on the Internet.[76] The CDA criminalized the intentional sending or displaying of messages that depict or describe to persons under 18 years of age sexual or excretory activities or organs in terms that are deemed offensive by contemporary community standards. The Supreme Court noted that the CDA did not allow parents to consent to their children's use of restricted materials. In addition, the Court ruled that the CDA lacked the precision required by the First Amendment when regulating the content of speech. Thus, in its attempts to deny minors access to potentially harmful materials, the CDA also denied adults access to a great deal of material that they have a constitutional right to receive and address to one another. In a critical step, the Court held that unlike broadcast media, the receipt of information on the Internet requires a set of affirmative steps by the user making the odds slim that a user would encounter harmful materials on the Internet by accident. Consequently, the Court accorded communications on the Internet the same level of protection as printed literature and public speech.

Internet filtering software has been embraced by some libraries as a defense against the growing frequency of lawsuits against public institutions for offering unrestricted Internet access to children. A survey by the First Amendment Center at Vanderbilt University showed that 58% of adults support the use of Internet filters in public libraries.[77] In 1997 a parent in Broward County, Florida, sued the School Board for failing to install filtering software on the computers in the school.[78] In 1998 a parent sued a public library in Livermore, California, after she discovered that her 12 year-old son downloaded sexually explicit material using a computer in the library.[79] The parent asked the court to close the library as a public nuisance unless it either installed filtering software or required parental consent for children's use of the Internet. The suit was eventually dismissed.[80] Unfortunately, instead of reducing their legal exposure, libraries that use filtering software are now becoming the targets of legal action. In 1997 after the Board of Directors of the Loudon County Public Library System in Leesburg, Virginia, adopted Internet filtering over the objections of its library director, the county was sued by a citizens' group known as Mainstream Loudon. After hearing the case, in November 1998 the U.S. district court for the Eastern District of Virginia struck down the policy as a violation of the First Amendment and a priori restraint on publication. In her opinion, Justice Leonie Brinkema, a former librarian, noted that the filtering software as used in Loudon County restricted adults' access to constitutionally protected materials. Loudon County had argued that the use of filters was equivalent to a library's decision to refrain from adding particular books to its collection. The court disagreed, finding the use of filters to be comparable to removing materials from a collection. In effect, once a library invests in an Internet connection, it acquires the contents of the Internet without physical or financial restraints.[81]

Based on court opinions to date it would appear that filtering software could be applied in libraries if only, with respect to adults, it prevents the viewing of materials that meet the legal definitions of obscenity and child pornography or constitute engagement in illegal activities by the user. Taking a view of the library as a limited public forum for receiving information, one might interpret court opinions as also permitting libraries to restrict other Internet activities such as commercial transactions, gaming, and chatting.[82]

One might ask whether filtering software is appropriate for use on workstations to be used only by children. The ALA holds the position that filtering software is not appropriate for use in the children's room of a public library or school library media centers. For children's rooms, ALA recommends developing a broad Internet use policy that is part of the overall library use policy, educating users about the policy, and guiding users in the selection of websites to locate information.[83] In contrast to ALA's policies, there are leaders in the profession who advocate strict safeguards in school media centers that include not only the use of filtering software but also placing all students' use of the Internet under adult supervision and ensuring that all Internet sites students visit are preapproved and curriculum-related.[84]

In addition to the need to protect children from harmful material on the Internet, proponents of filtering argue that filters help prevent a sexually hostile environment. This point was made in the Loudon case but not addressed in detail by the court. Although courts may accept a compelling state interest in preventing sexual harassment, the equally important interest of the state in protecting First Amendment rights of adults that is declared in the Loudon and CDA cases seems likely to require that libraries seek less restrictive measures than filters to solve this problem. For example, privacy screens and strategic placement of computer workstations could accomplish the same goal of preventing women from being exposed to offensive images.[85]

The next generation of Internet filters will use content labeling conventions developed by a cross-industry working group within the World Wide Web Consortium known as the Platform for Internet Content Selection

(PICS).[86] PICS offers a standard format for labels but does not prescribe a naming vocabulary. Labels would be provided as metatags by Internet publishers and third-party labeling services. Selection software would determine whether access to materials is permitted. PICS specifications govern the interoperability of selection software and ratings services but do not specify how those pieces work.[87] Once PICS standards are in widespread use, parents may decide which content dimensions and their labels should be used to block access to their children's material. Parents may choose to block all unlabeled material. If the honesty of publishers who self-label is questioned, parents may rely on third-party labeling. Libraries will be encountering PICS-compatible software in a variety of forms, as it may be incorporated into Internet browsers, installed on a proxy server, or included in commercial filters.

While Internet filtering software imposes a local barrier between library users and Internet content, lawmakers have also sought to erect barriers at the source of the content. Following the Supreme Court's rejection of the constitutionality of portions of the Communications Decency Act, Congress made another attempt to restrict children's access to material on the Web by passing the Child Online Protection Act in October 1998.[88] This law prohibits commercial websites from making sexually explicit material available to anyone under the age of 17. The penalties to violators include a $50,000 fine per offense and up to six months of imprisonment. Sites that post such material are granted an affirmative defense to prosecution if they restrict access by requiring use of a credit card, debit account, adult access code, adult personal identification number, or a digital certificate that verifies age.

Led by the American Civil Liberties Union, a coalition of publishers, Internet-industry groups, and free speech organizations immediately filed a motion in federal court for a temporary restraining order to block enforcement of the law before it was scheduled to take effect. Following arguments, a district court issued the order on the basis that fear of prosecution under the new law will likely result in censorship of constitutionally protected speech.[89] At this writing a federal appeals court has upheld the injunction citing the impossibility of determining "community standards" for the World Wide Web. The appeals court judges noted that the law would in effect require every Web publisher to adhere to the most restrictive and conservative community standards to avoid criminal liability.[90] Meanwhile, in the U.S. Congress, legislation continues to be proposed to mandate filtering for libraries that receive e-rate subsidies, so that children are denied access to obscene material on the Internet.[91]

As library administrators and publishers continued to grapple over the translation of fair use practices from the print arena to the digital arena of the Internet, a major revision of copyright law was effected with the passage of the Digital Millennium Copyright Act in 1998.[92, 93] Due to lobbying on the part of professional organizations such as the American Library Association, the law manages to preserve the concept of fair use and incorporate safeguards for libraries while protecting the interests of copyright owners. The law provides for legal remedies for the circumvention of technological measures designed to prevent unauthorized access or copying of copyrighted works. An exception is made for nonprofit libraries, archives, and educational institutions, allowing them to circumvent technological measures to make a good-faith determination as to whether to acquire a copy of a work, but the accessed copy of the protected work may not be kept for longer than needed to make the determination and may not be used for any other purpose. One of the unanswered questions posed by this exception is how the library may circumvent the protection measures as allowed, if the selling of the equipment necessary to do this is illegal.[94]

For preservation purposes the law allows libraries and archives to make up to three copies which may be digital provided that the digital copies are not made available to the public outside the library premises. Libraries are also allowed to make a copy of a protected work if the original format becomes obsolete, such as when a reading device is no longer manufactured or reasonably available commercially. The law also included a limitation on liability for copyright infringement by Internet service providers, a role that many libraries have chosen to assume. Essentially, providers are excluded from monetary liability for simply transmitting information over the Internet provided that they comply with the provisions of the law, have no knowledge of the copyright infringements, and immediately remove material that is in violation of the law.

One of the provisions of the Digital Millennium Copyright Act required the Copyright Office to conduct a study of how to promote distance education while balancing the rights of copyright owners and the needs of users of copyrighted works in a digital environment. In its subsequent report,[95] the Copyright Office offered a set of recommendations to Congress that include revising the language of the Copyright Act of 1976 to include digital as well as analog transmission; expanding the rights covered to include digital transmission only to the extent required to transmit a performance or display as authorized by the original exemption; eliminating the requirement for display or performance in the physical classroom; requiring educational institutions to implement safeguards against copyright violation; focusing legislative attention on cases where the owner of a work cannot be located; asserting that fair use language applies in a digital environment.

In contrast to the acquisitions process for print materials, subscribing to electronic publications, such as Web-based resources, requires libraries to enter into a licensing agreement with a publisher. In most cases libraries accept standard licenses provided by publishers without question, whether it is due to the lack of legal expertise necessary to review a document or the belief that an agreement may not be subject to negotiation. As the number of electronic products acquired by libraries increases, library administrators have become more willing to challenge the standard terms of agreement. As discussed in an earlier section, library consortia have concentrated on, and collectively bring more clout into, the process of negotiating these legal agreements. With funding from the Council on Library and Information Resources, Yale University has undertaken the LIBLICENSE project to provide libraries with the information required to negotiate licenses.[96] The project maintains a website that includes a glossary of licensing terms, samples of licenses supplied by publishers, links to licensing resources, and downloadable software that library administrators may use to create and customize licenses. The project also maintains a searchable ongoing and archived discussion list (LIBLICENSE-L) for the discussion of issues relating to the licensing of digital information by academic and research libraries.

CONCLUSION: NEW SKILLS FOR LIBRARY ADMINISTRATORS

What has been the impact of the Internet on the skills required of library administrators? As noted above, in many cases the Internet and its related technologies have contributed to the expansion of job responsibilities for library directors, who may now be expected to manage computer operations, electronic publishing, distance learning, and computer literacy programs. Technology-related job qualifications for directors are not Internet-specific. The references to technology in position descriptions are still stated broadly with phrases such as "knowledge of information technology," "skill in library service technology," "planning, and evaluation of library and information technology services," and the all-inclusive "vision for technology."

The Internet has influenced the scale, competitiveness, and speed of responsiveness associated with traditional administrative responsibilities. In terms of scale, the Internet has provided libraries with a user base and an information resource pool that is potentially worldwide. Library administrators must understand how to position their institutions to take advantage of these global opportunities. The sharing of information over the Internet offers library users many alternatives to the sources of information traditionally associated with libraries. Through the World Wide Web, libraries now compete with commercial information providers, nonprofit organizations, individuals, and other libraries for the attention of their user communities. Consequently, library administrators face having to make a stronger case for the added value that their institutions bring to mediated information services. The pace at which the world of information use operates requires library administrators to respond rapidly to keep their institutions current and relevant to their user communities. Administrators must develop systems that satisfy rising expectations of information seekers especially with regard to speed and ease of access. Library administrators who want their institutions to stand at the forefront of the profession must be able to assess opportunities rapidly within a changing information environment and make decisions that are inherently riskier than in the past.

Increasingly, the successful library administrator will be the one who can leverage the possibilities of the extensive reach of the Internet to further the mission of a library. This creativity will take a variety of forms. Administrators will need to understand how to shape a new form of organization, create new user communities, and project and maintain an institutional image by applying new communicative media and norms. To an increasing degree, libraries will have to look to the private sector for models that strategically use Internet-based technologies to support information services as they map future directions for their libraries.

NOTES

1. Schelle Simcox, "IPL: The Internet Public Library," *Ariadne* 7 (1997) (URL http://www.ariadne.ac.uk/issue7/ipl).
2. Prashant Bordia, "Face-to-Face versus Computer-Mediated Communi-cation: A Synthesis of the Experimental Literature," *Journal of Business Communication* 34 (January 1997): 99-120.
3. Jong-Young Kim, "Social Interaction in Computer-Mediated Communi-cation," *American Society for Information Science Bulletin* 26 (Feburary/March 2000): 15-17.
4. Richard W. Boss, "Facilities Planning for Technology," *Library Technology Reports* 31 (July/August 1995): 389-483.
5. Benton Foundation, "Buildings, Books, and Bytes: Libraries and Communities in the Digital Age," *Library Trends* 46 (Summer 1997): 178-223.
6. Trends Awareness Committee. Public Relations Section. American Library Association, "The Virtual Library: Pros and Cons for Public Relations," *Library Administration and Management* 14 (Spring 2000): 95-96.
7. Oswald M. T. Ratteray, "A Survey of Librarians in the Middle States Region on the Role of the Library, Electronic Resources, and Information Literacy Training in Higher Education," Middle States Association of Colleges and Schools Commission on Higher Education, November 1999 (URL http://www.smcm.edu/cald/Goto/survey.htm).
8. See also Larry Hardesty, "Do We Need Academic Libraries? A Position Paper of the Association of College and Research Libraries," December 1999 (URL http://www.ala.org/acrl/academiclib.html).
9. David M. Levy, and Catherine C. Marshall, "Going Digital: A Look at Assumptions underlying Digital Libraries," *Communications of the ACM* 38 (April 1995): 77-84.
10. Richard E. Lucier, "Building a Digital Library for the Health Sciences: Information Space Complementing Information Place," *Bulletin of the Medical Library Association* 83 (July 1995): 346-350.
11. Simcox, "IPL."
12. Ann Peterson Bishop and Susan Leigh Star, "Social Informatics of Digi-tal Library Use and Infrastructure," *Annual Review of Information Science and Technology* 31 (1996): 301-403.
13. Nancy Pickering Thomas, "Reading Libraries: An Interpretive Study of Discursive Practices in Library Architecture and the Interactional Construction of Personal Identity" (Ph.D. diss., the State University of New Jersey at Rutgers, 1996).

14. Rob Kling, "Hopes and Horrors: Technological Utopianism and Anti-Utopianism in Narratives of Computerization," in *Computerization and Controversy: Value Conflicts and Choices*, 2nd ed. (San Diego: Academic Press, 1995), pp. 40-58.
15. Eric Lease Morgan, " MyLibrary: A Model for Implementing a User-Centered, Customizable Interface to a Library's Collection of Information Resources," (URL http://my.lib.ncsu.edu/about/paper).
16. For example, Case Western Reserve University Law Library, (The URL is http:// lawwww.cwru.edu/library/libMission.htm); Fisher-Watkins Library of Cushing Academy (URL http://www.cushing.org/ academic/ text/ap _as _li_text.htm).
17. John Carlo Bertot, and Charles R. McClure, *The 1999 National Survey of U.S. Public Library Outlet Internet Connectivity: Final Report,* September 1998 (URL http://www.nclis.gov/statsurv/survey98.pdf), p. 6.
18. American Library Association, "MCI Study Shows Internet Use at Libraries on the Rise," ALA News Release, April 27, 1998 (URL http://www.ala.org/news/archives/v3n19/v3n19a.html).
19. Ekos Research Associates, Inc., *Canadians, Public Libraries and the Information Highway: Final Report*, March 1998 (URL http://www.schoolnet.ca/ln-rb/e/ekos/ekos4.html).
20. Jeremiah Sullivan, "What Are the Functions of Corporate Home Pages?" *Journal of World Business* 34 (Summer 1999): 193-210.
21. Elaine K. F. Leong, Xueli Huang, and Paul-John Stanners, "Comparing the Effectiveness of the Web Site with Traditional Media," *Journal of Advertising Research* 38 (September/October 1998): 44.
22. Stuart L. Esrock and Greg B. Leichty, "Social Responsibility and Corporate Web Pages: Self-Presentation or Agenda-Setting?" *Public Relations Review* 24 (Fall 1998): 305-319.
23. Ibid.
24. Sullivan, "What Are the Functions?"
25. Ibid.
26. Baruch Student Protest (URL http://home.onestop.net/119910).
27. Jay L. Lemke, "Discourse and Organizational Dynamics: Website Communication and Institutional Change," *Discourse and Society* 10 (1999): 21-47.
28. Bob Travica, "Organizational Aspects of the Virtual Library: A Survey of Academic Libraries," *Library and Information Science Research* 21 (1999): 173-203.
29. For example, Mary Ellen Bates, "The Newly Minted MLS: What Do We Need to Know Today?" *Searcher* 6 (May 1998): 30-33 (URL http://www.infotoday.com/searcher/may98/story1.htm).
30. Sara L. Nesbeitt, "Trends in Internet-Based Library Recruitment: An Introductory Survey," *Internet Reference Services Quarterly* 4 (1999): 23-40 (URL http://bubl.ac.uk/journals/lis/fj/irsq/v04n0299.htm# trends).

31. Deanna B. Marcum, "Transforming the Curriculum, Transforming the Profession," *American Libraries* 28 (January 1997): 35-37.
32. Scott Hays, "Hiring on the Web," *Workforce* 78 (1999): 76-81.
33. Christopher Caggiano, "The Truth about Internet Recruiting," *Inc.* 21 (December 1999): 156 (URL http://www.inc.com/custom_publishing/dotcomseries/articles/954274156.html).
34. Nesbeitt, "Trends in Internet-Based."
35. Roy Tennant, "The Most Important Management Decision: Hiring Staff for the New Millennium," *Library Journal* 123 (February 15, 1998): 102.
36. Anne Woodsworth, "Learning for a Lifetime," *Library Journal* 123 (January 1998): 62.
37. Kathleen O'Brien, "Taking Advantage of the Mobile Office: Homeward Bound," *New York Times* April 5 2000, G1.
38. JALA International, Inc., *Telecommuting Forecast*, 1999 (URL http://www.jala.com/ustcforecast.htm).
39. Joan M. Leysen and Nancy L. Pelzer, "Telecataloging: A Consideration of Present and Future Practices," *LIBRES: Library and Information Science Research* 6 (June 1996) (URL http://aztec.lib.utk.edu/libres/libre6n1/leysen-pelzer.html).
40. Paul Starr, "The Electronic Commons," *American Prospect* 11 (March 27 2000): 30 (URL http://www.prospect.org/archives/V11-10/starr-p.html).
41. Andrew J. Eaton, "Fund Raising for University Libraries," *College and Research Libraries* 32 (1971): p. 351.
42. Association of Research Libraries, *Library Development and Fund-raising*, SPEC Flyer 193 (Washington, DC: ARL, Office of Management Services, June 1993).
43. The New York Public Library (URL http://www.nypl.org).
44. Kathleen V. Schmidt, "E-Giving: Charity Begins at the Home Page," *Marketing News* 33 (October 11, 1999): 13.
45. University of Pennsylvania, "Friends of the Penn Library" (URL http://www.library.upenn.edu/friends/changes.html).
46. Adam Corson-Finnerty and Laura Blanchard, *Fund-raising and Friend Raising on the Web* (Chicago: American Library Association, 1998).
47. Ibid.
48. "Survey: E-commerce: Shopping around the Web," *Economist* 354 (February 26, 2000): s5-s6.
49. FYI Information Services (URL http://fyi.co.la.ca.us).
50. University of New Mexico Library, "UNM Library Offers 'Virtual Library' to WGU," *Lexicon: UNM General Library Newsletter* 4.1 (February 1998) (URL http://www.unm.edu/~libfunds/develop/ WGU .html).
51. Jay D. Hair, "Fund Raising on the Internet: Instant Access to a New World of Donors," *Fund Raising Management* 30 (October 1999): 16-18.
52. J. P. Frenza and Leslie Hoffman, "Fund-raising on the Internet: Three Easy Strategies for Nonprofits," *Nonprofit World* 17 (July/August 1999): 10-13.
53. City College Libraries (URL http://www.ccny.cuny.edu/library).

54. American Library Directory, 1999-2000, 52nd ed., "Networks, Consortia, and Other Cooperative Library Organizations" (New Providence, NJ: R. R. Bowker, 1999).
55. Kate Nevins, and Bonnie Juergens, "Library Networking and Cooperation in 1997," in *Bowker Annual*, 43rd ed. (New Providence, NJ: R. R. Bowker, 1998), pp. 262-271.
56. International Coalition of Library Consortia, "COC6 Meeting. Lisle, Illinois, Sept. 30 through Oct. 2, 1999," Notes taken by Tom Peters (URL http://www.wiu.edu/uers/mstap/coc6.htm)
57. Bonnie Juergens and Kate Nevins, "Library Networking and Cooperation in 1998," in *Bowker Annual* 44th ed., (New Providence, NJ: R. R. Bowker, 1999), pp. 293-301.
58. William Gray Potter, "Recent Trends in Statewide Academic Library Consortia," *Library Trends* 45 (Winter 1997): 416-423.
59. Rona Wade, "The Very Model of a Library Consortium," *Library Consortium Management* 1 (1999) (URL http://www.emerald-library.com/brev/24701aa1.htm).
60. Rollo Turner, "National Site Licensing and Consortia Purchasing," *Library Consortium Management* 1 (1999) (URL http://emerald-library.com/brev/24701ad1.htm).
61. Arnold Hirshon, "The Development of Library Client Service Programs and the Role of Library Consortia," *Library Consortium Management* 1 (1999) (URL is http://www.emerald-library.com/brev/24701cb1.htm).
62. Phyllis Spies, "Libraries Around the World," OCLC May 2000 Users Council Meeting, May 23, 2000, Dublin, Ohio (URL http://www.oclc.org/oclc/uc/20000523/ppt/phyllisspies/index.htm).
63. Wade, "The Very Model."
64. Simcox, "IPL."
65. Norman Oder, "MI Town Cuts Net in Preemptive Move to Save Legal Fees," *Library Journal* 125 (January 14 2000): 14.
66. Bertot and McClure, "The 1999 National Survey," p. 6.
67. American Library Association, "MCI Study."
68. Bertot and McClure, "The 1999 National Survey," p. 4.
69. Intellectual Freedom Committee, American Library Association, "Statement on Internet Filtering," July 1, 1997 (URL http://www.ala.org /alaorg/oif/filt_stm.html).
70. American Library Association, "Resolution on the Use of Internet Filters," (Chicago: American Library Association, July 2, 1997) (URL http://www.ala.org/alaorg/oif/filt_res.html).
71. Bertot and McClure, "The 1999 National Survey," p. 4.
72. "California Internet Survey: 28 Percent of Sample Use Filters," *LJ News* (April 3, 2000) (URL http://www.ljdigital.com/articles/news/thisweek/ 20000403_14133.asp).
73. American Library Association, "Resolution on the Use of Internet Filters."

74. Intellectual Freedom Committee. American Library Association. "Statement on Internet Filtering."
75. Ibid.
76. *Reno v. ACLU*, 521 US 844 (1997).
77. Freedom Forum, "State of the First Amendment, 1999: A Survey of Public Attitudes" (URL http://www.freedomforum.org/first/sofa/1999/ welcome .asp).
78. "Broward County Library Seeks Dismissal of Internet-Filtering Suit," *American Libraries* 31 (February 7, 2000) (URL is http://www.ala.org/ alonline/news/2000/000207.html).
79. Beverly Goldberg, "Suit Watch," *American Libraries* 29 (August 1998): 17.
80. "Bay Area Report: Court Rejects Suit over Sexy Photos in Library," *San Francisco Chronicle* October 22, 1998, C18.
81. *Mainstream Loudoun v. Board of Trustees of the Loudon County Library*, 24 F. Supp.2d 552 (E.D. Va. 1998).
82. Junichi P. Semitsu, "Burning Cyberbooks in Public Libraries: Internet Filtering Software vs. the First Amendment," *Stanford Law Review* 52 (January 2000): 509-545.
83. American Library Association, "Frequently Asked Internet Questions," June 1988 (URL http://www.ala.org/alaorg/oif/interfaq.html).
84. Carol Truett, "Censorship and the Internet: A Stand for School Librarians: Opinion," *School Library Media Quarterly* 25 (Summer 1997): 223-227.
85. Semitsu, "Burning Cyberbooks."
86. World Wide Web Consortium, "Platform for Internet Content Selection" (URL http://www.w3.org/pics).
87. Paul Resnick, and James Miller, "PICS: Internet Access Controls without Censorship," *Communications of the ACM* 39 (1996): 87-93.
88. Child Online Protection Act, 105 PL 277, 112 U.S. Statutes at Large 2681 (1998).
89. *ACLU v. Reno*, U.S. District Ct. for Eastern District of Pennsylvania, Civil Action 98-5591, 1998 U.S. Dist. LEXIS 18546; 27 Media L. Rep. 1026 (November 20, 1998) (URL http://www.aclu.org/court/ acluvrenoII _order.html).
90. *ACLU v. Reno*, U.S. Court of Appeals for the Third Circuit, 99-1324, 217 F.3d 162; 2000 U.S. App. LEXIS 14419; 28 Media L. Rep. 1897 (June 22, 2000) (URL http://pacer.ca3.uscourts.gov:8080/C:/InetPub/ftproot/ Opinions/ 991324.TXT).
91. "Competing Filtering Measures Attached to Senate Bill," American Libraries (July 3, 2000) (URL http://www.ala.org/alonline/news/2000/ 000703.html.
92. Digital Millennium Copyright Act, 105 PL 304, 112 Statutes at Large 2860 (1998).
93. U.S. Copyright Office, "The Digital Millennium Copyright Act of 1998. U.S. Copyright Office Summary," December 1998 (URL http://www .loc.gov/copyright/legislation/dmca.pdf).

94. Arnold P. Lutzker, "Primer on the Digital Millennium: What the Digital Millennium Copyright Act and the Copyright Term Extension Act mean for the Library Community," Washington, DC: Association of Research Libraries, 1999 (URL http://arl.cni.org/info/frn/copy/primer.html).
95. U.S. Copyright Office. "Report on Copyright and Distance Education," May 1999 (URL http://www.loc.gov/copyright/docs/de_rprt.pdf).
96. Ann Okerson, "The LIBLICENSE Project and How it Grows," *D-Lib Magazine* 5 (September 1999) (URL http://www.dlib.org/dlib/september9/okerson/09okerson.html).

CHAPTER THREE

THE INTERNET AND COLLECTION MANAGEMENT IN ACADEMIC LIBRARIES: OPPORTUNITIES AND CHALLENGES

Thomas E. Nisonger

INTRODUCTION

A decade ago many librarians had never heard of the Internet. Today the Internet (often simply termed "the Net") makes headlines in the national media. It has been observed that since the 1960s moon race, no technological issue has received as much publicity as the "information superhighway."[1]

This chapter examines the relationship between the Internet and collection management in libraries on three levels: (1) the Internet's use to perform traditional functions for traditional materials (i.e., using the Internet to help select books and serials or evaluate the collection); (2) the application of traditional collection development functions to the Internet (i.e., evaluation and selection of Internet resources); and (3) the impact the Internet's existence will have on traditional functions and materials (i.e., selecting fewer print resources because they can be accessed electronically on the Internet. There are at least five major variables in analyzing the relationship between the Internet and collection management): (1) collection management functions (e.g., selection, evaluation, etc.); (2) library type (i.e., academic, public, school, or special); (3) information resources on the Internet (e.g., electronic journals, listservs, databases, etc.); (4) access modes for Internet resources, such as telnet, File Transfer Protocol (FTP), or the World Wide Web; and (5) time frame. However, this chapter focuses on collection management functions in academic libraries in the context of the present technological environment.

This chapter explores, in the context of the Internet, such collection management functions as identification, microevaluation, selection, macroevaluation, acquisitions, resource sharing, and document delivery. Although intellectual freedom and censorship are usually considered within the domain of collection management, these topics will not be discussed here. The chapter's objective is to outline major issues rather than provide definitive answers. Both descriptive (describing what libraries are actually doing) and prescriptive (suggesting what libraries can or should do) approaches are used. The focus is on the utilization of the Internet rather than on technological issues. Information for this chapter is based on reviewing the literature, surfing the Internet, monitoring several listservs pertinent to collection management, and the author's background as a collection development practitioner, teacher, and researcher.[2]

Because the word "traditional" is frequently used in this chapter, a working definition is in order. Traditional resources include books, serials, government documents, maps, audio-visuals, and microformat materials. Traditional library functions are the identification, selection, evaluation, acquisition, borrowing, processing, and interpretation of information resources, usually in the form of distinct bibliographic units.

THE INTERNET

This section is relatively brief because it is assumed that most readers are generally familiar with the Internet. The Internet is a "network of networks." Its origin has been traced to the ARPANET, founded in 1969 by the U.S. Department of Defense for military purposes.[3] In January 1995 there were estimated to be over 25 million Internet users from more than 100 countries with Internet traffic growing 10% a month.[4] Librarians' initial use of the Internet focused on three applications: electronic mail (including listservs and discussion groups), remote login via telnet (most frequently to other libraries' online public access catalogs, i.e., OPACs), and file transfer using FTP. Later, librarians' attention began to focus on gophers and then on the World Wide Web. A gopher, first developed at the University of Minnesota in 1991, is a software application that produces a menu-driven directory structure providing access to Internet resources. Gophers can be created for campus-wide information systems, libraries, academic departments, nonacademic organizations, and/or organized on a subject or geographical basis. There were at least 520 gophers by June 1993 and reportedly 1,000 in early 1994.[5] The World Wide Web (often abbreviated WWW or "the Web") uses hypertext transfer protocol (HTTP) to provide links among textual and multimedia documents. The Web was developed at the European Particle Physics Laboratory in Geneva, Switzerland, beginning in 1989. The number of sites on the Web has grown exponentially, increasing from 1,000 in April 1994 to 110,000 by October 1995.[6] The World Wide Web can be accessed through such graphics-oriented Web browsers as Mosaic or Netscape Navigator as well as text-only browsers such as Lynx. An

Internet gopher or website can contain both primary information created by the site's sponsor and secondary information in the form of links to external sites.

OPPORTUNITIES OFFERED BY THE INTERNET

"Access versus ownership" and "just in time" versus "just in case" have been catchy, but somewhat simplistic, collection development slogans for a considerable period of time. Likewise, the "virtual library," the "digital library," and "the library without walls" are frequently heard but ill-defined terms. It does not take much imagination to perceive that the Internet offers an opportunity to give real meaning to these terms by facilitating rapid access to information resources external to the library. At a minimum, the Internet offers a potential to save money, shelf space, and library staff time while simultaneously increasing the rapid provision of information to patrons in effect, helping address the issue articulated by Melvil Dewey in 1877, "the problem before us...is to make libraries better -- their expenses less." [7]

The phrase "serendipitous use of automated technology" has been used to describe the utilization of technology for performing functions apart from the technology's original, intended purpose.[8] Numerous examples pertaining to collection management could be cited. *BIP Plus*, the CD-ROM version of *Books in Print*, was originally created as a technical services tool but has been used for collection development and research. Bibliographic utilities (e.g., OCLC, RLIN, or WLN) were created to support the cataloging function, but their archival tapes of cataloging records can be used for collection management, such as longitudinal analysis of a single library's collecting patterns or overlapping holdings among a group of libraries. In many ways the Internet's entire history illustrates the serendipitous use of technology. It was created for military reasons during the Cold War but soon became a scientific research tool. Only in recent years have librarians realized its potential applications to their profession. There are undoubtedly innumerable opportunities for collection management librarians to use the Internet in new and creative ways that are not now readily apparent.

At a maximum, the Internet could fundamentally alter library operations or even the definition of what constitutes a library, resulting in what Lynch terms "transformation."[9] Because the Internet can deliver information directly to the end user, a question arises whether libraries will even be needed in the future. These issues are speculated upon briefly later in this chapter.

PROBLEMS WITH AND LIMITATIONS OF THE INTERNET

At present, there are a number of generally recognized problems that hinder the effective utilization of the Internet; (1) the Net is not particularly "user-friendly," (2) one often experiences technical glitches such as dropped lines or traffic jams, (3) the Internet is undergoing dynamic, rapid change, (4) surfing the Internet can become addictive and waste one's time, (5) numerous unresolved copyright issues abound, (6) some of the available resources require passwords, (7) numerous ostensible links on the World Wide Web are unavailable because they are still "under construction," (8) intrusive advertising is beginning to appear on the Net, and (9) security is a problem.

There are additional difficulties more directly relevant to the collection management of Internet resources; (1) the totality of resources on the Net is unknown, (2) good bibliographical control of known resources is lacking, (3) resources on the Internet are inherently unstable, i.e., here today, gone, changed, or moved by tomorrow, (4) available information may be inaccurate, outdated, or generally useless since there is relatively little quality control on the Net (the opposite side of this issue is that the Internet is more democratic because anyone can post information without a gatekeeper), and (5) many of the Net's resources are not archived. However, it is reasonable to assume that some of these problems will ultimately be resolved.

These and other issues complicate planning for, as well as writing about, the Internet's effective utilization by librarians. Due to rapid technological change, the near future may witness presently unforeseen innovations. As the 1990s began, who would have guessed the World Wide Web's present importance? Moreover, how such issues as copyright, cost, and scholarly acceptance are eventually resolved will significantly influence the way collection management librarians use the Internet and its impact on their work.

THE INTERNET AS A COMMUNICATIONS DEVICE TO ASSIST COLLECTION MANAGEMENT OF TRADITIONAL MATERIALS

While computers were originally invented for number-crunching purposes, it is generally recognized that computers now facilitate communications. This section will discuss how, through the communications process, the Internet can assist traditional collection management and acquisitions.

There are at least 700 to 1,000 library OPACs that can be accessed on the Internet.[10] One can directly telnet to their addresses or access them through gophers or websites. Holdings information for other libraries can assist both selection and deselection decisions. For example, one wishing to assist selection by identifying titles in a specific subject could access the OPAC of a library with strong holdings in the area. Whether a busy collection manager would spend the time to assess OPACs to assist routine book selection is debatable. Nevertheless, serials selection or cancellation decisions could be assisted by checking availability in nearby libraries. This technique's use in resource sharing and the checklist evaluation method are discussed in subsequent sections.

Discussion lists or listservs on the Internet assist the performance of traditional library functions by serving as a communications medium among librarians and sometimes nonlibrarians such as vendors. The current *Directory of Electronic Journals, Newsletters and Academic Discussion Lists* annotates 161 "academic discussion lists" for library and information science.[11] Lists most relevant to collection management are enumerated below:

LISTNAME	TOPIC
COLLDV-L	collection development
ACQNET	acquisitions
SERIALST	serials in general but covers serials collection management
COLLIBS	collection development in Australian academic and research libraries
CONSERVATION DISTLIST	preservation
GIFTEX-L	gift and exchange issues
BACKSERV	duplicate exchange among libraries
BackMed	duplicate exchange of medical back issues

An interesting but unanswered question concerns how collection management librarians actually utilize listservs. Based on their analysis of three listservs relevant to reference, Cromer and Johnson identified eight categories of messages; specific queries, responses to queries, summaries of responses, presentations of issues, discussions of issues, general announcements, conference announcements, and job postings.[12]

There are home pages on the WWW for most types of major players on the contemporary library and information science scene, including academic libraries, national libraries, publishers, journals, bibliographic utilities, book wholesalers, serial subscription agents, standards organizations, library and information science education programs, and professional organizations. Access to publisher home pages and catalogs can obviously assist the selection and acquisitions process. As a specific example, using the Internet to verify the cost and availability of a video can save the cost of a long-distance phone call.[13] As of November 28, 1995, the WWW Virtual Library provided access to 508 publishers. Another use of the World Wide Web is the creation of web pages by collection managers to communicate information to their constituents.

Specific types of information available on the WWW that would assist the collection management or acquisitions function are summarized below. Most of these can be accessed through AcqWeb:

Bookstore Names and Addresses
Book and Video Reviews
Lists of Award-Winning Books
Best-Seller Lists
Serial Back Issue Dealers' Catalogs
Stock Availability and Price
Currency Exchange Rates
Publisher Electronic Mail Addresses
Publishers' Catalogs and General Information
Vendor Policies and Services
Bibliographic Utility Policies and Services
Postal Information
Telephone Information

That electronic mail facilitates communication among librarians and with vendors is so self-evident that no further discussion is required. Finally, readers interested in relevant Usenet newsgroups are referred to Makulowich and Balas, who list about a dozen devoted to books.[14]

SELECTION OF INTERNET RESOURCES

Selection of information resources has been the oldest and most fundamental collection development function. In abstract terms both traditional and Internet resources are selected through an essentially identical three-step process: identification, microevaluation, and selection. (Microevaluation refers to the evaluation of a specific item, while macroevaluation is the evaluation of a collection or set of resources.)

The Internet's use in the selection (and acquisition) of traditional library materials was discussed in the preceding section. This section's major focus will be on the identification, microevaluation, and selection of Internet information resources.

Identification

Identification of a particular resource's existence is a logical prerequisite to selection. Traditional library materials are identified through reviewing sources, publishers' advertisements, approval plans, and so on. Identification or, as sometimes used in the literature, "discovery" of Internet resources presents more of a challenge because of rapid changes on the Net and its continuing lack of good bibliographical control. Yet, the Internet's resources can be identified through both print publications and the Internet itself. Printed guides to Internet resources abound. As examples, one can mention *Internet World: On Internet 94: An International Guide to Electronic Journals, Newsletters, Texts, Discussion Lists, and Other Resources on the Internet* or the *Gale Guide to Internet Databases*.[15] *Internet Resources: A Subject Guide* compiles a series of Internet guides in various subjects from *College & Research Libraries News*.[16] Moreover, published "webographies" are beginning to appear.

Many tools are simultaneously available in print and on the Net itself. One could cite, among numerous possible examples, the *Directory of Electronic Journals, Newsletters, and Academic Discussion Lists*, edited by Ann Okerson, which is available on the Association of Research Libraries' gopher, or the three-volume *Internet Compendium* by Rosenfeld, Janes, and Vander Kolk, which is available on the Internet through the Clearinghouse for Subject-Oriented Internet Resource Guides.[17]

A number of Internet tools have been developed for identification of information sources on the Net. Archie locates information on anonymous FTP sites, while VERONICA and Jughead perform subject searches of gopherspace and provide access to identified gophers through customized menus. Use of these tools is explained in innumerable Internet guidebooks, so there is no need for further elaboration here. As of November 1995, an Indiana University School of Library and Information Science web page provided access to 17 Internet search tools.[18]

Tools for identifying sites on the World Wide Web include Yahoo, Lycos, the WWW Virtual Library, and the World Wide Web Worm.[19] Web tools usually are based on the following approaches; (1) menu-like subject directories or indexes, (2) keyword searching, or (3) both. Most Web searching tools are fairly primitive and do not include Boolean searching. The present effectiveness of these tools in identifying Internet resources for collection management librarians remains an unanswered question. For a useful evaluation of numerous Web searching tools see Courtois, Baer, and Stark.[20] Other approaches for identifying Internet resources include; (1) patron or staff suggestions, (2) monitoring other gophers and websites, (3) listservs (for example NewJour can help identify new electronic journals), (4) published reviews, (5) Usenet groups, and (6) serendipity while surfing the Net.[21]

Microevaluation

In the second step, the identified item's intrinsic merit is evaluated. Microevaluation can be internal (i.e., done by the selecting librarian) or external, (i.e., furnished by a third party such as a book or software reviewer). The two are often combined as the selector reaches an internal evaluation that incorporates external evidence.

Most traditional microevaluation criteria, including factual accuracy, currency, overall quality, and nonbiased perspective, also apply to Internet resources. The author's qualifications and publisher reputation are separate traditional criteria. On the Internet the distinction between author and publisher is often blurred, but the issuing agency's authority remains a critical factor. Several traditional microevaluation criteria (e.g., factual accuracy, currency, and assessment of quality) may actually be more important for Internet than for print resources. This reflects the well-known fact that with the exception of some peer-reviewed electronic journals the Internet lacks gatekeepers to perform a quality control function. There are additional microevaluation criteria unique to the Internet. Reliability of access and the source's stability are, due to the Internet's volatility, particularly critical criteria.[22] Other criteria are ease of access and whether there is documentation, so-called About Files, or FAQs that can assist with its use.

Microevaluation of Internet resources can be challenging because, as pointed out by Johnson, many items on the Net do not have a formal title page that provides basic information about the source.[23] Nevertheless, a number of Internet tools provide evaluation of World Wide Web sites. McKinley, as of the fall of 1995, included a brief descriptive annotation for each of the 80,000 websites it accessed.[24] Moreover, 20,000 of these were evaluated through a one to four star-rating system applied to the overall site and to each of four criteria: coverage, organization, currency, and ease of access. Pointcomm rated 3,500

World Wide Web sites (each considered by Pointcomm to rank among the top 5% of all websites) using a 0 to 50 scale for content, presentation, and "experience" (i.e., subjective reaction to the site).[25]

Beginning in 1994, the "Best of the WWW Contest" provides annual "Best of the Web Awards," based on voting, for the best overall website as well as for the best campus information system, commercial service, educational service, entertainment site, professional service, navigational aid, and the most important service concept.[26] Four technical awards are also granted for the best in document design, use of interaction, use of multimedia, and technical merit. While the validity of these awards and their relevance to Internet selection by librarians are not yet established, one is tempted to speculate that someday there might be Internet awards with the same prestige as the Pulitzer Prize, National Book Award, or Newbery Medal.

Selection

In the final step, a decision to select or not select the item is made. What does "selection" of an Internet resource mean? Buckland cogently argues that it means "privileging" the resource by providing patrons easier access to it than to other resources, such as including it in a gopher.[27] Other examples not explicitly mentioned by Buckland would be creating a link on a library's World Wide Web home page or deciding to subscribe to an electronic journal available on the Internet.

As with microevaluation, most traditional selection criteria also apply to the Internet. Foremost among these are relevance to user need, projected use, whether the source's intended audience and purpose match the library's clients, and the library's collecting priorities. Additional criteria unique to the Internet include: whether an Internet site is the best source of information on a subject and whether the Internet is the best format for conveying the information. [28] Cost, a significant selection criteria for traditional materials, is usually not a factor in Internet selection since most resources are free.

RELATIONSHIP BETWEEN COLLECTION MANAGEMENT OF TRADITIONAL AND INTERNET RESOURCES

Many observers have stressed that traditional collection management principles also apply to the selection of Internet resources -- a point with which I agree. For example, Seiden and Nuckolls state that "any issues which are considered in the development of policies for traditional library materials should also be considered in developing electronic library collections."[29] Swann and Rosenquist-Buhler assert "Providing collection development in an electronic environment is really quite similar to traditional collection building, since evaluators attempt to select information they feel will be most relevant to the academic community they serve."[30] Collection management of Internet and traditional resources is fundamentally the same in many respects. The three-step process, outlined above, applies to both. Internet selection and traditional selection are both done for the primary objective of meeting user information needs. Both require knowledge of those needs, subject expertise, stated objectives, policy making, and priority setting. Librarians or information professionals using the Internet face the same responsibility outlined several decades ago by Ortega Gasset in *The Mission of the Librarian*: the obligation to separate out from the vast number of available resources (Ortega used the term "torrent of books") the small portion that best meets their clients' information needs.[31] In fact, as the Web increases in size, the filtering process will become even more critical.

How does collection management of Internet resources differ from traditional library collection management? A number of key distinctions (not listed in priority order) are enumerated below.

One selects rather than collects[32]

This is a self-evident yet crucial distinction. One usually selects Internet resources in order to provide access to them, whereas traditional resources are collected for the purpose of ownership and housing in the library. In exception to this generalization, software or electronic journals on the Net might actually be acquired.

Traditional space and cost restrictions generally do not apply to Internet resources

Resources accessed on the Internet do not consume library space. There are, of course, costs associated with establishing and maintaining an Internet connection. However, once connected to the Internet, most resources can presently be accessed free of charge. There are exceptions to the above statement. Some resources on the Internet (e.g,, the *Encyclopedia Britannica*), are not free, while such traditional resources as books and periodicals are occasionally received for free. The extent to which Internet resources continue to be free is a critical, but uncertain, issue.

The Internet offers resources that have not generally been collected by libraries in the past

An example is preprints. As of June 1995 an estimated 70 preprint servers were available on the Internet, of which the bestknown were probably the Los Alamos National Laboratory, Physics Service, founded by Paul Ginsparg, and the International Philosophical Preprint Exchange, managed by the University of Chiba's Philosophy Department.[33]

Internet selection decisions are often macro, whereas traditional selection decisions tend to be micro

Macro refers to "en bloc" selection of an entire group of resources with a single decision; micro selection is on a title-by-title basis. Linkage to a website (or including a site in a gopher) is clearly macro because every resource on the site is simultaneously selected. Again, there are exceptions to the preceding generalization. Selection of an electronic journal on the Internet would be at the micro level, while a traditional blanket order for all the publications from a particular publisher would be macro selection.

Duplication is a less important issue on the Internet

Innumerable gophers and websites provide links to the same original sources. Consequently, when a library selects other gophers and websites to be included on its own gopher or web page, many of the same original resources will be duplicated. Since Internet resources can be accessed free of charge, this is not, at present, an important concern.

One might select unneeded and unwanted sources[34]

Because much Internet selection is at the macro level on a "take it or leave it" basis (i.e., when one links to a web page, a connection is made to all resources on the site), many unneeded resources may be included. As with the point made above, this is seemingly not a major concern as long as Internet resources continue to be generally accessible free of charge. Nevertheless, the inclusion of "fun" resources that would not normally be collected by libraries has been questioned.[35]

Internet resources tend to be dynamic, while traditional resources tend to be static

It is generally well-known that many Internet sites undergo rapid change. In fact, the adjective "volatile" is often used to characterize the Internet. Some traditional resources, such as serials, do change from issue to issue, but most remain in a fixed format after they are selected.

Traditional and Internet resources require different kinds of collection maintenance

Collection maintenance is defined as the handling of resources after their acquisition. For traditional materials it entails decisions concerning binding, weeding, relegation to remote storage, multiple copies, and replacement of missing items. Due to the Internet's rapidly changing nature, gophers and World Wide Web pages require constant maintenance to ensure that external links have not changed their address, ceased existence, or lost their currency. For example, links on the University of Michigan's ULibrary Gopher are checked at least once every two weeks.[36]

Most traditional selection/microevaluation criteria apply to Internet resources, but the relative importance of specific criteria may vary while additional criteria also become relevant.

This point has been elaborated upon in the text of the preceding section.

Traditional resources are much more likely to be selected without direct examination than are Internet resources

With the exception of items received on approval, most books are selected without directly examining them. In fact, one reason for the founding of approval plans was to allow direct viewing before selection. In contrast, one presumes (there is no systematic research on the issue) that the creators of gophers and websites almost always examine Internet resources before creating links to them.

Most traditional resources are used by one patron at a time, while Internet resources can have multiple users[37]

Again, there are exceptions. Audio-visual items are sometimes used by more than one patron, while Internet resources requiring passwords can be limited to a set number of simultaneous users.

The library is more likely to create or "publish" Internet resources than traditional resources

A library's World Wide Web home page may be viewed as its own creation or publication. Only on rare occasions does a library publish traditional resources, as, for example, when it attempts to market its collection development policy.

Unlike traditional resources, many Internet resources are not packaged in bibliographical units

Traditional collection management tends to focus on information contained in such distinct bibliographical units as book or serial titles. While electronic books and serials are available on the Internet, the Net's information is often found in something other than a conventional bibliographical unit, such as a site, file, menu, or link.

Level of access is more critical in Internet than in traditional selection

Most traditional selection is a binary decision to select or not to select, although access level is occasionally a factor--for instance, the purchase of multiple copies to increase availability. At Cornell University's Mann Library, selectors must designate one of five "tiers of access" for a new electronic resource. Tiers 1 through 3 offer availability over the campus network through the Mann Library Gateway at declining access speeds ("instantaneous," "slower," and "not...continuously available"), tier 4 resources are available for use on a local-area network in the library, while tier 5 resources are used at a stand-alone workstation in the library.[38] In effect, higher level tiers offer quicker, more convenient access to patrons. Likewise, most gophers and websites have several hierarchical levels. Consequently, collection management of Internet resources often requires not only their selection but an assessment of their overall importance and relevance to patron need in order to determine the appropriate access level.

Unlike for traditional materials, there are many unresolved archiving/preservation issues for Internet resources

Libraries ensure that their traditional materials are adequately preserved through binding and preservation programs. Yet there are presently no mechanisms that guarantee the archiving of Internet resources. Internet publishers can not be depended upon to permanently preserve their own resources, while it is generally not feasible for libraries to do so, although some Internet resources, such as electronic journals, can be downloaded and preserved. At present there are several unresolved issues concerning the archiving/preservation of Internet resources. Who does the archiving: the resource creators, libraries, consortiums, national or regional agencies? Which resources are archived? For how long are they archived? What archiving methods are used? There is a real concern that unarchived Internet resources may eventually disappear from the scholarly record.

THE INTERNET AND MACROEVALUATION

Traditionally, macroevaluation focuses on the entire collection as opposed to the microevaluation of a specific item. In the evaluation of Internet resources the distinction between micro and macro blurs. A library's gopher or website could, depending on one's perspective, be viewed as a single source or a collection of sources. Nevertheless, evaluation of the Internet's overall effectiveness and efficiency in fulfilling patron information needs is clearly at the macro level.

Over the last several decades a host of techniques has been developed for macroevaluation of traditional library collections. Collection-centered techniques, which focus on the collection itself, include the checklist method, comparative statistical data, the Clapp-Jordan formula, and the RLG Conspectus. Client-centered methods, which concentrate on the client's use of the collection and how well client information needs are being met, include use studies, Orr's Document Delivery Test, and Kantor's availability study. The American Library Association's *Guide to the Evaluation of Library Collections* outlines the established evaluation approaches along with their benefits and drawbacks.[39] The literature on academic library collection evaluation through early 1992 is summarized by Nisonger.[40]

Established, authoritative methods for evaluating the Internet's effectiveness in libraries have not yet been developed. Present evaluation appears to be in an early, exploratory stage and frequently draws on general evaluation methods. For example, the Woodstock Library (in New York state) reportedly used "structured interviews, evaluation forms, logs, background data, questionnaires, and site visits" for Internet evaluation.[41]

The Internet can be used in traditional collection evaluation. One of the oldest most traditional approaches to collection evaluation is the checklist method, whereby a list of items is checked against the holdings of the library under evaluation. A basic issue in this approach's implementation concerns locating an appropriate list to check. The American Library Association's *Guide to the Evaluation of Library Collections* lists 15 possible sources for checklists, including "printed catalogs of the holdings of important and specialized libraries," an often used source in evaluation projects.[42] A checklist for evaluating one's own library could easily be generated by remote login to the OPAC of a library known to have a strong collection in a particular subject. Subject or keyword searches in the OPAC would identify titles for the checklist. An obvious question concerns how one determines which library holds an appropriate subject collection. Ash and Miller's *Subject Collections* is a classic print work that would be of assistance.[43] The creation of an online directory to the strengths of collections accessible by OPACS, as advocated by Drabenstott and Cochrane, would also be helpful.[44]

Remote login to an OPAC can also be used to evaluate another library's collection. This tactic could be used by researchers to assess whether it would be worthwhile to visit a distant collection on a research trip or by academics considering where to spend a sabbatical or whether to accept a job offer from an institution.[45] This technique's effectiveness would be limited if the library being accessed has not completed retrospective conversion of its entire collection.

A number of traditional collection evaluation methods have potential application to Internet evaluation. An availability study tests whether a patron can successfully locate an item on the shelf at the time he or she is searching for it. Lack of success may be because the item was not acquired by the library (acquisitions failure); the item was checked out (circulation failure); the item was lost or misplaced (library operations failure); or the patron was unable to find a correctly shelved item (user failure). Kaske claims that the concept of availability is no longer relevant in the electronic age because many patron needs are fulfilled by resources external to the library.[46]

I would argue that with some modification the availability model is applicable to Internet evaluation. Just as a patron may be frustrated because a desired book is checked out, someone accessing an electronic resource might receive a message "file server not responding." A test could be designed to measure patron success on the Net as well as analyze the causes of failure. If the patron was unsuccessful, was it due to technological error, the fact a password was required, the patron's lack of skill, or some other factor? A complicating, but not insurmountable, problem would be that most traditional availability studies presuppose the patron is seeking a specific bibliographical item: a condition that often might not apply to Internet users. (Research is needed to determine how patrons actually use the Internet in a library setting). The checklist approach, discussed above, could be used to evaluate the coverage of a website or gopher. Perhaps the biggest difficulty would be locating a valid, up-to-date list of Internet resources in a particular subject, although the evaluator could compile such a list himself or herself.

In the past, data on volumes held, current serial subscriptions, and material expenditures were major components for evaluation of a library's entire collection and specific disciplines as well as for comparison among libraries. A significant unresolved issue, at present, concerns how electronic journals and books are counted in library statistics, as they can be accessed by patrons but are not physically housed in the library. It seems exceedingly probable that in the future such collection-centered evaluation approaches as holdings statistics will decline in importance.

In the final analysis, the most critical evaluation criteria concern how well and how cost-effectively patron information needs are met. McClure, cited above, has recently emphasized the importance of user-based evaluation of networked information services.[47] There is also need for new, client-centered evaluation approaches to assess how well the library, as a system that integrates both print and electronic resources, is responding to patron need.

THE INTERNET AND THE CORE COLLECTION

The "core collection" has long been an important concept in collection development thought. The core refers to the most basic, fundamental, and important materials that form the center or heart of the collection. In the words of Sheila Intner, "core collections are the nucleus of needed materials no self-respecting library would be without the 20% of existing information stock that satisfies 80% (or more) of users' requests."[48] Core lists have been compiled for subjects, formats, and library type as well as these variables in combination with each other. They can assist in selection, collection evaluation, plus deselection and weeding.

The Internet has been used to identify core materials for the print collection. Stein reports that during a serials cancellation project at the University of Delaware Library, core periodicals in the "fashion, textile, and apparel merchandising/manufacturing" field were identified by accessing the OPACs of eight other large university libraries with strong collections in that area. Titles held by five of the eight libraries were defined as core. Furthermore, the Internet was found to be a better method than the OCLC database or mailed surveys for obtaining serials holding information from other libraries.[49] This approach could also be used in serials selection and cooperative collection development decisions.

The core concept is obviously applicable to Internet resources, especially when constructing a gopher or World Wide Web site. It is evident that one would want to include links to the core items. How does one know what constitutes a "core" Internet resource? This question is not answered in the published literature. Yet, it seems clear that many of the methods used to identify core print and other traditional items, such as subjective judgment, identification of highly used items, overlap analysis, and published lists, could also be used for determining core Internet resources.

One can cite examples of research that might be used to ascertain core Internet resources, even though this was not necessarily the authors' intended purpose. Tillotson, Cherry, and Clinton found that of 1,325 sites available to University of Toronto Library users, the top 10 accounted for 33% of the total connections, while 80% of the connections were to 13% of the sites-a finding reminiscent of Trueswell's famous 80/20 rule that 80% of the circulation is accounted for by 20% of the books. The three authors note that similar Internet usage patterns have been observed at Texas A&M, University of California at Santa Cruz, and Memorial University of Newfoundland Libraries.[50] Parenthetically, Haworth Press announced that a forthcoming issue of *Collection Management* will be devoted to the 80/20 rule in cyberspace.[51] A 1993 study of nearly 100 gophers by Seiden and Nuckolls found that some sources such as the *CIA World Fact Book*, the *Chronicle of Higher Education's* "Academe," and U.S. Supreme Court decisions were repeatedly included.[52] In the fall of 1995, Kuster was tabulating the external links on over 150 public library World Wide Web sites in order to determine, among other things, the most frequently linked sites.[53]

Published lists of the "best" Internet sites may be viewed as the equivalent of core lists. As examples, one should note lists of the 100 "most interesting" websites and the 10 best government Internet sites.[54] As with traditional core lists, it would be prudent to consider the list's authority, scope, and purpose before using it.

One is tempted to speculate that due to the Internet and electronic resources the core concept will assume a more significant role in collection management. As print collections become smaller, a trend already suggested by Perrault's research on the United States' declining national research collection, libraries may tend to concentrate on collecting the core, while providing non-core materials to patrons through external access mechanisms.[55] Under this scenario, identification of core print materials will be more critical because the core will make up a larger proportion of the print holdings.

In the past most core lists were restricted to a specific format, but a trend toward multiformat core lists that integrate print with Internet resources can already be discerned. For illustration, Musser's recently published list of titles dealing with climate and global change included both print periodicals and Internet discussion groups.[56]

THE INTERNET AND ACQUISITIONS

Acquisitions is closely connected to collection management, yet it is an analytically distinct function. For the purpose of this discussion, acquisitions is defined as the technical process of ordering, receiving, and paying for an item, after the intellectual decision to select it has been reached. One can cite numerous ways in which the Internet facilitates the acquisition of traditional library resources: electronic transmission of orders, cancellations, and claims; access to vendor databases; transmission of approval plan information; general communication with vendors through electronic mail; and preorder verification by accessing other library OPACs.

By early November 1995, more than a dozen academic library acquisitions departments had established their own home pages on the Web. These pages typically provide clients information about departmental staff and book ordering procedures, while containing links to other sites pertinent to library acquisitions.

The application of the acquisitions function to Internet resources is problematic because the Net's resources are generally not ordered, physically received, and paid for in the usual sense. Nevertheless, standard acquisitions procedures will still be relevant in some circumstances. For example, an electronic journal subscription over the Internet might require ordering, payment, monitoring that issues have been received, and claiming missing issues. (While a majority of electronic journals on the net are now free, this will probably change in the not-too-distant future). In other instances payment for Internet resources may take the form of licensing, pay per use, or payment for a set number of simultaneous users.

THE INTERNET AND COOPERATIVE COLLECTION DEVELOPMENT

Cooperative collection development and resource sharing have been major collection management themes for at least two decades, although many observers have been disappointed with the results. The Internet can support traditional cooperative collection development by facilitating the dissemination of holdings information and the rapid transmission of documents between libraries. To illustrate the former, libraries could check each others' OPACs to insure they are not ordering duplicate copies of a title already held by a cooperative collection development partner. As an example of the latter, in 1992 and 1993 the Pennsylvania State University's life sciences and medical libraries (separated by approximately 120 miles) cancelled a combined total of almost $12,000 worth of current serials subscriptions. Then, using Ariel, the library that retained a subscription would transmit over the Internet copies of requested articles to the library that canceled the title. Copyright fees were paid.[57]

Innumerable opportunities abound for modified forms of cooperative collection development in regard to Internet resources. A gopher or Web link to another library's gopher or website clearly represents a form of resource sharing and, unlike conventional interlibrary cooperation, can usually be implemented without a formal agreement or the other library's permission. The WWW Virtual Library, administered by CERN in Geneva, Switzerland, compiles subject-oriented websites created at many different institutes. Britten advocates an American Library Association Virtual Library Collection modeled on the WWW Virtual Library to avoid "needlessly building dozens of similar collections" on the World Wide Web by academic libraries.[58] As with traditional cooperative collection development, there is always the danger that another library whose resources are being relied upon will discontinue its efforts.

Likewise, electronic journal collections may be viewed as a form of cooperative collection development on the Net. The "Ejournal SiteGuide," accessible through AcqWeb, contains links to approximately 30 electronic journal collections including the WWW Virtual Library and the Library of Congress.[59] Particularly noteworthy is the CICNet Project which, as of April 1995, archived 880 electronic journals.

THE INTERNET AND DOCUMENT DELIVERY

In an era emphasizing access, document delivery is inextricably connected with collection management. The Internet supports traditional Interlibrary Loan (ILL), commercial document delivery, and access to external information resources that transcend the traditional ILL/document delivery model.

The Internet, in a number of ways, can facilitate the traditional ILL function for print materials. Both initial patron requests and library requests to lenders can be sent through electronic mail. Ariel, a system developed by the Research Libraries Group for transmitting documents over the Internet and installed in over 350 libraries by the spring of 1993, allows more rapid, higher-resolution, and less expensive transmission than provided by facsimile machines.[60] Some libraries also use Ariel to transmit the original request to the lending library.[61] The British Library Document Supply Center in conjunction with the University of East Anglia is experimenting with document delivery over the Internet.[62] The Association of Research Libraries' North American Interlibrary Loan/Document Delivery (NAILDD) Project for upgrading ILL and document delivery services among academic and research libraries includes support for electronic document delivery.[63] An increasing number of libraries now post information about ILL policy on their web pages along with electronic forms for patrons to submit requests. Accessing other library OPACs for holdings and circulation information can also facilitate the ILL function. Lynch notes that the Z39.50 standard allows software programs to search remote OPACs for this purpose.[64]

During the last half decade an increasing number of libraries have turned to commercial document delivery services. A noteworthy feature of these services on the Net, such as CARL's UnCover, is that the end-user can directly order a document without the intervention of a librarian. The issue of "disintermediation" presents an interesting set of questions that are beyond this chapter's scope.

Both ILL and commercial document delivery are tied to the old paradigm of providing print documents to patrons. Yet the Internet offers the opportunity to completely bypass the print format through electronic access to electronic documents. The number of electronic journals on the Internet is constantly increasing. *Alex: A Catalog of Electronic Texts on the Internet* provides direct access on the Net to 1,800 book titles, as of March 1995.[65]

However, as cogently argued by Lynch, it is unlikely that conventional ILL will, to any appreciable extent, be applied to electronic resources on the Internet.[66] Free items can usually be accessed directly without the intervention of another library. Paid-for resources will be licensed rather than sold and the license agreements will probably prohibit sharing with other libraries.

THE INTERNET AND STAFFING FOR COLLECTION MANAGEMENT

The Internet can potentially impact numerous collection management and acquisitions staffing issues, including workflow, education and training, staffing level, and departmental organization. However, it is difficult to isolate the Internet's impact on collection management staffing from that of other factors such as downsizing, budgetary considerations, and the increasing importance of electronic resources in general. This chapter focuses on one unresolved, but fundamental, issue: Who will select Internet resources? Possible theoretical models for organizing Internet selection responsibilities include subject, format, genre, committee, or a combination of approaches.

Organization by format implies that Internet resources will be selected by individuals with technological expertise who probably do not take part in other collection management activities. On the other hand, organization by subject implies that the collection development staff who select traditional materials will also be responsible for Internet resources within their subject domain. Cornell University's Mann Library has organized electronic collection development according to "genre." So-called genre specialists perform collection management functions for a particular type or "genre" of electronic information, such as applications software, bibliographic files, full text, numeric files, or multimedia regardless of the format, which might be CD-ROM, floppy disk, magnetic tape, or remote access through the Internet.[67] Committees can incorporate a variety of perspectives, including both subject and format expertise. In actual practice, many libraries use a mixture of approaches.

More research is required to ascertain how libraries are assigning Internet responsibilities. Organization by subject seems the best approach because Internet resources would be "mainstreamed" with regular selection.

Some Internet collection maintenance functions, such as checking that gopher and Web links are still valid, can be handled by nonprofessional staff.

THE INTERNET'S CHALLENGES FOR COLLECTION MANAGEMENT LIBRARIANS

It is almost a cliché to state that the Internet offers one of the most exciting and fascinating challenges confronting the library profession in this century. Specifically, what are these challenges for collection management specialists? They must demonstrate that their traditional skills and knowledge base (i.e., subject expertise, setting priorities, interpreting user information needs, evaluating resources etc.) are both relevant and needed in an electronic environment. Collection managers must master basic Internet skills themselves. Libraries will soon be expected to have their own home pages on the World Wide Web, and selection skills will be needed. Countless issues require research. A major challenge is to analyze the Internet with dispassionate objectivity, identifying areas of effectiveness and ineffectiveness while viewing the Net as neither panacea nor threat. New evaluation techniques must be developed. Written policy statements will be necessary concerning selection criteria, access issues, archiving and preservation for Internet resources. In the near future, an increasing number of resources will be simultaneously available in both print and electronic format, especially as commercial and university press journal publishers begin issuing their established journals electronically while continuing the paper version. Consequently, collection managers will frequently have to decide whether a specific title will be housed locally in print format, accessed electronically, or, in some cases, both. Both policy guidelines and title-by-title microdecisions will be required. As Demas succinctly states, "The challenge to this generation of librarians is to seamlessly knit together a multiplicity of formats and access mechanisms into one intellectually cohesive, user-friendly set of information resources and services." [68]

FUTURE PROSPECTS

This chapter's focus has been on the Internet and collection management in the context (late 1995). Some speculation concerning the Internet's future impact on collection management seems warranted.

Lynch's distinction between "modernization" and "transformation" can help clarify the discussion.[69] Modernization means doing better and more effectively what libraries have always done. Most of this chapter has focused on the Internet's role in modernization. In contrast, transformation represents a fundamental change in what libraries do. I would contend that while the Internet may lead to the transformation of libraries in the long run, in the near term it can contribute to modernization by assisting the performance of traditional functions.

In the short and perhaps the intermediate term, the Internet will undoubtedly help accelerate already existing trends toward smaller collections and an increasing emphasis on access rather than ownership. The Net will enhance, through providing access to externally held resources, the meeting of patron information needs. Yet collection management will become more complex because collection managers will face more choices; for example, should patron need for a journal title be met through a print subscription, access to the electronic version on the Internet, or document delivery?

Basic changes will almost certainly occur on a gradual, incremental basis. Zhou outlines a three-stage process for the migration from the print to electronic format over several decades: traditional acquisition of traditional resources, computerized acquisition of traditional resources, and computerized acquisition of electronic resources.[70] Bauwens offers a similar three-level framework: electronic access to real libraries, OPACs; electronic access to virtual collections with delivery of print documents (e.g., UnCover); and "electronic access to virtual collections consisting of electronic documents."[71] These schemes might seem to imply a uniform linear progression from stages 1 through 3.[72] In reality, the transition pace may vary among disciplines and among institutions.

The Internet's long-term impact on libraries cannot be foreseen. Potentially, the Internet might "transform" or alter the definition of what constitutes a library. For example, digital libraries could replace collections of print materials. This outcome is alluded to in statements by Lee Teng-hui, the President of Taiwan, and the computer guru Nicholas Negroponte, among others. President Lee recently commented to a distinguished American library consultant that the concept of a traditional library is as antiquated as the village well. Lee expects to receive both water and information in the modern way, delivered to him personally through a plumbing system or a computer network, rather than the outdated approach of having to journey to an external point, such as a well or library, and carry the commodity home.[73] Nicholas Negroponte recently expressed a similar concept in *Wired* magazine, proclaiming that in the future "every book" can be obtained "with a keystroke, not a hike."[74] Will the Internet, through its capacity to deliver information directly to homes and desks, eventually replace the library? If so, within what time frame? Will librarians be active agents or passive pawns in the Internet's ultimate impact on their profession? Will cybrarians replace librarians and webographers replace bibliographers? Answering these questions is probably impossible at this time and certainly beyond this chapter's scope.

SUMMARY AND CONCLUSIONS

This chapter's major themes may be summarized as follows; (1) the Internet can be used for more effective performance of traditional collection management functions, "modernization" in Lynch's terms, (2) the Internet presents numerous opportunities and challenges to collection management librarians, (3) traditional collection management skills are necessary for effective utilization of the Internet, (4) there are many similarities as well as critical differences between collection management of traditional and Internet resources, and (5) the Internet's ultimate impact on libraries and collection management cannot, at present, be predicted, especially since there may be unforeseen technological developments in the future.[75]

NOTES

1. William A. Britten, "Building and Organizing Internet Collections," *Library Acquisitions: Practice & Theory* 19 (Summer, 1995): 243.
2. Readers interested in Internet resources pertaining to collection management /acquisitions are advised to consult the AcqWeb home page on the World Wide Web (URL http://www.library.vanderbilt. edu/law/acqs/ acqs.html). All Web addresses reported in this chapter were current as of early December 1995.
3. Dennis G. Perry, Steven H. Blumenthal, and Robert M. Hinden, "The ARPANET and the DARPA Internet," *Library Hi Tech* 6, no. 2 (1988): 51.
4. Lucy A. Tedd, "An Introduction to Sharing Resources via the Internet in Academic Libraries and Information Centres in Europe," *Program* 29 (January 1995): 43.
5. Peggy Seiden and Karen A. Nuckolls, "Developing a Campus-Wide Information System Using the Gopher Protocol: A Study of Collection Development and Classification Issues," *The Reference Librarian* nos. 41-42 (1994): 276, 278, 281-282; Dan Lester, "I May Be a Cyclops, But I'm Not an Internaut," *Technicalities* 14 (March 1994): 8.
6. "Energizing the 'Net." *USA Today*, October 30, 1995, B1.
7. Evan St. Lifer, "A New Era for ALA?" *Library Journal* 120 (October 1, 1995): 38, who cites *Library Journal's* March 31, 1977 issue.
8. Thomas E. Nisonger, "The Use of CD-ROM to Investigate the In-Print/Out-of-Print Subject Patterns for Books," *Library Resources & Technical Services* 39 (April, 1995): 123.
9. Clifford A. Lynch, "The Transformation of Scholarly Communication and the Role of the Library in the Age of Networked Information," *Serials Librarian* 23, nos. 3/4 (1993): 7-8.
10. Tedd, "An Introduction to Sharing Resources," p. 48.
11. Lisabeth A. King and Diane Kovacs, comps., *Directory of Electronic Journals, Newsletters_and Academic Discusion Lists*, 5th ed., ed. Ann Okerson (Washington, DC: ARL Office of Scientific and Academic Publishing, 1995), pp. 383-405 (URL gopher://arl.cni.org:70/11/ scomm/ edir/edir95).
12. Donna E. Cromer and Mary E. Johnson, "The Impact of the Internet on Communication among Reference Librarians," *Reference Librarian* nos. 41-42 (1994): 150-154.

13. Telephone conversation with Kristine Brancolini, Indiana University Libraries, Media Services, on November 21, 1995.
14. John S. Makulowich, "Books, Books, Books -- Browsing in Cyberspace," *Database* 18 (June/July 1995): 88; Janet Balas, "In Celebration of Books," *Computers in Libraries* 15 (May 1995): 29.
15. Tony Abbott, ed., *Internet World's: On Internet 94: An International Guide to Electronic Journals, Newsletters, Texts, Discussion Lists, and Other Resources on the Internet* (Westport, CT: Mecklermedia, 1994); *Gale Guide to Internet Databases* (Detroit, MI: Gale Research, 1995).
16. Hugh A. Thompson, comp., *Internet Resources: A Subject Guide* (Chicago: Association of College & Research Libraries, 1995).
17. King and Kovacs, *Directory*; Louis Rosenfeld, Joseph Janes, and Martha Vander Kolk, *The Internet Compendium* (New York: Neal-Schuman, 1995) (URL is http://www.lib.umich.edu/chhome.html).
18. School of Library and Information Science at the Indiana University (URL http://www-slis.lib.indiana.edu/Internet/search_me.html).
19. Yahoo.com (URL http://www.yahoo.com/weblaunch.html); Lycos.com (URL http://www.lycos.com/); WWW Virtual Library (URL http://www.w3.org/hypertext/DataSources/bySubject/Overview.html); and the World Wide Web Worm (URL http://wwwmcb. cs.colorado.edu/ home/ mcbryan/WWWW.html).
20. Martin P. Courtois, William M. Baer, and Marcella Stark, "Cool Tools for Searching the Web: A Performance Evaluation," *Online* 19 (November/ December 1995): 14-32.
21. Susan Grajek and R. Kenny Marone, "How to Develop and Maintain a Gopher," *Online* 19 (May/June 1995): 38.
22. Gale A. Dutcher and Stacey J. Arnesen, "Developing a Subject-Specific Gopher at the National Library of Medicine," *Bulletin of the Medical Library Association* 83 (April 1995): 230.
23. Peggy Johnson, "Desperately Seeking Sources: Selecting OnLine Resour-ces, " *Technicalities* 15 (August 1995): 4.
24. McKinley.com (URL http://www.mckinley.com/).
25. Pointcom.com (URL http://www.pointcom.com/); "Web Site Rating Directories Increase," *Library Journal* 120 (October 1, 1995): 14; the author's direct examination of McKinley and Pointcom.
26. The Contest's Website (URL http://wings.buffalo.edu/contest/).
27. Michael Buckland, "What Will Collection Developers Do?" *Information Technology and Libraries* 14 (September 1995): 158.
28. Grace Ann York, "New Media/Traditional Values: Selecting Government Information on the Internet," *Collection Building* 14, no. 3 (1995): 8.
29. Sedien and Nuckolls, "Developing a Campus-Wide," p. 292.
30. Julie Swann and Carla Rosenquist-Buhler, "Developing an Internet Research Gopher: Innovation and Staff Involvement," *Journal of Academic Librarianship* 21 (September 1995): 373.

31. Jose Ortega y Gasset, *The Mission of the Librarian*, trans. by James Lewis and Ray Carpenter. (Boston: G. K. Hall, 1961), p. 22.
32. Rachel Cassel, "Selection Criteria for Internet Resources," *College & Research Libraries News* 56 (February 1995): 92.
33. "Darwinism and the Internet: Why Scientific Journals Could Go the Way of the Pterodactyl," *Business Week* (June 26, 1995): 44 (URL http://xxx.lanl.gov/); The International Philosophical Preprint Exchange's Website (URL http://phil-preprints.l.chiba-u.ac.jp/ IPPE. html).
34. Pat Ensor, "The Volatility of Electronic Collection Development, or, the Care and Feeding of a Gopher, Part 2," *Technicalities* 14 (September 1994): 4-5.
35. Mary Ann McFarland et al., "Developing a Health Sciences Library Gopher: More Involved than Meets the Eye," *Bulletin of the Medical Library Association* 83 (April 1995): 218.
36. Ruth A. Riley and Barbara Lowther Shipman, "Building and Maintaining a Library Gopher: Traditional Skills Applied to Emerging Resources," *Bulletin of the Medical Library Association* 83 (April 1995): 223.
37. Neal K. Kaske, "On My Mind: Materials Availability Model and the Internet," *Journal of Academic Librarianship* 20 (November 1994): 317.
38. Samuel Demas, "Collection Development for the Electronic Library: A Conceptual and Organizational Model," *Library Hi Tech* 12 no. 3 (1994): 76-80.
39. American Library Association, Resources and Technical Services Division, *Guide to the Evaluation of Library Collections*, ed. Barbara Lockett. (Chicago: American Library Association, 1989).
40. Thomas E. Nisonger, *Collection Evaluation in Academic Libraries: A Literature Guide and Annotated Bibliography* (Englewood, CO: Libraries Unlimited, 1992).
41. Denise A. Garofalo, "Internet Use by Rural Public Libraries: An Examination of Two Programs in the Hudson Valley of New York State," *The Internet Initiative: Libraries Providing Internet Services and How They Plan, Pay and Manage*, ed. Edward J. Valauskas and Nancy R. John (Chicago: American Library Association, 1995), p. 87.
42. *Guide to the Evaluation of Library Collections*, pp. 5-6.
43. Lee Ash and William G. Miller, comps., *Subject Collections: A Guide to Special Book Collections and Subject Emphases as Reported by University, College, Public, and Special Libraries and Museums in the United States and Canada*, 7th ed., rev. and enl. (New Providence, NJ: R.R. Bowker, 1993).
44. Karen M. Drabenstott and Pauline A. Cochrane, "Improvements Needed for Better Subject Access to Library Catalogs via the Internet." *Emerging Communities: Integrating Networked Information into Library Services: Papers Presented at the 1993 Clinic on Library Applications of Data Processing, April 4-6, 1993*, ed. Ann P. Bishop (Urbana-Champaign, IL: Graduate School of Library and Information Science, University of Illinois at Urbana-Champaign, 1994), p. 79.

45. Laine Farley, ed. *Library Resources on the Internet: Strategies for Selection and Use* (Chicago: American Library Association, Reference and Adult Services Division, 1992), p. 6.
46. Kaske, "On My Mind," p. 317.
47. Charles R. McClure, "User-Based Data Collection Techniques and Strategies for Evaluating Networked Information Services," *Library Trends* 42 (Spring 1994): 592-595.
48. Sheila S. Intner, "The Meaning of Core Collections," *Technicalities* 13 (July 1993): 4.
49. Linda Lawrence Stein, "What to Keep and What to Cut? Using Internet as an Objective Tool to Identify `Core' Periodical Titles in a Specialized Subject Collection," *Technical Services Quarterly* 10, no. 1 (1992): 3-14.
50. Joy Tillotson, Joan Cherry, and Marshall Clinton, "Internet Use through the University of Toronto Library: Demographics, Destinations, and Users' Reactions," *Information Technology and Libraries* 14 (September 1995): 192-193.
51. From a Haworth Press advertisement dated July 1995.
52. Seiden and Nuckolls, "Developing a Campus-Wide," pp. 279, 284.
53. Richard Kuster is a Ph.D. student in Indiana University's School of Library and Information Science.
54. Don Willmott, "The World-Wide Web: A Guided Tour of 100 Hot Websites," *PC Magazine* 14 (April 11, 1995): 37-42; Bruce Maxwell, "The 10 Best Federal Government Internet Sites," *Database* 18 (August/September 1995): 42-47.
55. Anna H. Perrault, "The Shrinking National Collection: A Study of the Effects of the Diversion of Funds from Monographs to Serials on the Monograph Collections of Research Libraries," *Library Acquisitions: Practice & Theory* 18 (Spring 1994): 3-22.
56. Linda R. Musser, "Climate and Global Change Serials and Internet Discussion Lists," *Serials Review* 20 (Spring 1994): 59-80.
57. Nancy I. Henry and Esther Y. Dell, "Ariel: Technology as a Tool for Cooperation." *Bulletin of the Medical Library Association* 82 (October 1994): 436-437.
58. Britten, "Building and Organizing," p. 247.
59. URL http://unixg.ubc.ca:7001/0/providers/hss/zjj/ejhome.html.
60. Mary E. Jackson, "Document Delivery over the Internet," *Online* 17 (March 1993): 15, 17.
61. Based on a conversation with Jay Wilkerson, Indiana University Library, on November 15, 1995.
62. Tedd, "An Introduction to Sharing Resources," p. 50.
63. Mary E. Jackson, *North American Interlibrary Loan/Document Delivery Project ILL/DD Management System: Summary Description* (Washington, DC: Association of Research Libraries, 1995) (URL gopher:// arl.cni.org: 70/00/ access/ill/naildd/mgt).

64. Clifford A. Lynch, "System Architecture and Networking Issues in Implementing the North American Interlibrary Loan and Document Delivery (NAILDD) Initiative," *Journal of Library Administration* 21, nos. 1/2 (1995): 146.
65. *Alex's Home Page (*URL http://www.lib.ncsu.edu/stacks/alex-index.html).
66. Clifford A. Lynch, "The Roles of Libraries in Access to Networked Information: Cautionary Tales from the Era of Broadcasting," *Emerging Communities: Integrating Networked Information into Library Services: Papers Presented at the 1993 Clinic on Library Applications of Data Processing, April 4-6, 1993*, ed. Ann P. Bishop (Urbana-Champaign, IL: Graduate School of Library and Information Science, University of Illinois at Urbana-Champaign, 1994), pp. 123, 124, 130.
67. Demas, "Collection Development," p. 74.
68. Ibid., p. 72.
69. Lynch,"The Transformation of Scholarly Communication," pp. 7-8.
70. Yuan Zhou, "From Smart Guesser to Smart Navigator: Changes in Collection Development for Research Libraries in a Network Environment," *Library Trends* 42 (Spring 1994): 652-657.
71. Michel Bauwens, "What Is Cyberspace," *Computers in Libraries* 14 (April 1994): 44.
72. These authors do not claim a uniform, linear progression from lower to higher levels.
73. This anecdote was related to the author by David Kaser, Distinguished Professor Emeritus, Indiana University, School of Library and Information Science.
74. Nicholas Negroponte, "Bits and Atoms," *Wired* 3 (January 1995): 176.
75. The author gratefully thanks Judith Serebnick, Associate Professor Emerita, and Howard Rosenbaum, Lecturer, at Indiana University's School of Library and Information Science, for providing valuable feedback on a draft of this chapter and Cynthia D. Bergquist, my graduate assistant, for photocopying articles.

CHAPTER FOUR

THE IMPACT OF THE INTERNET ON CATALOGING

William J. Wheeler and Matthew Beacom

Cataloging practice and cataloging service in libraries have been greatly affected by the advent of the Internet. In this chapter, we address three major impacts: the impact of Internet-enabled communications on cataloging workflow, the impact of Internet-enabled content on cataloging theory and practice, and the impact of Internet-enabled functionality on the catalog itself. Since the Internet enables faster communications and text sharing, it can be (and is) used as a tool for cataloging work. Because of increases in content and the expansion of types of content available through the Internet, the Internet has affected acquisition, description, and organization of materials in library collections. These changes, in turn, have pushed and pulled catalogers in different directions with respect to their job and role in the library. The functionality of the Internet, especially linking to resources outside the library, has allowed new uses for the catalog and has changed nearly everyone's sensibilities and expectations about what the catalog can be and should do. The cataloging world continues to be affected by these changes in functionality and expectation. This chapter represents only a snapshot of current issues.

Internet-enabled communications, such as discussion lists, email, gopher menus, Telnet and FTP, Z39.50, SGML, XML, and the World Wide Web, have radically altered cataloging workflow because these fast, ubiquitous, and independent communications enable better and easier resource sharing. Catalogers now share information in a wide spectrum of ways that has speeded up their work and promote cooperation. This impact can be seen as part of a long series of developments in cooperative cataloging from the early days of semiautomated receipt of LC cards to the development of computer terminals with dedicated connections to outside databases, and to the introduction of networked workstations. The Internet has speeded up and magnified this capacity.

Internet-enabled content, both new kinds of materials (e.g. electronic from initial publication, the so called born digital) and the reformatting of more familiar library materials (e.g., print items) in digital form are a completely new arena of publication to be cataloged. Furthermore, the networked electronic medium itself has the potential to incorporate all other kinds of publishing into this intangible format. Among the "born digital" are such things as e-journals, e-journal databases, e-news feeds, e-information-based services, and web pages of all kinds. Among the reformatted materials are such things as digitized journals and books, networked encyclopedias, and scanned image databases. Catalogers are faced with a great increase of items that may be potentially useful to include in library holdings. Although we have never cataloged the world's publishing output, publishing of the materials we are likely to catalog is increasing at a faster rate than ever before. There is a lot more to catalog. A corollary impact of the increased publishing via the Internet is a highly energized and engaged group of catalogers who are working hard to promote theoretical changes in the field and guide practical changes at the item-by-item level. These changes in the cataloging world have broader implications and engagements beyond traditional boundaries of library practice that touch on nearly every aspect of librarianship.

Internet-enabled functionality has had a huge impact on how the catalog can be used. The basic listing function of the catalog is transformed by hypertext linking that allows simultaneous discovery and delivery of the listed items. When a catalog points out from the traditional listing of physical items in a building to electronic resources not held but licensed for use, the catalog now acts as an intermediary of proprietary concerns. In addition, cataloging becomes collection development (where no license is in question) when merely pointing to a "free" web page and adding it to the library's holdings. The catalog now, via hyperlink, also connects to other lists, other catalogs, other bibliographies that also can deliver content as well as citations. Thus Internet functionality greatly expands the role of the catalog. It changes the catalog's fundamental nature and the context in which the catalog operates. This expansion of the role of the catalog complicates further the issues of workflow and content and poses challenges to catalogers. They and other librarians must reconceive what they should be doing together. Richard Meyer in *The Cataloger's Future: A Director's View* notes that a cataloger's work has always been determined by others (i.e., they do not select what to catalog but are given items to catalog), but this is changing in the Internet world, where a wider array of choices of what can be or should be cataloged is under discussion. Catalogers, reference librarians, collection managers, technical services staff, and top administrators must work with each other more closely across traditional work boundaries to consider the implications of intangible Internet content with respect to library collections and services. Meyer also notes that cataloging is heavily "dependent on the technology available at the time," and the effects of technology have been to magnify options, increase the skill levels needed of staff, and augment the range of materials that could be brought under control efficiently." Meyer sees opportunities in technology. He argues that "We can go beyond our traditional role of "acquiring, organizing...physical artifacts to...systematically identifying and providing access to all the information regardless of format." He sees the cataloger's role as providing important procedures for authority control and subject access. He argues that the impacts of technology on catalogers are major changes in job definition, skills required, and increasing demands to adapt to changing work flows.[1]

Norm Medieros suggests some key perceptual changes that the Internet has fostered. First, it has clearly caused a renaissance in cataloging and catalogers "in part because a need for database maintenance exists as a side effect of the online catalog - issues such as authority control (for example) ...remain a stumbling block for removing catalogers from the mix." While there remains a host of traditional materials that require cataloging, it is the "mass of unorganized information" on the Internet that "has revitalized the role of catalogers," and "the decision to catalog Internet resources was made well before the emergence of the Web-based catalog." Internet resources are part of the information world libraries attempt to provide access to. The common debate between cataloging what is held versus what is actually held outside the library continues to challenge catalogers to go beyond simply what they are told to catalog and face their own choices (including telling others what can be cataloged).[2]

IMPACT OF INTERNET-ENABLED COMMUNICATIONS ON CATALOGING WORK

The Internet has changed how catalogers and other cataloging department staff communicate with each other, with peers in other libraries, and with users. The Internet has created a cadre of virtual coworkers within and outside any given library. Email is the most visible instrument of this change, but Web pages and Web-based catalogs are also new communication tools used by staff in cataloging units. These communications tools have dramatically changed how cataloging staff share work information within one library and across many libraries. With these new tools catalogers now share more information with each other. The overall effect of this communication revolution is to draw the profession closer together as a working community.

The Internet has further affected the cataloging environment by changing the hardware and software commonly used in cataloging. Although the movement toward workstations or personal computers for staff in cataloging units preceded the Web, the popularity of the Web has superseded the older communications technology developed around dedicated terminals. OCLC, for instance, has switched from dedicated lines to TCP/IP. The Web is practically becoming the universal interface and platform for all cataloging operations from input to display because the use of the Web requires a networked, multipurpose computer, and Web OPACs require Web browsers. The possibility that

Web-appliance-style computers may replace workstation-style computers is growing as Web-oriented applications become more common and robust.

The Internet's enhancement of communications pathways is a key change in cataloging workflow. Chris Evan Lon notes a number of ways catalogers are using the Internet to enhance their cataloging practices, but they boil down to two basic findings: catalogers use the Internet to search other catalogs and to communicate with other catalogers.[3] Searching other catalogs has enabled better and faster copy cataloging and authority work for many librarians. It can also be cheaper for smaller libraries to check other trusted libraries' catalogs than paying for access to RLIN or OCLC. Communications among catalogers has been greatly enhanced by such things as discussion lists and simple email communications. Such tools speed up the communication process among coworkers and allow for a much wider range of people inside and outside ones own library to become virtual colleagues. Through email, especially such discussion lists as AUTOCAT-L, cataloging staff around the world are able to discuss issues, ask and answer questions, and solve work-related problems on the spot. Before the Web age, cataloging staff worked in relative isolation from peers at other libraries. Only those in geographically proximate libraries could share ideas and work strategies on a daily basis. Issues often waited in a long queue.

In addition to Internet-enhanced direct communications, the Web has enabled asynchronous virtual communications. Many catalogers and cataloging units have made websites to support their own or their unit's work. These websites are available to other catalogers and other libraries to a degree undreamed of with printed materials. Manuals, policies, reports, and other documents that were only locally distributed in the print era are now shared throughout the profession. Such websites have become a vital source of published practices, policies, and other documents. A particularly important example of this is the website produced by the University of California at San Diego, called Technical Processing Online Tools or TPOT at http://tpot.ucsd.edu/ Cataloging/Electronic.[4] This site has been an exemplary source of new ideas, processes, and actions within the cataloging community.

The Internet has also linked the world's online catalogs together, and the Web has provided them with a relatively similar interface. Z39.50 has opened catalogs as sources of MARC records to catalogers, and searching several library catalogs with one search has opened a whole new range of opportunities for catalogers (and for users). With Z39.50, catalogers and cataloging agencies have each other as viable alternatives to OCLC, RLIN, and LC as sources of MARC records for copy cataloging. While there is occasionally controversy on the use of MARC records from other libraries, the practice is common and follows a long tradition of record sharing. The shift is part of a general shift to more peer-to-peer relationships within the cataloging community. The hegemony of bibliographic utilities and the Library of Congress is loosened by such opportunities for peer-to-peer collaboration.

The Internet has made outsourcing cataloging operations more affordable and more manageable. Although some outsourcing of cataloging operations (such as the Library of Congress' catalog card distribution service) is almost a century old, the communications revolution caused by the Internet has enabled far greater flexibility. Not only can catalogers more easily share information about their work, but so can administrators and vendors. As Alan Poulter points out, the Internet enables enhanced communications with suppliers, vendors, publishers, and reference needs of catalogers. Librarians have better access to checking their decisions, and the Internet entails a broader work profile. Electronic processes enable publishers and vendors to supply a wider array of information about items pre- and post- publication that enhance cataloging accuracy and speed, such as tables-of-contents and CIP data. Z39.50 and various Web guides for catalogers (USMARC, OCLC, Catalogers toolbox) add new dimensions to catalogers work resources.[5]

There are other impacts of Internet-enabled communications on cataloging workflow. We have noted that Internet-enabled communications allow a wider array of real and virtual colleagues and that the Internet, as a work tool, has changed the hardware of cataloging from specialized, dedicated terminals to ubiquitous, individualized, and Web-enabled workstations. But a corollary of the move to individual workstations is a change from a linear path of cataloging work (from individual to individual each with his or her own task) to the ability of all staff to work on all aspects at their own desks. This has caused realignment of staffing divided in new combinations. More technology has meant more skilled jobs, less of an assembly-line model and sure movement toward the team model where everyone does some work on nearly every aspect of the cataloging stream. Finally, the actual point at which cataloging occurs has also changed, from a traditional model where cataloging might be the last task before shelf to the first task before the item is even received (in the case of a vendor-supplied record attached during ordering) or the actual first task that puts an item in the collection (in the case where cataloging an external Internet resource means we now have it in our library).

The impact of Internet-enabled communications and tools in cataloging operations is tremendous and only beginning. These changes primarily affect how work is done and how it is organized rather than what work is done on what resources. Changes in the publishing stream, a workflow that is also being transformed by the Internet and related technologies, have had an equally important impact on catalogers. Thus assessment of the impact of the Internet on cataloging operations is incomplete until we have addressed the growth of information resources in multiple new formats.

IMPACT OF INTERNET CONTENT ON CATALOGING THEORY AND PRACTICE

The Internet is transforming the publishing industry, and this transformation is pushing libraries in new directions. Print publishing has always been of particular importance to libraries, and cataloging operations and libraries have long collected other media as well, including motion pictures, recorded music, video, archival materials, and artifacts of various sorts. Thus catalogers have experience in cataloging all forms of media. The new media have caused the creation of new job titles for catalogers and new responsibilities for catalog units in libraries. E-resource catalogers are now fairly common, metadata librarians are not unknown, and catalogers routinely work with information technology professionals on campuswide information systems. However, it is networked digital content provided through the Internet that has created a number of new problems for catalogers while exacerbating a few older ones.

The inundation of networked digital media (the intangible content of the Internet) is driving a concerted effort to rethink and revise Anglo-American cataloging rules, theory, and practice in the modern era. The new non-physical "items" have unsettled our old ways - the intangible material of the Internet falls outside our usual work habits and disrupts normal relationships among publishers, vendors, acquisitions, cataloging, collection development, circulation, and reference. In the face of aggregations of e-journals and full-text databases, e-books and websites, virtual realities, and virtual communities, concepts such as "publish," "copy," "edition," "reproduction," and "original" descend into imperfect analogies that we apply in our work with increasing doubt about their utility.

Michael Buckland is one in the library world who has reminded us of the expanded role of information and the necessity for information specialists to be able to understand all of its ramifications. Interestingly, he points to the documentation movement of the 1930s-1950s (precursors of the indexing and abstracting field) that anticipated our current Internet and multimedia cataloging quandary. An influential documentalist defined a "document" as "any concrete or symbolic indication, reserved or recorded, for reconstructing or providing a phenomenon, whether physical or mental" (Briet, 1951 quoted in Buckland p. 355). A wide array of tangible and intangible things is included in this broad definition, and we seem to have recognized early on that there is much more than print material that is worth organizing. We heirs of the documentalists (catalogers), then, have no justification for excluding intangible Internet resources from the catalog - they are potentially valuable information resources we should be and are collecting.[6]

Bella Hass Weinberg in reporting on a session of the American Society for Information Science Special Interest Group on Classification Research (ASIS/SIGCR) provides a cautionary note about our assumptions of the impact of Internet documents on cataloging. Instead of panicking about all the new and different aspects, she looks back at many similar situations that have gone before. First, she notes we have never cataloged the universe of print materials; thus we should not allow ourselves to be too alarmed by the sheer magnitude of the Internet. She goes on to mention the documentation movement which engaged in questions of fine-grained indexing and notes the hundreds of thousands of humanly indexed things, reckoning that the DIALOG database alone may have as many as 1.6 billion assigned index terms - thus the Internet's billions are not too many for us to organize for access. An example of the prior existence of solutions to moving targets (like unstable URLs) is the common practice of book indexers to provide for the revision process. She notes that indexers embed information in sections of documents to enable retrieval even if pagination changes; thus the bewailing and gnashing of teeth over URL changes should not be considered as a new development; rather strategies to overcome this difficulty will simply have to be created. Ultimately she notes a host of reinventions that are occurring across the field. Her article is a much needed island in our ocean of worry.[7]

The library community, especially the cataloging community, is responding to the changes in communication and publishing by both adapting rules and procedures and strategically rethinking the theory and practice of our profession. Examples of adapting practices and rules can be seen in recent changes to the MARC format and the cataloging guidelines issued by CONSER. In the mid-1990s, the MARC format was changed to allow the addition of information relating to the "electronic location" of digital media that are accessible remotely via the Internet (MARC 856 field). The addition of this field to the MARC record in catalogs allowed the catalog record to link directly to the resource it describes for the first time and fundamentally changed the nature and use of the library catalog.

In the mid-1990s, staff with CONSER, the national cooperative serials cataloging project, wrote a new module, *Module 31,* [8] for its cataloging manual to instruct or guide catalogers who catalog remotely accessible electronic serials. This module became the basis for widespread cataloging practices, and the serials cataloging community generally began to rethink cataloging in light of the new media. This effort has taken many hands and has been driven by many institutional and community needs and is now culminating in a profound revision of the Anglo-American cataloging rules for serials.

The new media are driving the creation of new rules for cataloging. In 1997 an international conference was held in Toronto entitled: "The Principles and Future of AACR" to consider whether and how much the Anglo-American cataloging rules and practices should be changed. The follow-up actions to this conference include a logical analysis of the structure of the rules by Tom Delsey,[9] analysis and proposed new rules for serials led by Jean Hirons,[10] and efforts led by the ALCTS Committee on Cataloging: Description and Access (CC:DA) to rethink and rewrite a "cardinal principle" of the cataloging rules, rule 0.24 (item in hand, reference all characteristics so that the characteristics or nature of networked, digital media is accommodated).

Jennifer Younger notes some of the history of resource description (cataloging and indexing) and the host of changes caused by developments on the Internet. Clearly, one impact implied by these notes about resource description is that the impact of the Internet on cataloging is the sheer volume of information resources that require/need some sort of retrieval. Librarians and information specialists, at least, seem to have recognized this early on and initiated processes to organize and to point to these resources. Younger notes a host of early experiments and ongoing initiatives in the library world. Reviewing the host of initiatives and new metadata standards, she argues that no single scheme will work for all types of materials. One problem associated with cataloging resources on the Internet is the traditional relationship of one MARC record to one document which is now in question. Younger calls for a need to map across various formats, MARC, SGML, XML, Dublin Core, and develop cooperative arrangements between various metadata and cataloging standards. Thus impacts (again) include a wider array of choices, a diversity of tools, a broadening of demands on catalogers, as well as calls for rule changes about what an "item" or "work" may be.[11]

Other impacts of Internet content on cataloging theory have been widespread experimental projects. Among the earliest projects investigating the impact of the Internet on cataloging and catalogs in the United States, was OCLC's early 1990s study of Internet resources. It identified a body of materials similar to those traditionally collected by libraries.[12] This study and the attention it generated led OCLC staff and others to experiment with actually cataloging Internet resources. This further test demonstrated two things critical to applying traditional library cataloging to Internet resources. First, it showed the potential of AACR2/MARC cataloging for supporting intellectual access to Internet materials. Second, it highlighted the need for a means to link the bibliographic record to the networked resource.[13] This latter need was addressed in 1994 by the creation of the MARC tag field 856 (Electronic location and access). The addition of this tag field made library cataloging Internet ready. The next step was OCLC-led cooperative Internet cataloging project-InterCat that involved hundreds of libraries in identifying, selecting, and cataloging thousands of Internet resources culminating in the publication in 1995 of *Cataloging Internet Resources: A Manual and Practical Guide.*[14] Following the formal end of the InterCat project, the database continues to be supported by OCLC and used by many libraries.

Building on the success of the InterCat project, OCLC initiated in 1999 another cooperative cataloging project, the Cooperative Online Resource Catalog (CORC). CORC went beyond the goals of the earlier project. Rather than testing the value of cataloging for Internet resources, CORC would be a suite of tools and a production environment for cataloging Internet resources. CORC's immediate claim on the attention of librarians was its use of two formal types of metadata within one catalog-AACR/MARC and Dublin Core. The CORC effort, both project and product, represents a particularly potent confluence of new tools, new content, and new ideas. The CORC project may also prove to be an important milestone for cataloging and the Internet in another way; it became a commercial product on July 1, 2000.

In addition to the efforts of the cataloging community, parallel developments can be seen for other media: the EAD (Encoded Archival Description) and SGML Document Type Definition (DTD) for archives; the

Dublin Core Metadata Initiative and its element set for Web resources; the Data Documentation Initiative (DDI) DTD for numeric data; the Visual Resources Association (VRA) core for digital images; and the FGDC for geospatial data.

IMPACT OF INTERNET-ENABLED FUNCTIONALITY ON THE CATALOG

The role of the catalog is changing due to the enhanced functionality enabled by the Internet. It is more than simply a list of local holdings; it is now operating in a context of other catalog-like entities, and it can be seen as a collection development tool. Earlier work in subject access, indexing and abstracting, and information retrieval (heirs to the documentalists mentioned above) anticipates some of the impacts catalogers are now feeling. The following section addresses how catalogers are facing these changes. In fact, much of our debate today in an Internet environment is preceded in the literature on indexing and information retrieval (see especially Cochrane's work as early as 1985 [15] and Fugmann 2000[16]).

If one accepts the Oxford English Dictionary's (2nd edition)[17] earliest, simplest definition of basic "catalog(ue)" as "A list, register, or complete enumeration," one can see how a resource like the Internet, with its millions of items potentially valuable to a library's collection, would challenge the library cataloger. The more modern definition (usually distinguished from a mere list or enumeration, by systematic or methodical arrangement, alphabetical or other order and often by the addition of brief particulars, descriptive or aiding identification indicative of locality, position, date, price, or the like) highlights the added challenges presented by the Internet's disaggregated chaos. Librarians define the catalog principally by identifying the functions of the catalog. The most recent work on the revision of AACR2 expands on the Paris Principles. The IFLA Study Group on the Functional Requirements for Bibliographic Records *Final Report* identifies four functions to enable users: (1) to find, (2) to identify, (3) to select, and (4) to obtain materials.[18] The 1999 summary report of the CCDA Task Force on Metadata (1998-2000) suggests that a fifth use be incorporated to reflect the library's ultimate purpose: use of materials. Without knowing it, those who suggest this fifth function are rediscovering one of the five laws of library science outlined by Ranganathan in the 1960s.[19] His five laws are remarkably prescient of our age stating that: (1) books are for use, (2) every reader served his book, (3) every book helped to find its reader, (4) save the time of the user, and (5) the library is a growing organization. If we replace books in these laws with resources, we have a good definition of the purposes of a library, and looking closely at laws 2, 3 and 4, one can note the clear call for accurate cataloging.

We can see from these definitional developments alone that the catalog is conceived of as much more than a listing of library holdings - it is a critical tool for library access. In the Internet environment, even as a list, the catalog now fails to be comprehensive while at the same time including more than a library's collection - crossing the barriers from old notions of local holdings to point to the holdings of other libraries and other resources not locally held. The catalog, in effect, at least part of the time, is a kind of virtual interlibrary loan operation. The list concept is also intimately tied to the concept of tangible items held, whereas now there is a host of intangible items made accessible via the catalog. As librarians have moved to home pages and gateways, catalogs have moved to become portals to content, a notion which expands more traditional concepts of the collection.

Solutions to identifying and pointing to Internet resources in the library have varied. One very common approach is not to catalog, but rather to make lists and lists of lists. This follows in an age-old tradition in libraries of bibliography. The fine-grained subject nature of much of the Internet has perhaps presented itself as easier to list. Its gray and ephemeral quality has perhaps suggested to librarians not to spend too much effort. But in fact a great deal of effort has been assigned to creating these lists. Another age-old tradition in libraries includes handouts, signage, stack guides, and various sorts of research guides. We have never bothered to catalog them - they change, they are simpler to create, destroy, use, and discard. In fact there is (and was) rarely a single tool to find all materials in any library; people have nearly always had to learn about the library through multiple catalogs, lists, indexes, and bibliographies. Guides of this nature continue and are now prevalent in libraries websites. Additionally, this pointing and listing function in a Web environment is being taken on by many other entities besides the catalog. While libraries have always had finding aids, bibliographies, and signage, the new similarity of all of these equally published on the library's web pages in effect creates a host of catalogs (in a user's mind) or a dismayingly large number of lists of stuff held in (or outside) the library. If one takes a historical view, one can see almost every kind of work librarians traditionally have done being replicated in the Internet environment – bibliographies, subject guides, dictionary catalogs, alphabetical lists, and so on. It is yet to be determined how we will break out of this replication and find truly new capabilities in the Internet environment, a Kuhnian revolution away from normal library science to a new paradigm.

The familiar notion of a library as a *place,* and as a *collection* is fundamentally challenged in the electronic environment. So too is the catalog as a description of the items in that place. The boundary between the local and the distant is blurred, one could see connection to Internet resources as a kind of instantaneous ILL, but we rather tend to see ourselves as collecting a number of virtual items that are worthy of our collection, organization, and notification to patrons of access.

A traditional model of collection development follows a pattern something like this: a book is published (or is announced); a librarian receives notice and decides to add it to the collection, and submits an order; the item is shipped and arrives, is processed and cataloged, and appears on the shelf ready to be found, identified, selected, obtained, and borrowed (used) by the user. Nowadays, a cataloger who adds an URL to a cataloging record (or other librarian who links from his or her library web page) virtually adds an item to the collection circumventing some or all of these processes. By virtue of pointing, an item becomes part of the collection.

CONCLUSION

In this chapter we have spoken in mostly theoretical terms about the impact of the Internet on cataloging practice and the catalog. In general, the impact of the Internet on cataloging has been to change how we catalog, what we catalog, and why we catalog. The impact of the Internet has revitalized basic issues regarding cataloging theory and practice. Like the context in which cataloging and catalogs undergo transformative changes, catalogers and catalogs change too. Users, librarians, and others in the information and communication industries are all looking for ways to organize the resources available on the Internet, to make it accessible, and to make it usable. Libraries, catalogs, and catalogers continue to play an important role in organizing information for access and use. Whether or not they will be important in the future is an open question. Will catalogers become knowledge managers? Will catalogs become networked information work spaces rather than simply finding aids? Or will other professions fill the roles for knowledge managers, other tools replace the catalog, and other institutions replace the library?

The most recent discussion of this open question is taking place as part of the Library of Congress Bicentennial Conference on Bibliographic Control in the New Millennium. The papers and other information about this conference are at http://lcweb.loc.gov/catdir/bibcontrol/.[20] All of these articles speak to specific issues also raised in this chapter. Sarah Thomas suggests that (among other things) we will have to be freer in working with other metadata standards (like Dublin Core), accept copy from vendors, work with authors, and increase collaboration worldwide in order to deal with the increasing amount of work we should do to serve users.[21] Tom Delsey argues for increased attention to the interface between the catalog, databases, and indexing as well as notes the increasing issue of rights access/licensing versus the traditional kind of ownership a library has had over its material.[22] Both Ann Huthwaite[23] and Matthew Beacom [24] call for significant changes in AACR and harmonization of AACR with ISBD. Karen Calhoun's descriptions of the typical, very labor-intensive acquisitions process for electronic products and the multiple lists (of library resources beyond the catalog) problem[25] are right on target. Lois Mai Chan's article on subject access and the untapped potential of LCSH, LCC and DDC for Web retrieval speaks to a whole area we have avoided here.[26] The discussions on information retrieval using human indexing versus automatic indexing and natural language versus controlled vocabulary searching go far back in the library literature but remain one of the most difficult issues to handle.

NOTES

1. Richard Meyer, "The Cataloger's Future: A Directors View," *Cataloging & Classification Quarterly* 24 (1997): 195-204.
2. Norm Medieros, "Delivering the Goods: Web OPACs and the Expanding Role of the Cataloger," *Issues in Science and Technology Librarianship*, (Spring 1998): 1-2; (URL http://www.library.ucsb.edu/istl/98-spring/article3. html).
3. Chris Evan Lon, "The Internet's Value to Catalogers: Results of a Survey," *Cataloging & Classification Quarterly* 23, no. 3/4 (1997): 65-74.
4. Technical Processing Online Tools or TPOT (URL http://tpot.ucsd.edu/ Cataloging/Electronic/).
5. Alan Poulter, "The Internet as a Tool for Descriptive Cataloging," *Cataloging and Classification Quarterly* 24, no. 1/2 (1998): 187-191.
6. Michael Buckland, "Information as Thing," *Journal of the American Society for Information Science* 42, no. 5 (1991): 351-360.
7. Bella Haas Weinberg, "Improved Internet Access: Guidance from Research on Indexing and Classification," *Bulletin of the American Society for Information Science* (December/January 1999): 25-28.
8. Jennifer Younger, "Resource Description in the Digital Age," *Library Trends* 45 (Winter 1997): 465-485.
9. CONSER *Cataloging Manual: Module 31: Remote Access Computer File Serials* (URL http://lcweb.loc.gov/acq/conser/module31.html).
10. Tom Delsey, "Modeling the Logic of AACR," *in Papers, International Conference on the Principles and Future Development of AACR* (Toronto: Joint Steering Committee for Revision of AACR, 1997). (URL http://www.nlc-bnc.ca/jsc/ r-bibun.pdf).
11. Jean Hirons and Crystal Graham, "Issues Related to Seriality," *in Papers, International Conference on the Principles and Future Development of AACR.*
12. Martin Dillon, Erik Jul, and Mark Burge, "The OCLC Internet Resources Project: Toward Providing Library Services for Computer-Mediated Communication," *in Emerging Communities: 30th Clinic on Library Applications of Data Processing* (University of Illinois at Urbana-Champaign, Graduate School of Library and Information Science, 1993).
13. Erik Juhl, "Cataloging Internet Resources: An Assessment and Prospectus," *Serials Librarian* 34, no. 1/2 (1998): 91-104.
14. OCLC, *Cataloging Internet Resources: A Manual and Practical Guide*, 2nd ed. (Dublin, Ohio: OCLC, 1999). (URL is http://www.purl.org/oclc/ cataloging-internet).
15. Pauline Cochrane, *Redesign of Catalogs and Indexes for Improved Online Subject Access: Selected Papers of Pauline A. Cochrane* (Phoenix, AZ: Oryx Press, 1985).

16. Robert Fugmann, "Obstacles to Progress in Mechanized Subject Access and the Necessity for a Paradigm Change," in *Saving the User's Time through Subject Access Innovation*, ed. William J. Wheeler (Urbana: Board of Trustees of the University of Illinois, 2000).
17. Oxford English Dictionary, 2nd ed., s.v. "catalogue."
18. IFLA Study Group on the Functional Requirements for Bibliographic Records, *Final Report*, UBCIM Publications - New Series Vol. 19, (Munchen: K. G. Saur, 1998).
19. S. R. Ranganathan, *Five Laws of Library Science* (Madras: Madras Library Association, 1931).
20. Library of Congress, *Papers Presented at the Conference on Bibliographic Control in the New Millenium at the Library of Congress, November 2000* (URL http://lcweb.loc.gov/catdir/bibcontrol/).
21. Sarah E. Thomas, "The Catalog as Portal to the Internet," in *ibid.*
22. Tom Delsey, "The Library Catalog in a Networked Environment," in *ibid.*
23. Ann Huthwaite, "AACR2 and Its Place in the Digital World: Near-Term Solutions and Long-Term Direction," in *ibid.*
24. Matthew Beacom, "Crossing a Digital Divide: AACR2 and Unaddressed Problems of Networked Resources," in *ibid.*
25. Karen Calhoun, "Redesign of Library Workflows: Experimental Models for Electronic Resource Description," in *ibid.*
26. Lois Mai Chan, "Exploiting LCSH, LCC, and DDC to Retreive Networked Resources: Issues and Challenges," in *ibid.*

SUPPLEMENTARY READING

ALCTS/CCS/Committee on Cataloging: Description and Access. Task Force on the Review of the IFLA Guidelines for OPAC Displays. "Report" (URL http://userwww.sfsu.edu/ ~turitz/ccdatf3. htm).

ALCTS/CCS/ Committee on Cataloging: Description and Access. Task Force on Metadata. "Summary Report," June 1999 (URL http://www.ala.org/alcts/organization /ccs/ccda/tf-meta3.html).

ALCTS/CCS/SAC/Subcommittee on Metadata and Classification "Final Report," 1999 (URL http://www.ala.org/alcts/ organizations/ccs/sac/ metaclassification.pdf).

The Alex Catalogue, A Collection of Digital Texts with Automatic Methods for Acquisition and Cataloging, User-Defined Typography, Cross-searching of Indexed Content, and a Sense of Community (URL http://sunsite.berkeley. edu/alex/).

Bates, Marcia. "Indexing and Access for the Digital Libraries and the Internet: Human, Database, and Domain Factors." *Journal of the American Society for Information Science* 49, no. 13 (1998): 1185-1205.

Calhoun, Karen. "Redesign of Library Workflows: Experimental Models for Electronic Resource Description." In *Papers Presented at Conference on Bibliographic Control in the New Millenium at the Library of Congress, November 2000* (URL http://lcweb.loc.gov/ catdir/ bibcontrol/ Calhoun_paper.html).

Caplan, Priscilla. "Cataloging Internet Resources." *The Public-Access Computer Systems Review* 4: no. 2 (1993): 61-66.

Chan, Lois Mai. "Exploiting LCSH, LCC, and DDC to Retreive Networked Resources: Issues and Challenges." In *Papers Presented at the Conference on Bibliographic Control in the New Millenium at the Library of Congress, November 2000* (URL http://lcweb.loc.gov/catdir/ bibcontrol/chan_paper.html).

CONSER "Cataloging Manual: Module 31 - Remote Access Computer File Serials" (URL http://lcweb.loc.gov/acq/ conser/module31.html).

CONSER "Cataloging Manual: Module 33.18 - Electronic newspapers" (URL http://lcweb.loc.gov/acq/conser/ enewsppr.html).

CORC Cooperative Online Resource Cataloging Project (URL http://corc.oclc.org/).

Data Documentation Initiative (URL http://www.icpsr.umich.edu/DDI/ codebook.html).

Delsey, Tom. *The Logical Structure of the Anglo-American Cataloguing Rules - Part I,* 1998 (URL http://www.nlc-bnc.ca/jsc/index. htm).

Delsey, Tom. *The logical structure of the Anglo-American Cataloguing Rules - part II,* 1999 (URL http://www.nlc-bnc.ca/jsc/ index.htm).

Dillon, Martin, and Erik Jul. "Assessing Information on the Internet: Toward Providing Library Services for Computer-Mediated Communication." *OCLC Systems and Services* 10 (Summer/Fall 1994): 86-92.

Delsey, Tom. "The Library Catalog in a Networked Environment." In *Papers Presented at the Conference on Bibliographic Control in the New Millenium at the Library of Congress, November 2000* (URL http://lcweb.loc.gov/catdir/bibcontrol/ delsey_paper.html).

Delsey, Tom. "Modeling the Logic of AACR" in *Papers Presented at the International Conference on the Principles and Future Development of AACR Toronto: October 23-25, 1997.* Toronto: Joint Steering Committee for Revision of AACR (URL http://www.nlc-bnc.ca/jsc/ r-bibun. pdf).

Dublin Core Metadata Initiative. *Dublin Core Metadata Element Set, Version 1.1: Reference Description* (URL http://purl.org/dc/documents/ rec-dces-199809.htm). This document has also been published as: Weibel, S.; J. Kunze ; C. Lagoze; M. Wolf. *Dublin Core Metadata for Resource Discovery. IETF #2413*. Reston, VA: The Internet Society, September 1998.

Electronic Resources: Selection and Bibliographic Control. *Cataloging & Classification Quarterly* 22, no. 3/4 (1996); entire issue.

Encoded Archival Description (EAD) Official Web Site (URLhttp://lcweb. loc.gov/ead/).

Federal Geographic Data Committee. *Content Standard for Digital Geospatial Metadata* (URL http://www.fgdc.gov/metadata/ contstan.html).

Hirons, Jean and Crystal Graham. "Issues Related to Seriality." In *The Principles and Future of AACR: Proceedings of the International Conference on the Principles and Future Development of AACR, Toronto, Ontario, Canada, October 23-25, 1997.* Ottawa and Chicago: Canadian Library Association; American Library Association, 1998.

Hirons, Jean. *Revising AACR2 to Accommodate Seriality: Report to the Joint Steering Committee for Revision of AACR, with the Assistance of the CONSER AACR Review Task Force, April 1999* (URL http://www.nlc-bnc.ca/jsc/ser-rep0.html).

Hudgins-Bonafield, Christine. "Who Will Master Metadata?" *Network Computing* 6, no. 8 (July 1995): 102-108.

Huthwaite, Ann. "AACR2 and Its Place in the Digital World: Near-Term Solutions and Long-Term Direction." In *Papers Presented at the Conference on Bibliographic Control in the New Millenium at the Library of Congress, November 2000* (URL (http://lcweb.loc.gov/ catdir/ bibcontrol/ huthwaite.html).

IFLANET "Digital Libraries: Cataloguing and Indexing of Electronic Resources" (URL http://www.ifla.org/II/ catalog.htm).

INTERCAT *Proceedings of the OCLC Internet Cataloging Colloquium Jan 1996* (URL http://www.oclc.org/oclc/man/ colloq/toc.htm).

ISBD(ER) *International Standard Bibliographic Description for Electronic Resources* (URL http://www.ifla.org/VII/s13/pubs/isbd.htm).

Jeng, Ling Hwey. "A Conversing Vision of Cataloging in the Electronic World." *Information Technology & Libraries* 15, no. 4 (December 1996): 222-229.

Jul, Erik. "Why Catalog Internet Resources?" *Computers in Libraries* 16, no. 1 (January 1996): 8-10.

Landesman, Betty and Steve Oberg. "What's in It for Us? Internet Use in Technical Services." *Serials Librarian* 28, no. 3/4 (1996): 317-321.

LC Draft Interim Guidelines for Cataloging Electronic Resources (URL http://lcweb.loc.gov/catdir/cpso/ dcmb19_4.html).

Martin, Susan K. and Don Bosseau. "Organizing Collections within the Internet: A Vision for Access." *Journal of Academic Librarianship* 22, no.4 (July 1996): 291-297.

OCLC *Cataloging Internet Resources: A Manual and Practical Guide,* 2nd ed. (URL http://www.purl.org/oclc/ cataloging-internet).

OCLC InterCAT Project (URL http://www.oclc.org/oclc/research/projects/ intercat.htm).

Porter, Margaret G. and Laura Bayard. "Including Web Sites in the Online Catalog: Implications for Cataloging, Collection Development, and Access." *Journal of Academic Librarianship* 25, no. 5 (September 1999): 390-394.

Simpson, Pamela and Patrricia Banach. "Finding the Missing Link: How Cataloging Bridges the Gap Between Libraries and the Internet." *Serials Librarian* 31, no.1/2 (1997): 245-230.

Stewart, Barbara. "Cataloging: Related Sites on Technical Services Benefits of Home Page Development" (URL http://tpot.ucsd.edu/Cataloging/ Misc/ cataloging.html).

Thomas, Sarah E. "The Catalog as Portal to the Interent." In *Papers Presented at the Conference on Bibliographic Control in the New Millenium at the Library of Congress, November 2000* (URL http://lcweb.loc.gov/ catdir/bibcontrol/ thomas_ paper.html).

Visual Resources Association Data Standards Committee VRA Core Categories, Version 3.0 (URL http://www.gsd.harvard.edu/~staffaw3/vra/ vracore3. htm).

Weibel, Stuart L. "The World Wide Web and Emerging Internet Resource Discovery Standards for Scholarly Literature." *Library Trends* 43, no. 4 (Spring 1995): 627-645.

CHAPTER FIVE

THE IMPACT OF THE INTERNET ON INTERLIBRARY LOAN AND DOCUMENT DELIVERY PRACTICE

Cindy Kristof

Interlibrary loan has always meant change.[1]
-Virginia Boucher

INTRODUCTION

Long gone are the days when ILL practitioners had only the union catalogs to assist them in locating materials not held locally. A variety of technological changes have occurred over the last 33 years: the use of Teletype equipment to transmit ILL requests, the birth of ILL messaging systems (OCLC, RLIN, WLN, and Docline), and the fax machine. The Internet promises to have the largest impact of all, from the way bibliographic utilities are accessed (such as OCLC Multidrop[2] vs. Internet access), to the way users submit and receive their requests, and to the way librarians communicate with each other. As these changes are implemented, the Internet promises to deliver to ILL practitioners some of the greatest challenges ever faced, as well as some of the greatest assistance ever possible. This chapter will outline these challenges and changes and their impact on ILL service everywhere.

Early Impact: An Example

During the latter half of the 1980s, librarians in Wisconsin and Pennsylvania began to utilize bulletin board systems (BBS) to communicate with each other. Cathy Moore (1987) describes the Wisconsin Interlibrary Services (WILS) ILL Network.[3] An IBM PC with 640K and a 10MB hard disk was used at WILS, together with BBS shareware (RBBS-PC). Librarians dialed into the BBS to post ILL requests, making requesting between member libraries much quicker. Likewise, David Belanger describes a similar system used by the Delaware County Library System in Pennsylvania,[4] which sliced the time it took to fill an ILL request from 7.1 days to 3.2. Though in a strict technical sense, these BBSs did not use the Internet, they illustrated the early power of electronic communications and served as a harbinger of the changes soon coming for ILL practitioners.

Visions That Shaped ILL Technology

In 1992, Shirley K. Baker and Mary E. Jackson prepared a paper for the ARL Committee on Access to Information Resources entitled "Maximizing Access, Minimizing Cost: A First Step toward the Information Access Future," which describes the "ideal system" for resource sharing. Due to continued increases in demand for interlibrary loan services (between 1981 and 1992 lending by ARL libraries grew by 52%, and borrowing grew by 108%), it was apparent that current systems could not support continued growth. Their vision included, but was not limited to, a patron-initiated system which would verify the current status of the patron and directly submit the request and the patron information to the bibliographic utility or document supplier. Automated billing and gathering of statistics would be automatic in this system and increased use of the Internet to transmit articles.[5] Soon thereafter, in 1993, the North American Interlibrary Loan and Document Delivery (NAILDD) Project, undertaken in collaboration with over 40 vendors and systems suppliers, was established by ARL in order to "facilitate the development of standards, software, and system design capabilities to improve interlibrary loan and document delivery services for users, and to make them more cost effective for research libraries."[6] Due to the efforts and initiatives of ARL, IFLA, the National Library of Canada, and other organizations, as well as advances in technology which utilize the Internet, ILL practice continues to grow closer to this ideal.

Two years later, in 1994, Harry S. Martin III and Curtis Kendrick published a paper entitled "A User-Centered View of Document Delivery and Interlibrary Loan." This paper presents a scenario in which Professor Sonia Hillel-Garcia sits at her office workstation for less than 30 minutes ordering items that she needs for her research and teaching. During this time, she orders full-text articles (some available to her immediately), books (some delivered directly to her office), and items to be placed on reserve.[7] This scenario was an amazing one at the time it was written. Advances in technology and the use of the Internet have pulled many libraries closer to this vision, with such services as electronic journals and desktop delivery.

The Kaleidoscope of ILL Technology

It would be impossible to describe in chronological order the impacts the Internet has had on ILL because many of these changes developed—and are still developing—simultaneously. They include electronic document delivery, electronic ordering and processing, electronic journals, and electronic mailing lists.[8] They also include the availability of databases and other information on the Web that are both a source of ILL requests for library users and a reference resource for ILL practitioners. This chapter outlines each of these aspects of Internet impact on ILL from the three perspectives of history, current practice, and future developments.

ELECTRONIC DOCUMENT DELIVERY SYSTEMS

Ariel

Since sending photocopied articles through the post office has always added extra days to ILL turnaround time, librarians have sought ways to expedite delivery. An early example of this was a detailed, one-month study of the use of the fax machine to transmit ILL articles between the Berkeley and Davis campuses of the University of California by William D. Schieber and Ralph M. Shoffner.[9] Though faster than traditional mail, fax transmission has always been plagued, however, by a host of problems including equipment failures, paper jams, thermal paper, telecommunications costs, and poor resolution.

In 1989, the Research Libraries Group (RLG) formulated a set of goals which eventually became its Shared Resources Program (SHARES), one of the goals of which was to develop an improved method of delivering photocopied materials. This goal gave birth to Ariel, which was beta-tested in October 1990 by six institutions: the University of Pennsylvania, the University of Michigan, Colorado State University, Dartmouth College, the University of California at Berkeley, and the University of California at Davis. On October 24, 1990, the University of Pennsylvania transmitted the first document via Ariel.[10]

In the fall of 1991, when Ariel was first officially released, its advantages over the fax machine were immediately apparent. Libraries could scan printed materials directly from the original, eliminating the need to photocopy the article first. The scanned images, TIFF files (Tagged Image File Format), had a compressed file size to save disk space yet also had a high resolution of 300 x 300 compared to a fax machine's high resolution setting of 100 x 200. Images were scanned into the Ariel software using a compatible commercially available scanner, then transmitted via FTP through the Internet to another Ariel workstation, where they were printed using a compatible commercially available laser printer. Because Ariel used the Internet rather than phone lines, telecommunications charges did not apply. Libraries could realize cost savings in both photocopy paper and in phone bills.[11] A copyright statement, which could be individually tailored by each library, was automatically transmitted with each article, thus helping libraries to comply with copyright guidelines.

Among the early disadvantages: Ariel workstations could transmit only to other Ariel workstations. Since many libraries did not own Ariel workstations, libraries that did were limited as to where they could send transmissions. Also, the scanned image could not be previewed before sending. Therefore, the receiving library would need to request retransmission of poor copies.[12] Ariel was not free of transmission problems either since documents could not always be sent successfully if there were a problem with the receiving workstation.

Systems similar to Ariel were being developed and tested around the same time Ariel was released commercially. Two such projects were The Ohio State University's CIC Network Fax Project and North Carolina State University's Digitized Document Transmission Project (DDTP).[13] Both projects utilized the Internet to transmit documents; the CIC Network Fax Project utilized a fax gateway, and the DDTP used a Macintosh HyperCard interface. However, neither project developed into a commercially available system with widespread use as did Ariel.

Studies have since proven the usefulness of Ariel to a variety of institutions. Two 1994 studies describe the use of Ariel between health sciences libraries in Pennsylvania and Delaware; in both, turnaround time for article delivery was reduced to 48 hours or less.[14] A 1997 study describing the State University of New York (SUNY) Ariel Project concluded that Ariel "can be considered a cost-effective, low-risk investment since most of the equipment needed to run it includes items that many campuses own, such as a PC, a laser printer, a scanner, and access to the Internet."[15] A 1999 study in which data were collected from a small, private Southern California undergraduate institution found that use of its courier service produced a statistically significant reduction in turnaround time compared to both fax and Ariel, but that use of fax or Ariel produced a significant reduction in turnaround time when compared to U.S. mail.[16]

As of February 1997, with Version 2.0, many of Ariel's shortcomings were eliminated. Ariel migrated to a Windows environment. Ariel became capable of transmission via the Internet to either another Ariel workstation or to a MIME-enabled electronic mail account. A preview feature for viewing scanned page images before sending was developed. A wide variety of commercially available scanners is now supported, including overhead scanners, such as the Minolta PS 3000, [17] which make scanning less laborious and are more preservation-friendly. Ariel continues to be labor-intensive at times, requiring staff attention, especially when scanning and sending, but the advantages continue to outweigh the disadvantages.

Because Ariel image files are TIFF files, if the file is sent to an email account, the end-user either will need a TIFF reader, such as National Library of Medicine's Docview,[18] or will need to convert the TIFF file to another file type for reading. An example of this is the conversion of a TIFF file to a PDF (Portable Document Format) file in order to read it with the free-of-charge, widely available Adobe Acrobat Reader.[19] Software from Adobe can do this, as can National Library of Medicine's DocMorph Server.[20] Recently, other programs, including some ILL management software, have been developed in order to make transmission and conversion of Ariel files and other electronic documents easier by utilizing the Web.

Electronic Document Delivery via the Web

High-volume delivery of Ariel TIFF files to users' email accounts can cause problems such as overloads on disk storage space allotted to users and slow downloads of large files. Programs were developed for local use at Marshall University (Web-EDD) and at Yale University (EDD) that allowed users to download documents in PDF format, with some scanned locally, and some converted from Ariel TIFF files.[21]

Systems staff at the John A. Prior Health Sciences Library at Ohio State University further developed Yale's EDD source code. This program, called Prospero, offers Web delivery of Ariel TIFF's files converted to PDF format. Documents coming from outside institutions as well as documents scanned in-house without having ever been transmitted can be converted. Prospero automatically sends an email message to end-users, informing them that their document is ready to be downloaded. After users download their articles, the files can be removed from the system after they have been viewed a specific number of times or after a certain number of days, depending on local copyright policies.[22]

Other systems that have been developed or are in the process of developing Web delivery modules include, but are not limited to, the ILLiad ILL management system developed at Virginia Tech and Docutek's ERes electronic reserves system originally developed at Santa Clara University.[23] The future is certain to bring more systems; we have seen only the beginning of electronic document delivery.

Web Request Forms

With the advent of widespread use of the Web, libraries began to develop their own web pages and complete online ILL request forms which enabled patrons to submit requests without completing a paper request form. Use of Web request forms has now become widespread. A 1997 check of the Netsearch icon of Netscape revealed almost 500 web pages related to ILL and "order forms."[24] A search at press time of Google[25] for the phrase "interlibrary loan request form" produced 1,830 hits. While this does not mean that there are 1,830 ILL Web forms in existence, this does indicate just how widespread their use has become.

Web request forms are useful in that patrons can submit ILL requests from any workstation with Web connectivity, 24 hours a day, seven days a week. For ILL practitioners, this means that messy handwriting does not need to be interpreted. The construction of Web request forms for ILL involves writing some HTML codes and some CGI scripts. This is just a recent practice.[26] Creating these forms is easier now than it ever was, thanks to HTML authoring tools, such as Dreamweaver and Microsoft FrontPage. An example of a more advanced system is the one used by participating libraries of the Library Association of Singapore. Their system is not just a Web form but also a system that allows ILL staff to manage back-end processing of ILL requests.[27]

ILL Prism Transfer and Beyond

While many ILL departments still print out electronic information and process it along with paper forms, a more efficient use of electronically submitted information is its transmission directly into an ILL request system such as the OCLC ILL Subsystem, so that library staff do not have to retype information. The results of the 1995/1996 ARL ILL study recommend this and other available technologies because they reduce staff involvement, thus saving staff time, when processing requests.[28] Such a system authenticates the patron (no more checking users against the OPAC's patron database), transmits the electronic request information directly into the ILL subsystem workform (no more retyping), allows immediate searching and bibliographic verification (no need to write down accession numbers), and then sends the request along to randomly chosen reciprocal or consortial libraries which have the desired item in their collections.

One library's success story is found at Southern Illinois University at Carbondale (SIUC), where a plan for comprehensive, patron-initiated borrowing was developed. In 1993, patron-initiated book borrowing, called ILLINET Online, was implemented for 45 Illinois Library Computer Systems Organization (ILSCO) libraries, including SIUC. In 1995, the FirstSearch Interlibrary Loan Link was initiated, allowing users to search FirstSearch databases, retrieve bibliographic records, and make requests directly from the databases. These requests were transferred directly into the OCLC ILL Review File. Soon thereafter, the library developed an ILL form on the Web, with the assistance of OCLC, which also transferred requests into the Review File. Though their system involved multiple systems, re-keying of ILL requests was thus eliminated, and ILL processes were successfully streamlined. Future plans included tracking and management systems for ILL requests and for copyright.[29]

An example of an initiative that evolved from a simple Internet request form to a powerful, time-saving, and commercially available system is Colorado State University's ZAP program. ZAP began in 1990 as a plan to develop a request form on the Internet. The Internet was not a familiar word to most at this time, and this request form predated the Web. However, this early system was sophisticated enough to store patron information in the system so that users did not have to retype it. Later, with the assistance of OCLC staff, ILL/PRISM Transfer was developed and implemented, which saved staff from having to rekey data into the OCLC ILL Subsystem. Soon thereafter, CSU developed a set of keystroke macros so that staff would save keystrokes when processing requests.[30] ZAP has since been developed into WebZAP, a Web-based ILL management system that can be purchased by other libraries for their use.[31]

With some ILL management systems, patrons can log into them to track the progress of their requests. This means that ILL practitioners do not have to answer the phone calls of patrons concerned about the status of their requests. As discussed in the previous section, other systems allow electronic document delivery via the Web, which saves patrons the time it takes photocopies to arrive in the mail and saves libraries postage costs. One system that does both is ILLiad, developed at Virginia Tech. Like WebZAP, ILLiad also provides its customers with a Web request form. Request information is captured and transferred into the OCLC ILL work form via a macro, eliminating the need to rekey information. Like WebZAP, ILLiad has been made commercially available.[32]

ISO ILL Protocol Standards

Ideally, all ILL management systems will eventually conform to the ISO ILL Protocol Standards (ISO 10160, ISO 10161-1, and ISO 10161-2). The ISO protocol allows, among other things, different ILL systems to communicate not only with ILL messaging systems, but also with each other, based on a client-server communications model.

The history of ISO ILL Protocol begins in Canada in 1983, when work began on protocol specification long before the vast majority of librarians were using the Internet. The National Library of Canada (NLC) launched PEB/ILL, the very first protocol-based ILL management system in 1987. During the late 1980s and early 1990s, Canadian libraries developed protocol-based systems so that by October 1996, 46 Canadian libraries were exchanging messages with the NLC. During the early 1990s, a European-based project began, which involved three national bibliographic centers in Great Britain, the Netherlands, and France. However, due to ILL messaging systems that were serving their constituents well, such as OCLC and RLIN, there was not much interest in ILL Protocol development in the United States until 1995.[33]

In 1995, the NAILDD established the ILL Protocol Implementers Group (IPIG) in order to explore the feasibility of developing protocol-based systems in the United States. An invitation was sent out by Mary Jackson on November 27, 1995, urging organizations and vendors to participate.[34] As of May 2000, 35 official representatives from eight countries from a variety of ILL vendors and organizations committed to implementing the ISO ILL Protocol Standards. Among these are the National Library of Medicine, OCLC, and RLG.[35] Projects include, but are not limited to, RLG's ILL Manager and Colorado State Univeristy's WebZAP.[36] Currently, OCLC's ILL Direct Request Service will accept an ISO-10161 ILL request from an external system.[37]

The technical aspects of ISO ILL Protocol are lengthy and complex and will not be reviewed in this chapter. However, the Protocol allows ILL systems to do the following:

- Exchange ILL messages between a wide variety of ILL management systems, despite their differences

- Allow two or more systems to communicate with each other; one can even act on behalf of another
- Manage the information in the ILL office, allowing tracking of ILL requests, including status and current location of materials.[38]

Each separate ILL action, such as "ILL-Request," "Shipped," "Received," "Returned," or "Renew," has been mapped to an ILL protocol "service." These services allow various systems to communicate with each other in a specific sequence so that an item cannot be "returned" before it is "received," for example. "ILL-Request" identifies the library, the desired item, and the preferred method of shipment. These technical complexities should be transparent to the user, provided that the end-user interface is well designed.[39]

Recent "protocol developments would not bear as much promise without the existence of the Internet's ubiquitous network."[40] Internet communications channels make communications between systems smooth and reliable. Additionally, Web-based interfaces for both end-users and ILL practitioners are being developed.

Despite nearly two decades of development, the use of ISO ILL-compliant systems is not yet widespread; we are "very much in the experimental stages of this ILL model."[41] It is not difficult to imagine the impact that these systems will have once in place and fully developed. Consider this scenario: an ILL practitioner at Kent State University in Ohio requesting a copy of a book chapter from Germany for a Modern and Classical Languages faculty member will no longer need to type an IFLA request form or send a free-form email message. Instead, with a few clicks of the mouse, a formal, electronic request will be sent via the OCLC ILL Subsystem, for example, and received by a German library using GBVdirekt/North America.[42] Ideally, the worried faculty member will be able to track the status of the item from her own office workstation, without calling the ILL office. Indeed, she may not need to leave her office at all; the book chapter will be made available in electronic format on the Library's website, ready to download once it is received from Germany. Resource sharing will reach unprecedented ease and efficiency. And we will be the lucky witnesses of ILL history.

Electronic Journals

Though outside the realm of traditional ILL services, the availability of electronic journals has grown dramatically over the past decade. Some journals, about 90% in 1996,[43] are published independently of major publishing houses and are available for free to all. On the other end of the spectrum are electronic journals published in both print and electronic formats by such giants as Elsevier. The Internet, specifically the Web, has made delivery of both easy for the end-user, as most are now available either in HTML or PDF format.

Free to All

There are many examples of electronic journals that require no subscription fee of their readers. Two journals, because they are listed in OCLC as Kent State University publications, are frequently requested from the Libraries' ILL department. The first is the *Online Journal of Issues in Nursing*, or OJIN (available at http://www.nursingworld.org/ojin/). The second is *LIBRES: Library and Information Science Electronic Journal* (available at http://utklib.lib.utk.edu/libres/). They are both peer-reviewed electronic journals and serve as good examples of electronic journals available on the Web, free to all. The ILL department typically responds to OCLC requests for articles from these journals with a conditional response, pointing toward the URLs for each. In the future, as ILL departments and their users adapt to electronic journal availability, it is likely that fewer such requests will be received.

Fee-Based Electronic Journals

The burden of publishing an electronic journal is likely to make many of the free publications carry a subscription price in the future. However, the focus here is on electronic availability of journals that are also available in print format, published by major publishers. A specific example of this is the OhioLINK Electronic Journal Center, which is a collection of such journals.

In order to avoid the copyright entanglements of large-scale electronic transmission of articles as well as the labor involved and as a solution to cooperative collection management for serials, OhioLINK sought consortial agreements with publishers for a shared collection of full-text electronic versions of print journals. This resulted in the OhioLINK Electronic Journal Center (EJC). The first publisher involved, beginning in 1996, was Academic Press, followed closely by Elsevier.[44] As of June 2000, other publishers included the American Physical Society, the Institute of Physics, Kluwer, MCB University Press, Project MUSE, the Royal Society of Chemistry, Springer-Verlag, and Wiley. All journals published electronically by these publishers are included; the total title count is over 3,000. Available issues for many titles go back as far as 1995.[45]

The expected result of the OhioLINK EJC is a reduction in ILL sharing.[46] With nearly 440,000 articles downloaded from the EJC during the 1998-1999 fiscal year,[47] the impact is not difficult to imagine. To date, OhioLINK has not measured or studied this. Not everything that every OhioLINK patron will ever want will be incorporated in the EJC. Recognizing this, OhioLINK continues its work through its Article Sharing Task Force, which seeks to enhance patron-initiated article requesting.

The overall impact of electronic journals on traditional ILL requesting has not yet been measured in a major study. ILL borrowing in ARL libraries continued to rise by an average of about 7.9% per year from 1986 to 1999.48 However, for the first time since 1986 when ARL began gathering these statistics, ILL lending decreased from the previous year by 3.9%. Are we beginning to witness the impact of electronic journal availability? If so, why did borrowing rates not follow suit? Are other, unrelated factors responsible for the ARL lending drop?[49] There are no answers to these questions right now, and any assumptions would be premature. Indeed, as Stephen Prowse writes, "electronic journals are poised to make a considerable impact on ILL – but not yet."[50] Their ease of use and instant availability are tremendously appealing to users and libraries alike. Their impact on the future of ILL will be interesting to observe as it unfolds.

Electronic Mailing Lists

Electronic mailing lists have played a major role in the way ILL practitioners communicate with each other. Problems are solved, policies are clarified, and professional contacts are made through these lists. Never before have ILL practitioners had such an easy way to connect with their colleagues and find solutions to problems. What follows is a list of major electronic mailing lists and their scope. This list is not meant to be a comprehensive guide; rather, it serves to illustrate the current ease of drawing on the profession's greatest resource: other ILL practitioners.

ILL-L

ILL-L, which began in November 1990,[51] is the most active of the lists devoted to ILL. It serves as a forum for common practice, copyright issues, policy changes, etiquette discussions, job postings, workshop announcements, calls for papers/presenters, citation verifications, last-resort requesting, and general discussion. Announcements from major ILL vendors and library associations are almost always made on this list. Traffic on this list is relatively heavy, at approximately 20 or more messages per day. Regional ILL lists, such as Texas' LoanStar, and the United Kingdom's LIS-ILL serve similar purposes for their constituencies.

IFLA-L

Sponsored by IFLA, this is a general list about the organization's activities and about issues related to librarianship from an international perspective. However, this list has a high proportion of ILL-related postings,[52] which make it worthwhile and valuable for ILL practitioners.

DOCDEL-L

This list was established in 1995 as a commercial document delivery-based discussion.[53] Previously hosted by EBSCOdoc and currently hosted by DocDel.net, it serves as an unmoderated forum for the discussion of document delivery issues. List traffic is generally slower than ILL-L. Since discussions often have a different focus, it is an important list for ILL practitioners.

ARIE-L

ARIE-L serves as a forum for discussion of the Ariel electronic document transmission system. Generally, traffic consists of announcements of libraries' new Ariel installations, new Ariel addresses, and Ariel downtime. Problems libraries experience with the system are frequently posted, and Research Library Group's Ariel technical support responds to inquiries over this list.

CLIO-L

CLIO-L is an example of a list devoted to support of an ILL management system. Problems experienced with the system are discussed, and Clio's technical support addresses problems with the system. Suggestions for improvements to the system are made via this forum, as well as announcements of new product releases such as ClioRequest. One of the first such lists, SAVEIT-L, was devoted to the now-extinct management and statistical software. Other examples of such lists include, but are not limited to, WebZAP-L (a forum for WebZAP users and other interested parties), ILLiad-L (a forum for users of the ILLiad system) and QUICDOC-L (a forum for users of National Library of Medicine's Quickdoc software).

UNCOVER-L

CARL UnCover's UNCOVER-L is an example of a list devoted to a commercial document delivery service. Announcements by UnCover regarding corporate changes, such as new services, are made through this list, which also provides a forum for users of this service.

Other Lists

Lists more peripherally related to ILL also prove useful for the ILL practitioner, depending on the focus of one's primary job responsibilities. FISC-L, for example, is devoted to the discussion of fee-based services in libraries. The OFFCAMP listserv is devoted to the discussion of library services for distance learners. The CNI-COPYRIGHT Forum can provide valuable discussion of copyright issues directly related to ILL practice. Occasionally, LIBREF-L, a list for reference librarians, contains valuable information related to ILL and document delivery, and it can serve also as a valuable reference resource. However, it is especially important for those involved in the busy field of ILL to choose wisely among electronic mailing lists, as their combined traffic has the potential to become overwhelming.

WEB RESOURCES

A multitude of general Web resources now exist that are particularly valuable for the ILL practitioner. They have made information that, only a decade earlier, may have taken days to find—or processes that would have involved much more paperwork—available almost instantly. An excellent listing of websites for ILL practitioners is available at the DocDel.net website at http://www.docdel.net. It has also become apparent that, on the user's end, the Internet is a significant potential source of ILL requests. Both aspects of Web resources are discussed below.

Verification of Questionable Citations

Citation verification for ILL practitioners has traditionally been a chore. Before the advent of networked CD-ROM databases and databases made available over the Web, it was always necessary to consult paper indexes, a laborious task often involving dusty tomes. The proliferation of web pages of all sorts have made this task easier, often an enjoyable challenge. For example, tables of contents of journals are often made available for free on publishers' websites, even if access to the journal itself is subscription-based. Publishers' websites also often contain forthcoming books, a convenient way to demonstrate to ILL users that the book they requested will not be printed for six more months. The web pages of researchers of all sorts often contain their curriculum vitae, an invaluable way to verify citations that cannot be found in available electronic databases. Since their web pages almost always have contact information, such as phone numbers and email addresses, obtaining ephemera, reprints, or more current information about research is often possible through direct contact with researchers. In turn, researchers are often flattered that their obscure document is being sought out.[54]

ILL Department Websites

ILL department websites, discussed previously in the context of Web request forms, have made it easy for ILL practitioners to check on policies, prices, and personnel. While directories such as OCLC's Name and Address file (NAD) and Leslie R. Morris' *Interlibrary Loan Policies Directory* (1999) also make it possible to check on library policies and other pertinent information, websites are frequently more updated. Importantly, library Web pages more often than not contain links to libraries' OPACs, whether those are Web- or telnet-based. OPAC access is especially useful when one has a need to find out circulation status, or when a library does not use an ILL messaging system, such as OCLC or RLIN.

Overseas libraries such as national and university libraries, particularly those in Europe and Asia, are often especially difficult for U.S. ILL practitioners to access. The Web has enabled those libraries to be accessed quickly, often by email. IFLA has developed guidelines for libraries to use when sending non-ISO ILL requests by email. This has increasingly become common practice, and the email messages that result are often "free-form" and thus may not contain all the necessary information.[55] Since the Web has made finding international libraries much easier, these email requests are likely to continue for years until ISO technology is developed and acquired on a broad scale.

Commercial Document Delivery Vendor Websites

Today, any commercial document supplier would be foolhardy not to have a website. Users, often but by no means always ILL practitioners, can check on prices and availability and order directly from the supplier. An example of this is the CARL UnCover Website, where users can open accounts for their Reveal table of contents and searching services, as well as order documents for which copyright royalty fees have been paid. Another example of a vendor website is UMI (Bell & Howell) ProQuest Digital Dissertation site. This site, available by subscription, serves as a database, in essence providing access to *Dissertation Abstracts International*, as well as a place to purchase dissertations, including a "shopping cart." Some dissertations are now available in digital format and can be downloaded for a fee.

Some national libraries and research centers also function as commercial document suppliers. General library, collection, and ordering information are all available on their websites. Examples of this include the British Library (http://www.bl.uk), the Canada Institute for Science and Technology Information, or CISTI (http://www.nrc. ca/cisti/lib_docdel_e. shtml), and Germany's DBI-LINK (http://www.dbilink.de/en/).

Copyright Reporting

The Copyright Clearance Center, Inc. (CCC) was formed in 1978, at the request of Congress, to facilitate compliance with U.S. copyright law. CCC provides a way for royalties to be paid to publishers, 9,600 of which are currently represented by CCC. CCC's users include not only libraries, but also commercial document suppliers, copy centers, bookstores, law firms, government agencies, and corporations.[56] When CCC began, users had to register and report their copying, all by mail. Looking up titles of copyrighted works to see if they were covered by CCC involved paging through a thick book. CCC's website makes all these processes possible online, thus ensuring that complying with copyright law and guidelines is as easy as possible.

OCLC Online Assistance

Yet another example of how the Internet has impacted and improved the work of the ILL practitioner is with online availability of a variety of assistance and services. Most notable among these are the services available from the OCLC Website (http://www.oclc.org). Reports on OCLC IFM (ILL Fee Management) usage, Management Statistics Service, and "Reasons for No" can all be downloaded from the OCLC Website after entering the library's user number and password. Keyboard macros, scripts, and software also are available at the click of a button, along with support services. In the not-so-distant past, ILL practitioners had to wait for similar types of reports to come in the mail.

The Internet as a Source of ILL Requests

Just as the Internet serves as a resource for ILL practitioners, it also serves as a resource for the end-user. Users are likely to find an interesting title on Amazon (http://www.amazon.com) and request it through ILL the very next moment (using the Web request form, of course). Unverifiable citations have always come from both reliable and non-reliable sources, which now include Internet resources and web pages. Naturally, databases made available over the Web in increasing numbers by libraries are a tremendous source of ILL requests.

Jonathan Miller conducted a study (1993) of Rochester Institute of Technology Library's Electronic Library Information System (ELIS) as a source of ILL requests. The ELIS was a gateway that included a link to the library's catalog, to remote online databases, to the Internet, and to networked CD-ROMs. Within the first 18 months of operation, patrons had come to rely on the ELIS as much as on traditional library resources, and the overwhelming majority of ILL requests originating from sources on the ELIS were periodical articles. Thirty-one ILL requests were found on the Internet. Miller came to the cautious conclusion that the ELIS had a marked effect on ILL requests, both as a source of ILL requests and on their total numbers. This conclusion was cautious because the ELIS CD-ROMs had been available in the Library for years. However, Miller speculated that the use of the Internet would transform traditional ILL function, both because of the information available there and because it would become a medium for article requesting and transmission.[57]

THE FUTURE

In an intriguing article by Steve Coffman, the success of "Amazon-dot-com" is reviewed. The author also envisions a future for resource sharing in which the OCLC Worldcat catalog morphs into something closer to Amazon, containing enhanced records with scanned cover art, jacket blurbs, reviews by customers and professionals alike, author interviews, and more. Through this enhanced catalog, users could more easily choose items to read. This would be combined with his proposed user-initiated requesting system, which would also track the item, sending updates by email, as it makes its way to the user. Collaborative collection development could be further utilized in this global catalog. The financial end of this would be partially covered by links to online bookstores at which users could purchase items rather than merely borrow. Coffman points again to Amazon, asking, "if they can do it, why can't we?"[58]

Coffman's vision of a global borrowing system could be realized only with the help of the Internet, specifically the Web. Amazon would not have been possible only a few short years ago. With changes in ILL technology being developed, such as the ISO ILL Protocol Standards, Coffman's vision may be closer than we think, as impossible as it seems today. The Internet has brought about changes to ILL practice that were out of the grasp of the imaginations of most ILL practitioners only 20 years ago and will without a doubt continue to do so.

NOTES

1. Virginia Boucher, *Interlibrary Loan Practices Handbook*, 2nd ed. (Chicago: American Library Association, 1997).
2. "With this access method, a synchronous, multidrop dedicated line, reserved exclusively for accessing OCLC services via the OCLC network, [was] installed at the library." OCLC supported this access method until March 31, 2000. "Accessing OCLC," OCLC Newsletter, No. 214, March/April 1995 (URL http://www.oclc.org/oclc/new/n214/n214sr.htm).
   Sharon Knowlton, "Product News: Ensuring a Smooth Transition from Multidrop Access," *OCLC Newsletter* No. 239, (May/June 1999) (URL http://www.oclc.org/oclc/new/n239/product/07product.htm).
3. "A Bulletin Board for ILL," *Small Computers in Libraries* 7 (May 1987): 42-44; Cathy Moore, "Do-It-Yourself Automation: Interloan Bulletin Boards," *Library Journal* 112 (November 1, 1987): 66-68.
4. David Belanger, "Bulletin Board and Interlibrary Loan EL-MAIL: The Electronic Library Mail Network," *Library Software Review* 9 (May-June 1990): 153-154.
5. Shirley K. Baker and Mary E. Jackson, "Maximizing Access, Minimizing Cost: A First Step Toward the Information Access Future," November 1992; revised December 1994 (URL http://www.ifla.org/documents/libraries/resource-sharing/ill.txt).
6. Harry S. Martin III and Curtis Kendrick, "A User-Centered View of Document Delivery and Interlibrary Loan," *Library Administration and Management* 8 (Fall 1994): 223-227.
7. Association of Research Libraries, "Information Access and Delivery Services: A Strategic Direction for Research Libraries" (URL http://www.arl.org/ access/infoaccess.html).
8. Lewis-Guodo Liu, *The Internet and Library and Information Services: A Review, Analysis, and Annotated Bibliography* (Champaign: Graduate School of Library and Information Science of the University of Illinois at Urbana-Champaign, 1995).
9. William D. Schieber and Ralph M. Shoffner, *Telefacsimile in Libraries: A Report of an Experiment in Facsimile Transmission and an Analysis of*

Implications for Interlibrary Loan Systems (Davis: Institute of Library Research, University of California, February 1968).

10. Mary E. Jackson, "Library to Library," *Wilson Library Bulletin* 65 (April 1991): 84-87.
11. Mary E. Jackson, "Document Delivery over the Internet," *ONLINE: The Magazine of Online Information Systems* 17 (March 1993): 14-15, 17-18, 20-21.
12. Ibid.
13. Ibid; Eric L. Morgan and Tracy M. Casorso, "Digitized Document Transmission using HyperCard," (North Carolina State University Libraries, June 1992) (URL is http://www.lib.ncsu.edu/staff/ morgan/ ddtp/).
14. Valerie M. Bennett and Eileen M. Palmer, "Electronic Document Delivery Using the Internet," *Bulletin of the Medical Library Association* 82 (April 1994): 163-167; Nancy I. Henry and Ester Y. Dell, "Ariel: Technology as a Tool for Cooperation," *Bulletin of the Medical Library Association* 82 (October 1994): 436-438.
15. Sonja Landes, "The Ariel Document Delivery System: A Cost-Effective Alternative to the Fax," *Journal of Interlibrary Loan, Document Delivery, and Information Supply* 7 (1997): 61-72.
16. Mary Sellen, "Turnaround Time and Journal Article Delivery: A Study of Four Delivery Systems," *Journal of Interlibrary Loan, Document Delivery, and Information Supply* 9 (1999): 65-72.
17. "Ariel® Frequently Asked Questions (FAQs)," March, 2000 (URL http: // www.rlg.org/ariel/arifaq.html).
18. Docview Website (URL http://archive.nlm.nih.gov/projects/docview/pro ject.htm).
19. Adobe Acrobat Reader (URL http://www.adobe.com).
20. DocMorph Server (URL http://docmorph.nlm.nih.gov/docmorph).
21. Eric H. Schnell, "Freeing Ariel: The Prospero Electronic Document Delivery Project," *Journal of Interlibrary Loan, Document Delivery, and Information Supply* (1999): 89-100.
22. Ibid.
23. ILLiad is a product of Atlas Systems, Inc. (URL http://www.atlas-sys.com). ERes is a product of Docutek.com (URL http://www.docutek. com).
24. Mounir A. Khalil and Raja Jayatilleke, "Increasing Utilization of the Internet/WWW in the Interlibrary Loan and Document Delivery Services," *Computers in Libaries* (1997): 66-77.
25. Google Web search engine (URL http://www.google.com).
26. James McCloskey, "Web-Based Forms for ILL using HTML." *Journal of Interlibrary Loan, Document Delivery, and Information Supply* 7 (1996): 79-85. Selena Wang and Glenn Manino, "Creating Interlibrary Loan Request Forms on the Web," *Journal of Interlibrary Loan, Document Delivery, and Information Supply* 8 (1997): 79-86.

27. Schubert Foo and Ee-Peng Lim, "An Integrated Web-Based ILL System for Singapore Libraries," *Interlending and Document Supply* 26 (1998): 10-20.
28. Mary E. Jackson, *Measuring the Performance of Interlibrary Loan Operations in North American Research and College Libraries* (Washington, DC: Association of Research Libraries, 1998).
29. Barbara G. Preece and Susan Logue, "Empowering the Patron: Redesigning Interlibrary Loan Services," *Journal of Library Administration* 23 (1996): 155-166.
30. Tom Delaney, "ZAP: An Electronic Request System. Planning, Development and Adaptation in a Network Environment," *Journal of Library Administration* 23 (1996): 141-153.
31. WebZAP ILL Service (URL http://www.web-zap.org/info.html).
32. Harry M. Kriz, M. Jason Glover, and Kevin C. Ford, "ILLiad: Customer-Focused Interlibrary Loan Automation," *Journal of Interlibrary Loan, Document Delivery, and Information Supply* 8 (1998): 31-47.
33. Barbara Shuh, "The Renaissance of the Interlibrary Loan Protocol: Developments in Open Systems for Interlibrary Loan Message Management," *Interlending & Document Supply* 26 (1998): 25-33; Barbara Shuh, "The Interlibrary Loan (ILL) Protocol: An Introduction," *Network Notes* 40 (December 1996; rev. May 1998) (URL http://www.nlc-bnc.ca/pubs/ netnotes/ notes40.htm).
34. Mary E. Jackson, "North American Interlibrary Loan and Document Delivery (NAILDD) Project, Call to Participate in the ILL Protocol Testbed," (November 27, 1995); the URL is http://www.arl.org/ access/ naildd/ipig/res/participation-call.shtml).
35. "North American Interlibrary Loan and Document Delivery (NAILDD) Project, ILL Protocol Implementors Group (IPIG), Official Representatives as of May, 2000" (URL http://www.arl.org/access/ naildd/ipig/members-ipig.shtml).
36. Interlibrary Loan Application Standards Maintenance Agency. *ISO ILL Protocol Standards* (URL http://www.nlc-bnc.ca/iso/ill/stanprf.htm).
37. OCLC Interlibrary Loan (ILL) Direct Request Service (URL http:// www. oclc.org/oclc/menu/drill.htm).
38. Shuh, "The Interlibrary Loan;"
39. Ibid.
40. Shuh, "The Renaissance;"
41. Karen G. Schneider, "Internet Librarian: Loan Rangers: New ILL Method Supplies the Goods," *American Libraries* 29 (October 1998): 78.
42. Mary E. Jackson, "Strengthening Access to Overseas Library Collections," *ARL Bimonthly Report* 206 October 1999 (URL http:// www.arl.org/ newsltr/206/access.html).
43. "Electronic Publishing Explodes on the Web," *ARL Newsletter* 187 August 1996 (URL http://www.arl.org/newsltr/187/explode.html).

44. David F. Kohl, "How the Virtual Library Transforms Interlibrary Loans – the OhioLINK Experience," *Interlending and Document Supply* 26 (1998): 65-69.
45. OhioLINK Website (URL http://www.ohiolink.edu).
46. Kohl, "How the Virtual Library."
47. OhioLINK Website.
48. Association of Research Libraries, "Supply and Demand in ARL Libraries, 1986-1999," *ARL Statistics* (May 2000) (URL http://www.arl.org/stats/arlstat/1999t3.html).
49. Mary E. Jackson, "Research Library Interlibrary Lending: An Isolated Drop or the Beginning of a Trend?" *ARL Bimonthly Report* 211 (August 2000); (URL http://www.arl.org/newsltr/211/ill.html).
50. Stephen Prowse, "Trends and Developments in Interlending and Document Delivery in the UK in 1997," *Interlending and Document Supply* 26 (1998): 83-92.
51. Suzanne S. Rice, "ILL-List Conspectus," *Journal of Interlibrary Loan, Document Delivery, and Information Supply* 6 (1995): 11-16.
52. Sara Gould, " 'Apologies for Cross-Posting': A Brief Look at Internet Discussion Lists in Interlibrary Loan and Document Delivery," *Interlending and Document Supply* 26 (1998): 21-24.
53. "Introduction to the DocDel listserv" (URL http://www.docdel.net/Information_DocDel.html).
54. David Flaxbart, "Document Delivery: Interlibrary Loan, and Beyond," In *Library without Walls: Plug in and Go,* ed. Susan B. Ardis (Washington, DC: Special Libraries Association, 1994): 17-33.
55. *IFLA Guidelines for Sending ILL Requests by E-mail* (URL http://www.ifla.org/VI/2/p3/g-ill.htm).
56. Copyright Clearance Center (URL http://www.copyright.com).
57. Jonathan Miller, "The Electronic Library Information System as a Source of Interlibrary Loan Requests," *Journal of Interlibrary Loan, Document Delivery, and Information Supply* 42 (1993): 17-28.
58. Steve Coffman, "Building the Earth's Largest Library," *Searcher: The Magazine for Database Professionals* 7 (March 1999): 34-47.

CHAPTER SIX

INFORMATION SERVICES IN ELECTRONIC COMMUNITIES

Bryce Allen

INTRODUCTION

Reference or information services have long been part of the services libraries offer to their user communities. The Internet has influenced library information services in two important ways: it has revolutionized the mechanisms by which information services can be provided, and it has transformed the user community to which library information services are offered. The first effect is the most obvious. There are now a wider range of information resources available to users, and more ways of contacting library information services for assistance. But the second effect is more far-reaching and substantial. User communities in the past have been geographically defined. Libraries offered information services primarily to people who were physically present in the library. For the most part, these users were members of a local community, defined by tax districts or by membership in an organization or a school. However, when the users, the information resources, and the librarians are all located in cyberspace, the geographical and physical limitations on the user community become irrelevant. The resulting transformation of the user community is gradually transforming library information services and the libraries that provide those services.

The Evolution of Electronic Information Resources

When electronic information resources first became commonly used in library reference services in the 1970s, many librarians thought of these resources as a new type of information resource. They recognized that they had to master new searching techniques and to understand how electronic resources could be used to respond to patron information needs. However, many librarians thought that this additional set of tools constituted a familiar phenomenon: an incremental change in the resources available to provide existing services.

In a sense, this perception of electronic resources in the information services environment occurred because of the incremental introduction of such resources and the fact that early electronic information resources resembled traditional print information resources in many ways. The first type of electronic resource introduced into reference work was "print equivalents." These resources were created, in the first place, by the physical production of print reference works. For example, indexing and abstracting databases, electronic dictionaries, and the first electronic encyclopedias, were created as a by-product of printing the paper reference tools. These databases, accessible for the most part only through dial-up access, added a new dimension to reference work. They provided enhanced access because of keyword indexing and Boolean search capabilities. They allowed information to be tailored for individual users. But, typically, they were regarded as supplements to traditional resources. In some cases, libraries charged patrons for the costs of accessing these supplementary resources. It was only with time that some libraries began to view remote databases as a possible replacement for print reference tools.

The second type of electronic resource introduced was the "print plus" resource. These databases, although based upon print materials, had added features that distinguished them from the print resources. For example, electronic encyclopedias started to incorporate sound and video clips that had never been part of the print reference tools. Similarly, indexes and abstracts could be transformed by digital storage. *The Readers' Guide to Periodical Literature*, for example, became *Readers' Guide Plus Abstracts.* As these "print plus" resources began to penetrate the market for reference tools, librarians began to regard electronic resources more as a replacement for traditional resources than as a supplement.

The third type of electronic resource is the "electronic only" resource. These are information resources available only in electronic form, with no print equivalent. Some of them resemble the "print equivalent" resources. For example, the *Infotrac* databases or *ABI/Inform* have no print equivalent but are essentially the same as the print equivalent indexes and abstracts. Other electronic resources have no resemblance to earlier genres of information tools. Websites, for example, must be regarded as a new genre. Some websites incorporate some print-equivalent or print-plus elements, but others have no connection to the traditional print-on-paper reference tools. As these new types of electronic information resources have become widely available, librarians have increasingly come to view electronic resources as a replacement for traditional resources. For example, large-scale bibliographic databases have in many cases replaced the voluminous national bibliographies that at one time were found in most reference collections. Electronic encyclopedias have significantly reduced the necessity of buying a new set of paper encyclopedias every year. Many government publications are more easily accessed on the Web than from the massive collections of paper documents that still are found in depository libraries.

All three of these types of electronic resources are present in, or accessible by, most library information services. It is clear that they have substantially influenced the nature of such services. Electronic resources typically provide enhanced access to information by superior indexing and search techniques. They have the potential to be more usable than traditional resources, and they can be available in any library. Even a small school library or public library branch can have access to the substantial resources that are available free on the Web.

The Evolution of User Communities

The impact of electronic resources is, however, more profound than this view recognizes. Remote databases and other remote information resources have proliferated. There is now far more information *outside* most libraries than *inside* those library collections. Increased ease of end-user access to these remote information resources via the Internet means that it may be easier for users to find information *outside* the library than *inside* the library. The nature of user communities and the services libraries provide for them has been altered. This change can be illustrated by considering one example: the role of distance education in academic libraries. In traditional academic libraries, specialized services were established to meet the needs of distant students, usually defined as those students taking courses off campus. These special services were based on the understanding that on-campus students could come into the library to ask reference questions, use the reference collection, or check out circulating materials from the collection. Distance education students were perceived as representing a special case, since they were prevented by distance from using traditional library information services.

In today's electronic environment, however, a vast number of information resources are available on the Internet. It is quite possible for a student to obtain information services without physically entering the library. One academic library in Missouri offers a free current awareness and document delivery service to its faculty and graduate students. A commercial full-text journal resource provides monthly updates of newly published articles that match the interest profiles of library users. From this "table of contents" service, library users can request electronic document delivery of the articles in which they are interested. Traditional library information services built around reference desks and collections of print materials are far less important to students and faculty who can obtain access to the full text of the documents they need from electronic resources available on the Internet. In effect, all users have become "distant" users, whether they are sitting in a dorm room two blocks from the library, in an apartment across town, or in a different state or country taking

Web-based courses. The special case has become the rule. This example illustrates how the availability of information resources on the Internet has brought about a structural change in library information services.

Similarly, public libraries are providing access to information to patrons who are located outside the library. One public library in Missouri offers free access to dozens of Internet information sites to individuals who use an Internet service provider with whom the Library is a partner. Again, it is far less important for users to be physically present in the library to obtain information resources and services. Many public libraries offer access to electronic resources to patrons who are physically present in the library (often accompanied by training in how to use these resources). But the structural change that has occurred is that some public libraries are emphasizing services to patrons who might be located in a wide variety of locations: homes, schools, offices or industrial plants. In effect, the real location of these information services is cyberspace.

So, rather than just introducing new information resources into an existing service structure, the Internet has transformed that service structure. Of course, traditional services continue to be offered. As a result, the transformed service structure is built on top of a traditional, face-to-face service structure. The resulting extra demands on resources are the major limiting factor in the development of information services to electronic communities. Because of the structural changes that are occurring in library services and library user communities, it is essential, in considering the impact of the Internet, to begin with an analysis of the new electronic user communities that are emerging.

ELECTRONIC COMMUNITIES

Dictionary definitions of "community" include "a group of people living in the same locality and under the same government," "the district or locality in which such a group lives," and "a group of people having common interests." In defining a community, the geographical boundaries, the "district" or "locality," are important. But perhaps more important are the shared interests, and the participation in shared activities by members of the community.

Traditional communities were defined by a combination of location and interests. In virtual, electronic, or cybercommunities, the importance of the locality vanishes, and the importance of shared interests and activities becomes paramount. This transformation occurs because cyberspace is not limited geographically. The distance-independent nature of computer-mediated telecommunications means that communities can be formed around common interests and activities even when large geographic distances separate members of the community.

Comparisons of physical communities with electronic communities help to clarify the transformation that the Internet has brought about. In a physical community, an individual might shop regularly at a particular bookstore. The staff at the store comes to know that shopper's interests and suggests new books that match those interests. Other shoppers at the store may also offer their suggestions or opinions about books. This is a community of people, somewhat loosely organized, but sharing an interest in books and reading and patronizing a particular bookshop. When someone shops at a Web-based bookstore (and there are many of them), the bookstore site may send the customer emails about book sales and new items that might correspond to previous items purchased. The shopper can read reviews of books that other shoppers have posted. The cybercommunity matches many aspects of the physical community.

Similarly, there are electronic parallels to many other local communities. There are communities of faith (e.g., websites that bring together people who believe in a certain religion). There are communities of interest: sports, movies, hobbies, and so on. In fact, it would be hard to think of a topic or interest that doesn't have its electronic community, represented by a web page, listserv, newsgroup, MUD, or some combination of these technologies. Cybercommunities are everywhere, and they share many characteristics with traditional physical communities.

However, there are significant differences that should be emphasized as well. In physical communities, people can regulate the degree of their community involvement. One can go to a college football game and sit with 50,000 or 60,000 other people watching it. Or, one can sit at home alone and watch the game. The choice is in the hands of the individual. Sometimes, people go to great lengths to insulate themselves from contact with the community. But electronic communities may provide fewer opportunities to regulate community contact. That may be why some people develop "Internet addiction." They get too involved with their electronic communities.

Traditional communities frequently are structured by their history. The "important" people are easily distinguished from the "unimportant" people by their family background, or where they live. Similarly, within a physical community, some people are identified as having authority over certain kinds of activities. Police and fire department employees are identified as having authority by their uniforms. So also (in many cases) are clergy. But, electronic communities may have little or no structure. Radical equality is frequently the founding principle of electronic communities, although over time authority figures may emerge. What that means is that people don't know where they stand or who's in charge, the way they might in a traditional community.

Just as the structural cues that exist in a traditional community are missing (or transformed) in an electronic community, so also is the electronic communications environment different. It lacks many of the verbal and nonverbal cues that help people understand what is being said in ordinary interactions. As a result, communications patterns among members of the electronic community may be rather different from those among members of a physical community.

In summary, electronic communities are similar in some respects to traditional communities, but there are enough differences to produce important effects on society. Their similarities make it relatively easy to develop electronic communities. For example, the existence (for centuries) of bookstores made the concept of the electronic bookshop easy to accept. At the same time, it is important to note how far electronic bookshops have evolved beyond the bookstore concept. They are selling other kinds of merchandise and providing services that many traditional bookstores would not normally consider. So the differences between traditional and electronic communities provide tremendous opportunities for new electronic services to traditional communities. The differences in social structures and communications methods also present challenges.

Library User Communities

The potential user community of any public library is normally taken to be the residents of some municipality, county, or other geographic region. Sometimes, municipal regulation or state law encodes this definition of the user community. On the basis of this definition, some public libraries refuse to serve people who reside outside the geographic region, or they may charge a service fee for nonresident borrowers. The potential user community of any academic library is normally taken to be the faculty, students, and staff of the college or university. Again, some selected services may be offered, with or without payment, to members of the city or state in which the college is located. School library communities have traditionally mirrored those of academic libraries, although the information needs of parents of students are sometimes considered as well. Special libraries, as one might expect, exhibit greater diversity in their potential user communities. Some libraries serving corporations may limit their services to employees of that corporation. On the other hand, a special library such as the National Library of Medicine has a much broader and more diffuse potential user community.

The actual user community of any library (people who use any of the library's services) is a subset of this broader community of potential users. Actual users may be different from potential users in systematic ways. They may exhibit different demographics such as age, income, and gender. Actual users may be distributed among occupations and family characteristics differently than the potential user community. Users of information services are a subset of those who use the library for any reason and, again may be distributed differently from the broader user community.

The identifying characteristics of those users of the library who use library information services (primarily reference) are frequently poorly defined. Clearly, they have information needs. But that is not a very strong identifying feature. Many people with information needs do not approach library information services. Certain types of information needs that they are experiencing might identify actual users of information services. Or actual users might be a miscellaneous group of people who have heard about the library's information service from other satisfied users or who have successfully used the reference services in the past. Defining the actual user community of library information services is a crucial component in identifying the role and function of those services. To put the same idea in different language, it is essential for library information services to ascertain those areas in which they have a competitive advantage over alternative sources of information.

This advantage can come about because of the specific topic being searched for. There is, in other words, a good fit between the information service and the information sought. Or it can come about because the library information service is particularly easy to use, to approach, and to work with. Possibly, some other characteristics of the user, the topic, or the service act to give the library information service a competitive advantage.

Electronic Library User Communities

In traditional libraries, there are three types of user communities: those who reside in a geographical area, those who actually use the library, and those who actually use library information services. Since electronic communities are unlikely to be defined geographically, it is important to re-think the nature of library user communities in the electronic age.[1]

If we combine the distance-independent nature of electronic communications on the Internet with the three definitions of traditional user communities, the broadest definition of the library's electronic user community is "anybody, anywhere, who is on the Internet." There are obvious differences between this electronic user community and the geographically defined user community of the traditional library. People on the Internet are likely to be significantly different from residents of any particular community. They may be more affluent, better educated, younger, and so on.

The second definition of the electronic user community can be approached by asking, "Who (from those millions of people worldwide who have access to the Internet) would be likely to approach a library site for information? And, what would be the features of the site that would attract them?" These people are the equivalent of the actual library user community in the traditional world. The idea of competitive advantage reemerges here. An individual who is seeking information on the Web can do so in many ways. There are classified sites that lead people to the information they seek. There are hundreds of different search engines, some of which offer highly sophisticated retrieval capabilities. Why would a student, or a businessperson, or an ordinary citizen trying to find information on a topic select a library site over all of these other information services?

Perhaps library information services can offer information that no one else can. If the local public library has digitized a set of historic photos of the city and mounted those photos on its website, that library information service may be the only place in cyberspace that can satisfy certain information needs. Similarly, an academic library can obtain a competitive advantage by creating and maintaining an electronic journal in a specialized field as part of its information services.

Perhaps libraries can compete by using price competition. Some people come into libraries to borrow videos when the local video rental agency may be much more convenient, largely because library videos are free. People may come to a library information service on the Web because that service offers free access to information that would otherwise be costly. Alternatively, libraries may be able to compete in the electronic information environment by offering services that are different from those offered by other information providers. Fast, personalized access to expert information searchers (i.e., reference librarians) as part of library information services may attract those users who prefer personal assistance to do-it-yourself surfing of the Web.

The third level of definition of electronic user communities can be approached by asking this question, What would lead a person who has Internet access and who is predisposed to consulting a library information service to select one particular library information service over any other? The competitive advantage is now expressed in terms of one library over another. There may be areas of topic expertise that will attract users to a specific library. A botanical garden or science center library may be the obvious choice for horticultural or science information, for example. In addition, there may be price competition. In academic libraries, this can be done by assigning a password to all students that will provide them with access to a number of information services free of charge. Finally, there are service advantages that may attract users to a particular site. If a specific library electronic information service has a reputation for quick, courteous, expert assistance, users may be attracted to that site.

Electronic User Communities for Library Information Services: Summary

Libraries have now, and will continue to have for the foreseeable future, traditional user communities. These will be people from the local potential user community who have first selected themselves as library users, then as users of the reference function of the library. However, grafted onto this existing user community is a different group of users. These are people who are seeking information on the Internet and who are drawn to a library site because that type of site offers advantages that make it competitive with all of the other possible information sources on the Internet. At the same time, they are attracted to a specific library's electronic services by the competitive advantages enjoyed by that one library. This new user community may overlap with the traditional user community to some extent. For example, individuals who have come to rely on traditional reference services in a library may on occasion make use of the electronic information services of that library, thus becoming part of both user communities. The extent of overlap between traditional and electronic user communities may be controlled by library policy. A library may refuse to answer email reference queries from someone outside the physical boundaries of the community served. Or, fees may be charged to electronic users who are not also traditional users. These issues of policy are discussed in more detail below.

INFORMATION SERVICES BASED ON ASYNCHRONOUS COMMUNICATION

Asynchronous communication is not at all new or revolutionary: it goes back to the invention of writing. In electronic communities, however, asynchronous communication has taken new forms. There are three main types of technology to be considered: one-to-one, one-to-many, and many-to-many. In one-to-one technologies, individuals correspond privately with each other. Traditional examples include personal letters. In the electronic world, the best example is email. In one-to-many technologies, one individual sends a recorded message to many readers. Traditional examples include books, journals, newspapers, and other print technologies. In the electronic world, there are electronic books, journals, and newspapers. There are also websites, for which there appears to be no clear precursor in the analog era. The communities that are formed by those who read or use specific websites or other one-to-many asynchronous communications technologies are similar to those communities that read the same books, journals, or newspapers. The main many-to-many asynchronous technologies are listservs and bulletin boards or news groups. These technologies enable members of communities to communicate with each other about specific topics. These communities vary in cohesiveness depending on the interests and also on the communications technology employed.

The Website as Information Service

A large number of libraries have websites. They may have been established for a variety of purposes, and with a variety of audiences in mind. But they do represent an excellent vehicle for creating an asynchronous information service for libraries.[2] It is now important to consider how library websites can be transformed into information services for electronic communities. To be an information source in an electronic community, a member of that community must first of all be knowledgeable. Information that is not expert, not correct, or not appropriate will not be gratefully received, and the informant will be ostracized in the community. Second there must be a reasonable response time. Although asynchronous communication does not depend on "real time" responses, information resources that respond quickly will be likely to be sought out. Third, an information resource that is pleasant, chatty, and nontechnical may be perceived to be a better informant than someone who is unpleasant or needlessly technical. So, communications skills help to create valued information resources.

If a library wishes to establish an information service based on one-to-many asynchronous communication using its website, there are a number of steps that may be taken to ensure that this information service will be valued by its user community. The technology of the information service will be considered separately, but the most important matter is the planning of the service.

Step 1: Identify the target market

What is the nature of the electronic community the library wants to serve? Who is included? This is the first and arguably the most difficult step in developing an information service. Libraries have long been accused of trying to be all things to all people. This is not true, of course, but frequently library services are diffuse and without focus, probably because libraries have tried to develop information services that everyone can use. Information services that have this general purpose cannot be tailored to meet any user's real and specific information needs. So what starts off as a service that tries to satisfy everyone ends up satisfying no one.

It is possible for library information services to achieve the goal of serving a broad spectrum of users, but only by approaching this goal in an incremental fashion. The library can identify one or two groups of users, design information services to meet their needs, then progress to the next one or two target markets, and so on. Like any planning process, planning for information services must begin with setting of priorities. For example, a public library might establish its first priority as meeting the needs of children in local schools. A second priority might be meeting the information needs of local businessmen who need information about manufacturers and investments. A third priority might be meeting the information needs of historians and genealogists interested in the history and people of the community. And so on. By the time a library has developed information services to meet the needs of its top 20 or so target markets, it will have a highly developed and articulated set of information services that might come close to the objective of having a general-purpose information service. The same process of priority setting can be applied in an academic library. The library may establish as its first priority meeting the needs of undergraduate students taking elements of the general education curriculum. Then it could move on to selected departmental course offerings where electronic information resources are particularly appropriate. In a sense, this planning process for developing electronic information services closely parallels the process associated with creating a collection policy statement for the academic library. It identifies the areas that will receive the most attention and the greatest proportion of library resources.

Step 2: Identify the information needs of the target market

The next step in the planning process requires the library to get closer to its users. Any target market might have dozens or hundreds of information needs. If a public library, for example, establishes a priority for meeting the information needs of children in local schools, the library will have to investigate what those needs are. Clearly, these children have information needs associated with the courses they are taking. The library could, for example, design a specific web page to provide information that would help a grade 5 student complete a social studies assignment on American history. Or it could create a web page that would help a student in a science class understand photosynthesis a bit better. At the same time, the library will be investigating the environment in which these information needs exist. Other libraries in the community (e.g., a school library) might be better equipped to meet these information needs. Perhaps children in local schools want information about rock stars or sports figures. Should this kind of information be the library's priority? Or, the library may find that students need information about school violence and mental health or about the dangers of illicit drugs. Should these topics be the focus of the public library's Web-based information service?

Again, planning means the setting of priorities. Once the target market is identified, it is essential to analyze the kinds of information that people in that target group feel they need, then decide whether the library's electronic information service is the best mechanism for providing that information. If the library succeeds in defining, then providing the information that people need, marketing the library website to users will be straightforward.

Step 3. Select the information

One thing that has been the hallmark of librarianship over the centuries has been the process of selecting information that will meet users' information needs. Collection development is the key to this selection process in traditional information services. When libraries begin to meet the information needs of electronic communities, the same principles and practices are relevant. The best information should be selected from what is available. If the library has decided to focus on science information for secondary school students as one of its priorities, the library will find a variety of websites that deal with photosynthesis, for example. In evaluating them, however, the library will see that some of the websites are written at a reading level far above that of secondary school students. Perhaps they were designed for college students. Others might be written at an appropriate level but may come from sources that might be regarded as problematic (such as a term paper plagiarism site). So, applying all of the evaluative criteria for judging the quality of information, the library can identify the websites to which its information service will link.

In some circumstances, the information that has been identified as meeting the needs of the target market may not be available on the Web. For example, there may be local history and genealogy information that isn't on any existing website. In such circumstances, the library may be in a slightly unfamiliar role: that of creating information resources needed to provide information services. This role provides a new opportunity to work with library users to develop and create the new information. In doing so, the library will be giving itself a competitive advantage: it will be providing information that is unique and not available elsewhere in cyberspace.

Frequently the best information to meet some information needs can be found on the Web, but it is on a fee-based website. If the library decides to subsidize access to this information by licensing access to that information for its users, it can create another competitive advantage: a price advantage.

Step 4. Organize the information

Once the information has been selected from the best the Web has to offer, licenses are in place for the commercial sites, and local information has been created or digitized, the information service site must be organized to provide convenient and easy access. Again, organization of information is something that librarians have been doing for centuries, and we can make use of all of this background and expertise. That is not to say that we should be applying traditional cataloging and classification techniques to our websites. But, given the hypermedia nature of the Web, there may be a variety of organizational schemes that will work. The library might, for example, use a timeline as one means of organization. Images and documents related to a specific decade could be accessed from that timeline. Or, the library could develop a spatial approach to organizing its information services. An interactive map of the state, county, or city would permit users to click on specific locations to find images and documents associated with that location. Alternatively, a thematic approach would organize information resources by topic. Images and documents on sports could be grouped together, while images and documents on industry and commerce could be grouped together, and so on. But, given the nature of hypermedia, the same information resources could be found in a number of possible places in the topical structure.

Step 5. Make the information accessible

Once the information service has been created (i.e., selected and organized), it can be placed on the library's website. Access to the website will occur in a couple of different ways. People may be using the library's website for a variety of other purposes (e.g., consulting the OPAC), and may be led to the information service just because they see it there on the site. More likely, however, is that users will be drawn to the information service because of specific marketing and indexing activities. The library can add appropriate metadata to each of its specialized information pages to ensure that search engines will index the pages appropriately. In addition, the library can submit its pages to the various search engines rather than waiting patiently for the search engines to discover the pages and index them. Following these simple steps will bring users who are searching for content using the general search engines to the library's site.

But more specific promotion can be done. If the library has been working with a local historical association or a group of genealogists in developing its information service, there is a ready-made avenue of promotion. If the library creates an information service for students, then appropriate links from the websites maintained by the schools in the area would be an obvious mechanism of promotion. Because the information service is focused upon a set of target markets, the promotional campaign can be equally targeted on those markets.

Step 6. Beyond the website

All of the above discussion is based on the idea that if we know our users, we can anticipate the information that they need and can prepare information services to meet those needs. While this is no doubt true in some cases, there are other information needs that may arise that could not have been anticipated even with the most thorough analysis. Libraries will need a mechanism through which the user can ask for information and be provided with information on demand. In asynchronous information services, this mechanism is usually in the form of an email reference service or ask-a-librarian function, discussed below.

Step 7. Constant updating

Dynamic updating of any information collection is essential. In the case of a website, however, dynamic updating of the information is even more crucial. Because sites to which there are links may change, move, or disappear, it is important to check all links to ensure that they are still valid. This task can be automated using link-checking software. However, even when the links remain valid, the information provided may not remain the best possible information for users. Checking for new sites that provide good (or better) information on a topic is an ongoing task that requires the attention of professional librarians who can evaluate the content and ensure that their patrons are being given the information they need.

The Technology of the Website

There are many excellent resources, both electronic and print, on Web design. There is no need to repeat this information here. But, from the perspective of information systems design, there is one small aspect of Web design that must be considered because it relates to the marketing of the information service. The assumption here is that a library wishes to attract a wide range of users to its information service. This assumption may not, in fact, be correct if the library has decided to restrict access to its services to a definable geographic or institutional area. If the assumption is correct, however, then the major access point to the library's Web-based information service will be the major search engines. In order to ensure that the information service is adequately indexed in these search engines, two steps are necessary. First, the library should include sufficient metadata to ensure that the indexing will be effective. Here is an example of the metadata included on a well known commercial information service on the Web:

> <META name="description" content="The New York Times on the Web: Daily international, national and local news coverage from the newspaper, breaking news updates, technology news, sports, reviews, crosswords, classified ad listings.">
> <META name="keywords" content="New York Times, international news, daily newspaper, national, politics, science, business, your money, AP breaking news, business technology, technology, Cybertimes, circuits, new york times, navigator, sports, weather, editorial, Op-Ed, arts and leisure, film, movie reviews, theater, stock quotes, arts, classified ads, automobiles, books, crossword puzzle, job market, help wanted, careers, real estate listings, travel, Web glossary, new york region, Navigator, cybertimes, op-ed, job listings, forums, business connections, theater reviews, auto classifieds, newspaper archives, travel forecasts, NY Yankees, Mets, Giants, Jets, boxing, pro football scores, major league baseball, college basketball, Knicks, Rangers, Islanders, college football, sports commentary, fashion and style, hockey, tennis, major league soccer, global issues, associated press, regional news coverage, quick news, women's health, obituaries, stock quotes, charts, market indexes, sports update, politics, science, political news, science times">

Here are the comparable data from the New York Public Library:

> <META NAME="description" CONTENT="Information about the programs, services, and collections of The New York Public Library, along with access to its catalogs and other information databases.">
> <META NAME="keywords" CONTENT=" new york, public, library, nypl, libraries, research, branch, branches, center, humanities, schomburg, black culture, science, industry, business, sibl, performing arts, lpa, donnell, heiskell, mid-manhattan, bronx, manhattan, staten island, catnyp, leo, nypl express, teen link, on-lion">

It should be clear how helpful these additional search terms would be in allowing search engines to retrieve library websites. It would be appropriate for a library to add keywords to the metadata in its websites describing each of the user communities and information needs it has elected to cover.

The second step that libraries should take to market their electronic information services is to submit their sites to the major search engines. For example, one may submit a site to Excite by using the URL: http://www.excite.com/info/add_url. Taking the time to submit one's site to the 25 or so major search engines will increase the probability that users will find the library's website while conducting searches for information.

Ask-A-Librarian Functions

The one-to-one form of asynchronous communication, represented by email, can serve as the technical foundation for information services to electronic communities. Of course, anyone can send an email to a librarian at any time, but the ask-a service makes such contact easier and more standardized. As a result, many libraries have forms on their websites that allow users to submit questions to the reference staff. Libraries are not alone in the creation and use of ask-a sites. There are literally dozens of ask-a sites available on the Web, ranging from experts in science and engineering who answer questions, primarily from students, on their areas of specialty, to experts on gardening who are available to answer questions about plants. Included in this mix are a number of health-related ask-a sites that provide medical information to the general public.

In this context the idea of competitive advantage again appears. If there are physicians to answer medical questions and vulcanologists to answer questions about volcanoes and expert gardeners to ask about roses, what role is there for ask-a-librarian sites? One tempting answer is that library information services are generalists, able to field questions in a wide range of areas. As tempting as that answer is, it seems unsatisfactory. Knowing a little about a lot of things may not provide much advantage when there is ready access to real experts. Nor should librarians be satisfied with a "residual" role, being available to answer questions in those areas where there are not experts in ask-a sites on the Web. As in the case of library websites, it seems clear that market analysis and planning are required to recognize competitive advantages that the library's email reference service might have.

A thorough examination of ask-a-librarian sites currently found on the Web does not engender confidence that libraries are engaging in the requisite market analysis and planning. Few sites mention an area of expertise that the library's information services might be able to address. Few mention specific users to whom the ask-a-librarian site might be addressed. Rather, what one finds in abundance are rules, usually negative in nature. There are restrictions on the type of question that may be asked, about the type of user who can ask a question, and about the amount of effort that librarians are allowed to invest in an answer. Examining ask-a-librarian sites leads to the idea that libraries are trying to discourage use of the service, rather than actively to market it.

If a library wishes to establish an information service based on one-to-one asynchronous communication using an ask-a-librarian service on its website, there are a number of steps that may be taken to ensure that this information service will be valued by its user community.

Step 1. Identify the target market and its information needs.

As in website development it is essential to designate the nature of the electronic community the library wishes to serve. The process outlined above can be replicated here to establish the target market for the ask-a-librarian site.

Step 2. Prepare the respondents

Provision of expert information is the goal of an ask-a-librarian service. It follows that the information services staff members who respond to email questions must be experts. While they will undoubtedly have access to information resources such as databases and reference books, personal knowledge will allow them to understand questions readily, select appropriate information, and respond quickly. Subject expertise is frequently found in academic research libraries where the practice of requiring a second master's degree is common. In other types of libraries, however, subject expertise may be less systematic. In such libraries, it is important to be able to route the email reference questions directly to an information services staff member with expertise in the area of the question. When a question is received that does not match any staff expertise, the ask-a-librarian service may want to respond with an honest avowal that no staff expertise exists in that area. Even when the information services staff has expertise in an area, it is unlikely to have several experts. Because of varying work schedules, expert responses may be delayed. It is essential to communicate this to questioners, so that they have reasonable expectations of the amount of time it may take to receive a response.

Step 3. Give the ask-a service a personality

One of the chief drawbacks of an email reference service is that it is impersonal. When there is a group of experts responding to a large number of questions, it is difficult to maintain a consistent personality in the responses. Yet, although it is difficult, it can be achieved. Most library users know the attributes they prefer in a reference librarian: personable, patient, expert, open, and with a good sense of humor. It is possible to train information services staff so that they convey these attributes through their responses to email reference questions. In one library, a personality sketch of the collective respondent was maintained. This personality sketch was used in drafting responses to questions received through an email reference service so that a consistent and positive attitude was conveyed to the users.

The Technology of the Ask-A-Site

Developing an ask-a-librarian site is relatively straightforward. Most libraries use a simple email message system, frequently using a form that users complete and submit over the Internet. Oddly enough, in a profession that has produced hundreds of articles about the reference interview over the years, there is little sophistication in the types of questions that are asked of the users on the email form. Traditional reference practice makes it clear that a better understanding of the user's information need will lead to better information service. Accordingly, the questions posed to users to elicit their information need must be carefully designed. Some sites, for example, ask not only about the topic that the patron wants information about, but also about how the patron intends to use the information. Although some might view this question as unnecessarily intrusive, it has the potential to reveal essential details about the amount of information needed, the reading level and existing knowledge levels of the patron, and the type of answer expected. Another question that might reveal more about the patron's information need would ask the patron to imagine an ideal document or website, then to describe that ideal information resource. In the email environment, the reference interaction can be slowed down dramatically by the communications medium. It might take a day, for example, for a librarian to read a question, ask for clarification, and receive a response. In this circumstance, it is essential to get as much detail as possible about the information in the initial query, and carefully designed questions on search forms can elicit that detail.

It seems unnecessary to argue that a web page should be visually attractive. Clearly, visual attractiveness is also important in an ask-a-librarian site. In keeping with the idea of giving the service a personality, libraries might want to consider incorporating a photograph of "the librarian." For reasons of personal security, photographs of actual employees may pose a problem. But a visual image of a "generic librarian" can add to the personality of the ask-a-librarian site.

Earlier it was mentioned that many ask-a-librarian sites are laden with rules and restrictions. Here are some examples, drawn from actual ask-a-librarian sites:

> Ask a librarian is intended for short, factual answers to your questions. Detailed information requires a trip to the library.
> We will respond to your request within 24 hours.
> Who may use this service? This service is open to all but if you do not live in the xxx area you may wish to contact your local library about this type of service.
> We can provide brief answers to factual questions or suggest locations or sources which might help to answer your question.

> This service is restricted to members of the xxx community or to questions relating to xxx. For all other questions, contact your local library for assistance or try the Internet Public Library.
> Who may use this service? This service is intended for the students, faculty and staff of xxx. If you are not affiliated with xxx, we are sorry that we can reply to your inquiry only if it concerns xxx or some unique resource of the xxx Libraries.

Placing this type of restriction on the initial page of the ask-a-librarian site presents a predominantly negative impression, which may be sufficient to counteract the positive personality of the site. If such policies are necessary (see the discussion on service policies below), the policies can be presented in less obtrusive and less negative ways on the site.

Bulletin Boards, News Groups, and Listservs

The preceding sections have discussed one-to-many and one-to-one information services using asynchronous communications technologies. To complete the review of possible information services using such technologies, it is necessary to consider many-to-many communications mechanisms. In such communications, any member of a community may contribute a question or an answer on a topic under discussion, and all members of the community will see these contributions. There are many examples of listservs that librarians have established for professional communication on a variety of issues. But there are apparently no examples of library information services based on this kind of technology. Nor are there library-based news groups, although public libraries frequently participate in freenet community information resources that maintain news groups. Since libraries have embraced other forms of asynchronous communication for the provision of information services, the absence of many-to-many information services deserves exploration.

Any library has two distinct options when it comes to providing information services in electronic communities. The first is to create its own electronic community around its own information resources and personnel. The second is to move into existing electronic communities and to act as information sources within them. This second option might be recognized as the "outreach" option that many public libraries have adopted. They have moved outside the library, providing services in communities that have a variety of different information needs. For example, public libraries have created deposit collections within schools or nursing homes. Or they've placed branch libraries in neighborhoods to meet the needs of residents of those areas. It is possible that libraries can find electronic neighborhoods into which they can move and become information resources within those communities.

The first option would lead the library to set up a listserv or news group that would meet the needs of an identified community of users. Suppose, for example, that a public library supports the information needs of a reasonably large number of people who are doing genealogy. The library could establish a listserv or a news group through which these users could communicate with each other (and with reference librarians) about their work. In an academic community, there might be a number of faculty and students who are interested in a topic such as space exploration. Again, the library could establish a listserv or a news group linking these users and, of course, include information services staff who could respond to information requests from all members of the group.

The second option would require information services personnel to become members of existing listservs or news groups and to assume the role of information provider in that community. This sounds easy but, of course, it raises many questions. Into what electronic communities should the library attempt to "reach out"? There are hundreds of listservs and news groups in existence. There are some examples of a clear "fit" between electronic communities and the information resources and personnel of libraries, but exploring that "fit" and assigning personnel resources to the outreach function require extensive planning on the part of the library.

In the case of developing Web-based information services or creating ask-a-librarian sites, the first steps in the library's planning process were to identify the target market for their information services and to establish the information needs that the library's information service might address in those markets. The same process is essential in developing information services based on many-to-many communications technologies. Once the library's priorities have been established, information services personnel can explore electronic communities, establishing whether existing listservs or news groups provide appropriate mechanisms for the library to begin to meet users' information needs. If there are no existing communications mechanisms for the targeted user communities, the library may wish to establish, as part of its suite of electronic information services, a suitable many-to-many communications forum.

Since the services discussed thus far have been Web-based, it would seem appropriate to create a Web-based discussion forum rather than using email lists or a separate news group server. Fortunately, there are a number of software support packages that create threaded discussions on websites, using Java scripting. For those libraries that prefer to develop their own Java scripting, code for creating discussion forums can be found on the Web.

INFORMATION SERVICES BASED ON SYNCHRONOUS INFORMATION

If someone had predicted, 20 years ago, that virtual worlds called dungeons would exist on computers, the prediction would have been regarded as science fiction. What a bizarre development! These are "places" where people "go" to "meet" each other. They may play games, or they may just chat. In some "places," the people adopt alternative identities, false names, or avatars.

Whether it's a multiuser dungeon, or a plain chat room, synchronous electronic communication mechanisms create interesting and novel types of electronic communities, and provide new challenges for information services. Synchronous communication goes back to the preliterate (and in that sense, prehistoric) reality of human culture. In synchronous communication, the messages sent and received are temporary, occurring at one place in one time. Yet they are also tremendously powerful. The power of political oratory, religious preaching, commercial salesmanship, or even library storytelling seems to lie in the power of synchronous communication. So also is the power of conversational interaction in groups. That's why business meetings are so prevalent and such a powerful way of making decisions.

It is perhaps not too surprising that synchronous communication has been the basis for library information services for as long as these services have existed. With very few exceptions, individuals have approached a librarian for assistance. The standard reference desk interaction is taught as the paradigm for information service interactions. The two most frequent ways of obtaining information services are both synchronous: walking up to a reference desk is probably still the most common, with telephone reference service as the second most common. It is strange that when faced with electronic communities, libraries have opted for asynchronous communications for the most part, moving away from their long tradition (and excellence) in synchronous communication.

Implementing library information services using synchronous computer-based communication can best be visualized by thinking of the librarian in the chat room. There are some parallels that can be illuminating. For example, some news organizations (CNN, MSNBC) put their reporters in a chat room, sometimes with pundits or other guests. It's the electronic equivalent of having viewers phone in with questions. If a library has a website that is already serving an electronic community of users, it is relatively easy to add a chat room to the web page. Reference staff, either at the reference desk or during their time off the desk, would monitor this chat room and answer questions when they occur just as if the questions were coming into the library by phone. The objection to this service is likely to be that it increases the workload of reference staff. At the time of writing, there are some examples of operational synchronous reference services offered by libraries. For example, the Cornell University Libraries have a "Live Help" service. The Library of Congress has undertaken a leadership effort entitled Reference Services in a Digital Age (http://lcweb.loc.gov/rr/digiref/). One of the projects that grew out of that effort is a "collaborative remote reference service" project, which is considering synchronous communication as at least one mechanism for service provision. The literature discussing synchronous information services to electronic communities by libraries is currently full of many question marks, and experimentation seems to be the order of the day.

As technology evolves, it will be possible to combine voice and video with data communications. If this occurs in a timely and cost-effective manner, two-way synchronous communications between librarians and users can be significantly enhanced. The librarian and the user will be able to look at the same search engines and the same data and chat back and forth about the progress of the search for information.

ECONOMICS OF SERVICE EXPANSION

The services discussed above represent an addition to traditional library information services. Although it is no doubt true that some users of traditional information services will switch completely to electronic information services, it seems probable that some users will use both traditional and electronic information services. And it is to be expected that information services that are developed with specific user groups in mind will attract new users to the library's services. As a result, libraries may expect to see the level of activity of their information services increase overall as they add electronic information services.

At the same time, most libraries find themselves in situations in which available funds to finance the provision of information services are either constant from year to year or decreasing in real terms over time. In such situations, libraries can add electronic information services to the job tasks of existing personnel, recognizing that some (usually unspecified) aspect of current job tasks will be neglected as a result. Or libraries can make a conscious decision to allocate funds to information services provision from other parts of the overall library budget (e.g., by reducing collection building). Since these options are both unpalatable, libraries may wish to consider the option of using electronic information resources as a source of revenue.

There are two possibilities for revenue generation from electronic information services. The first is a direct fee-for-service arrangement, in which electronic information services are priced so as to cover the incremental costs of offering such services. The second is indirect revenue generation via advertisements. There exist ample precedents for both of these approaches in existing Web information services. For example, a firm like Dun and Bradstreet (http://www.dnb.com) can offer a subscription-based service that includes a variety of payment options for credit card customers. On the other hand, the Thomas Register Website (http://www. thomasregister.com) offers free searching of its manufacturer's directory, supported at least in part by on-site advertising.

Librarians share a tradition of valuing free access to information. They are likely, therefore, to shy away from revenue generation as an alternative economic strategy. It is possible, however, that the absurdity of increasing demand for services while restricting resources to provide those services will convince librarians that alternative economic models need to be considered. In most libraries, revenue received is not tied in any direct way to service provided. In an academic library, a proportion of a student's tuition payments will be allocated to the library whether or not that student actually uses the library. Similarly, two homeowners with comparable properties will pay comparable property taxes to the library, whether or not they are comparable users of public library services. There may be an indirect link between the provision of information services and library revenues. An argument can be made that high-quality services will increase the willingness of students to pay higher tuition or of residents to pay higher taxes to support library services. There is little evidence to support this indirect link between services and revenues, however, and those who advance this argument seem to be guided primarily by wishful thinking.

Given the lack of a solid association between services and revenues, a rational approach to library information services will be to minimize the services provided and thus maximize the revenue per service transaction. Suppose a library reference department receives a budget of $100,000. If it answers 10,000 questions per year, revenue per question will be $10. If it answers 50,000 questions per year, revenue per question will be $2. Now, it is within the realm of possibility that a reference department could provide high quality service with resources of $10 per question. But it is clearly impossible to provide high-quality service with the lower amount. Accordingly, the rational action on the part of the department is to reduce reference questions to the lowest figure it can reasonably achieve.

When faced with the possibilities of expanding library information services via services to electronic communities, libraries seem to be faced with the undesirable alternatives of restricting access to information services or of generating new revenue to support the new services. This author prefers the entrepreneurial approach, while recognizing that it goes against some of the valued traditions of our profession.

SERVICE POLICIES

It is against the background of the economics of service expansion that policies for information services to electronic communities can be viewed to advantage. Examples of policies restricting access to electronic reference services were cited above. These are to be viewed as mechanisms for minimizing extra service provision given constant resources. Another aspect of information service policies was introduced in the planning process described above. This planning process leads libraries to establish their priorities in service provision and to seek positions of competitive advantage in the overall information marketplace. This planning process is an essential precursor to the establishment of service policies.

The service policies that relate to information services to electronic communities must incorporate the following elements:

- A description of the user groups who have been identified as target markets for the service (and, as a result, a description of those user groups who are not members of the target electronic communities)

- An outline of the information needs that are the priority of the information service
- A description of the types of service that are to be offered to members of the target market (and, as a result, a description of the types of service that are to be offered to people who are not members of the target electronic community)
- A description of the types of service that are to be offered to users who present queries that are associated with the priority information needs of the service (and, as a result, a description of the types of service that are to be offered to users who present queries that are not associated with the priority information needs of the service)

For each description of a type of service, the policy should include:

- Expected qualifications of personnel who will be responding to queries
- Time deadlines to be met
- Information resources that may or may not be used
- Referral policies
- Pricing policies

It is recognized that in a rapidly evolving area such as the provision of information services to electronic communities, these policies will evolve rapidly. However, they are essential mechanisms for ensuring that policies are based on proper planning and consistent thought and are shared by all information service providers.

CONCLUSIONS

The advent of the Internet has introduced a number of transforming technological changes: the digital storage of information resources and new telecommunications methods that have established electronic communities. It is the task of libraries to invent new information services that will deliver the new information resources to the new user communities. These new information services can be sufficiently different from traditional information services to transform the economics and the policies of information service provision. While it can be argued that traditional information services, offered to individuals who are physically present in the library, will continue to be an important part of the jobs of reference librarians, it also seems true that offering information services to electronic communities is beginning to change those jobs in important ways.

NOTES

1. Redmond Kathleen Molz and Phyllis Dain, "The Institution: Services, Technology and Communities," in *Civic Space/Cyberspace: The American*

Public Library in the Information Age (Cambridge: MIT Press, 1999), pp. 183-216.

2. Charles Anderson, "Proactive Reference," *Reference and User Services Quarterly*, 38, no. 2 (1998): 139-140; Nancy K. Reger, "Redefining Reference Services: Transitioning at One Public Library," *Reference and User Services Quarterly*, 38, no. 1 (1998): 73-75.

SUPPLEMENTARY READING

Abels, Eileen G. "The E-mail Reference Interview." *RQ* 35, no. 3 (1996): 345-358.

Baym, Nancy K. "The Emergence of On-line Community." In *Cybersociety 2.0: Revisiting Computer-Mediated Communication and Community,* ed. Steven G. Jones. Thousand Oaks, CA: Sage, 1998, pp. 35-68.

Bristow, Ann and Mary Buechley. "Academic Reference Service over E-mail: An Update." *College and Research Libraries News*, 56, no. 7 (1995): 459-462.

Bromberg, Heather. "Are MUDs Communities? Identity, Belonging and Consciousness in Virtual Worlds." In *Cultures of Internet: Virtual Spaces, Real Histories, Living Bodies*, ed. Rob Shields. London: Sage, 1996, pp. 143-152.

Bushalow-Wilbur, Lara, Genna DeVinney, and Fritz Whitcomb. "Electronic Mail Reference Service: A Study." *RQ* 35, no. 3 (1996): 359-371.

Curtis, Pavel. "Mudding: Social Phenomena in Text-Based Virtual Realities." In *Cultures of the Internet*, ed. Sara Kiesler. Mahwah, NJ: Erlbaum, 1997, pp. 121-155.

Fernback, Jan. "There Is a There There: Notes toward a Definition of Cybercommunity" In *Doing Internet Research: Critical Issues and Methods for Examining the Net*, ed. Stephen G. Jones. Thousand Oaks, CA: Sage, 1999, pp. 203-220.

Fishman, Diane L. "Managing the Virtual Reference Desk: How to Plan an Effective Reference E-mail System." *Medical Reference Services Quarterly* 17, no. 1 (1998): 1-19.

Frank, Ilene. "E-mail References Services at the University of South Florida: A Well-kept Secret." *Art Documentation* 17, no.1 (1998): 8-9.

Harrison, Teresa M. and Timothy Stephen. "Research and Creating Community Networks." In *Doing Internet Research: Critical Issues and Methods for Examining the Net*, ed. Stephen G. Jones. Thousand Oaks, CA: Sage, 1999, pp. 221-241.

Igbaria, Magid, Conrad Shayo, and Lorne Olfman. "Virtual Societies: Their Prospects and Dilemmas." In *Psychology and the Internet: Intrapersonal, Interpersonal, and Transpersonal Implications*, ed. Jayne Gackenbach. San Diego: Academic Press, 1998, pp. 227-252.

Jones, Steven G. "The Internet and Its Social Landscape." In *Virtual Culture: Identity and Communication in Cybersociety,* ed. Steven G. Jones. London: Sage, 1997, pp. 7-35.

Jones, Steven G. "Information, Internet and Community: Notes toward an Understanding of Community in the Information Age." In *Cybersociety 2.0: Revisiting Computer-Mediated Communication and Community,* ed. Steven G. Jones. Thousand Oaks, CA: Sage, 1998, pp. 1-34.

Lagace, Nettie. "Establishing Online Reference Services." In *The Internet Public Library Handbook*, ed. Joe Janes et al. New York: Neal-Schuman, 1999, pp. 153-183.

Lankes, R. David and Abby S. Kasowitz. "Planning: Creating a Plan for Building and Maintaining an AskA Service." In *The AskA Starter Kit.* Syracuse, NY: ERIC, 1998, pp. 41-73.

Parks, Malcolm R. and Lynne D. Roberts. "'Making MOOsic: The Development of Personal Relationships On Line and a Comparison to their Off-line Counterparts." *Journal of Social and Personal Relationships* 15, no.4 (1998): 517-537.

Reid, Elizabeth. "The Self and the Internet: Variations on the Illusion of One Self." In *Psychology and the Internet: Intrapersonal, Interpersonal, and Transpersonal Implications.* ed. Jayne Gackenbach. San Diego: Academic Press, 1998, pp. 29-42.

Reid, Elizabeth. "Virtual Worlds: Culture and Imagination." In *Cybersociety: Computer-mediated Communication and Community*, ed. Steven G. Jones. Thousand Oaks, CA: Sage, 1995, pp. 164-183.

Riva, Guiseppe and Carlo Galimberti. "The Psychology of Cyberspace: A Socio-Cognitive Framework to Computer-Mediated Communication." *New Ideas in Psychology* 15, no. 2 (1997): 141-158.

Schiano, Diane J. "Convergent Methodologies in Cyber-Psychology: A Case Study." *Behavior Research Methods, Instruments & Computers* 29, no. 2 (1997): 270-273.

Schilling-Eccles, Katherine and Joseph J. Harzbecker. "The Use of Electronic Mail at the Reference Desk: Impact of a Computer-Mediated Communication Technology on Librarian-Client Interactions," *Medical Reference Services Quarterly* 17, no.4 (1998): 17-27.

Stahl, Joan. "'Have a Question? Click Here': Electronic Reference at the National Museum of American Art." *Art Documentation* 17, no. 1 (1998): 10-12.

Summers, Robin. "Meeting Education Information Needs through Digital Reference." *Art Documentation* 17, no.1 (1998): 3-4.

Tibbo, Helen. "Interviewing Techniques for Remote Reference: Electronic versus Traditional Environments." *American Archivist* 58 (Summer 1995): 294-310.

CHAPTER SEVEN

BIBLIOGRAPHIC INSTRUCTION ON THE INTERNET

Gillian Allen

INTRODUCTION

Bibliographic instruction, as traditionally practiced in libraries of all types, helps library patrons to make better use of a library's materials and services. Library orientation exercises, such as the guided or audiocassette tour of the library, and library instruction lectures or workshops on such topics as how to search the library's online public access catalog or how to design a search strategy have formed the nucleus of traditional bibliographic instruction activities. These traditional bibliographic instruction activities and indeed the whole philosophy of instruction have been greatly influenced by the Internet. The patrons of a particular library no longer have to come into that library to receive the instruction that will enable them to make better use of the specific materials and services of that library. In its simplest form, the Internet allows a library to make its instructional materials available to anyone using its web pages. In a broader sense, it is now theoretically possible that anyone, anywhere can make use of any instruction provided on any library's website on the Internet to make better use of any library's (or other information providers') materials and services.

TRADITIONAL BIBLIOGRAPHIC INSTRUCTION

The American Library Association recommended in 1980 that libraries adopt instruction as one of the primary goals of library service.[1] Instruction began with librarians providing one-on-one, just-in-time instruction to their patrons. Over time, as it became necessary to cut costs and improve the efficiency of instruction (and all other library services), libraries started to organize larger instruction classes for groups of users who were seen to have instruction needs in common. This more efficient instruction complemented the less efficient, individualized instruction that was still offered, but to a lesser extent, at specific points-of-use throughout libraries. Librarians lectured to groups of public library patrons on how to perform typical searches using the online public access catalog. They held workshops for all new students at a university who needed to know how to select a term paper topic. Special librarians held demos in the corporate library of the latest CD-ROM databases purchased by a professional firm.

Librarians have learned to incorporate sound educational principles into their bibliographic instruction. A large number of learning theories explain how library users (and students in general) learn and how library instruction (and other course work) should be organized to meet the needs of users. Not all learning theories are useful in all instruction, but the careful librarian thinks about applying appropriate learning theories in the design of each library instruction module. An example of a useful learning theory used in instruction is active learning. Dabbour suggests benefits of incorporating active learning in instruction[2]:

1. Less emphasis is placed on transmitting information and more on developing skills;
2. Students are involved in higher-order thinking (i.e., analysis, synthesis, evaluation);
3. Students are engaged in activities (e.g., reading, discussing, writing); and
4. Greater emphasis is placed on students' exploration of their attitudes and values.

The use of active learning techniques in instruction is also discussed in an article by Allen.[3] These techniques include modified lecture (which include quizzes, questions, demonstrations, and assignments), brainstorming, small group work, cooperative projects, peer teaching and partnering, and note-taking or journaling. Reliance on the use of the lecture in instruction is discouraged according to this learning theory, and as a result many instruction librarians have rethought how instruction should be undertaken in their libraries. The focus of much traditional instruction has been shifting, as many students are now encouraged by their instruction librarians to search actively for information. Learners are now able to seek out their answers to their own questions using the library's resources; they complete exercises which test their understanding of new concepts; and they practice using their new research and evaluation skills.

BIBLIOGRAPHIC INSTRUCTION ON THE LIBRARY'S WEBSITE

The Internet provides a relatively convenient and inexpensive means for libraries to reach their users (and their nonusers). Virtually all academic libraries, most public libraries, and many special libraries have established sites on the Internet to provide selected information and to publicize the materials and services offered by the library. Library websites represent a vehicle by which libraries can reach their intended users. These websites also allow other self-selected users to access a library's materials and services, which might be seen as a problem by some libraries.

The home page of a library can be used to provide many types of information. Administrative details, such as hours of opening, location, and library policies, are frequently found on the home page. In addition, community information might be found on the public library's web pages, and many libraries now use their websites to provide bibliographic instruction for their users. The library must decide what type of instruction to provide on the Internet. Types of instruction range from specialized to generalized, with each type of instruction of particular interest to a distinct group of users. Specialized information, like how to use "our" online public access catalog, would be useful to library patrons, who intend to visit the library sometime. More generalized information, like how to use a generic online public access catalog—an example would be instruction on how to use Boolean logic in searching, would be useful for distant users of the library (who may never even enter the library itself). The type and amount of instruction to be provided on the library's website vary, and depend on the chosen mission of the library and its target market for services. Regardless of the type and amount of instruction offered, the Internet offers great opportunities to libraries for providing bibliographic instruction. Libraries can provide basic library orientation on the home page: teasers like "Look what you can find in your library!" can be used to attract new users to the website and to the library. Location information, contact phone numbers, and email addresses can be provided, and a map of the physical layout of the library can be included. The advantages of incorporating the Internet into instruction are obvious. Multimedia files can be created on a web page. Audio, video, image, graphics, and text in one file can be integrated into the presentation of the instruction. Links can be incorporated to other useful Internet sites within the instruction. Learners can access or review this instruction at their own convenience from wherever they happen to be located, as long as they have access to the Internet. Sounds wonderful, doesn't it? But there is also possibly a downside to providing instruction on the Internet. The learners are learning from a distance. This means that they are usually learning alone. Much traditional instruction takes advantage of collaborative learning principles and uses groups as the focus of learning. But the very nature of learning on the Internet means that learners do not have the help and support of other learners in a group. They also do not have direct access to a library's materials and services when they learn from a distance. Finally, they do not have the personalized help of an instruction librarian, who can demonstrate a technology or make sure the learner has understood the directions as to how to proceed in traditional, face-to-face instruction. This means that the instruction on the Internet must be very carefully designed to take advantage of the opportunities and reduce the limitations of the Web-based system in instruction.

INTERNET BIBLIOGRAPHIC INSTRUCTIONAL DESIGN

Librarians often try to adapt methods that have been traditionally used in face-to-face bibliographic instruction to the Web environment. For example, classroom lectures used in a traditional library can be turned into electronic instruction notes that can be incorporated into a library's website. Some of the elements of design are the same for traditional instruction or Internet instruction. Nipp points out that the instructional designer must consider the content, instructional design, programming, and evaluation of instruction.[4] The content is what you will teach the user that will help that user make better use of the library and its resources. Instructional content is the same in traditional and Internet design, but there will generally be less content on a library's web page (than the amount of instruction that can be included in a traditional BI session).

At this point, however, traditional and Internet instructional design diverge. Instructional design using the Internet includes the effective use of screen space, computer logic, the keyboard, and other peripherals to facilitate learning and a solid understanding of computer memory and its constraints on response time. Programming refers to the ability to create text in HTML and to integrate it with graphics files. Evaluation of Internet instruction involves both the testing of the Web product and the testing of the success of the learner in using the instruction site. Nipp provides a series of steps to work through in developing instruction using the Internet.[5]

Step 1: Review other instructional sites on the Web. This will help you understand the medium, see innovative uses, and learn from the most obvious blunders.

Step 2: Provide for the four competencies. You have two choices: develop your own skills in content, instructional design, programming, and evaluation, or work with a team in which each member brings a different competency (or competencies) to the project. The librarian and webmaster present a good combination of personnel for working together to develop Web instruction.

Step 3: Write instructional goals and instructional objectives. Instructional goals are the broad outcomes that will be seen in the students as a result of the instruction. Instructional objectives must be measurable. An example: "following instruction, 95% of the learners will be able to find periodical articles on a particular subject."

Step 4: Determine organizational design. Different designs are appropriate to different learning experiences. A hierarchical design with links between levels and among pages on each level is most like the Web experience itself and fits many types of instruction. A linear design, like reading through a book, is appropriate for presentation of a process in which each step depends on mastery of the one before. Drill and practice are appropriate for presenting a series of problem-solving questions. A tutorial is appropriate for initial presentation of material. Testing must be included at appropriate points in the design to measure and record student performance.

Step 5: Write the script and graphic support for each objective. Plan for consistency in layout and presentation. Plan for consistency in font type and size and in the use of underlining, bold letters, and italics. Remain consistent in the use of technical language. Use the fewest possible words to teach each instructional objective. Use examples. Consider the use of a chart or a diagram. Use short sentences. Provide plenty of white space. Use wording which motivates the learner to move forward. Review every aspect of the project for accuracy as you proceed.

Step 6: Create the HTML text and the graphics files. Often, well-designed software, such as Word for MacIntosh, can be of great assistance in this step.

Step 7: Evaluate. The first form of instruction evaluation is pretesting the instruction on individuals (like those who will be in the intended audience). That is difficult, of course, when you expect at least some of your users to be distant users of the library, and you have no way of knowing exactly who those distant users might be. Then, evaluate further by interviewing actual users of the instruction about problems they encountered in the instruction.

Step 8: Revise. The evaluation will identify parts of the instruction that are not working. Changes you make at this point will improve the instructional design.

Step 9: Reevaluate. Reevaluation leads to further revision and to further improvement of the instruction.

There are other general rules of design which apply specifically to the design of Web-based instruction, as opposed to traditional instruction. DeWald explains:[6]

1. Web-based library instruction is not primarily semester-long but consists of modules that can be used to complement and supplement the one-shot library instruction.
2. Web-based library instruction most often consists of short modules designed to teach specific library skills and concepts... Material is presented online in the order determined by the librarian, and students are queried frequently during the instruction.
3. A variety of learner ability level can be accommodated when the student is allowed some degree of choice in the learning path to follow. For example, a linked table of contents in a separate frame not only provides a continual

overview of the material but it also allows the user to select the elements and their order.

4. Modules that provide information in small blocks, breaking it up into parts and subparts with summaries and reviews, help learners absorb material gradually and organize the material in their own minds.
5. Librarians can use page elements such as arrows, color, highlighting, white space, small icons, and different fonts and font sizes to structure information for better learner understanding.
6. The level of multimedia use in Web-based training should be determined by the program design needs, not just by a desire to use the latest technology. For example, graphics, including pictures and charts, are valuable in clarifying information and maintaining students' attention and interest. Nonetheless, use of multimedia can be costly and requires users to have high-end computers.
7. Extrinsic motivation can be provided in a Web module by immediate feedback to the learner's practice questions.

Perhaps an example of instructional design using the Internet will help. Pixey Anne Mosley and Daniel Xiao described the Texas A & M experience in developing the virtual library tour.[7] One hundred and sixty-five hours of professional time were needed to create and release the tour, which was intended to replace the typical 45-minute walking tour of the library. The authors decided it was not feasible to put the entire tour in one HTML file, and separate files were used for each tour stop. Target sizes for the files were 20K to 25K, with graphic sizes targeted at 10K (big enough for realness without detracting from the descriptive information). The basic structure of each tour stop was a photographic representation of some aspects of the area, a few bulleted points for emphasis, a brief description of the area, and hypertext links for pursuing in-depth information. The HTML scripting was done with a simple text editor. The maps were created using Windows Paintbrush. Problems were encountered with graphics displaying incorrectly (so the developers changed to an earlier—and more tested—version of the software), photograph resolution (so they suggest that developers use a digital camera), and browser version incompatibilities (the authors note that less sophisticated users may be running older versions of the software). A large number of hypertext links were used in the program—and this meant that constant checking of the URLs was needed to ensure that each URL was current.

Libraries do have one major limitation in what instruction can be provided on the Internet. A library is not usually permitted (by a number of outside parties) to provide instruction in using all of its materials and services. Although many libraries now can allow patrons to access the online public access catalog and some library collections on the Web, they are usually prevented from allowing unrestricted access to certain licensed library resources. First-time users of such "protected" parts of the library's website are asked for their library card number as a preliminary to accessing some databases of the library, and Cookies (software downloaded onto Netscape for identifying acceptable user status to access the library's resources) are frequently needed for accessing some resources of the library.

WRITING INSTRUCTION FOR THE INTERNET

The Internet provides a way for libraries to provide just-in-time, on-demand instruction that can be accessed by users at their convenience. Tutorials can be written that provide instruction on a wide range of topics, from how to use technologies found in all libraries, like the online catalog, to how to search for information on the Internet (and evaluate the quality and usefulness of the information found using a number of different search engines). This writing for the Internet must be clear and brief, with lots of examples to reinforce the instruction. Ongoing help must be built into the lessons for users who don't understand a particular component of the instruction, and tests included to ensure that the learner understands one instruction module before proceeding to more advanced instruction. A number of tools exist to help the instruction librarian write for the Web. For example, the following website, http://bones.med.ohio-state.edu/eric/papers/ primer/webdocs.html, was created as a Web-writing guide for librarians.

It is difficult to put into words the complicated instructions needed to help library patrons to search better, to use better, or to understand better what is going on in the library (or on the Internet). Users need to be able to ask the instruction librarian for further clarification, they need lots of examples to help them understand, and they need to have their work checked (so they know they are "doing it right"). How can you allow necessary (or appropriate) communication while discouraging overuse of your instructional resources (including the time and patience of the instruction librarian)? You need to build into the instruction site a means to communicate with the instruction librarian and make clear to the users the conditions under which it is appropriate to use that communication link. Nancy DeWald considered the degree of help provided in 19 "good" Web-based instruction tutorials.[8] "The offer of help by a librarian, whether that help is provided online, by phone, or in person, is a vital part of any instruction and should be included in Web tutorial. Web tutorials may contain an email connection to the reference desk, an online form or worksheet for the student to fill out, which should preferably include space for student questions, or at least a referral to the reference phone number or the location and possibly times of availability of a reference [or instruction] librarian."

Another issue related to Internet instruction focuses on how to publicize and increase use of the instruction provided by the library on the Internet--finding ways to get users to take advantage of the instruction offered (and finding ways to get them to provide feedback in return to the library on the usefulness of that instruction). We know that most library users do not take advantage of library instruction voluntarily. Kaczor and Jacobson stated that library users preferred to learn on their own (rather than in the library).[9] This suggests that learners should be more comfortable learning about the library or about the Internet at the library's website on the Internet rather than in the traditional bibliographic instruction sessions offered in the library. Have you seen the ads on TV for the personalized shopper service on the Land's End website? Many companies are starting to offer such customized advisory and help services in the retail sector. The user asks for help and the person at the other end of the Internet connection immediately responds with suggestions or pictures of sample merchandise that seem to match the user's request. The interview proceeds, with the client revising the question or request and the helper making further suggestions and providing more information, until a point when the communication is successfully completed, and the client makes a final selection from among the merchandise offered. Couldn't this be a model for the communication mechanism between the instruction website user and the instruction librarian? Can/should the instruction librarian provide online consultation hours (similar to the online reference hours provided by some libraries)? The instruction librarian could be available to answer questions, and provide further clarifications or examples as needed on a real-time basis, and otherwise assist the distant (or local) user of the library to better understand what the library and its staff have to offer. Would this work?

EVALUATION OF THE INTERNET INSTRUCTION

The instruction on the library's website must be evaluated before use, during use, and after it has been put into use by library patrons. The instruction, as initially written, must be assessed for usability before it is made available to the public. Day-to-day success of actual users of the system must be tested on a continuing basis. The effectiveness of the instruction, in terms of cost and required resources, must also be considered by the library as the instruction is being used.

Evaluation before Use

As you plan and create instruction for the library's website, you will be guided by certain evaluation criteria. Instruction website developers will be influenced by a number of self-selected (or even user-imposed) standards for website quality, such as accuracy, objectivity, currency, comprehensiveness of coverage, or user-friendliness. Even when a lot of care is used in preparing the content and design of your instruction, the job is not finished when your instruction is "put up on the Web." Many instruction librarians emphasize the need to pretest the instruction site before it is used by library patrons. Even when the instructional materials are created and mounted on the site by a team of professionals representing library and computer science professionals, it is important to recognize that users may still have trouble understanding the instructions for using the site or the content of the site. It is therefore important to make sure your site is tested by a large number of individuals representative of each user group you anticipate using the site when it becomes operational. Based on the comments (and errors made) by people pretesting the site, you may have to do minor (or major) revisions to the site before it is ready for use by your intended audience(s).

Evaluation during Use

Nipp states: "When the package is put into actual use, observe students to see where they have problem most users will have at least one insight they are willing to share."[10] This points to the necessity of continued attention to, and revision of, the site content. The "lurking" instruction librarian can see evidence of users having difficulty following directions within the instruction materials. The instruction librarian should also provide a "Comments" communication space at the end of each instruction module, so users can mention problems encountered during the instruction or make recommendations for improving the instruction site that will benefit future users of the site. The evaluation methods available to the librarian in charge of instruction on the library's website are few and simple. The evaluation must be "short and sweet" because the user cannot be forced to remain at the library's website to complete lengthy evaluation(s). The user must also see that he/she is getting something from completing the evaluation(s)--or the user won't spend a lot of time simply to help the library gather its statistics. Consider the applicability of the following evaluation methods: a very brief post-test on the user's ability to use the online catalog; a very brief questionnaire on the user's attitude toward using certain Web search engines; the use of transaction logging to trace the (successful and inappropriate) progress of users through the instruction and library resources encountered during the Web visit; games incorporated into the site, such as a word seek to show the user's familiarity with the terminology associated with the instruction subject or a small crossword puzzle focusing on the keywords of the instruction; or a series of very brief exercises that are self-scoring and that provide immediate feedback to the learner, spread throughout the instruction module to test the ability of the patron to understand and use the library resources in question.

Evaluation after Implementation of the Instruction

The costs of providing electronic services in libraries, including the costs of providing instruction on the Internet, are very difficult to measure. Bertot considers issues related to the costs of Internet services offered in libraries.[11] Intuitively, we believe that instruction using the Internet should be cost-effective. If you carefully create instruction that can be understood by the intended user group, the instruction can be placed once on the Web (and therefore it will not have to be repeated for each individual user or group of users who comes into the library). The instruction librarian's time can be put to better use helping users with specific problems not covered by the Web instruction or providing advanced library instruction. If we "buy into" this basic assumption, it will be helpful to keep statistics to provide support for the assumption. Collect the numbers! How many people are still coming into (or calling or emailing) the library to ask for the instructional content that is included on the library's website? How many patrons are now asking for advanced instruction (because their basic instruction needs have been met by the instruction on the website)? How many individuals accessed each instruction module on the library's website? Were more individuals looking for instruction on how to use an OPAC, or how to evaluate Web resources or instruction involving access to and use of the library's special collections?

Look at the comments you receive from users of your website. Analyze trends in the comments you receive and revise your instruction module(s) on the website as needed. Add modules to your instruction that are frequently requested by your users, keeping track of the costs of such additions in terms of equipment and manpower requirements (to create, provide, and support the instruction). Be prepared to demonstrate the cost-effectiveness, in terms of physical resources and in terms of user response, of your Web-based instruction.

SIMPLE AND COMPLEX INSTRUCTION SITES ON THE INTERNET

At the time of writing of this chapter, a large number of instruction sites on the Internet were examined. These can be differentiated as simple instruction sites which provide one type of instruction and complex instruction sites which provide several instruction modules within a site (and need special tools that assist the learner to make the best possible use of the site). Examples of the simple instruction site include:

1. The Customized Pathfinder

At times, an instruction site will be customized to serve a unique purpose. Sloan describes the process implemented at the University of New Brunswick to custom design pathfinders. “If the user chooses a subject like Psychology, the script writes back an HTML document that contains preformatted hypertext links for finding information on that subject. A Psychology Pathfinder, as such, does not actually exist until the user requests one.”[12]

2. The Specialized Site

Alternatively, a website might exist to serve a particular population or to provide a particular product on a continuing basis. Cox’s article introduces a website built around a poem, which can be accessed at http://info.ox.ac.uk/departments/humanities/roes.[13] A seminar was developed around the poem, which can be accessed by anyone using the website.

However, this separate and specialized instruction site might not be easily found by all interested parties (as compared with instruction that is accessible from the library's home page).

3. The Tutorial

A third type of simple site is the common tutorial site. This website teaches how to use, or to make the best use of, a particular product. TONIC, described in Cox's article, presents the case of a tutorial exploring basic Internet skills. It covers all the main internet protocols. Although there is a systematic path through the information, it is possible to jump to the main menu to access a particular part of the tutorial. Access TONIC at http://www.netskills.ac.uk/TONIC. A very interesting tutorial intended to teach interview skills is located at: http://www.kaplan.com/career/hotseat. The site provides a game to teach interview skills, in addition to some funny but helpful quotes. Such a site could be provided by any library with a large career assistance service.

Complex instruction sites provide more than one type of instruction for users. There are a number of navigational and instructional tools that you can use to organize and provide better access to complex instruction modules. Here are some examples of tools to help the learner make use of the complex instruction site:

1. The Site Map or Guide

http://www.city.palo-alto.ca.us

This website offers a site map, a site search feature, and a site guide (or index) for the city of Palo Alto. The site search feature provides very useful relevance indexes for the documents retrieved in response to each keyword search query. The site guide places library-related modules at appropriate levels of the overall site structure (e.g., the library advisory board is listed in council-appointed boards and commissions and the library itself is shown as one of the city services). Unfortunately, the library does not appear on the first level of the site map. Note what happens when you click "site guide" on the city's home page: instant navigational and instructional aids!

2. The Screen Layout or Menu

http://www.ci.glendora.ca.us/library

This example provides a very nice choice of options for searching. The user can choose keyword search, dictionary, thesaurus, browse search, other databases, or search assistant from a central screen. Search assistant provides step-by-step instructions for searching the resources of the library.

3. The Help Provided
http://www.dekalb.public.lib.ga.us

This public library provides a troubleshooting feature that allows the user to obtain guidance in solving some common problems in using the library's website. Unfortunately, the troubleshooting section is not prominently displayed on the home page of the website. The user must be able to access the catalog module of the site before troubleshooting help is offered. Then, the user can obtain assistance with problems accessing the browser, or with other problems such as dealing with "error connecting" messages or inability to print.

4. The Instructions for Users
http://library.ci.mtnview.ca.us/screens/mainmenu.html

This site provides instruction on "what button to push" in order to continue to use the system. It is interesting that the site provides a menu of instructions according to type and version of software being used.

5. The Links
http://www.bham.lib.al.us

The Genealogy module on this website provides links to 10 other sites (or aggregations of sites). One of the links is to Cyndi's List, which is in itself a link to 56,300 Internet links to useful genealogy sources.

6. The Appropriateness of the Site for Intended Users
http://www.bham.lib.al.us

This site provides specialized searching instructions for the young user. Children can use Searchasaurus or ProQuest KidQuest to search the databases of the library.

http://www.lib.ci.tucson.az.us

The user is able to access from this site Spanish websites, magazines, and search engines. Unfortunately, the descriptions of these resources on the library's website are in English!

As you can see, a wide variety of simple and complex instruction sites can be found on the Internet.

INSTRUCTION ON THE ACADEMIC LIBRARY WEBSITE

Bibliographic instruction in its traditional form began in the academic library, and academic libraries generally provide extensive instruction using the

Internet. Academic libraries normally offer instruction to homogeneous groups of users who accept that they need to be able to make the best possible use of the university's library system. Instruction is offered in the use of library technologies and in the development of research strategies—topics needed across the board by all of these library users (to a greater or lesser extent). With the recent move of most universities to providing courses through distance education, it follows that it was logical for academic libraries to begin to offer a variety of interactive instruction using the Internet. This on-line instruction ranges from simple instruction (the library tour on the Web) to providing course-integrated instruction.

A survey by the Association for Research Libraries reported that 93% of their member libraries provide Internet training on a regular basis and that 91% of their member libraries plan to continue to provide Internet training.[14] Eighty-six percent of these libraries have a full-time bibliographic instruction coordinator, and 66% of the libraries use the library websites in their instruction. As an example, the State University of New York has recognized several Internet-related competencies for their students, including being able to understand and use the Internet, being able to use information technologies, being able to access the Internet, and being able to navigate the information superhighway. Universities have found that there are many advantages to offering library instruction on the Internet. Instead of offering a standard instruction program for all users (the one-size-fits-all approach), the Web instruction program can offer alternative training content, alternative methods of training, and alternative assignments (and the user can select training to match his or her specific instruction need). In addition, Web instruction can provide assignments throughout the course to ensure that the learner has learned and provide possibilities for communication with other learners in the course and with the instructor.

The simplest form of library instruction on the Web is the virtual tour. The Texas A&M University Virtual Library Tour can be examined at http://www.tamu.edu/library/reference/virtual/tour00.html. This is a very interesting website that offers two versions of the library tour. The user can select the walking tour, which provides floor plans of the library. Or, the user can opt to go directly to a particular point of interest on the point-of-interest tour. The design and development of this tour are described by Mosley and Xiao.[15] Of considerable interest in this article is an extensive list of extremely valuable tips for developing such a Web tour of the library, which can be adapted and used in developing any instruction module. An abbreviated list of these tips follows:

- Define the scope and purpose of the tour;
- Identify the target audience and write to their needs;
- Present the material in stages;
- Establish targets for file size limitations and graphic size and quality parameters;

- Define guidelines regarding individual responsibilities and editorial input;
- Set a maintenance/updating schedule;
- Use as many relative URLs as possible;
- Use title fonts, graphic positioning, and color bars for variations in appearance of the tour stops;
- Keep the first release simple;
- Use consistent text editors and Web clients during the development process;
- Gain HTML experience prior to a project of this magnitude;
- Design pages so low-technology users can still access the basic information;
- Review the nearly finished product;
- Encourage peer review and user feedback;
- Be prepared to make quick changes and corrections after public release.

An example of Web orientation to more advanced library services on an academic website is PLUTO at Purdue University. An article by Scholz et al. describes the design and development of PLUTO (Purdue Libraries Undergraduate Tutorial Online).[16] Objectives of the instruction included helping the student to:

- Define and formulate keyword searches on a given topic;
- Retrieve information on a topic from THOR, the libraries' online system; and
- Locate information from THOR within the Purdue Libraries System (p. 347).

The original PLUTO (described in this article) included the tutorial and two quizzes which provided immediate feedback to the students. You can consider the development of library instruction at Purdue over just a few years by comparing the original PLUTO with the current form of library instruction (CORE+) at Purdue. This system now contains three modules (on research skills, using the library technologies, and advanced search skills). The URL for this instruction is http://thorplus.lib.purdue.edu/core/.

Bowling Green University offers Falcon, an interactive tutorial on its online public access catalog. Users proceed at their own pace in this tutorial and must understand the instruction and the system well enough to answer questions on the correct way to use the system as they proceed throughout the tutorial. At the time of writing, this extremely well designed and written tutorial can be found at http://www.bgsu.edu/colleges/library/ infosrv/tutorial/ tutor1.html

INSTRUCTION ON THE PUBLIC LIBRARY WEBSITE

The public library has been slower to begin to offer traditional library instruction than the academic library. Yet, real needs for instruction can be easily identified. On any given day, public librarians might encounter public library patrons who need to know how to use the CD-ROM version of the

Reader's Guide to Periodical Literature (if that technology is in use in the library). They might meet patrons who need to be able to locate primary materials to do genealogical research. They might talk to library users who want to be able to identify new authors in a genre to expand their recreational reading opportunities. Children might want help to do research for school projects or to successfully complete their homework at the library. The public library, therefore, offers a variation on the type of traditional instruction provided by the academic library. Instead of having a relatively few fairly homogeneous groups of users (e.g., freshmen, graduate students, and faculty) with common needs (e.g., the tour, research strategies) who are accustomed to coming to the library for instruction at regular intervals, the public library has:

- Individuals who approach the library one at a time;
- Individuals with needs for a greater variety of instruction; and
- Individuals who may (or may not) be familiar with the concept of library instruction.

Because of the nature of this bibliographic instruction, it is almost always done on a one-to-one, just-in-time basis. The instruction is simplified because it is in direct response to the immediate instruction need. The instruction librarian simply shows the patron what he or she needs to know. The downside of traditional public library instruction is that it is very time-intensive (and therefore costly for the library); the instruction is continuously repeated for all patrons who need particular information or a particular skill at a particular time. The first problem for the patrons is that they must recognize a need for instruction (which may not be apparent). Then, they must come to the library to try to get the needed instruction (which might be impossible because there may not be someone available to provide the instruction when it is needed). Hundreds of public libraries in the United States have begun to provide bibliographic instruction on their websites, and others have shown an interest in providing instruction on the Internet. Many librarians believe that, if libraries provide library instruction to public library users using the Internet, they should not have to repeat their instruction sessions for every library patron who comes to the library with an instruction need. This might be an appealing thought for many public librarians. Further, library patrons would not even have to come into the public library for their instruction. Perhaps a less appealing thought? Theoretically, the recipients of distance instruction might not even be from your community, but they could still receive your instruction. This might be a strange and perhaps disturbing concept for many public librarians. It calls into question the appropriate mandate and service community of the public library.

The LIRT (the Library Instruction Round Table) Website will introduce you to LOEX (the Library Orientation Exchange) at http://Diogenes.Baylor.edu/Library/LIRT/. At this site, you will find a good starting place to discover the vast array of public library instruction on the Web. Look at some of the over 500 public library websites now in existence (according to the PLA link from this site). The amount of library instruction available on the Web is indeed mind-boggling! Library users are no longer bound by the physical boundaries of library districts to obtain instruction. Of course, this might also be seen as a problem. First, there appears to be considerable duplication of the instruction offered on individual public library sites. Most libraries provide the same types of instruction. How is the library user to choose where to look for help to make the best use of public library resources, including instruction? A partial solution has arisen to deal with the question of "how to choose" good library instruction. One of the many resources intended to help students evaluate the quality of Web instruction can be found at http://www.personal.psu.edu/users/w/x/wxh139/evalu/ topic.htm. A large number of "nice" features can be found in sample public library websites. Birmingham Public Library (http://www.bham.lib.al.us/) has a very nice screen layout (pull-down search menu) and offers detailed instructions (for searching databases). The site for Mountain View Library (http://library.ci.mtnview.ca.us/screens/mainmenu.html) explains clearly what users should do on the top of each screen. For example, on the home page, it says, "To move through the catalog, click on the underlined text using the mouse or use the TAB key to make a choice." This is very useful for the users who are not familiar with computer technology. The website of Redwood City Public Library at http://www.redwoodcity.org/library/rcpl.html provides the "little something extra." If you look at the Local History collection, you are presented with a very nice slide picture show of scenes from Redwood City's past. Pikes Peak Library District (http://library.ppld.org/) provides a very interesting kids' section, divided into separate sites for young kids and for young adults. It is important that the content and language of your instruction suit the intended audience! The website of the DeKalb County Public Library (http://www.dekalb. public.lib.ga.us/) was accessed over 240,000 times in an eight-month period in 1999. Why do users like this site? It has a nice graphic design and a Web-accessible catalog. The instruction includes a user guide, a troubleshooting section, and a step-by-step guide for users. It's nice to have appropriate contact with an individual when you are learning to use library resources. Meet Judi Wolinsky, instruction librarian, at the Homewood Public Library website (http://homepage.interaccess.com/ ~home wood/). The screen layout of Hennepin County Library site (http://www.hennepin.lib.mn.us) provides a pull-down menu that makes browsing the site very easy. There is a "search the library catalog" section offering instruction for the text-based catalog (and the Web-based catalog has its own instruction). However, one is concerned about information overload at this site: numerous topics lead to pages of links to other useful sites! Mount Clemens Public Library (http://www.macomb. lib.mi.us/ mountclemens/) is one of the many libraries willing to share its special collections with the distant user: the genealogy and local history collections can be accessed from the Web.

THE FUTURE OF INTERNET BIBLIOGRAPHIC INSTRUCTION

One way to improve instruction on the Web in the future is to look at criticisms of Internet-based instruction now. Laurie Sabol was involved in a project to design and deliver Web instruction and received a number of criticisms of the instruction offered.[17]

- "Add more examples in the citation List." As a general rule, try to provide lots of examples for the users.
- "Most of us know how to do research already." Sabol and I agree that most users can improve their research skills, and instruction can help them to improve their skills. A big part of the job of the instruction librarian in the future might be to sell the usefulness of instruction!
- "I would have much preferred a tutorial with a librarian." Although many users report that they prefer to learn independently, some want personalized help. Maybe this is where the "Land's End-Type" of instruction librarian fits in!
- "Navigating back and forth was a big aggravation." There's lots of good "stuff" on the Web. One of our jobs in instruction is to teach the users to be able to obtain the best "stuff" by using sound searching techniques.
- "I had no one to ask when I had questions." So, give the user someone to ask!

I asked some librarians in two public libraries recently how they saw the future of instruction on their library's website. Both libraries currently offer traditional bibliographic instruction in using the OPAC and in using the special collections of the library. Library A currently provides instruction on the Web, a tutorial intended to help the users of the library evaluate Internet sources. Library B is "thinking about" providing such a tutorial. The administration and librarians of Library A seem to welcome distant users to their instruction and other services (although they would serve distant users after they have served their "own" library patrons) but feel limited in what they can do faced with limited public library resources. An instruction librarian from Library B (which seems slower to adapt to using the Web in instruction) thought that a course to help users to become "cyber-savvy" might be a good idea (and might be developed if time ever permits). It became clear that the administrators and librarians of Library B do not see helping distant users make better use of the (generic) library as being within their mandate. Further, they do not see why or how distant users can or should be helped except on a user-pay basis.

Will libraries use the Internet more and more in providing bibliographic instruction? I think so. Because of the continuing cutbacks in libraries' funding today, which have limited the amount of instruction taking place in libraries, librarians and library administrators will continue to search for ways to provide their services more efficiently. The Internet provides a means by which instruction can reach larger numbers of users (and nonusers) with advantages over traditional instruction methods. As librarians learn to design, write and evaluate their instruction, learners will become more accustomed to and accepting of bibliographic instruction on the Internet.

NOTES

1. American Library Association, *Policy Statement: Instruction in the Use of Libraries,* Council Document 45 (Chicago: American Library Association, 1980).
2. Katherine Dabbour, "Applying Active Learning Methods to the Design of Library Instruction for a Freshman Seminar," *College and Research Libraries* 58, no. 4 (July 1997): 300.
3. Eileen Allen, "Active and Teaching: Improving Postsecondary Library Instruction," *Reference Librarian* 51/52 (1995): 89-103.
4. Deanna Nipp, "Innovative Use of the Home Page for Library Instruction," *Research Strategies* 16, no. 2 (1998): 93-102.
5. Ibid. pp. 96-101.
6. Nancy DeWald, "Web-Based Library Instruction: What Is Good Pedagogy?" *Information Technology and Libraries* (March 1999): 26-31.
7. Pixey Mosley and Daniel Xiao, "Touring the Campus Library from the World Wide Web," *Reference Services Review* 30 (Winter 1996): 7-14.
8. Nancy DeWald, p. 31.
9. Sue A. Kaczor and Trudi E Jacobson, "Bibliographic Instruction for the Internet: Implications of an End-User Survey," *Research Strategies* 14, no. 4 (1996): 214-223.
10. Deanna Nipp, "Innovative Use of the Home Page for Library Instruction," *Research Strategies* 16, no. 2 (1998): 11.
11. John Carlo Bertot and Charles R. McClure, "Measuring Electronic Services in Public Libraries," *Public Libraries* (May/June 1998): 176-180.
12. Steve Sloan, "The Virtual Pathfinder: A World Wide Web Guide to Library Research," *Computers in Libraries* 16 (April 1996): 53-54.
13. Andrew Cox, "Using the World Wide Web for Library User Education: A Review Article," *Journal of Librarianship and Information Science* 29, no. 1 (March 1997): 39-43.
14. Association for Research Libraries, *Internet Training in ARL Libraries,* (Washington, DC: ARL, Office of Management Services, 1997).
15. Mosley and Xiao, "Touring the Campus Library," p. 8.
16. Ann Margaret Scholz, Richard Kerr, and Samuel Brown, "PLUTO: Interactive Instruction on the Web," *College & Research Libraries News* (June 1996): 346-349.
17. Laurie Sabol, "The Value of Student Evaluation of a Website," *Research Strategies* 16, no. 1(1998): 79-84.

PART III

THE IMPACT OF THE INTERNET ON LIBRARY AND INFORMATION SERVICES

CHAPTER EIGHT

THE EMERGENCE OF BUSINESS INFORMATION RESOURCES AND SERVICES ON THE INTERNET AND ITS IMPACT ON BUSINESS LIBRARIANSHIP

Lewis-Guodo Liu

INTRODUCTION

In recent years, various business activities and transactions on the Internet have increased and continue to grow rapidly. Electronic commerce has been transformed from tentative and risky business adventures into legitimate and sophisticated business practices. While the traditional ways of doing business are still in existence, e-commerce has opened up a new frontier for individuals and companies to engage in economic, business, and trade activities. Sales volumes in e-commerce are counted in billions of dollars. The growth of business on the Internet has had a considerable impact on business information services in terms of information production, organization, distribution, access, and retrieval. Websites providing business information on the Internet are proliferating in a variety of formats and cover virtually every business area. While governments at all levels and well-established publishing companies that traditionally provide business information are still dominant in providing major products, thousands of small businesses have created their own web pages to market and sell their products and services. Internet service companies serving millions of individuals and businesses have sprung up worldwide. Examples are Freeserve in the U.K.; T-Online International in Germany; Club Internet in France; Tin.it in Italy; Softbank Corp. in Japan; Terra Networks that provides

Internet services in Spain, Brazil, Mexico, Peru, Chile, and Guatemala; and Yahoo, America Online, Amazon.com, and eBay in the U.S. Many of these companies are heavily traded on stock markets. Commercial websites with detailed information on product specifications, various services, price ranges, and order and purchase information have become an important source of business information that did not exist before the "Web age." Electronic business information products have become increasingly complicated and dynamic in content and organization. A business data service can consist of multiple databases covering various areas of business and may contain large amounts of data from financial reports and stock markets that can be used for various statistical analyses. Wharton Research Data Service (WRDS) is a good example of this kind of dynamic data service. The emergence of e-commerce and rapid changes in business information provision have had notable effects on business information services. This chapter presents and discusses business information resources and services on the Internet and their impact on business librarianship.

Business Information

Information can be understood differently in different contexts. It can be defined as a commodity, communication, facts, data, knowledge, and energy.[1] Information is considered communication when people communicate and exchange ideas and data with each other. People become informed during the communicating and exchanging process. Information is often considered as facts, such as an event that took place. But facts may have an effect on people's decisions regarding what they plan to do. Information is often regarded as data. Digital symbols of zeros and ones may mean nothing to many people but contain a great deal of information for computer scientists. Information is often viewed as knowledge. But knowledge goes far beyond awareness of facts and symbols. It is involved with reasoning and analysis based on facts and experiences and reaches a high level of intellectual capacity. When information is viewed as a commodity, it has an economic value and can be demanded and supplied at a certain price level in a competitive market. Individuals or organizations possessing information relevant to their decision making can maximize their well-being and minimize risks and costs and have better control over the situations they are in. The most relevant and useful definition of information for the field of business is that information is a valuable commodity. Some people obtain information for entertainment. Others obtain information for making business decisions. Regardless of the purpose of getting information, they are all willing to pay for information. When an information product is priced, demanded, and sold in a competitive market, it has an economic value.

The scope of business information is as broad as the field of business and can be better understood by conceptually classifying it under standard business disciplines or subjects, such as accounting, economics, finance, marketing, management science and statistics, operations and production, management information systems, real estate, insurance, and international business. Like information in other subject areas, business information can be in print and electronic formats. It can be stored on microfilm or microfiche, databases, datasets, CD-ROMs, websites, and magnetic tapes. Types of business information can be found in directories, dictionaries, encyclopaedias, handbooks, newspapers, magazines, scholarly journals, working papers, annual reports, indexes and abstracts, bibliographies, manuals and guides, and biographies.

Business information is produced by individuals (business researchers, scholars, librarians, and other information professionals) and organizations (commercial organizations, such as small businesses and large corporations; and nonprofit organizations, such as federal, state, and local governments, and institutions of higher learning). While governments at all levels and nonprofit organizations provide a large amount of business information, a great deal of business information is produced by commercial organizations. Like any other goods and services produced in a capitalist economic system, business information produced by commercial organizations is intended to generate profits.

Business information is acquired, stored, organized, maintained by, and disseminated through various types of libraries, including academic libraries, corporate and other kinds of special libraries, public libraries, federal, state, local government libraries, and information centers. Some research libraries, such as those at Ivy League schools, top state universities, and some large public libraries in cities have extensive business collections.

The Emergence of Electronic Commerce

The number of Internet hosts in August 1981 was only 213. By July 1999, the number of Internet hosts had reached 56,218,000.[2] The number of websites has been growing exponentially since 1994, when Web browsers (Mosaic and its commercial version, Netscape) were developed. Web browsers greatly facilitate the use of the Internet. The emergence of the Internet, particularly the World Wide Web, makes it possible to do business online. E-commerce has become a fast-growing industry. Businesses have been pouring onto the Internet in recent years. By 1999, dot.com registrations had accounted for 79 % of total dot.net, dot.org, and dot.com registrations combined.[3] The commercial sector is becoming a dominating and driving force on the Internet. Businesses use the Internet to market products, negotiate business deals, fill out orders, and conduct commercial transactions. Many corporations have already integrated the Internet into their strategic planning, as the Internet has become an indispensable part of their business operations. Financial and investment services are increasingly common on the Internet. Millions of small investors can get real-time stock quotes from services provided by many online brokerage firms. Banking transactions can be done over the Internet. Consumers can shop in virtual malls. New-car buyers are able to examine the features of new cars in virtual showrooms. There are reasons for the growth of commercial use on the Internet. The ultimate goal of private enterprises is to make a profit, which is, of course, a driving force of the capitalist economy. Private enterprises play a crucial role in improving productivity and creating wealth. In general, there are a number of ways of making profits: by increasing revenue (if expenses are constant) or reducing expenses. Increasing sales will increase revenues. Total business expenses can be reduced by cutting administrative and operating expenses. The Internet can be used to achieve both purposes. A company can reach out to its customers and market its products and services by using email and creating web pages. Customers not only can receive information on the company's products and services but can also communicate with the company's sales and service representatives if they have questions about the products. The company can save a great deal of its financial resources by using the Internet to deliver services, provide training programs, hold virtual conferences, cut traveling expenses, strengthen internal communications, speed up purchasing cycles, and reduce long-distance phone call and fax expenses.

BUSINESS INFORMATION ON THE INTERNET

The fast-growing use of the Internet has not only dramatically changed the way business is conducted but also has had a tremendous impact on the way business information is provided and used. Business information resources that have emerged on the Internet can be classified into major business areas, such as company information, economics, finance and investment, international business, real estate, and marketing. While the scope of this article is by no means exhaustive, it intends to highlight some important business information resources and services on the Internet in major business areas.

Information on Small, Private, and International Companies

One of the salient effects of e-commerce on business information services is that it has created millions of commercial websites which provide a great deal of information on small and private companies. Previously, it was very difficult to find information on small and private companies that were not local, such as jewelery and watch stores, small, high-tech companies, small banks and insurance companies, furniture stores, small publishing and printing companies, wholesale stores, and antique shops because they do not have legal obligations to report their financial activities to government agencies, and they are often ignored by commercial publishers. Print directories, such as *D&B Million Dollar Directory* (the private company part) and *Hoover's Handbook of Private Companies* provide information only on leading private companies. Reference librarians are almost always frustrated by questions related to small and private companies. The emergence of small and private companies' websites in many ways improves business information services. The websites of small and private companies normally provide information on company history, products, services, prices, payment, and contact information, such as telephone numbers, fax numbers, and mailing addresses. Finding information on small, international companies was also extremely difficult. The *International Directory of Company History*, one of the most comprehensive directories for international companies, covers over 3,000 international companies. But the *Directory* limits its coverage to leading international companies with a minimum of millions of U.S. dollars in annual sales. Now individuals and businesses can access the websites of companies of any size in virtually any country. National boundaries and geographical location are no longer an issue. Internet search engines, such as Altavista and Lycos, can be used as access and retrieval tools to facilitate searches for company information. *Business Information Sources on the Internet* is a good example (www.dis.strath.ac.uk/business/directories UK.html). It is developed and maintained by the Department of Information Science, part of the Business School of the University of Strathclyde in Glasgow, Scotland, and contains a comprehensive, worldwide directory of online business directories. It covers many kinds of companies: large, small, publicly held, private, domestic, and international in many countries and regions.

Company information is traditionally produced by a few well-established companies in business information, such as Dun and Bradstreet, Hoover's, the Gale Group, and Standard and Poor's. Users can access company information in libraries and other kinds of information centers. Now small businesses as well as large corporations have become not only business information producers but also business information providers. The advantages of the dual role of businesses are obvious. First, information provided by companies tends to be more current since they are motivated to update their websites because inaccurate and outdated information can eventually lead to decline of sales and loss of customers. Second, users can directly access and retrieve information from companies' websites. The connection between businesses and consumers is strengthened, and the provision of information on companies is greatly improved. In recent years, the role of traditional business information producers and libraries in providing general company information (such as company products, services, product prices, stock prices, and performance indicators) is increasingly diminishing due to the fact that a wealth of company information is readily available on the Web. However, library users still rely on libraries and commercial information providers for value-added business information, such as annual reports, financial analyses, and cross-section and time-series data which cannot be easily obtained from the Web.

Internet Resources in Economics

The field of economics is divided into macroeconomics and microeconomics. Macroeconomics studies the behavior of an economic system at the aggregate level. Macroeconomists are mainly concerned with a nation's aggregate demand and supply, unemployment, price stability, economic growth, productivity, government economic policies, national income account, interest rate, and so forth. Microeconomics studies the behavior of individual decision-making units, such as firms, households, and nonprofit organizations. Economists tend to deal with economic issues by constructing quantitative models. An econometric model is a conceptual and theoretical framework that integrates economic variables into a mathematical equation and reflects economic relationships between these variables. The domination of quantitative research methodology in the field of economics plays a significant role in the types of information sources provided in economics. The impact of the Internet on information resources and services in economics has been tremendous in recent years in terms of information production, provision, organization, and content.

Teaching materials on the Web

Traditionally, economic information is produced and controlled by authoritative institutions and individuals, such as government agencies, publishing companies, scholarly societies, and well-established scholars. There is a screening process regarding who can publish what. While it is true that these traditional publishing forces still produce and control economic information, many individuals and small businesses have begun to play a greater role in producing and providing economic information on the Web. Since anyone can publish on the Web, there is little control over who publishes what. For example, textbooks used to be produced by scholars and published formally by recognized print publishers. While this is still the case, many instructors have put their course syllabi, class notes, articles, and book chapters on the Web. A simple search using Altavista retrieved hundreds of web pages that provide economic course syllabi in virtually every area of economics, such as environmental economics, economics of industrial organization, principles of macroeconomics and microeconomics, health economics, managerial economics, labor economics, international economics, applied economics, economics of capital markets, economics of information technology, economics of the price system, economics and politics, home economics, forestry economics, business economics, economics of industrial markets, transportation economics, and economics of education. These economics syllabi not only cover a wide range of areas but also various levels, from introductory to advanced.

Many people, particularly instructors and students, can benefit from these online teaching materials, which often provide detailed definitions, concepts, terminologies, and lengthy discussions on the theory and methodology of economics. Instructors could use online teaching materials put up by their fellow instructors and thereby discover new teaching ideas and approaches. Instructors who use others' online course materials should be aware of copyright and ethical issues. As long as the motive is to improve teaching, and credit is given to the sources used, online teaching materials can be a good source for improving teaching and learning.

Students can use online teaching materials. It is very difficult to find a dictionary or encyclopedia that provides good definitions and descriptions of some economic terms. For example, *The New Palgrave: A Dictionary of Economics*[4] provides detailed discussions on the relationship between macroeconomics and microeconomics but does not give a definition for macroeconomics. The definitions of macroeconomics and microeconomics in *Economics Dictionary*[5] are too simple to be useful for conceptually understanding the two terms. Yet one can easily find detailed definitions, discussions, and illustrations in online teaching materials in economics. The course syllabus on the website of the Department of Economics at the University of Sheffield in the U.K. (www.shef.ac.uk/~ptn/mgt652/nature.htm) is such an example. It provides in-depth discussions on macroeconomics and covers some key concepts and theories in macroeconomics, such as the traditional Keynesian approach, new classical models, and post-Keynesian models. The description of macroeconomics on this web page is much more educational than the simple definitions in many dictionaries.

Plagiarism of online materials is a problem and has become widespread. Students may just copy what is online and hand it in as their own work. Another disadvantage is not knowing whether information on the Web is reliable, accurate, and authoritative. In the case of syllabi, such materials are prepared by university or college professors and instructors, and information in them tends to be reliable.

Cross-country and time-series research datasets

Economists have long been concerned with understanding economic growth and the development of nations. While formal interest in economic growth studies dates back to 1776, when Adam Smith wrote *An Inquiry into the Nature and Causes of the Wealth of Nations*, research on economic growth has expanded in recent years largely due to the successful construction of research datasets.[6] Many economic research datasets have emerged on the Web and can be readily accessed and retrieved. These include Barro-Lee, Summers-Heston Penn World, Levine and Renelt, Nehru and Dhareshwa, Bruno and Easterly, Deininger and Squire, DeLong-Summers, and Easterly and Fischer. These datasets provide international data on economic growth and its relationship to stock markets, banks, inflation, physical capital stock, income inequality, human capital, education, and equipment investment.

Some of these datasets can be accessed from the Department of Economics at Harvard University and the University of Pennsylvania. The World Bank home page (http://www.worldbank.org/html/prdmg/grthweb/growth_htm) also provides links to many of the datasets mentioned above. The other two notable datasets are Sachs and Warner, and the Bartelsman-Gray NBER productivity dataset that can be accessed from U.K.-based Nuffield College's Website (http://www.nuff.ox.ac.uk/Economics/ Growth/ datasets). The National Bureau of Economic Research's NBER Macro-history Database (http://www.nber.org/databases/macrohistory/ contents/index. html) assembles an extensive dataset that covers all aspects of the pre-World War I and inter-war economies, including production, construction, employment, money, prices, asset market transactions, foreign trade, and government activity. Many series are highly disaggregated, and many are updated monthly or quarterly. These datasets can be readily accessed through the Web and provide research, teaching, and learning tools for researchers, instructors, and students in economics. Researchers can use these datasets to verify existing research and to explore new research areas without spending a great deal of time reinventing the datasets. Instructors can use them to teach students empirical research methodologies and skills. Students can use datasets to learn conduct original research, to apply theories into practice, and to improve their analytical skills. The leading research universities, such as Harvard University, the University of Pennsylvania, and the University of Chicago, as well as the World Bank, are major producers of these datasets.

U.S.-based Internet resources in economics

Many professional and scholarly organizations have developed or sponsored individuals or organizations to develop websites with information resources for teaching and research. These websites bring together useful resources in their professional field and greatly facilitate teaching and research. Sponsored by the American Economic Association, the website of *Resources for Economists on the Internet* (www.rfe.org) provides over 1,000 Internet resources for teaching and research in economics. These resources are classified into categories, such as data and statistics; directional information on economists in academic departments and on organizations and associations; forecasting and consulting information; grants and jobs; information on professional conferences and meetings in economics; and resources related to scholarly communication, teaching, and other Internet guides.

The data section of *Resources for Economists on the Internet* provides extensive international, national, and regional time-series data. U.S. national and regional data include various economic indicators and statistics, such as gross domestic product, national income, personal income, corporate profits, business investment, producer price index, consumer price index, interest rate, unemployment, federal spending and revenue, macroforecasts, and federal budget. Major information providers are federal government agencies, such as Federal Reserve banks; the Bureau of Economic Analysis; Bureau of Labor Statistics; Congressional Budget Office; Council of Economic Advisors; STAT-USA; National Bureau of Economic Research; U.S. Census Bureau; U.S. International Trade Commission; Office of the U.S. Trade Representative; Social Security Administration; and Agriculture Economic Research Service of the U.S. Department of Agriculture. Many international organizations, such as the Economist Intelligence Unit, Organization for Economic Cooperation and Development (OECD), International Monetary Fund, the United Nations, U.N.

Conference on Trade and Development, U.N. Food and Agricultural Organization, U.N. Statistics Division/DESIPA, and the World Trade Organization also provide economic data and statistics on countries and regions around the world.

The data section contains links to many financial market data sources, including the Center for Research in Security Prices (CRSP) at the University of Chicago, financial data finder at Ohio State University, international financial services, global financial data, and Security and Exchange Commission's EDGAR. Another unique feature of the data section is the archived data and programs from a number of scholarly journals, such as *Economic Journal Datasets Online, Journal of Applied Econometrics, Journal of Business and Economic Statistics,* and *Journal of Money, Credit and Banking*. Economists can use these data to do in-depth analyses. Students can use these data to enhance their research skills and gain hands-on experience.

The online directory section lists over 4,000 economics-related institutions, including both domestic and foreign economics departments, economics departments with doctoral programs, research institutions, business schools, and the Association for University Business and Economic Research. This website greatly facilitates general communication within the field of economics. economists can easily find information about their colleagues worldwide and communicate with them for the purposes of research and teaching. The directory also lists economists worldwide.

The academic communication section provides online working papers, journals, books, publishers' websites, email newsletters, and library resources. Economists can find journal articles, books, working papers, and publishers' information at their fingertips. These online scholarly publications greatly improve communication, research, and teaching productivity.

The teaching resources section offers a variety of learning tools (guides, aids, tutorials, calculators, budget simulators) and learning resources (online macroeconomics and microeconomics textbooks, glossaries, tests, and web pages teaching how to run regressions). This section serves a wide range of users: undergraduate students, K-12 school students, and economics educators. It certainly provides rich resources and tools for learning and teaching economics at the school and undergraduate levels. The Internet Resources for Economists website also provides links to grants and jobs in economics; software and programs for econometric computation; forecasting and consulting; and professional conferences and meetings.

Many of these resources in economics can be used to provide basic economic literacy education for the general public. The National Council on Economic Education has been in the forefront of economics education. Its mission is:

> "To help all students develop economic ways of thinking and problem solving that they can use in their lives as consumers, savers, members of the workforce, responsible citizens, and effective participants in the global economy." (http://www.nationalcouncil.org/index.html)

A campaign by the National Council on Economic Education was launched in April 1999 with the goal to promote economic literacy for students and adults and educate them to understand how the global economic system works. Economic educators have long recognized the importance of economic literacy:

> "The need for such a concerted effort is urgent; the issue is critical. Young people entering the workforce cannot function effectively without knowledge of how the world works. The spiraling rate of personal bankruptcies and credit card debt; the lack of understanding of the importance of saving and investing; the inability to discern the consequences of powerful international economic changes, or even to know the meaning of "profit," are all evidence that we as a nation can no longer afford to make economics an option in our schools. It is especially necessary to give our young people—who are our future—a grasp of the basic principles of the American economic system" (http://www.nationalcouncil.org/index.html).

There is no question that the economics resources on the Internet can help economics educators to achieve the goals of economic literacy.

Other Internet resources in economics

The WebEc in Finland (www.helsinki.fi/WebEc) is a part of NetEc which is a collaborative project between the global economics community and the European-based counterpart of *Resources for Economists on the Internet.* WebEc contains a great deal of useful economic information and is free for economists worldwide. It provides a large amount of Web resources covering Asia, Europe, North America, and South America, including many countries, such as the U.K., Germany, Finland, Norway, France, Spain, Bulgaria, Croatia, the Czech Republic, Hungary, Poland, Romania, Slovakia, Slovenia, Russia, Ukraine, Australia, New Zealand, Japan, China, Mexico, Brazil, and Peru. They are classified under various topical categories, such as general economic resources, education and teaching, mathematical and quantitative methods, economics and computing, microeconomics and macroeconomics, international economics, financial economics, public economics, law and economics, economic history, economic systems, economics of networks, and agriculture and natural resources. While some parts of it overlap with *Resources for Economists on the Internet*, a large number of resources are provided by scholars, librarians, and other information professionals from countries other than the United States.

A New Zealand-based website, OFFSTATS (www.auckland.ac.nz/lbr/stats/offstats/OFFSTATSmain.htm), lists current and time-series social, economic and general data on countries from government and other official sources. Economists can use these data to perform econometric analyses of many countries. This site is developed and maintained by a business and economics librarian at the University of Auckland Library in New Zealand.

Full-text electronic journals: Academic Press' IDEAL and JSTOR

While a vast number of economic resources on the Internet are free, there are fee-based economics resources on the Internet. These resources provide global access and instant retrieval of fulltext journal articles, and therefore greatly accelerate the research process and make scholarly publications more productive. Academic Press' IDEAL is such a full-text electronic journal database. It provides articles in full-text from nearly 200 journals in scientific, technical, and medical fields. While its focus is not on economics, it covers economics, business, law, finance, and the social sciences and provides some important scholarly journals in economics, including *Explorations in Economic History, Games and Economic Behavior, Journal of Comparative Economics, Journal of Economic Theory, Journal of Environmental Economics and Management, Journal of Housing Economics, Journal of Urban Economics, Journal of the Japanese and International Economies, Research in Economics, Review of Economic Dynamics,* and *Ricerche Economiche.*

Almost all electronic journals on the Web, either free or fee-based, offer only the most recent articles. However, scholars often also need to locate older journal articles. JSTOR arose to meet this demand. While it provides full-text articles in many subject areas, it contains many influential scholarly journals in economics. The coverage of some of these journals goes back to as early as the 19th century. JSTOR offers *American Economic Review* (1911-1993), *Econometrica* (1933-1993), *Economic Journal* (1891-1993), *Journal of Economic History* (1941-1993), *Journal of Economic Literature* (1963-1993), *Journal of Industrial Economics* (1952-1993), *Journal of Money, Credit and Banking* (1969-1993), *Journal of Political Economy* (1892-1993), *Quarterly Journal of Economics* (1886-1993), *Review of Economic Studies* (1933-1995), and *The Review of Economics and Statistics* (1919-1993). These journals are indispensable resources for research, teaching, and learning. JSTOR was certainly instrumental in completing our research guide for the economic growth literature.[6] If we had not been able to use JSTOR full-text journals, we would have spent at least two more years and more human and financial resources trying to find articles published from the 1950s to the 1980s. Traditionally, researchers use indexes to find citations of articles and then find articles, a process that can be very tedious. To develop a research guide containing thousands of articles and hundreds of books in a subject area can take years to complete using print sources. With these full-text databases, the research cycle is tremendously shortened.

Internet Resources and Services for Finance and Investment

Finance is a subfield of economics dealing with the management of cash flows. Three key areas include corporate finance, financial markets and institutions, and investment.

Corporate financial information

Information resources for corporate finance have emerged on the Internet. These resources include corporate financial reports, corporate securities, and corporate laws. Corporate financial reports have never been accessed and retrieved more easily than they are today. FreeEDGAR (www.freeedgar.com) provides free and unlimited access to indexed SEC EDGAR. The user can instantly look at and download corporations' filings. FreeEDGAR's user-friendly interface makes the search for SEC filings much easier. The EDGAR Database of corporation information (www.sec.gov/edgarhp. htm), developed and maintained by the Securities and Exchange Commission, provides an archive of EDGAR documents that indexes from 1994 to 1999. Additional features include current events analysis, mutual funds retrieval, and an exhaustive mutual funds search that enables the user to search all the mutual funds available in the database. 10KWizard (www. ntenkwizard.com) is another value-added site that provides cross indexed filings search and financial analysis. Like FreeEDGAR, 10KWizard also offers a user-friendly interface. All of these Internet resources are free. Business librarians may want to take advantage of these websites and think about canceling fee-based databases their libraries currently subscribe to.

In addition to these free websites that provide corporate financial reports, there are fee-based websites, such as EDGAR Online (www.edgar-online.com) and Global Access (www.primark.com). EDGAR Online provides SEC filings as well as various search tools, such as full search, personal alerts, people search, IPO express, and today's filings. Global Access offers more value-added tools. The interfaces and the abilities to manipulate data of these fee-based services (e.g., sorting data by sales, assets, net income, and geographical area) are much better than their free counterparts.

Banking information

Traditional financial institutions (banks, savings and loan associations, savings banks, credit unions, investment companies, financial advisory services, and brokerage firms) have also emerged on the Internet. Internet banking has become a widely used service. Many banks allow their customers to pay bills online. Approximately 200 banks provided Internet or Web-based banking services in 1998 and 50% of all banks will provide home banking services in the near future.[7] It was estimated that this year, 65% of households in the United States will use electronic bill payment[8] and over 90% of North America's largest financial institutions will provide transactions using the Internet.[9] Internet banking is moving toward a commonly shared cross-platform electronic banking system as a result of the rapid growth of diverse banking systems.[10] Customers of many banks have already been able to access their accounts via the Web and move funds between their accounts.

Many websites provide a great deal of information on locations of banks, loans, interest rates, and various investment opportunities. There are virtually hundreds of bank directories on the Internet. BankSITE developed by the Forms Group, a Division of Credit Interchange of America, Inc. (www.banksite.com) is a good example. It provides directories of banks in all 50 states in the U.S. as well as directories of banks all over the world, including Africa Bank Directory (www.banksite.com/intbanks/ africa_banks.htm), Asia Bank Directory (www.banksite.com/intbanks/ asia_banks.htm), Australia-New Zealand Bank Directory (www.banksite.com/intbanks/ australia_new_zealand_ banks.htm), South America and Central America & Caribbean Bank Directory (www.banksite.com/intbanks/south_america_banks.htm), Europe Bank Directory (www.banksite.com/intbanks/europe_banks.htm), Middle East Bank Directory (www.banksite.com/intbanks/middle_east_banks.htm), and North America Bank Directory (www.banksite.com/intbanks/north_ america_banks.htm). Thousands of banks, both domestic and global, and banking information related to specific banks can be accessed through this website.

In addition to this global Internet directory of bank websites, worldwide regional banks are also readily available on the Internet. Examples are European Central Bank, African Development Bank Group, Reserve Bank of Australia, Reserve Bank of New Zealand, Asian Development Bank, Caribbean Development Bank, and Central American Bank of Economic Integration. The European Central Bank website (www.ecb.int) provides information on its history, development, objectives, organizations and legal framework. It also offers publications, bank statistics, information on Monetary Financial Institutions (MFIs), and links to websites of the national central banks of European countries. African Development Bank Group (www.afdb.org) was established in 1963, and its primary objective is to promote economic and social development through loans, equity investments, and technical assistance to its 77 member countries. This site provides information on bank policies, economic and research papers, and news releases. The Reserve Bank of Australia (www.rba.gov.au) is the central bank of Australia. Its website offers information on the bank's history, organization, monetary policy, reports, articles, speeches, and other publications. The Reserve Bank of New Zealand (www.rbnz.govt.nz) is New Zealand's central bank. This site contains a wide range of financial and banking information, including monetary policy, collector's currency, registry services, current inflation figures, and data release and forward release calendars. Websites for Asian Development Bank (www.adlb.org), Caribbean Development Bank (www.caribank.org), and Central American Bank of Economic Integration (www.bcie.hn) all contain information on their organizational and banking policies, news releases, and other publications. Economists, financial analysts, investors, and policy makers of national governments and international organizations can access these websites and use the information to study banking policies and financial and banking environments in these regions and for the purpose of making various economic, financial, and investment decisions.

Stock, futures, and options markets

Obtaining stock information in a timely manner is exceptionally valuable and critical for making investment decisions. Millions of dollars can be made by knowing a specific piece of information on the market, while millions of dollars can be lost without that information. The Internet provides instant and real-time stock information. That is why real-time quotes on the Web are so valuable for investors, particularly those who are engaged in day trading. Before the Web era, individual investors used to rely on print newspapers and magazines, such as *The Wall Street Journal, The New York Times, Investor's Business Daily*, and local newspapers, for stock, futures, and options information. Financial information in standard print newspapers is always one day behind what happened in the markets. Relying on financial newspapers to obtain stock quotes is not obsolete, but as Internet technology becomes more sophisticated, more financial information will be available on the Web.

Many stock exchanges have set up home pages on the Web, a development that facilitates stock trading activities. Domestic and international investors can find information on stocks at their fingertips at such sites as the New York Stock Exchange (www.nyse.com), American Stock Exchange (www.amex.com), NASDAQ (www.nasdaq.com), Chicago Stock Exchange (www.chicagostockex.com), Pacific Stock Exchange (www.pacificex.com), London Stock Exchange (www.londonstockexchange. com), Tokyo Stock Exchange (www.tse.or.jp), Athens Stock Exchange (www.ase.gr), Australian Stock Exchange (www.asx.com.au), Stock Exchange of Singapore (www.asx.com.au), New Zealand Stock Exchange (www.nzse.co.nz), and Vancouver Stock Exchange (www.vse.com). Trading of futures and options is also made much easier by using information from futures and options websites, such as Chicago Board Options Exchange (www.cboe.com), Chicago Board of Trade (www.cbot.com), Chicago Mercantile Exchange (www.cme.com), London International Financial Futures Exchange (www.liffe.com), Hong Kong Futures Exchange (www.hkfe.com), Sydney Futures Exchange (www.sfe.com.au), Swiss Options & Financial Futures Exchange (www.swx.com), New Zealand Futures & Options Exchange (www.nzfoe.co.nz), and Tokyo Grain Exchange (www.tge.or.jp).

Brokerage firms also use the Internet to offer stock services. Brokers connect investors with financial markets. *USA Today* reported that online brokerage accounts increased from 4.1 million in 1997 to 10.5 million in 1999, which were more than doubled in two years.[11] Hundreds of stock brokerage firms have now surfaced on the Internet. Many of these online brokerage firms provide financial information services related to stocks, IPOs, basic options, advanced options, and mutual funds. XOLIA.com (www.xolia.com) is a website that provides all kinds of financial information and information on brokerage firms. In addition, it offers a number of tools potential investors can use to make investment decisions, such as decision making, comparisons, and broker profiles. The decision-maker tool can be used to analyze the investor's unique financial background and to assist the investor in finding the online brokerage that best fits the investor's profile. The comparison tool enables prospective investors to compare potential brokerage firms in terms of their financial products, services, and strengths. Broker profiles include many online brokerage firms, including Datek, Discover Brokerage, DLJ Direct, Dreyfus, E*Trade, Empire Financial, Fidelity, Charles Schwab, Morgan Stanley, Merrill Lynch, and First Trade.

Wall Street Resources (www.geocities.com/WallStreet/Floor/ 8205/ wall.htm) also provides various online financial resources and services. The news and magazine resources section connects to USA Today (Money), Money Magazine, CNN, Kiplinger Online, Forbes Magazine, Reuters, Bloomberg, and CBS Market Watch. The stock research section contains a wide range of online research tools and resources, such as Investorhome, DailyStocks, Market Guide, Security APL Quote Server, Stockguide, Silicon Investor, and Zacks Investment Research. Investors can also find intraday stock index, charts, and quotes through CNNfn Markets, and Fidelity Investments.

These Internet investment resources and services have had a tremendous impact on the way people invest. Investment information has never been easier to obtain. Investors can gather data on a company; examine its products or services; find out how they are priced and marketed and their competitiveness; examine the company's financial status by looking at its annual reports (balance sheets, income statements, and cash flow statements for the past five years); and analyze the company's performance by looking at some important ratios (current ratio, quick ratio, debt ratio, total liabilities to net worth ratio), and important performance indicators (the growth rates of sales, net income, earning per share, and dividend payout ratio). Financial analyses that report total sales, net earnings, institutional stockholders, total number of shares, earning per share, year highs and lows, asking, bidding, and closing prices, trading volumes, insider trading, financial statements, and intraday charts are traditionally provided in print sources. While much of this kind of information is still available in paper form, investors can now take advantage of many websites with all of the financial information for free. A great deal of the information the investor needs for making investment decisions is now available.

While many stock brokerage firms are fee-based services, some websites provide free financial information. For example, Quicken.com. provides stock quotes, company and industry news, and a variety of graphical functions to analyze stocks. Small investors, who are not armed with Bloomberg, Reuters, or other expensive financial investment systems, can gather information on industry trends and evaluate a company's position in the industry and its market share using this kind of site. The Internet greatly facilitates the process of stock analysis by providing various kinds of financial information on companies and industries.

Financial analytical tools are readily available on the Internet, such as calculators for relocation, mortgages, insurance, investment, and retirement. These tools can be used to perform many kinds of financial and investment calculations, whereas in the past a professional financial analyst was needed to do many of these calculations.

The Global Guide for Internet Resources and Services for Finance and Investment coauthored by this author, includes more than 3,000 websites.[12] Investors can save a great deal of time using this guide to find finance and investment-related information on the Internet.

Internet Resources and Services for International Business

Organized trade activities are dated back to between about 4000 and 1500 B.C.[13] The developments of cross-nation and trade-related organizations in recent years, such as the EU and the World Trade Organization are moving world trade toward globalization of businesses.[14]

Internet resources for international business

Information sources for international business are indispensable since they help businesspeople to learn and understand cultures, religions, economic systems, infrastructures, and business practices in foreign countries. There is now a large volume of international business information on the Internet. Traditionally, a person has to look for this information in various print sources and it can take considerable time. However, Internet resources are not well organized. While search engines have been developed and improved to facilitate information searching on the Internet, they are still not sufficiently effective at finding specific pieces of information. A keyword search can generate thousands of records. To look through a long list of retrieved items can be time consuming and frustrating. To meet this challenge, many librarians and information professionals have started selecting and compiling Internet resources and services in specific subject areas. *Internet Resources and Services for International Business: A Global Guide*[15] was written to meet the information needs of international business. Over 2,500 websites, covering 175 countries, were selected. These websites were further classified into five sections (general information, economy, business and trade, business travel, and contact information). The general information section includes Internet resources with information on a country's geography, population, history, religion, culture, language, ethnicity, and political, social, and legal systems. The economy section focuses on Internet resources with information on countries' economic systems and macroeconomic indicators, such as GNP, GDP, unemployment rate, economic growth rate, government economic policies, and currency exchange. The business and trade section contains Internet resources with a wide range of information on natural resources, manufacturing, industries, companies, exports and imports, trade organizations, and business directories. The business travel section provides travel information, health conditions of countries, visa requirements, hotels, transportation, and weather reports. The contact information section offers business and government contact information.

Guides to doing business in foreign countries used to be in print format, but now they are readily available on the Internet. Examples are Free Globalization Tips on Doing Business in China, Japan, India, Russia, and the U.K. (http://ourworld.compuserve.com/homepages/Richard_Ishida/free.htm). The site provides general introductions to these countries' social, political, and economic systems and offers social tips and information on conventions, customary business practices, and general customs. These online guides are very helpful for people who have little knowledge about the political, social, economic, and cultural systems of foreign countries.

National Trade Data Bank, part of Stat-USA (free for federal depository libraries), contains extensive current and historical information on international trade, such as exchange rates, current and historical trade leads, market and country research, international trade statistics, press releases, market reports on various industry sectors, country commercial guides, imports and exports by commodity and by country, U.S. exporters yellow pages, and a national export directory. It is a very valuable online source for international business.

There are a number of online resources that provide profiles of countries all over the world. The CIA World Factbook (www.odci.gov/cia/publications/factbook/index.html) is an excellent source for country profiles. It provides maps and information on geography, people, government, economy, communications, transportation, and the military. The geography section contains information on countries' natural resources, such as natural gas, petroleum, coal, copper, iron ore, salt, precious and semiprecious stones; climate in four seasons; land use; and natural environment. The geography information is very important for business decision making. The people section offers information on population, ethnic groups, religious groups, languages, and education literacy. The government section provides information on political and legal systems. The economy section contains significant economic statistics, including an overview of the economy, GDP and GNP, labor force, inflation rate, unemployment rate, industries, imports and exports, currency, and exchange rate. The success or failure of an international business endeavor depends on the performance of the country's economy. An unproductive labor force, and high inflation, and unemployment rates are not a positive environment for international business. The communications section provides information on infrastructure consisting of telephone systems, radio stations, and television stations. It is almost impossible to conduct business without a sophisticated communication infrastructure since business communication and marketing and advertising goods and services must be done through these communication channels. The transportation section provides information on transportation infrastructure, such as highways, railways, waterways, and airports. Business activities rely on an effective transportation infrastructure. A country profile is a small but important step in getting information and gaining understanding.

Some international business websites are developed by business schools or libraries of universities, such as the Business School of the University of Kansas, the Center for International Business Education and Research at Michigan State University, and the University of North Carolina at Charlotte. These websites contain a tremendous amount of international business information.

WSU-Cyber: International Resources (http://ciber.bus.msu.edu/busres.htm) is developed and maintained by the Center for International Business Education and Research at Michigan State University. The site offers links with very useful information on international business. Resources are organized under news and periodicals; journals, research articles, and papers; regional- or country-specific information for Africa, Asia and Oceania, Europe, Central and South America, North America; statistical data and information resources; international trade information; international trade leads, company directories and yellow pages; international trade shows and business events; mailing lists; culture and travel; and various utilities and useful information. The news and periodicals section provides many general as well as country and region specific online newspapers and periodicals, such as *Business Week-Global Business, International Herald Tribune, Advertising Age-International, World Link Magazine, Trade Compass, Multinational Monitor, African Business Magazine, ArabiaBusiness, Asia Watch, Asia Week Online, The Australia Financial Review, Baltic Review Online, Brazil Financial Wire, The Brazil Special Report, Bulgarian Economic Review, Canadian Business,* and *Central Europe Online*. These online news and periodicals provide up-to-date business information on many countries.

The journal, research articles, and papers section links online scholarly journals, such as the *Journal of International Marketing, Journal of International Business Studies, European Journal of Marketing, Review of International Economics, Review of Development of Economics, The Journal of Business in Developing Nations, Russian Business Law Journal, International Treasurer: The Journal of Global Treasury and Financial Risk Management, Valore International Finance*, and research publications from the World Bank, International Monetary Fund, and other worldwide organizations. These online scholarly journals and research papers help to strengthen scholarly communication and facilitate research in international business. The country- and region-specific information section provides general business, investment, finance, economic, and trade information on countries in Asia and Oceania, Africa, Central and South America, North America, and Europe. Businesspeople can obtain a wide range of international business information on a specific country or region from this section. The statistical section contains economic, investment, and trade statistics for many countries and regions. These statistics are useful for analyzing a country's or region's economic, investment, and trade conditions and provide a basis for business decision-making. The government resources section contains finance, market, imports and exports, and economic information from the government agencies of many countries. These resources provide valuable and reliable information. Information on international trade and trade leads is available on this website. The company directories and yellow pages section lists exporters and importers and companies engaged in international business by region and country.

The Virtual International Business and Economic Sources website (http://libweb.uncc.edu/ref-bus/vibehome.htm) is developed and maintained by the Library of the University of North Carolina at Charlotte. It gathers more than 1,600 links with information on international business. Internet sources are organized under a number of sections, including agricultural and forest products, banking and finance, business and marketing, business periodicals, country information, and foreign exchange rates, foreign stock markets, international trade law, patents, petroleum and energy, taxation in foreign countries, and trade issues and statistics. Links are also arranged by region and country. While there are overlaps with the Michigan State University site, this site is certainly unique in terms of content and offers useful information on international business.

The Internet Business Library: International Business and World Trade site (http://www.bschool.ukans.edu/intbuslib/trade.htm), sponsored by the University of Kansas School of Business, also provides a fairly large amount of information on international business. Web links are organized under country and regional profiles, European Union and related documents, guides to international business, international company directories, international markets trade opportunities, international statistics, international trade organizations, North American Free Trade Agreement (NAFTA) and related documents, trade and international law, travel guides and world maps, and world news. Although this site is not well maintained, it is still a site with a great deal of useful international business information.

International organizations related to international business

A number of international organizations, such as the Global Chamber of Commerce (http://www.gcc.net/), World Trade Organization (www.wto.org), OECD, Online (www.oecd.org), and NAFTAnet (www.nafta.net) have already made their presence visible on the Web and provide valuable information and services for the international business community. The Global Chamber of Commerce site provides a search engine for worldwide trade and industry resources. Information is searchable by region and country. The World Trade Organization's website offers information on a wide range of trade topics, including goods, services, intellectual property, environment, development, regionalism, policy reviews, dispute settlement, government procurement, and research and analysis. It also contains many resources, such as legal texts, statistics, technical cooperation, trade policy courses, non-governmental organizations, and members of the World Trade Organization. OECD Online offers information on agriculture, energy, industry, health, transport, science and technology, public management, education and labor as well as economic statistics on members of the OECD. These international organizations' websites provide the most updated information and play a significant role in information provision and dissemination in international business.

Internet Resources and Services for Real Estate

The real estate is an important economic sector in many countries. In the U.S., for example, the real estate sector generates over $800 billion annually, accounting for over 11% of total GDP.[16] The Internet greatly facilitates real estate transactions. Many real estate agencies have set up web pages to provide information on real estate agents, home financing, property transactions, the neighborhood, and school districts. Mortgage payment calculators and relocation calculators are also available on these websites. Many banks use the Internet to process real estate loans. Marine Midland Bank has started using the Internet to handle appraisals and environmental reports. It is reported that considerable time can be saved in this way.[17]

Thousands of directories providing information on properties, realtors, lenders, and neighborhood information have emerged. Realtor.com provides information on over 1.3 million homes. The user can use this search tool to navigate properties in each state of the United States. It also provides buying, selling, moving, and ownership information. In addition, information on insurance, home improvement, and other homeowner topics is readily available on this site. Many real estate organizations have set up home pages on the Internet, such as the National Association of Realtors (http://nar.realtor.com/) and Realtors Associations (http://www.realtor.com/). These institutions play an important role in disseminating real estate information among buyers, sellers, and real estate agents. The National Association of Realtors has over 700,000 members and provides a wide range of information on real estate, including news, market trends and insights, profiles and evaluations of real estate firms, auction information, fair housing handbook, government policies, property disclosure guide, code of ethics and arbitration manual, conventional and trade shows, and community involvement. Realtor.com provides extensive real estate services that help home and property buyers to search real estate listings on the Internet. In fact, thousands of individual realtors have set up their own home pages on the Internet. *Internet Resources and Services for Real Estate,*[18] part of the *Internet Business Guides Series* edited by the author, has gathered over 1,000 websites related to real estate in all 50 states as well in other countries.

Real estate-related websites are also available for almost every country. Examples exist in Brazil (www.sitedoimovel.com.br), Japan (www.homes.co.jp), Australia (rainbow.24.com.au), New Zealand (www.nz.com/realestate), and Norway (www.husguiden.no). While many of these countries' websites use their native languages, some of them use English as well.

Given the global nature of the Internet, many international real estate directories are available online. The International Real Estate Directory (www.ired.com) and PropertyPoint's Global Real Estate Directory (www.propertypoint.co.uk) are two examples. The International Real Estate Directory lists over 25,000 real estate-related websites throughout the world. All the websites in the directory are reviewed by the directory staff before they are added. It covers countries in virtually every continent, including Africa, Asia, Canada, Caribbean, Central America, Europe, Middle East, North America, Oceania, South America, and the United States. The links are organized by continent and then country in alphabetical order. PropertyPoint's Global Real Estate Directory is a U.K.-based real estate Internet service. It lists both residential and commercial properties in Asia, Europe, Oceania, Australia, and New Zealand. This site particularly specializes in European real estate markets.

Internet Resources and Services for Marketing and Advertising

Marketing is not just about selling and advertising. It is "a social and managerial process by which individuals and groups obtain what they need and want through reacting and exchanging products and value with others."[19] Marketing consists of individual and organizational activities that facilitate satisfying exchange relationships in a dynamic environment through the creation, distribution, promotion, and pricing of goods, services, and ideas. Marketing deals with people and organizations, buying and selling, exchange, relationships, products, distribution, promotion, and price.

Traditional marketing tools include television, radio, newspapers, magazines, trade journals, posters, and direct mail. They are essentially one-way communication tools since there is no immediate personal interaction between advertisers and consumers. Door-to-door sales, telephone, and word-of-mouth communication are also traditional marketing tools, but they are two-way communication. Salespeople and consumers can talk to each other about products and services. While these marketing tools are still widely used by businesses, the Internet has added a new dimension to marketing and advertising. In fact, the impact of the Internet on marketing and advertising has been tremendous and growing. Thousands of Internet marketers have emerged. They not only help companies to set up, update, maintain, and publicize web pages but also help companies market their products and services; incorporate the Internet into their marketing strategies; examine competitors' Internet marketing plans; investigate customers' expectations of companies' web pages; and evaluate the effectiveness of companies' websites. Companies also market their products and services through well-established Internet services, such as Yahoo!, Altavista, and Lycos, to name a few. Millions of dollars have been poured into Internet marketing by both small and large companies. The Internet

Advertising Bureau and Coopers and Lybrand's New Media Group estimated that the amount of dollars spent on Internet advertising was $900 million in 1997, a 240% increase since 1996, and would be $2 billion in 1998.[20] As e-commerce continues to grow, spending on Internet advertising is expected to increase as well.

There are many kinds of marketing-related information on the Internet, such as teaching materials in marketing, directories of advertising agencies, market research, marketing consultants, market research suppliers, software, marketing support services, micromarketing, public relations, sales skills, telemarketing, advertising on the Internet and Web, antitelemarketing, marketing conventions and conferences, marketing courses, demographics, mailing lists, marketing organizations, and employment. This list is by no means exhaustive but rather representative. Marketing professionals and consumers can find a great deal of information relevant to their needs on the Internet.

Teaching materials in marketing

Marketing on the Internet (http://iws.ohiolink.edu/moti) is an effort made by Ohiolink institutions to use the Internet to supplement marketing courses at the college level. OhioLINK, the Ohio Library and Information Network, is a consortium of Ohio's college and university libraries. It connects 79 institutions and serves over half a million students, faculty, and staff. This site teaches market research and analysis and the marketing mix using the Internet, including the concepts of product, place, promotion, and price. It also provides reading and course review materials and panel discussions. The Marketing Plan Website (http://karn.ohiolink.edu/~sg-csu/) is another website offered by Ohiolink for marketing instruction. Its goal is to help students to learn the marketing planning process. It shows students how to develop a marketing plan using Internet resources and services. The site provides discussions on situation analysis, marketing strategy and tactics, and projected income statement and break-even analysis.

Directories of advertising agencies and marketing organizations

Hundreds of advertising agencies and marketing organizations have set up their home pages on the Web. Many online directories of advertising agencies and marketing organizations have emerged on the Internet to organize these websites. Advertising Agencies in America (http://www.americanadagencies.com) is a comprehensive directory of advertising agencies in 22 major cities in the United States and Canada. Entries are frequently updated. The Tilburg University Department of Marketing in the Netherlands (http://marketing.kub.nl/associat.htm) has gathered over 50 websites of marketing associations, institutes, and academies all over the world, including Asia Pacific Marketing Federation, Australia-New Zealand Marketing Academy, the Federation of European Direct Marketing, the European Society for Opinion and Marketing Research, Institute of Marketing Management South Africa, Association of Francaise du Marketing, Association Espanola de Marketing Directo, Japan Marketing Association, Dutch Association for Market Research, and so forth. These directories help to strengthen communication between marketing scholars and professionals worldwide.

Market research

Market research is a process of systematically gathering and analyzing data related to a specific market. It is an important tool used by market researchers to study the behavior of consumers in a particular market. Market research reports and analyses provide crucial information that can be used to make marketing decisions. A great deal of information on market research reports is now available on the Internet. MarketResearch.com (www.MarketResearch.com) is one of many websites that provide information on market reports, newsletters, and competitive marketing data on various markets, such as computers and telecommunications, electronics, food and beverages, household products, media and publishing, health care and pharmaceuticals, chemicals, and construction materials. The Cranfield University Library in the U.K. (www.cranfield.ac.uk/cils/library/ subjects/ market.htm) also provides various information sources useful for conducting market research, including general information sources, market research sources, professional associations, and Internet sources.

Research Services on the Web

The Internet provides tremendous opportunities for research in business. Academic researchers at Wharton School of Business of the University of Pennsylvania have developed a Web interface, Wharton Research Data Service (WRDS), that contains some of the popular business databases. WRDS makes it easier to access, retrieve, and analyze accounting, economic, financial, management, and banking data. The accessibility of databases depends on the subscriptions to databases by individual libraries or institutions. Only a handful of elite business schools subscribed to WRDS after it was initially released. But the number of business schools subscribing to it is increasing.

WRDS provides access to some widely used financial data services and financial analytical tools, including Compustat, CRSP, DRI, Dow Jones Average, FDIC, IBES, PHLX, and TAQ. Compustat contains data on balance sheets, income statements, cash flow statements, and other financial and accounting reports for over 7,500 public companies. For many companies, annual and quarterly financial data are available for the last 20 years. Data are searchable using the company name, ticker symbol, CUSIP symbols, and variables related to financial statements. CRSP provides historical standard and derived security data for the NYSE, AMEX, and NASDAQ stock markets. The CRSP U.S. government bond file contains daily data for over 3,000 U.S. government securities and monthly data for over 5000 bonds, notes, and bills.

The Dow Jones Average offers comprehensive and historical stock information, including highs, lows, and closing prices for 30 stocks in the industrial average, 20 stocks in the transportation average, and 15 stocks in the utility average. Searchable fields include the type of stocks and date. FDIC provides financial data, asset sales information, laws and regulations, news, analyses of financial, economic, and industry trends for commercial banks, and savings and loans institutions. Financial data include asset and liability schedules, income and expenses schedules, and historical statistics on banking. PHLX, the first organized stock exchange in the U.S., trades more than 2,600 stocks, 870 equity options, 14 index options, and 100 currency pairs. Stock sectors include computer manufacturers, banks, forest and paper products, gold and silver, oil services, the phone sector, semiconductors, the Internet, and the utility sector. The number of databases covered in WRDS is subject to change. More and more business databases are integrated into this service and provide a powerful research tool. The advantages of using WRDS are that it is easy to:

- access data;
- retrieve data using variables;
- manipulate data for various research purposes;
- transfer data to other computer systems; and
- incorporate data into statistical packages and spreadsheets, such as SAS and Excel.

This research data service can be accessed 24 hours a day and seven days a week. It greatly expedites the research process. Data gathering, organization, and maintenance have become much easier.

THE IMPACT ON BUSINESS LIBRARIANSHIP

The above sections have highlighted, described, and discussed the emergence of Internet resources and services in major business areas. It is apparent that business information on the Internet has been increasingly characterized by rapid growth, tremendous volume, great variety, and increasingly subject-oriented contents. The current trend in information provision and distribution in general and in business in particular is also characterized by continuing massive migration from print to electronic formats and from CD-ROM to the Web. This is particularly true for business directories, annual reports, financial analyses, cross-section and time-series databases, economic and financial indexes, and statistics. Business information also tends to be more subject-oriented. The Wharton Research Data Service, for example, puts together various economic and financial databases and analytical tools under one uniform interface. The user can access and retrieve various financial and economic data for analysis. Subject knowledge in business is crucial in understanding the subject-oriented business databases.

Many business librarians at academic institutions and public libraries play multiple roles. They provide reference services, participate in collection development, and offer instruction in library systems and databases. Academic business librarians are also liaisons with business faculties. The explosion of Internet resources and services in business has prompted business librarians to go beyond the traditional boundaries.

Typical reference sources that business librarians use include business directories, annual reports, financial statements and analyses of corporations, and information sources related to stocks, mutual funds, notes, bonds, and government securities. Traditionally, these kinds of sources are in print or CD-ROM formats. These print sources are inadequate to answer questions related to small, private companies' products and services and current financial, acquisitions, and merger information. Print sources and CD-ROMs can now be complemented by the use of the Internet. Information on small businesses that is not available in print may be found on the Internet since millions of small businesses have set up home pages. The challenge to business librarians is to be familiar with various search engines and skilled in search techniques. Business librarians should also be familiar with Internet resources and services in various business areas so that they can make better use of the Internet for answering reference questions. Getting familiar with Internet information sources is not an easy task since it is not well organized. The business librarian needs to spend a great deal of time navigating the Web and identifying valuable business information sources available on the Internet. Lack of knowledge and skills in the use of information on the Internet lowers the quality of reference service.

Many business librarians in academic, corporate, and public libraries are responsible for selecting and purchasing various library materials in business. The rationale behind this is that they are experts on the subject and have a better understanding of publications in business. Therefore they can effectively select library materials. Business librarians also normally work at reference desks and have direct contact with patrons, and therefore know their information needs. This fact also makes business librarians ideal candidates for selecting and purchasing library materials in business. Traditionally, librarians use collection development tools to facilitate selection of library materials, such as *Choice* book reviews. The emergence of the Internet adds a new dimension to collection development. Many business librarians have started playing a role in identifying, evaluating, selecting, organizing, and maintaining Internet resources and services in various business areas. This fact can be easily observed by looking at business web pages created by many business librarians at academic libraries. Many academic institutions have in fact developed web pages with extensive coverage on specific business areas. Business information on these websites is used not only by people at the institution that developed the websites, but also by people elsewhere. While some publications provide reviews of websites with business information, they are far from adequate due to the large volume of Internet information. Business librarians have to identify, select, evaluate, and organize business information on the Internet themselves to meet the information needs of their local patrons.

Business librarians in many academic libraries also outreach to faculties of business schools to meet their teaching, research, and information needs. Faculty members make purchase recommendations. Traditionally, business librarians receive book requests through campus mail, which is very slow. The Internet has greatly facilitated this process. Faculty members can make book purchase requests via email. Business librarians can also set up web pages with book request functions so that both faculty members and students can make book purchase recommendations online. Business librarians can display newly purchased books on the web page so that faculty members can use the most recent research results and publications for their teaching and research.

Business librarians in many academic institutions also conduct workshops to train faculty and students to use business-related resources and services. Until recently, business resources were mostly in paper format. In addition to finding print sources, business librarians now need to include Internet resources as well because they have become significant sources of information and knowledge. This requires business librarians to have substantial knowledge of various business areas and skills in identifying, selecting, organizing, and teaching Web resources.

Many business schools have established trading centers. The goal of these trading centers is to provide hands-on and real-time trading experience for students, particularly those in finance so that the gap between classroom education and real-world activities can be narrowed. Graduates with real-world experience can smoothly undertake job responsibilities as traders, portfolio managers, and other financial service administrators. Business schools, such as Baruch College of the City University of New York, the University of Texas at Austin, Illinois Institute of Technology, Bentley College, and Babson College are the leaders in providing such real-time trading facilities. While the role of librarians in many of these schools is not visible, librarians at Baruch College have undertaken to teach seminars and workshops related to the use of financial and trading information systems, such as Reuters. To be able to teach these systems, subject knowledge, such as knowledge of equities, commodities, currencies, futures, and options markets, is essential.

Challenges

One of the biggest challenges to business librarians today is subject knowledge. Many business librarians simply do not have formal education in business, yet subject knowledge in business is vital. It cannot be replaced by work experience since there is little chance that a business librarian would have time to engage in serious and rigorous studies in theories and methodologies of business. A working business librarian would not have time to do debit and credit postings on a ledger and transform it into a balance sheet or to run regressions on economic growth. Even if a business librarian would like to learn these things, proper guidance from highly trained faculty members is absolutely necessary. Subject knowledge is crucial in identifying, selecting, evaluating, and organizing business information.

A survey of 162 business librarians from over 570 business schools conducted years ago by Kendrick[21] shows that only about 10% of the business librarians surveyed had undergraduate degrees in economics or other business areas and about 17% held masters' degrees in business administration. The initial results of our recent survey indicate that this situation has not changed much. One reason for the lack of business librarians with business degrees is the competition between the business sector and libraries, where libraries lose out. The average starting salary, including bonuses for an employee with an MBA working for a company, is well above that of a business librarian working in a public or academic library.

Business information reflects the quantitative nature of business as an academic discipline. Business librarians with subject knowledge understand what these numbers mean and are able to interpret them for their patrons. Numbers are the language of accounting, finance, economics, and marketing. Statistics is a common tool for analyzing business, industry, financial market, and economic trends. While business students are required to take at least two quantitative statistical courses, many library science students have little knowledge about statistics or quantitative research methodologies. Without quantitative analytical skills, business librarians may face a tremendous challenge in understanding and teaching some business databases, such as the Wharton Research Data Service, which contains extensive time-series and cross-section data in accounting, finance, economics, and marketing.

The Internet has created many challenges as well as opportunities for business librarians. To fully utilize these opportunities, academics in library and information science, library administrators, and business librarians must focus on quality of business information services and quality of education and training for business librarians. Library and information science schools should have high standards for hiring faculty members teaching business information courses. Advanced degrees in business, such as an MBA, or Ph.D. in addition to advanced degrees in library and information science will ensure that instructors have formal training in both areas. Scholarly publications in business information or business-related areas are further proof of competencies in teaching business information. Library and information science schools need to reform their business information-related courses by incorporating subject knowledge into business information courses. Subject knowledge is crucial when it comes to interpreting business information. Basic knowledge in accounting, finance, economics, management, marketing, production and operations, and business statistics is essential in teaching business information-related courses. It is also important to set high standards for recruiting business librarians. A business librarian should have at least a bachelor's degree in business, preferably an MBA degree in addition to a library science degree. Working experience in business-related information services is helpful but it is far from adequate and should not replace formal education and training in business. Without high standards for faculty members, business librarians, and substantial subject knowledge, the quality of business information services will deteriorate. Business librarians without business degrees need to take courses to correct deficiencies.

SUMMARY AND CONCLUSION

This chapter has highlighted some effects of the Internet on business information, particularly business information services in academic libraries. While it is difficult to observe and discuss the impact for every aspect, it is possible to summarize some major trends.

- E-commerce is bringing about great changes in the way business is conducted and is shaping the way business information is organized, distributed, maintained, accessed, and retrieved.
- Business information on the Internet is increasing markedly in both variety and quantity and covers virtually every business area.
- Business information on the Internet has been increasingly interactive and spontaneous, for example, real-time streamers.
- Until recently it was difficult to obtain information on private companies since they do not have to file annual reports with the Securities and Exchange Commission as publicly held companies do. Now it is much easier to find information on privately owned companies since thousands of private companies have set up web pages with information on their products, services, and prices.
- Research databases and datasets are emerging on the Internet, such as the Wharton Research Data Service, the Barro-Lee dataset, the PennWorld dataset, and many others. These research databases and datasets greatly facilitate research in business and economics.
- Teaching materials, such as course syllabi in business and economics, are mushrooming on the Web. Business disciplines are among those that post the most course syllabi and teaching materials on the Internet. These materials have added a new dimension to business information services.
- While the Internet is still intended to be a free telecommunication network for everyone, business information on the Internet has increasingly become fee-based. Websites providing analytical reports on stocks, and up-to-date company news, more often than not, charge fees.
- The role of traditional print business sources is diminishing due to the fact that an increasing amount of business information is available on the Internet.
- The Internet has changed the way we live, learn, and work and has also changed business information services. Subject knowledge in business and technical skills is becoming increasingly critical to meet new challenges.

This chapter is written in the hope of helping business librarians and others to recognize some important business information resources on the Internet, improving business information services, and advancing business librarianship in the new information age.

NOTES

1. Anthony Debons, Esther Horne, and Scott Cronenweth, *Information Science: An Integrated View* (Boston: G. K. Hall and Co., 1988).
2. The Internet Software Consortium (ISC), *Number of Internet Host* (URL www.isc.org/ds/host-count-history).
3. "Dot-com Registrations," *Investor's Business Daily*, January 24, 2000, p. A6.
4. John Eatwell, Murray Milgate, and Peter Newman, eds., *The New Palgrave: A Dictionary of Economics* (London: Macmillan Press, 1987).
5 Donald Moffat, *Economics Dictionary* (New York: Elsevier, 1976).
6. Lewis-Guodo Liu and Robert Premus, *Global Economics Growth: Theories, Research, Studies, and Annotated Bibliography: 1950-1997* (Westport, CT: Greenwood Press, 2000).
7. Bill Orr, "Community Bank Guide to Internet Banking," *American Bankers Association (ABA) Banking Journal* 90, no.6 (June 1998): 47-53.
8. Michelle Clayton, "Monitoring PC and Internet Banking," *America's Community Banker* 7, no. 6 (June 1998):16-21.
9. Bill Orr, "Where Will Internet Banking Be in Two Years?" *American Bankers Association (ABA) Banking Journal* 90, no.3 (March 1998): 56.
10. Jeffrey Marshall and John W. Milligan, "Internet Standard Moves Closer," *USBanker* 108, no. 3 (March 1998): 26.
11. "Commercial banks on the Internet." *USA Today,* 20 December 1999 (URL www.usatoday.com).
12. Gerry Jiao Q. and Lewis-Guodo Liu, *Internet Resources and Services for Finance and Investment: A Global Guide* (Phoenix, AZ: Orxy, 2000).
13. Philip D Curtin, *Cross-Culture Trade in World History* (Cambridge, UK: Cambridge University Press, 1984).
14. Lewis-Guodo Liu, *Internet Resources and Services for International Business: A Global Guide* (Phoenix, AZ: Oryx Press, 1998).
15. Ibid.
16. Bureau of the Census. Economics and Statistics Administration. U.S. Department of Commerce. *Statistical Abstract of the United States* (Washington, DC: U.S. Government Printing Office, 1998), p.452.
17. Scott M. Schaffer, "Improving Real Estate Loan Turnaround with the Internet," *Journal of Leading and Credit Risk Management* 80, no. 11 (July 1998): 36-39.
18. Janey Chao, *Internet Resources and Services for Real Estate* (Phoenix, AZ: Oryx Press, 2000).

19. Philip Kotler and Gary Armstrong, *Marketing: An Introduction* (Upper Saddle River, NJ: Prentice-Hall, 1997).
20. Adriene Mand, "IAB Internet Ads Gead for $1 Billion Mark," *Adweek* (April 6, 1998).
21. Aubrey Kendrick, "The Educational Background and Work Experience of Academic Business Librarians," *RQ* 29 (Spring 1990): 394-399.

CHAPTER NINE

THE INTERNET AND GOVERNMENT INFORMATION SERVICES

Sherry Engel

INTRODUCTION

Governments create, compile, and maintain large amounts of information. Although some of this information is confidential or otherwise restricted, other government information can be released to the public. Traditionally, public access to government information was provided via printed publications. Several methods of dissemination were used. Some government agencies provided free copies of their publications upon request. Numerous government sales programs and clearinghouses were established to sell government publications. Commercial publishers repackaged and sold the publications. Libraries obtained publications through the above means or through depository library programs. They also provided assistance in locating and obtaining desired information.

The Internet originated as a means of disseminating government information. Originally, access was limited to the U.S. Department of Defense and affiliated contractors and researchers who used it to share computer resources. In the 1970s and 1980s, other government agencies began operating networks. In 1980, about 50 interconnected networks formed the Internet; by 1990, more than 1,000 networks were connected.[1] The Internet and connected networks were used for several purposes. Electronic mail (email) was the most popular feature. File Transfer Protocol (FTP) allowed users to download data files, image files, and software to local computers. Telnet permitted these users to log into remote computers. Government agencies began placing information on publicly accessible servers. The types and quantities of information were limited, as were the number of people with access. The development of the gopher at the University of Minnesota and the World Wide Web at the European Organization for Nuclear Research (CERN), publicly released in 1991, changed the Internet from a tool for specialists to one that could be used by nearly everyone. In 1993, U.S. government agencies began creating web pages. State, local, foreign, and international government agencies also began creating Web presences.

The last decade of the twentieth century was a period of dramatic change with respect to public access to government information. This chapter provides an overview of the dissemination practices prior to 1990 and some of the factors leading to the proliferation of government information on the Internet. The chapter then discusses the impact the Internet is having and resulting issues and concerns. The discussion centers on U.S. federal government information, although state, local, foreign, and international government information resources are mentioned. The U.S. government has long been a model for providing public access to government information. It has embraced the Internet as a means of publicly disseminating information.

U.S. GOVERNMENT INFORMATION

The public's right to access government information and the government's obligation to provide this access have been an issue for much of this nation's history. The First Amendment of the U.S. Constitution grants freedom of speech and freedom of the press. Many scholars have interpreted this as a public "right to know," although the Constitution does not explicitly state such a right.[2]

Early Congresses recognized the need for the public to have access to congressional information. The first 12 Congresses contracted with newspaper publishers to print extra copies of certain congressional publications. These publications were distributed to the states and territories. 13th Congress regularized this practice in an 1813 resolution (3 Stat. 140). The resolution stated that House and Senate journals, reports, and documents "of the present and every future congress" shall be printed and distributed to state and territorial governors, legislative bodies, colleges, universities, and historical societies.[3] In 1814, the American Antiquarian Society in Worcester, Massachusetts became the first depository library.[4]

Statutes, regulations, and other executive branch documents were printed and distributed under the direction of the secretary of state. This practice continued into the 20th century although the secretary had no statutory authority for doing so.[5] Some executive agencies also distributed publications. For example, when the Department of Agriculture was established in 1862, part of its mission was to provide public information on agriculture, including information about crops, rural economic development, forestry, and related topics.

Acts regarding the printing and distribution of government publications were passed throughout the 1800s and 1900s. The most significant of these acts were the Printing Act of 1895 and the Depository Library Act of 1962. Under the Printing Act, the Government Printing Office assumed responsibility for printing, distributing, and selling government publications. The types of publications distributed to depository libraries expanded to include those executive agency publications created specifically for public distribution. Prior to 1895, the only executive agency publications included in the Depository Library Program were reports prepared for or presented to Congress. The Depository Library Act of 1962 (PL 87-579) further expanded the number of publications in the program. It stated:

> Government Publications, except those determined by their issuing components to be required for official use only or for strictly administrative or operational purposes which have no public interest or educational value and publications classified for reasons of national security, shall be made available to depository libraries.

The act defines "government publication" as "informational matter which is published as an individual document at Government expense, or as required by law."

The Federal Depository Library Program

The guiding principles of the Federal Depository Library Program (FDLP) are

1. With certain specified exceptions, all government publications shall be made available to Federal depository libraries.
2. Federal depository libraries shall be located in each State and U.S. Congressional district in order to make Government publications widely available.
3. These Government publications shall be available for the free use of the general public.[6]

Currently, 1,339 libraries participate in the FDLP.[7] Depository libraries are scattered throughout the country. Since designation is largely based on the Congressional District, there are more depositories in densely populated areas than in rural areas. Most depository libraries are college or university libraries, followed in frequency by public libraries. These libraries receive publications free of charge from the Government Printing Office (GPO). In exchange, the libraries agree to "abide fully by the law and regulations governing officially designated Federal depository libraries."[8] These obligations are specified in the *Instructions to Depository Libraries*, the *Depository Library Manual*, and other publications of the GPO.[9] Depositories are required to provide free public access to depository and supporting reference materials. They must provide this access even if they do not provide public access to the remainder of their collections. Since 1996 depositories are also required to provide free public access to government information resources available via the Internet.

There are two types of federal depository libraries, regional depositories and selective depositories. Regional depository libraries, currently 53, receive all distributed titles. They are obligated to maintain these publications in perpetuity. Selective depositories profile with GPO to receive just those publications they feel are necessary to meet the needs of their users. These libraries may, with the permission of their regional depositories, remove materials from their collections after five years. The selective depositories rely on other depository libraries, especially regional depositories, to provide public access to the materials they do not select.

Depository versus non-depository publications

Per the Depository Library Act of 1962, all non-classified government publications of public interest or educational value are to be included in the depository library program. GPO has identified 17 types of publications that meet these criteria. They are:

- Public notices, informational memos, press releases, and newsletters
- Handbooks, manuals, and guides
- Advisory circulars
- Directories
- Proceedings
- Forms (e.g., survey, tax, and grant applications)
- Maps, atlases, and charts
- Posters, lithographs, and photographs
- Catalogs, bibliographies, indexes, and abstracts
- Reports
- Journals, periodicals, and newsletters
- Environmental impact statements
- Legal materials (includes legislative materials, laws, rules and regulations, decisions, legal opinions, treaties, and international agreements)
- Informational and explanatory flyers, brochures, booklets, and pamphlets

- Statistical publications
- Marketing and promotional flyers and pamphlets
- Monographs

Depository publications may be in any format including paper, microfiche, CD-ROM, floppy disk, video, multi-media, or Internet. If a publication is issued in multiple formats, only one format needs to be included in the program, even if other formats are available through sales programs. Depository libraries might, for example, receive the microfiche format of a publication while the paper version is available through the GPO Sales Program. If, however, there are multiple versions of a publication – draft, preliminary, interim, final, German, Spanish, Korean, or braille – all versions are to be included in the depository program. Appendixes, inserts, supplementary materials, and errata also are sent to depositories.[10]

Government publications classified for reason of national security are specifically excluded from the depository library program. Some agencies, for example, the Smithsonian Institution, create self-sustaining publications. That is, sales proceeds for these publications must cover production costs. Self-sustaining publications are excluded from the depository program.[11] GPO identified 13 additional types of nondepository publications. These publications, intended for internal agency use, are:

- Job vacancy notices
- Rules, notices, and handbooks concerning recreational and welfare activities, and services for federal employees
- Memos, directives, notices, and manuals relating to internal administrative operations of specific agencies
- Data input forms
- Internal agency forms and guidelines
- Personnel evaluation forms
- Procurement solicitations
- Identification cards
- Instructional signs and stickers (such as parking permit decals)
- Working drafts of publications that are not circulated outside the agency
- Form letters
- User manuals for computer programs if information is covered by the Privacy Act
- Agency control forms [12]

Some publications that should be part of the depository program also are excluded. Fugitive documents occur when agencies are noncompliant in supplying copies of non-GPO-published publications for distribution to depositories. Non-GPO publications include in-house publications created using desktop publishing software and materials printed under contract with private sector publishers. Reasons for noncompliance include agencies' lack of awareness that copies of these materials should be sent to GPO for depository distribution and executive agencies believing that as an equal branch of government, they are not obligated to supply materials to a legislative branch program. Publications that often are fugitive include technical reports, promotional materials, and press releases.[13] Estimates on the number of fugitive publications vary but may be more than 50% of all government publications.[14]

Volume of distribution

The quantity of materials distributed to depositories increased dramatically from 1895 through 1980. In 1900, the average depository received 400 items per year. By 1930, the average depository was receiving 4,300 items.[15] In 1979, 86,431 titles were included in the program (most libraries did not select all titles).[16] Until 1977, virtually all depository publications were distributed in paper. In that year, as a cost-savings measure, GPO began microfiche distribution of some titles. By 1982, microfiche titles outnumbered paper titles.[17]

The increased availability of government publications reversed in the 1980s. The Paperwork Reduction Act of 1980 directed the Office of Management and Budget (OMB) to develop policies and standards regarding federal information. The goal was to reduce record keeping and the amount of information gathered. OMB Circular A-130 required agencies to collect only the data needed to perform their duties. They also were to disseminate information via the private sector or on a cost recovery basis.[18] In 1981, President Reagan issued a moratorium on new periodicals and pamphlets. He believed that the government was spending too much money on "public relations, publicity, and advertising."[19] Between 1982 and 1989, one-quarter of government publications were eliminated (approximately 4,000 titles). The American Library Association tracked this loss in a series of pamphlets entitled *Less Access to Less Information by and about the U.S. Government.*

The number of paper and microfiche titles distributed to depositories continued to decline in the 1990s. Federal agencies continued to follow policies instituted during the Reagan and Bush administrations such as contracting with private sector publishers. The Clinton administration was much more public-oriented in regard to information policies. Between 1993 and 1995, OMB Circular A-130 was revised. The revised circular instructs agencies to avoid granting exclusive distribution contracts to the private sector. Agencies are encouraged to disseminate information through multiple channels, including the FDLP. The revisions also limit cost-recovery to the actual costs of dissemination.[20] The administration has encouraged agencies to disseminate information via the Internet.[21] As a result of federal agencies choosing to use electronic formats, the number of titles available in paper and microfiche has declined.

Electronic Information

Bibliographic Databases

The National Library of Medicine began providing batch searches of its Medical Literature Analysis and Retrieval System (MEDLARS) in 1964. It was the first publicly available, large-scale bibliographic search service. Requests submitted to the National Library of Medicine were coded and input. The average turnaround time was six weeks. (The system went online as MEDLINE in 1971.)[22]

Government agencies contracted with the private sector to create computer databases. For example, Lockheed developed DIALOG in the mid-1960s to provide access to NASA citations. The system was adapted for use by other government agencies, including the U.S. Atomic Energy Commission (Nuclear Science Abstracts and DOE/RECON), the Department of Education (ERIC), National Technical Information Service (NTIS), National Library of Medicine (MEDLINE), and the National Agriculture Library (AGRICOLA).[23] Initially, access was restricted to government agencies, contractors, and researchers. In the 1970s, Lockheed began offering other organizations access to its files. ERIC, NTIS, and AGRICOLA were among the first offered.

Public access to government citation databases was provided through the private sector. A 1982 article by Linda Futato identified 21 online databases available via the private sector consisting almost entirely of bibliographic citations to, or full text of, government publications.[24] Federal agency practices regarding bibliographic databases varied. ERIC, AGRICOLA, and GPO Monthly Catalog tapes were supplied to private sector vendors for very low fees and with few restrictions on their use. Vendors had to pay substantial fees for copies of files such as NTIS, DOE/Energy and MEDLINE. Vendors providing access to patent and trademark information had to create their own electronic files. This increased the costs to end-users. Depository libraries tried to gain free access to government bibliographic databases through the FDLP. They argued that the databases should be considered as government publications and therefore be part of the depository library program. The GPO General Counsel disagreed. In a 1982 opinion, he stated "Data which remain in a computer database without publication cannot be considered informational matter which is published as an individual document."

The Government Printing Office, therefore, was not required to provide free access to these databases.[25] Libraries wishing to have access to the citation databases subscribed to services such as DIALOG, BRS, and Mead Data (Lexis). A 1981 survey of depository librarians found that few were using online bibliographic files. The most commonly cited reasons for not searching these files were a lack of access to computer terminals and that librarians in other library departments provided this service.[26]

Statistical Data

Much of the statistical information collected and maintained by the government is not published in print format. For example, only a small portion of the data collected in the Census of Population and Housing is tabulated in printed reports. By 1976, more than 90 government agencies were collecting, analyzing and distributing statistical data. These agencies had accumulated some 9 million reels of magnetic tape.[27] Copies of the files often could be leased or purchased. The problem was locating them. There were additional access issues. Agencies created the files for internal use. File documentation was poor, in some cases handwritten. Agencies rarely had established distribution procedures and often lacked the funds to prepare their files for public use.[28]

In 1977, *Government Publications Review* began carrying a column entitled "Machine-Readable Datafiles." The column provided information on gaining access to and using these files. Agencies began creating catalogs of their data files in the 1970s. The Paperwork Reduction Act of 1980 called for agencies to increase cost-effectiveness by reducing duplication in information gathering. Agencies often did not know what information other agencies were collecting. NTIS and the Office of Statistical Policy and Standards compiled *A Directory of Federal Statistical Data Files* in 1981.[29] This directory helped make government statistical data files more accessible, and available to other agencies and the public by providing such information as descriptions of data files, geographic coverage, availability of technical documentation, and method of access (including costs).[30]

Despite the availability of statistical files, few libraries collected or provided access to them. Reasons included librarians' lack of statistical backgrounds, the absence of skills needed to manipulate raw data files, librarians' lack of access to computer resources, and librarians' traditional role of providing access to information resources but not interpretation of them. Many academic institutions established data archives. These archives tended to be associated with social sciences departments rather than libraries.[31] Organizations such as the Inter-university Consortium for Political and Social Research (ICPSR) obtained and archived copies of statistical files. Researchers at affiliated institutions have free access to the files; nonmembers must pay for access. ICPSR provides user support but researchers are expected to perform their own analysis.

Electronic Bulletin Boards

Agencies began using Electronic Bulletin Boards in the 1970s as a means to rapidly disseminate information, with usage increased in the 1980s. A number of factors limited access to bulletin boards. These included having access to computer hardware and software capable of accessing the files. The user needed knowledge of how to access, navigate, and FTP the files. Protocols were not standardized. Unless the user lived in the Washington, D.C. area, connecting to the bulletin board often involved a long-distance telephone connection. Users usually had to register before access was permitted and in some cases had to pre-pay subscription fees.[32] Bulletin boards were subject to rapid change, often appearing and disappearing without notice. Agencies used bulletin boards for current information, typically removing older files when new ones were added.[33]

Call for Action

The Reagan and Bush administrations believed it was the responsibility of the private sector to provide access to electronic government information. It granted sole rights to government databases to commercial entities. For example, WestLaw contracted with the Justice Department to create an electronic database of federal court opinions, statutes, regulations and related materials (JURIS). Access to JURIS was restricted.[34] The private sector added value to raw data by designing search and retrieval software. It did not want competition from the government and lobbied Congress to that effect. Citizens' groups lobbied for free or low-cost access to government information. The movement gained momentum in 1989 when the governor of South Dakota was outraged when he learned that he would have to pay several hundred dollars for information from a database created by the Department of Agriculture.[35]

In 1988, the Congressional Office of Technology Assessment produced *Informing the Nation: Federal Information Dissemination in an Electronic Age.* This report called for Congress to determine the roles of the public and private sectors in disseminating government information. It cited the need for clarification on electronic dissemination of information since it was not explicitly covered under previous legislation. The report stated that public access to federal information was of vital importance and that this access was impeded by current practices.[36]

The Clinton administration viewed government information as a resource to be used for the public good rather than as a marketable commodity. It created the National Information Infrastructure (NII) initiative and used it to promote public access to government information at all levels of government. The NII encouraged government agencies to make more information available to the public.[37] The administration believed electronic dissemination would increase the cost-effectiveness of the federal government.

The Internet

Two advances in computer technology helped ease Internet access for the ordinary person. The Gopher, developed at the University of Minnesota, was a client-server protocol that allowed users to connect to remote sites by following a hierarchical series of menu options. Gopher scripts could be written to provide access to FTP and Telnet sites, Wide Area Information Servers (WAIS), directories, and files. The World Wide Web developed by CERN, could be used to provide access to the same resources as a gopher, plus image, sound, and video files. The Web uses Hypertext Mark-Up Language (HTML) for navigation rather than a series of menus. The resulting ability to have links embedded in a page of text made the Web more flexible than the Gopher. The downside was that it required the end-user to have a higher-end computer and greater bandwidth capacity than did the gopher. Gopher and the websites coexisted, often linking to each other, for several years.[38] The Web gained in popularity after the National Center for Supercomputing Applications (NCSA) at the University of Illinois at Urbana-Champaign, released the Mosaic Web browser in 1993. Mosaic was a user-friendly, graphical interface browser available in PC and Macintosh versions (computers preferred by the general public) as well as in an X Window version (more popular with researchers).[39] Once the software was installed and configured on an Internet connected computer, the user could navigate the Web using a mouse (point and click). At the beginning of 1993 there were 50 Web servers worldwide. By the end of 1993, there were 5,000, and by the end of 1994, 10,000 servers.[40] For comparison in 1993 there were 750 gopher servers, 500 of them in the United States.[41]

Government agencies took advantage of these developments and became major content providers on the Internet. Federal law mandated some Internet sites, for example, FEDWORLD and GPO Access. A few sites such as STAT-USA are self-sustaining. Most federal agency sites, however, are intended for free public access.

FEDWORLD

The National Technical Information Service (NTIS) developed FEDWORLD in response to a mandate in the American Technology Preeminence Act of 1991 (PL 102-245). FEDWORLD went online in 1992 as a dial-up service providing an access point to federal electronic bulletin boards. It provided access to 49 bulletin boards. By the time it was connected to the Internet in 1993, FEDWORLD pointed to more than 100 bulletin boards.[42] Most of the bulletin boards it pointed to were free to the public, although parts of the site were fee-based.

Census Bureau

The Census Bureau began providing Internet access via a Gopher in 1993 and a website in 1994. The sites provided access to *County Business Patterns*, data from the *Statistical Abstract of the United States*, population estimates, and links to census data loaded on university servers. The website had more than a million hits within the first six months of operation.[43] The Census Bureau Website has expanded to include more data from the 1990 Census of Population and Housing, some earlier census data, *Current Population Reports*, other Census Bureau publications, economic census data and more. The bureau's newest feature is the *American Factfinder. American*

Factfinder allows the user to create customized tables and maps using data from Census Bureau microdata sets. It is the primary means of access to 1997 Economic Census data and is scheduled to be the primary method for distribution of 2000 Census of Population and Housing data.

GPO Access

The Government Printing Office Electronic Information Enhancement Act of 1993 (PL 103-40), or GPO Access Act, required GPO to provide online access to the *Congressional Record*, *Federal Register*, and "other appropriate federal databases." GPO expanded the files available on the Federal Bulletin Board and implemented a WAIS server. GPO Access went online in 1994 as a subscription service.[44]

GPO distributed EINet winWAIS software to subscribers. This software had to be loaded and configured on the subscribers' computer. Source files had to be updated when GPO added files to its server. The software allowed the subscriber to send queries to GPO Access database files and view retrieved ASCII and TIFF files. If Adobe Acrobat Reader software (available free of charge) was loaded, the subscriber also could view PDF files.

Depository libraries were entitled to free subscriptions. Some depositories volunteered to be gateway libraries. The Columbia Online Information Network (COIN) and Seattle Public Library were among the libraries offering Simple Wide Area Information Server (SWAIS) access through telnet, gopher, or library catalogs. SWAIS users could view ASCII files but not TIFF or PDF. Benefits of using a gateway were that they provided remote access free of charge, and no special software was required.[45] Purdue University went even further, providing a Web interface which allowed the user to view all formats. GPO also moved to a Web interface and changed GPO Access from a subscription to free service in 1995.

Library of Congress

The Library of Congress Information System (LOCIS) went online in 1993. It provided access to Library of Congress catalogs, federal legislation from 1973 forward, copyright information, and more. It could be accessed via telnet or through the Library of Congress Machine-Assisted Realization of the Virtual Electronic Library (LC Marvel) Gopher.[46] LC Marvel also provided access to electronic information from other federal agencies. The Library of Congress created THOMAS at the request of the House of Representatives in 1995. Unlike GPO Access, there was no legislative mandate involved in its creation.[47] It offers free public access via a Web interface to congressional information such as bills and the *Congressional Record.* Although the same information was available via GPO Access, THOMAS was much more heavily publicized as a means of public access to government information.

STAT-USA

The Department of Commerce's STAT-USA Website provides online access to business and economic data. Available resources include the *National Trade Data Bank (NTDB), U.S. Global Trade Outlook, Industry Sector Analyses*, and *Best Market Reports.* It was developed as, and has remained, a subscription service. By the end of 1996, agencies were abandoning gopher in favor of the Web. By the end of the decade, the U. S. Government was maintaining thousands of Web servers containing millions of pages.[48] These pages offer public access to a wide range of resources including data files, historical documents, satellite images, catalogs of publications, and more.

Electronic Information and Depository Libraries

Information in electronic formats remained outside the depository library program until 1989. In that year the GPO General Counsel partially reversed its 1982 opinion. The General Counsel stated:

> Whenever an agency "publishes" information, that is, intends to, and does, disseminate it to the general public – in whatever form – the information constitutes a "Government publication" within the meaning of [44 USC] section 1901. This would include, therefore, a publication in electronic format. Also, this would be so whether or not the electronic formatted publication had previously existed in any other format, such as the printed format.[49]

While the reversal did not include providing free access to bibliographic databases, it did clear the way for several pilot projects. GPO's first depository CD-ROM was *Census Test Disk No. 2,* sent to depositories in 1988 and 1989. It was followed by the *Toxic Release Inventory (TRI)* and the *1985 Congressional Record* on CD-ROM in 1990. Most depository librarians had little experience with this type of resource. Although many libraries had CD-ROM workstations, these workstations generally were located in the reference area of the library. The Census CD-ROM was the first nonbibliographic CD-ROM most librarians had encountered. Two online services also were piloted; the Department of Energy's *Integrated Technical Information System (ITIS)* in February through June 1990 and the Commerce Department's *Economic Bulletin Board* in July through December of the same year. Despite mixed reviews, plans to include electronic information went forward. GPO began providing depository access to the Project Hermes Bulletin Board in 1990. This bulletin board provided access to Supreme Court opinions. The site went through several evolutions and in 1994 became the Federal Bulletin Board.[50]

At the urging of the depository library community, GPO issued its first recommended minimum standards for depository library computer workstations in 1991. The recommended configuration was an IBM compatible 386 SX with 2 to 4 mega bytes of RAM, a modem with 2400 to 9600 BPS speed, and MS-DOS 3.3 or 5.0.[51] In 1993, GPO recommended a 486 DX with at least 8 mega bytes of RAM and suggested that libraries consider the Windows operating system since many CD-ROM products required it.[52] The recommendations have been subject to almost annual updates. Depositories were encouraged, but not required, to provide public access to the Internet and CD-ROMs on library workstations. As recently as 1993, one-third of all depositories lacked Internet access.[53]

Tangible electronic products, primarily CD-ROMs and floppy disks, created major problems for depository libraries. The lack of standardization was of particular concern. Each agency and in some cases each title from the same agency, used a different software interface. Some CD-ROMs were distributed without the software necessary to run them. Others were distributed with insufficient technical documentation. Rapid technological advances necessitated frequent hard and software upgrades. Librarians' lack of technological training and patrons' need for increased assistance when using these products also were issues.[54] Libraries typically chose one of three routes when dealing with tangible electronic products:

- The library did not select tangible electronic products.
- The library selected tangible electronic products, circulated them for use outside the library, but did not provide in-library use.
- The library loaded the products on workstations within the library. (Most libraries loaded only a small percentage of the titles they received.)

Despite all the problems tangible electronic products caused, they never accounted for more than a small percentage (currently less than 1%) of depository receipts.

Depository Program in Transition

The Internet has had a greater impact on depositories than have CD-ROMS. In 1995, GPO released *The Electronic Federal Depository Program: Transition Plans FY 1996-FY 1998*.[55] This plan called for all but 24 core titles to be distributed only in electronic format by the end of 1998. After much discussion, the list of core titles was expanded, and the transition period lengthened from two to five years.

In 1996, GPO began requiring all depository libraries to provide public access to the Internet.[56] Depository libraries in large academic libraries had had the necessary telecommunications infrastructure for several years. Many smaller libraries, especially public libraries, frequently lacked even staff access. The GPO mandate forced library administrators to choose between obtaining the necessary computer hardware, software, and telecommunications connections or relinquishing depository status.

By 1998, depository libraries were pondering the merits of remaining in the depository library program.[57] Although depository status bestows a certain prestige on the library, the costs of being a depository are considerable. Georgetown University's Lauinger Library performed a cost-analysis of its depository operations in 1993. Its library expenditures in support of depository materials totaled $217,970. The library found a minimum of a 4:1 ratio of library to government expense in its depository operations.[58] The number of depository libraries decreased slightly in the 1990s. The costs associated with providing electronic access and the increased availability of freely accessible electronic government information have been commonly cited reasons for relinquishing depository status.

Libraries have many reasons for remaining in the depository program. Items received through the FDPL are the property of the federal government. A library relinquishing depository status must get permission from its regional library to retain depository materials. The regional may require the depository to offer the publications to other depository libraries. The library would need to find other ways to obtain government information resources to meet the needs of patrons, probably through purchase. Depository libraries are eligible for free access to some government subscriptions services, for example, STAT-USA.[59] Not everything is on the Internet. Approximately 25,000 current depository titles are available only in tangible format.[60] Some of these publications are available only through the FDLP.

Beginning in 1999, GPO permitted depository libraries to substitute certain Internet-accessible publications for tangible products. Librarians considering making these substitutions were urged to consider the following:

- Is the title better suited in another format?
- What are its scope, purpose, and intended audience?
- Is the title authoritative?
- What is the date range or coverage?
- Is the information time-sensitive?
- Is the title's electronic presentation comparable to the tangible version?
- Are an adequate number of publicly accessible computer workstations available?[61]

As federal agencies increased the amounts of information they placed on their own Internet sites, tangible versions of publications began to be dropped from the depository program. For example, the March 1996 *Administrative Notes Technical Supplement* indicated three publications, *AIDS Bibliography*, *U.S. Energy Industry Financial Developments*, and *National Water Conditions*, were "discontinued in paper. Available on Internet."[62] The frequency of migration increased and occurred even when GPO printed and offered the print version through its sales program. By the first quarter of fiscal year 2000, 52%

of current depository titles were no longer distributed in tangible format. This compares to 20% being distributed in paper, 27% in microfiche, and less than 1% in other formats.[63]

Depository Library Contributions

Depository librarians had to find ways to handle the increasing flow of electronic government information. In the past, they needed to be familiar with government organization, the Superintendent of Documents (SuDoc) Classification System, and how to use specific indexing sources.[64] In the 1990s, depository librarians learned to install and use a variety of nonbibliographic CD-ROM products. The librarians learned to search and navigate the Internet to find and provide government information in a variety of formats. These new skills often were acquired through trial and error.

Depository librarians increasingly served as resources for each other. Librarians submitted copies of the user guides and pathfinders they created to *Administrative Notes* for publication in the "Reader's Exchange" column. They provided copies of the materials they created for inclusion in the American Library Association's (ALA) Government Documents Roundtable (GODORT) Handout Exchange. A more interactive means of communication became available in 1990, when Diane Kovacs began the GovDoc-L listserv.[65] This discussion group, open to anyone with an interest in government information, quickly became a valued resource. Early discussions on the list included automation, depository CD-ROM, government information on the Internet, and Marcive tapes.[66]

Some depository librarians created gopher sites to guide their patrons to online government information. After the development of the Mosaic and later Netscape Web browsers, even more depositories created Web presences. The advantages of the Web were that Web browsers could easily link to both Web and gopher sites and that information describing links could be provided on web pages.[67] Documentation on creating web pages was readily accessible, although many people simply found a page they liked and copied the coding. Depository web pages often provided information specific to the depository library such as location, hours of service, user guides, and collection strengths. They also organized and provided links to selected online resources. "Documents Center," created by Grace York at the University of Michigan, is perhaps the best known website produced by a documents librarian.

A few depository libraries entered into partnerships with GPO or other agencies. Gateway libraries were discussed above. The University of Illinois at Chicago Richard J. Daley Library is archiving information distributed via the Department of State Foreign Affairs Network (DOSFAN).[68] University of North Texas Libraries are archiving the electronic publications of selected "dead" agencies, the Advisory Commission on Intergovernmental Relations (ACIR), the Commission on Structural Alternatives for the Federal Courts of Appeals Research, and National Civil Aviation Review Commission. Louisiana State

University Libraries provide links to federal agency websites. These and other partnerships are discussed on GPO's "FDLP Partnership" web page.[69]

Other Methods of Accessing Federal Government Information

Agency Dissemination Programs

Federal agencies frequently distribute their own publications (including those published by GPO). The Department of Agriculture, for example, supplies copies of its publications to all land-grant university libraries. Agencies maintain mailing lists of individuals or organizations interested in receiving their publications. Rising costs and the use of electronic dissemination have curtailed distribution of nonsolicited print publications. Agencies, however, often will provide single copies of publications upon request. Some publications are provided free of charge (particularly if the requester is a library); others are available as sales publications.

Several agencies host their own depository programs. These programs are much smaller in scale and scope than the FDPL. The Patent and Trademark Depository Library Program, administered by the Patent and Trademark Office (PTO), was established in 1871. Patent depositories pay an annual fee (currently $50) and receive copies of design, utility, reissue, and plant patents along with the *Official Gazette* and other indexes. The libraries are required to provide free public access to at least the last 20 years' worth of patent and trademark information and are encouraged to maintain more complete collections.[70] The Census Depository Program, operated by the Bureau of the Census, began in 1950. It has never numbered more than a few hundred libraries. Most of the member libraries are public libraries and tend to be smaller than those in the FDLP. Census depositories receive seven core titles and may select additional census titles. They are obligated to maintain materials for a minimum of five years and provide public access to them.[71]

The Census Bureau established the State Data Center Program in 1978 to aid in the dissemination of information from the 1970 Census of Population and Housing. A lead agency within each state coordinates the activities for that state. This agency receives copies of printed reports, microfiche, magnetic tapes, and CD-ROMs for distribution to affiliates. Many lead agencies compile census data and data from other sources to provide composite views of the state, counties, and smaller geographic areas. Affiliates, including libraries, are the public's initial point of contact. They provide access to census materials for their state (and often surrounding states) and may provide access to data stored on magnetic tapes.[72]

In the 1990s the federal government came to view the Internet, particularly the World Wide Web, as a cost-effective means of disseminating information. Agencies created websites. The sites vary in size and content, but all provide basic information about the agency, including its mission. Agencies provided links to electronic versions of some publications on these sites, and many agencies provided bibliographic citations to other publications. Some agencies found that demand for print copies of publications increased when electronic versions were posted.

Government Sales Programs and Clearinghouses

The National Technical Information Service (NTIS) is a self-sustaining agency functioning as a repository and clearinghouse for government-funded scientific and technical research. Its predecessors were the Publications Board (1945), the Office of Technical Services (1946-1964), and the Clearinghouse of Federal Scientific and Technical Information (1964-1970).[73] In addition to U.S. government-sponsored research and development reports it collects and translates research from foreign sources. Unlike GPO, which prints and distributes publications but does not maintain a collection, NTIS keeps a copy of every report it indexes. Until 1996, NTIS produced *Government Reports Announcements & Index* (*GRA&I*), which indexed the reports in its collection. Citations for more recent reports can be found on NTIS' website or in an online index (available from NTIS and several private sector vendors). Only a small percentage of reports indexed by NTIS are distributed through the FDLP. Copies of reports can be purchased from NTIS.

The Educational Resources Information Center (ERIC) was established in 1966 as a series of clearinghouses for acquisition and indexing of materials in educational fields. Federal agency publications account for only 10% of the materials in the ERIC databases. ERIC publishes two indexes, *Resources in Education* and *Current Index of Journals in Education.* Online versions of ERIC databases usually offer the ability to search the indexes concurrently. Microfiche copies of most publications indexed in *Resources in Education* are available for purchase either through subscription services or as individual titles. Although free versions of ERIC databases are available on the Internet, many libraries continue to subscribe to commercial versions.

There are a number of other clearinghouses and sales programs, such as the General Services Administration's Federal Consumer Information Center (FCIC). The FCIC distributes free and low-cost, consumer-oriented government publications. The Government Printing Office not only prints government publications and administers the FDLP, but also sells publications through its sales program. In the past, clearinghouses and sales programs periodically issued catalogs and lists of available publications. Today, the catalogs and many publications are available on the Web.

Private Sector

U.S. government information is not copyrighted. GPO is required by law to provide at cost copies of its electronic files, printing plates, and negatives to the private sector.[74] The private and nonprofit sectors repackage and distribute government information, often adding value to it. Examples of valueadded resources include Bernan's large-print edition of the *Statistical Abstracts of the United States* and Westlaw's *United States Code Annotated.* Both depository and nondepository libraries purchase government publications distributed via the private sector to augment their collections.

Two companies of special note are the Readex Corporation and Congressional Information Service (CIS). Readex began producing microcard copies of nondepository government publications in 1951. A few years later it added depository items. (Since 1981, the company has produced microfiche as opposed to microcards.) In addition to U.S. government information, Readex provides microformat and CD-ROM access to foreign and intergovernmental agency publications. *British Parliamentary Papers* and *United Nations Documents and Publications* and the CD-ROM *Index to United Nations Documents and Publications* are just a few examples of its array of publications.[75] CIS began publishing the CIS index in 1970. This index provides indexing and abstracting of congressional hearings, prints, reports, and documents. CIS sells archival-quality microfiche to accompany the index. The company branched into statistical publications in 1973 with the publication of the *American Statistics Index (ASI)* and accompanying fiche. Today CIS publishes a variety of indexes in print, CD-ROM, and online versions. It continues to sell microfiche versions of indexed publications.[76] Readex and CIS provide archival-quality microfiche. Microfiche distributed via the depository program is not archival-quality. Some libraries substitute the commercial versions for depository titles.

Freedom of Information Act Requests

Some U.S. government information has always been available to the public. It was in the last decades of the twentieth century that most government information was publicly accessible.[77] Traditionally access to government information was provided through publications. Much of the information collected by the government resides in agency files and is never published. Throughout the early to mid-20th century access to federal agency information largely was based on "need to know." Agencies were not required to disclose even such basic information as their missions, programs administered, mailing addresses, or business hours until the passage of the Administrative Procedures Act of 1946.[78] Agencies' refusal to disclose information extended so far as to refuse congressional access to agency files. Agencies cited a need to protect their records in the interests of national security and their standing as an equal branch of government not under the purview of Congress. Disputes over access to government information led to the Freedom of Information Act of 1966.[79]

The Freedom of Information Act was the first law to state that all individuals had the right to access government information. This act required government agencies refusing to disclose information to justify their actions and gave the public the right to challenge refusals in court. Lauded by the public, this act was opposed by many government agencies. They discouraged requests for information by requiring detailed descriptions of desired information and imposing substantial copying fees. Requests could take months and access to entire files routinely was denied if any part of the files was confidential.[80]

The act was amended twice in the 1970s, once over a presidential veto. These amendments required federal agencies to release information unless there was a specific law requiring the withholding of the information. If a portion of a file was confidential, the remainder of the file should be released. For the first time, courts had the right to *in camera* reviews of materials agencies sought to withhold. Copying fees could be lowered or waived if it were in the public interest to do so, and time limits for responses were imposed. These amendments and increased public awareness of the ability to submit Freedom of Information requests greatly increased the number of such requests.[81]

The Freedom of Information Act was weakened in the 1980s. Executive Order 12356 increased the amount of classified government information. Automatic declassification arrangements were eliminated and agencies could reclassify previously available information in the interests of national security. The CIA Information Act of 1984 exempted most CIA files from Freedom of Information Act requests. The Freedom of Information Act Amendments of 1986 (PL 99-507) allowed agencies to deny requests relating to criminal investigations, informant records, and certain FBI records. The amendments also restructured fees.[82]

The Electronic Freedom of Information Act Amendments of 1996 (PL 104-231) required federal agencies to create electronic reading rooms for frequently requested information. This included information that formerly was available for inspection and photocopying in agency reading rooms and information that had been requested and released under the Freedom of Information Act in the past. Agencies were required to compile and provide access to lists of the statutes they used to deny Freedom of Information Act requests. The amendments also required that when agencies released only portions of records, they indicate the places where deletions occurred. Whenever possible, agencies are to release information in the requested format, regardless of the format of the original.[83] Although not specifically required to do so, many agencies now provide this information on their web pages.

STATE AND LOCAL GOVERNMENT INFORMATION

State Government Information

Each state operates its own depository system for state government publications. These programs vary considerably. In some states, depositories receive and must retain all distributed publications. In other states, the depositories profile for, or select, desired publications.[84] Margaret T. Lane proves an overview and historical background of state depository programs in her book, *State Publications and Depository Libraries: A Reference Handbook.* She found evidence of state depository libraries as early as 1902; many states, however, established their programs in the 1980s.[85] Most state depository programs are limited to libraries within the state.

State agencies often provide free copies of their publications upon request. The *Monthly Checklist of State Publications*, produced between 1910 and 1994, listed state publications sent to the Library of Congress. State libraries often produce lists of the publications they have received. They also add bibliographic records for the publications to the OCLC database.[86] State publications of, a statistical nature are indexed in the *CIS Statistical Reference Index.*

Each state publishes, or contracts with the private sector for publication of laws, regulations, and court decisions. Commercial editions of state laws and court decisions are available. State regulations can be harder to locate.[87] State legislative information has been available electronically since the 1970s. Few services, however, provided public access, and most were subscription services.[88]

Local Government Information

Local government information can be difficult to locate. Local government information, especially for smaller governments, rarely is published. The public must instead visit the city, town, or township hall and may have to complete Freedom of Information Act requests.[89] When local governments do publish information, publication runs tend to be small. The publications rarely are marketed.[90] A few states include local government publications in their state depository programs.[91] In most cases, however, librarians collecting local government publications must obtain them directly from the governmental units.[92]

State and Local Government Information on the Internet

By 1997, all states and 48% of cities with populations greater than 100,000 had official presences on the Web.[93] A sizable number of unofficial sites also existed. The primary focus of official sites has been economic development. To this end, information about tourism, education, business, community planning activities, and general economic development is readily available.[94] State sites usually provide information about the three branches of government. The amount and arrangement of information vary by state. Legislative branch pages often include legislative calendars, the text of bills, voting records, and legislators' addresses.[95] The number and content of state and local government websites continue to expand.

FOREIGN AND INTERNATIONAL GOVERNMENT INFORMATION

Foreign Government Information

A number of libraries in the United States are Canadian Depository Libraries. The Canadian program is similar to the FDLP. It has selective and 100% depositories. Unlike FDLP selective depositories, Canadian selective depositories do not profile for desired categories of publications. Instead they receive a *Weekly Checklist of Canadian Government Publications.* The libraries select the items they wish to receive and return the order form. The selection process is labor-intensive, but the libraries only receive the items they truly want.[96] Another important difference between the FDLP and Canadian Depository Program is that in Canada maps are distributed under a separate program.[97]

Obtaining publications from other countries can be difficult. Few countries have established programs like those of Canada and the United States.[98] Many foreign governments do not publish their records. This is particularly true of Third World countries. Budgetary limitations may prevent publication, as may a desire to keep government operations secret.[99] Libraries or individuals wishing to acquire foreign government publications must first identify the desired publications. They must then find a distributing publisher. Some governments, Great Britain, for example, have national publishers. Other governments contract with the private sector for publication.[100]

International Government Organizations Information

Many international government organizations (IGOs) maintain depository programs. One of the largest programs is that of the United Nations. Under its depository program, one library in each of 142 countries, usually the National Library, receives United Nations publications free of charge. Other United Nations depositories pay an annual fee to be part of the program. Currently there are 378 United Nations Depositories worldwide.[101] Other IGOs with depository programs include the European Union, World Trade Organization, and the World Health Organization.[102]

IGP depositories do not receive all publications issued by the IGO. Also, unlike the U.S. government, IGOs make a distinction between "publications" which are intended for public release, and "documents", which are intended for internal agency use. IGO policies regarding public access to documents vary. Individuals and libraries sometimes can obtain free copies of publications from the IGO. Publications can be purchased through the IGO's sales office or from a commercial publisher. Readex and Chadwyk-Healy market microform and CD-ROM versions of many IGO publications. Bernan sells many print volumes.[103] Detailed information about individual IGOs and their publications can be found in *International Information: Documents,*

Publications, and Electronic Information of International Government Organizations.[104]

Foreign and International Government Organizations Information on the Internet

Foreign governments and IGOs increasingly are using the Internet as a means of disseminating public information. The amount of information provided varies by country or IGO. One author has noted that even some countries that do not publish information in traditional formats are maintaining Internet presences.[105] IGOs see the Internet as a cost-effective means of increasing public access. They are providing access to materials not previously released to the public.[106] IGOs with especially strong Internet presences include the United Nations and the European Union.

BIBLIOGRAPHIC ACCESS TO GOVERNMENT INFORMATION

Monthly Catalog of Government Information

Bibliographic access to government information has long been an issue. After all, people can't use the material if they don't know it exists. Under the Printing Act of 1895, GPO was required to produce a monthly list of nonclassified publications printed during the previous month. This list, *The Monthly Catalog of Government Publications,* included both depository and sales titles. For many years, the *Monthly Catalog* was the primary source for identifying U.S. government publications.

From 1895 through June 1976, the *Monthly Catalog* consisted of short entries and a combined author, title, and subject index. In July 1976, GPO began using the Anglo-American Cataloging Rules and MARC format to create the *Monthly Catalog.*[107] This vastly increased the quality of the entries. The number of indexes and indexed fields also was increased. GPO added the records to OCLC and supplied magnetic tapes to the private sector. Vendors began marketing CD-ROM and online versions of the *Monthly Catalog.* They began offering tapes of GPO records and catalog cards tailored to libraries' GPO profiles. For the first time, many libraries found full card cataloging and electronic records for documents to be economically feasible.

GPO began cataloging Internet-accessible government publications in 1996. By the end of 1997, it had cataloged 2,300 of the online titles identified in GPO's "Browse Electronic Titles" web page.[108] In 1998, GPO assigned Persistent Universal Resource Locators (PURLS) as a means of assuring access to online resources. The PURLS provide a link between the bibliographic record and the resource in case of changing URLS.[109]

OCLC Bibliographic Database

Although GPO did not begin contributing records to OCLC until mid-1976, the database contains many records for older U.S. Government publications. Libraries that purchased government publications and depositories that integrated depository materials with other library collections contributed most of the records. The records vary in quality and usually lack SuDoc numbers. They are, however, very useful for verifying the existence of publications. Currently, there are several projects under way to retrospectively catalog pre-1976 depository materials.[110] Libraries also have contributed records for state, local, foreign, and IGO publications.

Other Indexes and Guides

A vast number of indexing resources can be used to identify and locate government information resources. Government agencies often create bibliographies and catalogs of their publications. The private sector's practice of contracting with the government or purchasing government information to create value-added products was discussed above. In the last decade, numerous guides to government resources on the Internet have been published. General indexes often include some citations to government publications, for example, PAIS International. Produced by Public Affairs Information Service, it indexes articles in English, French, German, Italian, Spanish, and Portuguese on topics of public concern. These topics include agriculture, business, economics, environment, government, law, political science, and public administration. Many U.S., foreign, and intergovernmental agency publications are among the titles it indexes. Both print and electronic versions are available.

THE IMPACT OF THE INTERNET

Changing Role for Libraries

In the past, people needing government information had to go to the information. Many public and academic libraries collected some government publications. Depository libraries, however, bore primary responsibility for providing public access to published government information. They maintained collections of print and microformat publications and supporting reference materials. Librarians provided assistance in locating desired information.

Today much government information is available on the Internet. Most of this information can be freely accessed by anyone with a computer connected to the Internet. In 1999, 42% of the adult population of the United States had access to the Internet at home or work.[111] Libraries serve as access providers for the remaining population. A 1998 survey found that 73% of public libraries provided public access to the Internet. Virtually all academic libraries provide Internet access.[112] Nondepository libraries have less need to refer their patrons to depository libraries. They instead, rely on online government resources.[113]

Depository libraries are shifting their focus from acquisition of government publications to provision of access to government information regardless of format. Unlike other libraries, which may select their own access policies, depository libraries are obligated to provide free public access to government information on the Internet. Access goes beyond providing public computer workstations. Librarians increasingly are acting as facilitators. Government information on the Internet is decentralized. Librarians are creating web pages to guide patrons to recommended resources and commonly requested information. They are adding bibliographic records for Internet-accessible publications to their library catalogs. Librarians also are providing assistance in using the resources. For example, when working with printed census volumes, librarians showed patrons how to use tables of contents to located desired statistical tables. When using the Census Bureau website, librarians may need to assist patrons in creating their own statistical tables. Librarians are supplying technological support. They answer questions about computer hardware and software requirements and how to retrieve data from government sites.[114] Often this assistance is provided over the telephone or through email.

Depository libraries continue to collect tangible government publications. Some government information is not available on the Internet. Other publications are easier to use in printed formats. Fewer of these publications are being issued in physical formats through depository programs. Libraries purchase, if possible, those publications their primary patrons most need. Many depository libraries, especially regional depositories, maintain historical government publications. Libraries will continue to archive these materials.

Issues and Concerns

The archiving and preservation of government information in electronic formats are of primary concern. Historically, regional depository libraries were responsible for maintaining copies of all titles distributed to depository libraries. Responsibility for preservations of online government information is unclear. Some depositories are working in partnership with federal agencies to ensure information is not lost. GPO is committed to providing permanent access to selected publications on its GPO Access website. The future of GPO itself, however, is uncertain.

Archived electronic information must be saved in usable formats. Many current electronic publications were created using proprietary software such as Adobe Acrobat. The problem with these files is that as computer technology advances, backward compatibility is lost. For example, many 1990 Census of Population and Housing CD-ROMs used the DOS operating system.

Libraries that have upgraded their computers are experiencing difficulty running these products.

Cost of access is another issue. Computer technology advances very rapidly. Libraries must constantly upgrade equipment and software. Libraries also must hire technical support staff and librarians with skills to handle both traditional and electronic resources. Libraries increasingly are subscribing to commercial databases that provide more user-friendly interfaces than government sites. They also are purchasing tangible materials that in the past, they received free of charge through depository programs. Some costs are being passed on to the public in the form of per page costs for computer printouts.

There are other areas of issue and concern. The media have reported several instances of computer hackers breaking into and altering government data files. The authenticity of government information is important. Computer viruses have caused some government servers to be shut down. Lost telecommunications connections result in denied access. Privacy issues also must be addressed. Telecommunications software allows tracking of people accessing specific Internet sites. The public must be assured these applications will not be misused.[115]

CONCLUSION

The Internet has had a profound impact on the accessibility and availability of government information. The U.S. Government views the Internet as a cost-effective means of disseminating public information. Publications once distributed through the Federal Depository Library Program are migrating to agency websites. Statistical agencies are producing fewer reports. They are, instead, placing data files on servers for public manipulation. U.S. federal government information is not copyrighted; the private and nonprofit sectors are providing added value sites (often for a fee). This decentralization of government information has spread beyond the federal government. State, local, and foreign governments and international government organizations also are creating Internet presences. Much government information can now be accessed by anyone with a computer connected to the Internet.

Government information on the Internet is not necessarily easier to find or use than traditional formats. Libraries facilitate access to online government information in a number of ways. They add bibliographic records for some Internet publications to their library catalogs. They subscribe to private sector resources offering more user-friendly interfaces than government sites. Librarians create web pages guiding users to recommended or frequently requested sites. Depository libraries, in particular, provide a place where those who otherwise lack access to the Internet can access online government information.

NOTES

1. Stephen B. Gould, "An Intellectual Utility for Science and Technology: The National Research and Education Network," *Government Information Quarterly* 7, no. 4 (1990): 415-425.
2. Herbert N. Foerstel, *Freedom of Information and the Right to Know: The Origins and Applications of the Freedom of Information Act* (Westport, CT: Greenwood Press, 1999), pp. 10-14.
3. LeRoy C. Schwartzkopf, "Depository Libraries and Public Access," in *Collection Development and Public Access of Government Documents*, ed. Peter Hernon (Westport, CT: Meckler, 1981), p. 9.
4. Peter Hernon, Charles R. McClure, and Gary R. Purcell, *GPO's Depository Library Program: A Descriptive Analysis* (Norwood, NJ: Ablex, 1985), p. 4.
5. Ibid.
6. Government Printing Office (GPO), *Instructions to Depository Libraries* (Washington, DC: GPO, 1992), p. iv.
7. *Keeping America Informed: Federal Depository Library Program,* February 7, 2000. [Cited May 13, 2000] (URL http://www.access.gpo.gov/su_docs/dpos/keepam.html).
8. GPO *Instructions to Depositories*, p. 2.
9. Government Printing Office, *Depository Library Manual* (Washington, DC: GPO, 1993).
10. "Types of Publications Included in the Depository Library Program," *Administrative Notes* 11, no. 16 (1990): 11-16.
11. Judith Schiek Robinson, *Tapping the Government Grapevine,* 2nd ed. (Phoenix, AZ: Oryx Press, 1993), p. 29.
12. "Types of Publications Excluded from the Depository Library Program," *Administrative Notes* 11, no. 16 (1990): 17-18.
13. Robinson, *Tapping*, p. 5.
14. Harold B. Shill and Sandra K. Peterson, "Is Government Information in Your Library's Future?" *College and Research Libraries News* (September 1989): 649-656.
15. Michael Waldo, "An Historic Look at the Debate Over How to Organize Federal Government Documents in Depository Libraries," *Government Publications Review* 4, no. 4 (1977): 319-329.
16. Hernon, McClure, and Purcell, GPO's p. 2.
17. Ibid.
18. Sara D. Knapp, "OMB A-130: A Policy Which Could Affect Your Reference Service," *Reference Librarian* 20 (1988): 35-54.
19. Peter Hernon, "Publications and Information of the United States Government in an Electronic Age," *Serials Review* 12 (Summer/Fall 1986): 133-147.

20. Peter Hernon, "Information Dissemination as Reflected in U.S. Government Policy and Practice," *The Internet and Higher Education* 1, no. 1 (1998): 59-81.
21. Harold B. Shill and Lisa R. Stimatz, "Government Information in Academic Libraries: New Options for the Electronic Age," *Journal of Academic Librarianship* 25, no. 2 (1999): 94-104.
22. Charles P. Bourne, "On-line Systems: History, Technology, and Economics," *Journal of the American Society for Information Science* 31 (1980): 155-160.
23. Ibid., pp. 156-157.
24. Linda Futato, "Online Bibliographic Database Searching for Government Documents Collections," *Government Publications Review* 9 (1982): 311-322.
25. "GPO Dissemination of Federal Agency Publications in Electronic Format," *Administrative Notes* 10, no. 15 (July 31 1989) : pp. 5-11.
26. Charles R. McClure, "Technology in Government Document Collections: Current Status, Impacts, and Prospects," *Government Publications Review* 9 (1982): 255-276.
27. John C. Beresford and Deborah S. Pomerance, "Federal Policy about Machine-Readable Statistical Documents," *Government Publications Review* 8A (1981): 221-229.
28. Judith S. Rowe, "Machine-Readable Data Files of Government Publications," *Government Publications Review* 5, no. 2 (1978): 195-197.
29. Technical Information Service and Office of Federal Statistical Policy and Standards, *Directory of Federal Statistical Data Files* (Washington, DC: U.S. Department of Commerce, 1981).
30. Joseph W. Duncan, "Accessing Social Statistics," *Library Trends* 30 (Winter 1982): 363-376.
31. Barton M. Clark, "Social Science Data Archives and Libraries: A View to the Future," *Library Trends* 30 (Winter 1982): 505-509.
32. Jim Jacobs. "U.S. Government Computer Bulletin Boards: A Modest Proposal for Reform," *Government Publications Review* 17 (1990): 393-396.
33. Susan M. Ryan, *Downloading Democracy: Government Information in an Electronic Age* (Cresskill, NJ: Hampton Press, 1996), p. 141.
34. Graeme Browning, "Dueling Over Data," *National Journal* (1993): 2880-2884.
35. Ryan, *Downloading*, p. 8.
36. U.S. Congress. Office of Technology Assessment, *Informing the Nation: Federal Information Dissemination in an Electronic Age.* (Washington, DC: GPO, 1988), pp. 257-260.
37. Harold B. Shill and Lisa R. Stimatz, "Government Information in Academic Libraries: New Options for the Electronic Age," *Journal of Academic Librarianship* 25, no. 2 (1999): 94-104.

38. Jackie C. Shane, "Administering World Wide Web Home Pages and Gopher Menus," in *Finding Government Information on the Internet*, ed. John Maxymuk (New York: Neal-Schuman, 1995), pp. 45-62.
39. CERN-European Organization for Nuclear Research, "History and Growth." [cited April 8, 2000]; (URL http://public.web.cern.ch/Public/ACHIEVEMENTS/WEB/history.html).
40. Ibid.
41. David L. Wilson, "Array of New Tools Is Designed to Make It Easier to Find and Retrieve Information on the Internet," *Chronicle of Higher Education.* May 26, 1993, pp. A17-19.
42. John T. Cocklin, "FEDWORLD, THOMAS, and CBDNET: United States Federal Government Information Dissemination in the 1990s," *Journal of Government Information* 25, no. 5 (1998): 397-412.
43. Jackson Morton, "Census on the Internet," *American Demographics* (March 1995): 52-53.
44. Duncan Aldrich, "The GPO and the Federal Depository Library Program in the Information Age: Past Present, and Future," in *Finding Government Information on the Internet*, ed. John Maxymuk (New York: Neal-Schuman, 1995): pp. 3-21.
45. Raeann Dossett, "The Online Interactive Service of GPO ACCESS: WAIS and SWAIS," in *Finding Government Information on the Internet*, pp. 63-75.
46. Greg R. Notess, "LC's Debut on the Internet," *Database* (October 1993): 84.
47. Cocklin, "FEDWORLD," p. 403-405.
48. Greg R. Notess, *Government Information on the Internet*, 2nd ed. (Lanham, MD: Bernan, 1998), p. xii.
49. "GPO Dissemination of Federal Agency Publications in Electronic Format," *Administrative Notes* 10, no. 15 (July 31, 1989), pp. 5-11
50. Ryan, Downloading; pp. 40-42.
51. "Recommended Minimum Technical Guidelines for Federal Depository Libraries," *Administrative Notes* 12, no. 19 (August 31, 1991), pp. 1-3.
52. "Recommended Minimum Technical Guidelines for Federal Depository Libraries," *Administrative Notes* 14, no. 19 (September 15, 1993), pp. 9-10.
53. Ryan, Downloading; p. 172.
54. Robert E. Dugan and Anthony Cipriano, "Making It Happen in a Depository Library: Those Pesky CD-ROMs," *Government Information Quarterly* 10, no. 3 (1993): 341-355.
55. Government Printing Office, *The Electronic Federal Depository Library Program: Transition Plans FY 1996-FY 1998* (Washington, DC: GPO, 1995).
56. "Public Access to Electronic Government Information Provided Through Federal Depository Libraries," *Administrative Notes* 17, no. 7 (May 15, 1996).

57. Lorraine Kram, "Why Continue to Be a Depository Library If It Is All on the Internet Anyway," *Government Information Quarterly* 15, no. 1 (1998): 57-71.
58. Robert E. Dugan and Ellen M. Dodsworth, "Costing Out a Depository Library: What Free Information?" *Government Information Quarterly* 11, no. 3 (1994): 261-284.
59. Kram, "Why Continue," pp. 64-65.
60. "GPO Response to Proposed Appropriations Cuts," *Administrative Notes* 21, no. 8 (May15, 2000): 1-8.
61. "FDLP Guidelines on Substituting Electronic for Tangible Versions of Depository Publications," *Administrative Notes* 20, no. 9 (May 15, 1999): 2-4.
62. "Update to List of Classes – Miscellaneous," *Administrative Notes Technical Supplement* 3, 3 (March 31, 1996)
63. "LPS Update," *Administrative Notes* 21, no. 6 (April 15, 2000): 8.
64. Julia Wallace, "Why Government Information?" *DttP* 28, no. 1 (2000): 17-23.
65. Diane K. Kovacs, "GovDoc-L: An Online Intellectual Community of Documents Librarians and Other Individuals Concerned with Access to Government Information," *Government Publications Review* 17 (1990): 411-420.
66. Ibid.
67. Shane, "Administering," p 46.
68. "GPO, State Department, University of Illinois-Chicago Join in FDLP Partnership," *Administrative Notes* 18, no.10 (1997): 3.
69. Government Printing Office, "FDLP Partnerships." [Cited May 25, 2000.] Available from the World Wide Web (URL http://www.access.gpo.gov/su_docs/dpos/partner.html).
70. Patent and Trademark Office, "The Patent and Trademark Depository Library Program. [cited May 1, 2000] (URL http://www.uspto.gov/web/offices/ac/ido/ptdl/ptdlgen.htm).
71. Peter Hernon, "Discussion Forum: The Census Depository Library Program," *Government Information Quarterly* 8, no. 1 (1991): 1-10.
72. Mary Redmond, "State Data Centers: Improving Access to Census Information," *Government Information Quarterly* 3, no. 3 (1986): 291-303.
73. Joe Morehead and Mary Fetzer, *Introduction to United States Government Information Sources* 4th ed. (Englewood, CO: Libraries Unlimited, 1992), p. 353.
74. Francis J. Buckley Jr., "GPO's Government Information Dissemination Programs: Sharing the Wealth," *DttP* 28, no. 1 (2000): 13-16.
75. Carolyn Dryer, "Readex United Nations Documents and Publications: A History of International Documentation Partnership," *International Information: Documents, Publications, and Electronic Information of International Government Organizations*. Ed. Peter I Hajnal (Englewood, CO: Libraries Unlimited, 1997), pp.347-353.

76. Susan Jover, "Index to International Statistics and Other Guides to IGO Information Published by Congressional Information Service, Inc.," in *International Information,* pp. 325-332.
77. J. Timothy Sprehe, "Government Information: From Inaccessibility to Your Desktop and Back Again," *Journal of the American Society for Information Science* 50, no. 4 (1999): 340-345.
78. Ibid.
79. Harold C. Relyea, "Public Access through the Freedom of Information and Privacy Acts," in *Federal Information Policies in the 1980's: Conflicts and Issues*, ed. Peter Hernon and Charles R. McClure (Norwood, NJ: Ablex, 1987), pp. 55-56.
80. Foerstel, *Freedom*, pp. 42-45.
81. Ibid., pp. 48-49.
82. Ibid., pp. 55-56.
83. Kristin R. Eschenfelder, John C. Beachboard, Charles R. McClure, and Steven K. Wyman, "Assessing U.S. Federal Government Websites," *Government Information Quarterly* 14, no. 2 (1997): 173-189.
84. Margaret T. Lane, *State Publications and Depository Libraries: A Reference Handbook* (Westport, CT: Greenwood Press, 1981), p. 174.
85. Ibid.
86. Sharon Walbridge, "OCLC and Government Documents Collections," *Government Publications Review* 9 (1982): 277-287.
87. Robinson, *Tapping*, pp. 176-177.
88. Maurie Caitlin Kelly, "State and Local Government Information Issues and Initiatives," in *Finding Government Information on the Internet*, ed. John Maxymuk (New York: Neal-Schuman, 1995), pp. 173-188.
89. Ibid.
90. Carolyn C. Sherayko and Diane H. Smith, "Acquisition of Government Information Resources," in *Management of Government Information Resources in Libraries*, ed. Diane H. Smith (Englewood, CO: Libraries Unlimited, 1993), pp. 31-42.
91. Lane, *State Publications*, pp. 114-115.
92. Sherayko and Smith, "Acquisitions," p. 40
93. Genie N. L. Stowers, "Becoming Cyberactive: State and Local Governments on the World Wide Web," *Government Information Quarterly* 16, no. 2 (1999): 111-127.
94. Ibid.
95. "There's Lots on the Web," *State Legislatures* 23 (January 23, 1997): 5.
96. Sherayko and Smith, pp. 38-39.
97. Carol A. Singer, "BGSU's Canadian Documents Collection," *Docs Prescriptions* 51 (Spring 2000): 5-6.
98. Sherayko and Smith, "Acquisitions," p. 39.
99. Catherine W. Lee, "The Impact of Electronic Globalization on Foreign Documents Collections in the United States," *Journal of Government Information* 23, no. 3 (1997): 203-212.

100. Sherayko and Smith, p. 41.
101. United Nations, Dag Hammerskjöiid Library, "United Nations Depository Libraries." [Cited April 24, 2000] (URL http://www.un.org/ Depts/dhl/dls.htm).
102. Peter I. Hajnal, "Collection Development," in *International Information: Documents, Publications, and Electronic Information of International Government Organizations*, ed. Peter I. Hajnal (Englewood, CO: Libraries Unlimited, 1997), pp. 401-422.
103. Ibid.
104. Peter I. Hajnal, *International Information.*
105. Wallace, "Why Government," p. 18.
106. Hajnal, *International Information,* p. 417.
107. Joe Morehead, "Inordinate Fondess: The Feds and the Internet," *The Reference Librarian* 57 (1997): 227-238.
108. "Cataloging Branch Update," *Administrative Notes* 19, no. 2 (1998): 5-6.
109. Ibid., no. 7 (1998): 42- 43.
110. Jan Swanbeck, Marda Johnson, Dan Coyle, Carolyn Kohler, Tim Byrne, and Arlene Weible, *Cataloging Pre-1976 U.S. Government Publications: Stakeholders and Strategies Summary.* January 11, 1998. [Cited May 6, 2000] (URL http://www2.lib.udel.edu/godort/cataloging/ summary.htm).
111. "Internet Access and Usage and Online Service Usage: 1999," in *Statistical Abstract of the United States* (Washington, DC: GPO, 1999), p. 582.
112. American Library Association, *"How Many Libraries are on the Internet?"* May 6, 1999 [Cited May 25, 2000] (URL http://www.ala.org/ library/fact26.html).
113. Shill and Stimatz, "Government Information," p. 98.
114. Joan K. Lippincott and Joan F. Cheverie, "The 'Blur' of Federal Information and Services: Implications for University Libraries," *Journal of Government Information* 26, no. 1 (1999): 25-31.
115. Ibid.

CHAPTER TEN

THE INTERNET AND INFORMATION SERVICES FOR THE SCIENCES

Carolyn Mills and Jonathan Nabe

INTRODUCTION

Many of the impacts of the Internet felt by science librarians are the same as those felt by other librarians, as described in previous chapters. Web catalogs, electronic databases and journals, publisher and vendor resources, interlibrary communications and lending, scholarly Internet resources, email and listservs all impact science librarianship in the same way as any other area of the field. However, because of the nature of the types of research which science libraries support and the types of scholarly communication through which that research is published, disseminated, and accessed, the *degree* of impact is often higher, and issues unique to the scientific disciplines are raised. In this chapter, we examine ways in which the Internet has changed science librarianship and the access to scientific information.

The Internet has been used extensively in the scientific community from early on. Indeed, the first electronic bulletin boards and journals were scientific ones. It is here that preprint archives were developed, electronic communities of scholars created, and multimedia applications on web pages exploited. New uses for the Internet are still being seen for the first time from within the sciences, note CrossRef, an effort among numerous science, technology and medical (STM) publishers to link the references among fulltext journals, which will have profound implications for librarians, faculty, and students.

Academic research in the sciences is heavily dependent upon journals, much more so than the humanities and social sciences. This cardinal fact about the field implies a great deal about the issues surrounding the use of the Internet within the sciences: the cost of electronic versus print publications, the necessity of developing reliable archiving methods, the potential for alternative publishing ventures, the power of preprint and reprint archives (and the subsequent impetus for developing their interoperability), and issues of access and ownership. It is with the latter that we begin, for it is here that the fundamental problems - and solutions - of the Internet make their greatest impact on science libraries and librarians.

ACCESS VERSUS OWNERSHIP AND THE INTERNET

Access versus ownership is certainly not a new concept, and it is not limited to the sciences. But the impact of the Internet on access versus ownership issues has been profoundly felt in science libraries. In brief, there has been a gradual but major change of focus in collection development in the sciences. The traditional library effort has been to attempt to own everything potentially needed by researchers and students, and to house anything users could possibly need within the walls of the library so that it is always available for use. No library has ever really been able to achieve that goal, though some have come impressively close. Libraries have traditionally been seen as storehouses of information and librarians as the caretakers of that information, whether in books, journals, or other formats. Because libraries could not collect comprehensively in all areas, some subject areas were supplemented by borrowing from the collections of other libraries through interlibrary loan, which has been in existence since at least the 1930s.

Over the past 20 or more years, a number of changes have eroded that policy of ownership, especially in the sciences. The reasons for these changes are familiar to most science librarians. Spiraling subscription prices force libraries to buy fewer titles for more money. Stagnant library budgets force libraries to cut subscriptions even further. A seemingly endless array of new journal titles requires researchers to have access to even more journal titles to adequately cover their fields. Journal publishing in many fields of science have migrated from society and not-for-profit publishers to commercially oriented for-profit publishers, increasing the likelihood that subscription costs will continue to escalate. The result is that researchers and students need access to more journal titles than ever before at the same time that libraries are less and less able to provide that information in-house.

The inevitable outcome is that libraries have had to cut journal titles, especially in the sciences, where costs and inflation rates are the highest. However, the need for information is still there and must be met. The access versus ownership model allows libraries to provide for the information needs of users by either purchasing the information and owning it in the collection *or* by accessing information not owned through either interlibrary loan (the borrowing of materials from other participating educational institutions) or document delivery (the purchase of information from commercial providers). For the purposes of this section, interlibrary loan and document delivery services will be referred to as DD/ILL. In the access versus ownership model, the library is serving the needs of its users through whichever means makes more sense, in terms of both collection development and financial feasibility.

Interlibrary Loan and Document Delivery

When a library cuts journal titles, there are actually two different informational needs that are no longer served. The first, more obvious one is the loss of the articles contained in the journal. The second is the decreased potential for browsing, the serendipitous gathering of information from glancing through recently arrived journals on a regular basis. Both losses have significant impact on information dissemination.

If a journal is no longer subscribed to, library patrons no longer have access to the full text at the library. This can be relieved to some degree by using DD/ILL to replace that information. Use of software to transmit documents over the Internet has radically transformed the ability of DD/ILL staff to provide for the needs of library users in terms of document transmission quality and speed of delivery.

Interlibrary loan is certainly not limited to the sciences. However, the sciences are much more focused on journals than are the humanities or social sciences, and journal cancellations have hit the sciences especially hard. Therefore, this trend toward dependence upon interlibrary loan is especially significant for science patrons and science librarianship. As journal titles have been progressively cut over the past 20 years, interlibrary loan is relied upon more and more, so that it has moved from an occasional supplementary service to a central cornerstone of information provision for scientific research. The past 10 years especially have seen an increasing reliance on interlibrary loan, and although science materials form the bulk of journal requests through interlibrary loan, the technology available until recently for transmitting documents has made it a poor replacement for print access. For years, photocopiers and facsimiles were the dominant means of sending documents from one institution to another. Reproduction of text and especially of graphics was often of very poor quality and generally very slow.

In the early 1990s a software product called Ariel was introduced to academic interlibrary loan. Ariel is a software tool created by the Research Libraries Group. This product enables articles and other materials to be transmitted (via FTP or email) over the Internet anywhere in the world, so long as the computer at the other end has the software as well. DD/ILL offices use the software both to send and receive requested documents to and from other participating institutions and commercial providers and also to distribute documents to requesters within an institution. For example, an article requested by a chemistry professor is sent from the lending institution to the DD/ILL office of the professor's institution via Ariel. The receiving DD/ILL office can then turn around and Ariel the document right on to the requesting professor at his desktop, provided he has either the Ariel-receiving software loaded on his or her PC or has an MIME-enabled email system and access to TIFF-viewing software. Therefore the requesting professor can potentially receive the document within minutes of its transmission from the lending institution. This is a dramatic increase in speed of delivery from the days when requesters had to wait days for delivery of a journal article through both the U.S. mail and campus mail systems. This speed of delivery makes the "access" part of access versus ownership much more useful to researchers and students.

Ariel transmission of documents over the Internet has also improved the quality of documents. With a scanner, DD/ILL office staff can scan directly from the original document to create an electronic version. This eliminates the photocopying step, which was necessary when sending documents either in the mail or via facsimile. Scanning produces a much higher resolution product, providing significantly higher-quality graphics and text. Poor graphics quality has been one of the major impediments to the use of DD/ILL to supply journal articles in the sciences, and the introduction of Internet-compatible software has gone a long way toward improving the acceptability of DD/ILL services in the sciences.

A second software product, Prospero, has recently been developed which complements the Ariel software. Prospero allows DD/ILL office staff to import incoming requested documents sent via Ariel, translate the document files to PDF files, and then post the requested documents on a secure Web server. With the Prospero system, library patrons who have requested an article no longer have to worry about having Ariel software on their own machines or having MIME compliant email. When the document is received and posted on the server, the Prospero software automatically sends email to requesters, alerting them that requested items are available and where to find them. Patrons are provided with PIN numbers for secure access. Therefore, any patron with access to email and the World Wide Web can receive incoming documents through the DD/ILL system at the desktop. The convenience and privacy of this improvement are only beginning to be felt as the Prospero software is integrated into academic, government and commercial DD/ILL systems around the world.

Current Awareness

The decreased ability to browse is the second negative impact of journal cancellations on information dissemination. So long as journals are available in print, scientists and students regularly scan new issues for interesting information as a means of keeping up-to-date in their fields and related areas. Once print titles disappear from the shelves, that kind of information gathering is no longer possible, and current awareness services come into play. Printed current awareness products have been available for years, as collections of reproduced tables of contents from journals within selected subject areas. The Institute for Scientific Information (ISI) had weekly printed table of contents publications for the life sciences, physics, and chemical

& earth sciences that science libraries kept on shelves as a means of keeping their patrons up to date on titles not owned. However, patrons had to come to the library to use them and more importantly had to *remember* that it had to be done.

The Internet has made available electronic alternatives to browsing in print journals or table of contents collections. There are many types of current awareness products available, but most incorporate some similar properties. In most products, users store personal contact information (such as an email address) in patron profiles. Users generally have two kinds of searches available: table of contents searches by journal name, which closely duplicate the old print current awareness products which libraries used to subscribe to, and keyword searches, which look for keywords in the titles (and sometimes abstracts) of new citations. Current awareness services also must have at least one database available to search as it is regularly updated with new information. Lastly, current awareness services deliver information to the user conveniently, generally through email but also sometimes via facsimile.

Electronic current awareness services are especially important in the sciences for several reasons. First, even without the collision between rising journal costs and decreasing journal budgets, no institution could hope to provide every scientist with every title needed. Current awareness services provide broad journal access to scientists in a scope that was not possible prior to their inception, except perhaps in the largest, best-funded research institutions. Second, current awareness services provide information quickly and conveniently. Instead of waiting several months for an open afternoon to spend at the library, researchers and students get results in their offices and labs on a regular basis. There is no need for them to remember to pursue the information; it comes to them via the Internet at the location where they spend most of their time. Third, citations are provided in electronic format. Many scientists keep their own records of research done in their areas of research by collecting relevant citations into databases. They use citation management software (like EndNote, ProCite or Reference Manager) to store records, manage them, and access them as needed. Electronic current awareness services generally provide new records in easily convertible formats which can be stored in these personal "libraries" of citation information by busy researchers for later perusal.

Commercial sources, like CARL Uncover and ISI's Current Contents, provide for the bulk of academic current awareness needs. Software vendors, such as Ovid and Silver Platter, provide current awareness platforms from which to search databases which they provide, such as Medline, Current Contents, Inspec, Agricola, CINHAL, and many other databases in the sciences, social sciences, and arts and humanities. An institutional subscription to these products allows any faculty, student, or staff members to store the information they wish to have searched and to receive the results regularly via email. The software products vary in how they manage patron profiles and search database records, but overall the quality of service provided is quite high. A further enhancement which will no doubt be expanded upon in the future is the increase of links between current awareness products and document delivery services. Several examples are CARL's Uncover Reveal and its document delivery system, and ISI's Current Contents database and Genuine Article document delivery service.

Current awareness-like services are also available directly over the Web to individual users. These may not have all the components of the more classic campuswide commercial services, but they are quite valuable in their own right and certainly are early versions of more sophisticated products to come. They use email to deliver their products right to the user on a regular basis, all the user has to do is subscribe.

A good example of a science news awareness product is ScienceWeek, a weekly summary of science research and policy distributed via email (www.scienceweek.com). ScienceWeek is edited by a professor emeritus from the University of Chicago and is a product of Spectrum Press, Inc. The service is available for a subscription fee, though contents are archived at the site for free. While the information received cannot be tailored to an individual scientist's interests, this is an example of a valuable source for browsing for new developments, with citation information included for the source documents.

Two resources are available for free which are excellent sources of information about new scientific websites. The first and better known site is the Internet Scout Project's Science and Engineering biweekly report for faculty, students, staff, and librarians in the life sciences, physical sciences, and engineering. The sites are chosen by librarians and other content specialists. Each report has two parts, a selection of Internet sites and information on published resources like books and journals as well as conference and grant announcements, and other information. The report is meant to be a sampling of information, not an exhaustive study. It can alert researchers, students, and librarians to new and interesting information on the Internet and in their professions which they otherwise might have missed. The Internet Scout Project, of which the Science and Engineering Report is part, is housed at the Department of Computer Sciences at the University of Wisconsin-Madison and has more than 45,000 subscribers via email. An archive of previous reports is stored at the site and available to all users for free.

The second example of a free source of interesting scientific information on the Web providing current awareness information is a lesser-known product from an employee of the National Science Foundation. (NSF) Stephanie Bianchi, an NSF librarian, publishes her newsletter for staff at NSF but also makes an abbreviated version of it available on the Web (www-sul.stanford.edu/hosted.html) and via email delivery for the general public. It is published once or twice a month and includes a wide range of topics that might be of interest to scientists and those personnel who support them (such as librarians). Recent issues have included information about science websites, analysis of search engines, electronic journals in the sciences, federal budget news, and grant reviewing. Both of these sources are examples of a grassroots effort by individuals which reach far beyond any individual institution, providing information in a broad, yet targeted, way that only the Internet can facilitate.

These are certainly not all the current awareness resources available - there are many of all types and topics. The Internet is such that new sources appear and old ones disappear every day. A common complaint about the Internet is simply the inability to ever really have a grasp of what is available out there. Current awareness resources like those outlined above simply provide glimpses of the world of possibilities available to all users.

THE INTERNET AND COLLECTION DEVELOPMENT IN THE SCIENCES

There are two components to consider when analyzing the impact of the Internet and electronic resources on collection development in the sciences: (1) the electronic resources which selectors must consider for purchase and support. (i.e., those that fall within the traditional role of the collection development librarian), and (2) the electronic resources that aid in the operations of collection development.

Concerning items for consideration of purchase, there are two types of e-resources that stand out: databases and journals. Free Internet resources must also be considered and are discussed below. Many of the issues involved in evaluating the potential purchase of electronic resources are the same as those for print versions - pricing, format, reliability, and currency. Each issue takes on new twists, however, within the digital domain. In addition, new issues are raised, most notably, licensing and archiving.

The availability of electronic databases and journals has not led to cost savings for libraries - in fact, the effect has been just the opposite. Both almost always require additional expense above the cost of print subscriptions, so that the provision of electronic versions of print resources leads to reduced discretionary buying power. With the uncertainty yet surrounding the issues of archiving of electronic journals in particular, most librarians have chosen to provide both formats to their users for the most important items in their collections. Since library budgets so often are flat or only slightly increasing, the only choice is to cut expenditures in some area - usually, other print subscriptions. Thus, the amount of *choice* exercised by the collection development librarian has declined as more electronic titles have been purchased.

Moreover, the practice of bundling titles for a set price exacerbates the problem, since in an all-or-nothing scenario, the expense is usually high. If a library chooses to provide access to ScienceDirect or IDEAL, for example, the funds available for other purchases are, obviously, adversely affected. The budget is not the only concern when considering bundled titles. By definition this type of purchase reduces choice for the librarian. Much of collection development involves tailoring the collection to support the research focus of the institution's faculty and courses, but this task is obviated with bundled packages. Few institutions require the type of high level support for ALL areas of a discipline which comes with the purchase of bundled journals. It may be a noble goal to provide access to the entire universe of scholarly information, but the superfluous information comes at a considerable cost. Responsible oversight of each precious dollar being a fundamental part of the collection development librarian's job, such purchases must be considered dubious at best.

Evaluation of the format of an electronic database or journal still depends on the concept of *ease of use*, just as with print resources. Questions to ask still include whether the interface is intuitive, and helpful, whether information is easy to locate, the level of indexing, and so on. Now, however, librarians are called upon to invest even more time and effort into new aspects of the evaluation of format. Previously, resources were evaluated primarily on their scope, content, and authority. The size of *Zoological Record*, for example, is more or less irrelevant to its use. It stands on the shelf as a functional resource on its own, and as long as the shelf space is there, no further concerns about its size or shape are needed. With the electronic product, considerations other than the usefulness of the content come into play. Is the server the database is loaded on adequate enough to provide quick response times? Is it mirrored anywhere? Is it compatible with all Internet browsers? For journals, what file format are the articles in? What cross-linking is available? These questions and more all require diligent examination before a sound decision regarding purchase can be reached. Collection development librarians have to develop the analytical skills necessary for answering these questions, and the ability to evaluate print resources is not always directly translatable to the digital realm.

One of the most contentious aspects of electronic resources is their *durability*. Will back files of a given journal continue to be made available? At what added cost? For print resources, once purchased, there is a certain confidence that they will be available forever, barring catastrophe. For electronic resources, this is far from true. The most common example given is 5 1/4 inch-floppies - almost universally unsupported now. There is no guarantee that PDF files are here to stay, HTML is constantly changing, and so on. But the concern is not only that platforms may change. Some vendors will not provide access to backfiles once the electronic subscription is canceled, meaning libraries do not really own the content; they just lease it. This further complicates collection decisions, especially in fields such as chemistry, physics, and biology, where the validity of research never goes out-of-date.

Licensing is probably the most contentious and complicated issue for libraries today. Often, collection development librarians are required to play some role in the licensing of electronic resources.[1] Even if at the preliminary level of evaluating a license, this demands specialized knowledge and training. This issue is discussed elsewhere in this volume and need not be repeated here. It is worth noting, however, that the high dependence in science on journals for scholarly communication means that science librarians are increasingly and necessarily drawn into the fray.

Nonetheless, the pressure is on to provide access to more and more electronic resources. Scientists have long recognized the usefulness of this relatively new medium over traditional print: faster access, incorporating multimedia, better search and retrieval methods, reader interaction, and so on.[2] Librarians are compelled to meet the demands of library users, and providing access to electronic resources is probably the greatest current demand in academic libraries. Fortunately, there have been some developments in electronic publishing in the sciences which promise a more manageable state of affairs for librarians. These are discussed in the section on alternative publishing, below.

Internet Resources

Internet resources which have no print counterpart also place demands on the collection management librarian. Simply in terms of an increased number of available resources and thus more content to evaluate, the Internet adds to the time necessary for collection decision making. Nowhere is this more true than in the sciences, where scholars have seized on the new technology to provide access to research, overcome the limited ability of print resources for the distribution of scientific results, and develop new lines of communication. The Scout Report Signpost, for example, listed 1,084 science websites as of May 2000 and claims to contain "only the best Internet resources."[3] While such resources are of unquestionable worth in the provision of reference and research support, they complicate the collection development librarian's life.

For example, take *Species 2000*, an Internet resource providing taxonomic information for organisms across several databases, which is of obvious benefit to librarians, researchers, and students. A biology bibliographer has to verify that this site is accurate, current, and user-friendly and that access is provided and its usefulness marketed and established among appropriate students and faculty - all of which takes time. It is even more difficult-impossible, really - to have responsibility for more than one subject discipline, as many science librarians do.

Internet resources demand more monitoring than do those in print, because of the notorious dynamic nature of the Internet.[4] Software tools exist which can help librarians validate URLs and thus ensure the reliability of the links on library web pages, but it not only takes time to use them, but also takes time to learn them. Content can change dramatically as well as the location of pages, and it is rare for older editions of sites to be archived, at least not for public access.

If a librarian, overwhelmed by the number of websites, chooses simply to link to an existing list of resources, then the collection - the electronic collection, in this case - is less adapted to the unique needs of the institution. This one-size-fits-all method may be the best choice for a bibliographer with too much to do, but it cannot serve the best interests of the user community. Reliance on already existing resource lists means dependence on those lists' authors to update and verify the content of linked pages. Moreover, this type of macroselection reduces the visibility of the library and librarians, with unfortunate consequences for both.

Online Scientific Communities

A recent development on the Internet is the establishment of online scientific communities, websites which are designed for practitioners of specific science disciplines. In general these communities offer a host of services and products oriented toward making the professional lives of their participants more enriched and convenient. Many offer access to electronic journals and books, either for free or via subscription, fulltext, or abstracts. Some sites make use of video and audio delivery capabilities. In addition there is generally information about professional societies, meetings, conferences, employment opportunities, and discussion groups.

Some examples of these communities are:

- GasNet, an anesthesia server network with mirror sites located around the world (http://gasnet.dundee.ac.uk/) and sponsored by a number of medical companies and professional societies
- the Computer Science Teaching Center (CSTC), a digital library of peer-reviewed teaching sources, funded by the National Science Foundation (NSF) and the Association for Computer Machinery (ACM) (http://www.cstc.org/index.html)
- ChemWeb, a product of Current Science Group which is owned by Elsevier Science, intended as an online information and communication service for chemists (http://chemweb.com)
- the Physics Forum, a global news and information service for physicists from the Institute of Physics (http://www.physicsweb.org)
- CogNet, an electronic community for researchers in the cognitive and brain sciences from the Massachusetts Institute of Technology (MIT) (http://cognet.mit.edu/)
- MDConsult, a medical information service targeting physicians, which is produced by a joint venture group of medical publishers (Saunders, Mosby and Lippincott, Williams & Wilkins) (http://www.mdconsult.com)

These websites are sponsored by an interesting mix of educational institutions, commercial entities and professional societies, but all clearly state as their primary goal the furthering of communication between practitioners. Most require membership and some require a subscription. These online communities are natural extensions of the "invisible colleges" of information sharing that have existed for decades among scientists working in the same subject areas. They are interesting in their various approaches and the principles that they emphasize. In providing online journals and texts, they do bypass, to some degree, the roles of traditional libraries in providing information to their members. However, researchers have always gotten information from sources beyond their libraries, and these focused online communities complement the more traditional services which librarians provide across a much broader range of subjects.

Internet Tools for Collection Development

If Internet resources have added to the complexity of collection development in the sciences, there are others that have simplified it. Listservs specific to scientific disciplines help subject librarians gain access to a far-flung network of colleagues with experience and knowledge. Publishers' catalogs, online book reviews, libraries' Web catalogs, vendor collection tools, and other websites make collection development easier and faster and allow for more thorough and comprehensive analysis of collections and resources available for purchase.

Listservs and/or mailing lists exist which can help science librarians reach beyond their own institutions and personal contacts and quickly get answers to reference questions, insider knowledge of databases, journals, licenses, and help and guidance on other library issues, all courtesy of the Internet. Some examples are:

BSDNET-L@LISTSERV.NCSU.EDU (Biomedical and Life Sciences Division, Special Libraries Association)
CHMINF-L@LISTSERV.INDIANA.EDU (Chemical Information Sources)
GEONET-L@IUBVM.UCS.INDIANA.EDU (Geosciences Information)
IAMSLIC@UCSD.EDU (International Association of Aquatic and Marine Science Libraries and Information Centers)
NATRESLIB-LCC.USU.EDU Natural Resources Librarians and Information Specialists
SLA-PAM@LISTSERVER.LIB.MUOHIO (Physics, Astronomy, and Mathematics Division, SLA)

The only online journal, *Issues in Science and Technology Librarianship*, published quarterly by the Science and Technology Section of the Association of College and Research Libraries, is another valuable Internet tool for science librarians. "It serves as a vehicle for sci-tech librarians to share details of successful programs, materials for the delivery of information services, background information and opinions on topics of current interest, to publish research and bibliographies on issues in science and technology libraries."[5] The journal began publication in 1991.

Book reviews for the sciences are notoriously difficult to locate, and even when present, they are often so slow to appear that a librarian relying on them will have a collection far behind the times. One of the more promising developments in this area has been E-Streams (http://www.e-streams.com/), a cooperative effort between H. Robert Malinowsky of the University of Illinois at Chicago and YBP Library Services. This site provides electronic-only reviews of books in the sciences in a timely manner, most written by librarians. It includes a search engine for retrieval of reviews across all of the published issues. Approximately 30 reviews appear each month, all of which are archived. An expansion of this service would be of enormous benefit to the academic science library community.

PubList.com, another useful tool, provides information about 150,000 serial publications worldwide, including frequency, indexing, formats, publisher addresses (including email addresses), circulation data, and ISSN numbers. Most entries contain hyperlinks to electronic versions. It is possible to search by subject and publisher as well as title. Although not a comprehensive list of all the journals and newsletters in the world, this is a convenient source which can eliminate much of the frustration of searching the Internet with a standard search engine.

Given the dependence of science librarianship on journals, an online service for locating back issues of science titles is a boon to collection librarians. Such a service is provided by Backserv (and BackMed for medical titles), a listserv used for the exchange of individual or bound volumes. The searchable archives are located at http://www.blackwells.com/quick links.shtml.

Book vendors, serials vendors, and other library service providers have responded to library demands for high-quality online resources in collection development. YBP provides publisher lists, information on book prices and the publishing industry, as well as E-Streams. Direct ordering of materials through its website promises to simplify the acquisitions process as well. EBSCO provides a single interface for electronic journals subscribed to by a library, which allows searching across all titles, maintenance of URLs, and the benefits of having one interface to learn instead of the multitude of idiosyncratic looks provided by individual publishers.

Online publishers' catalogs make it much easier to delve into the content and format of books being considered for purchase. Many librarians are faced with the problem of making a decision about purchase based on the ridiculously limited information provided on a yellow book slip. Now, in a timely manner, tables of contents and descriptions of content are accessible on publishers' web pages. Many lists of publishers' sites exist, but one of the most useful for libraries can be found via AcqWeb (http://www.library.vanderbilt.edu/law/acqs/pubr.html).

ALTERNATIVE PUBLISHING AND THE INTERNET

The traditional model of science research and publishing has been in trouble for 20 years. Even if the Internet hadn't radically transformed the way we view access and distribution of journal literature, there would have had to be fundamental changes in the researcher–publisher – librarian mode of interaction.

Much has been written about the evolution of the current system, including an informative discussion from the Association of Research Libraries, which reviews the historical relationships and how they have evolved over time.[6] There is a lot of uncertainty about the future of science journals. Few people involved question the value of research articles and the dissemination of information between scientists and clinicians, but the coming of the Internet has brought the traditional organization and distribution of those articles into question.

In the traditional mode, a researcher writes an article and submits it to a scholarly journal editor for consideration. The editor distributes the article to the author's peers, other scientists doing research in a related field, for review and evaluation. Based upon the comments of the peer reviewers the editor decides whether to publish the article in that journal. This is known as the referee or peer review process, and it's fundamental to the quality control of scholarly research.

The referee process is managed by the journal editor, who is part of the staff of the publishing entity, whether that's a professional society like the Ecological Society of America or a commercial publisher like Academic Press. The publisher has been almost exclusively responsible for collecting information from authors, evaluating it, and packaging it in journals to sell to individuals and libraries. It has been the most efficient process until recent years, but the arrival of the Internet has seriously shaken traditional thinking about what is the standard approach to journal publishing.

The Internet opens up new possibilities for collecting, evaluating, and distributing information. Rather than organizing information in the method that works best for paper – subject-oriented journals divided into volumes and issues and available as a block of information – why not organize information in a way that works with the best characteristics of the electronic environment? At the same time, the annual subscription method of payment has also worked well for paper formats, but that may not continue into the electronic medium.

Many publishers have made their journals available electronically over the past few years, but in nearly all cases it has simply been an extension of the paper model. Articles are issued in collections at specified times, and access to the articles is paid in advance for whole blocks of information regardless of how much of that information is actually relevant or needed by libraries and individual researchers and students. Scientists and librarians are questioning whether this paper-oriented mode of operation should be continued in the electronic environment.[7]

Preprint and Reprint Archives

An early pioneer in alternative publishing was Paul Ginsparg, a research physicist at Los Alamos National Laboratory. In 1991 he created a series of electronic bulletin boards on the Internet which allowed authors of papers in high-energy physics to upload their research and make it available for free to all interested parties. The preprints were unpublished and not refereed.

Within a year Ginsparg included additional bulletin boards in other subdisciplines of physics and more recently has opened up the preprint service to include computer science and mathematics. The service, called arXiv, has been an overwhelming success, with the number of weekly connections to the website reaching 800,000 in April 2000, and the number of submissions by authors topping 2,500 per month in late 1999.[8] The physics community is fairly unique in that preprints were actively distributed among researchers even prior to the advent of arXiv, so the notion of the value of nonrefereed articles was not new to participants. Physicists still submit their articles to scholarly journals; they simply do it as part of a larger distribution network. That way research developments are available immediately without the months-long delay needed for journal publishing. Also, the community of active physicists is fairly small compared to those in medicine, chemistry or biology.

However, in 1994 a cognitive science professor, Stevan Harnad, from the University of Southampton in England, made what was known as the "subversive proposal" on VPIEJ-L, an electronic journals discussion listserv based at Virginia Polytechnic Institute. Harnad suggested that researchers, in addition to submitting their articles to standard science journals, at the same time submit a version to a public e-print archive. This would make their work available for free to fellow researchers. Others in the scientific community would have immediate access to important information, rather than waiting months, and would be able to provide feedback, discussion and evaluation of the research and to refer to their own research. Those who insisted on refereeing could still wait for the version of the paper published in the standard journals.[9] Harnad argued that the two main reasons that researchers write papers are to make a contribution to the body of knowledge in their discipline and to be recognized for making that contribution. The current system of publishing in established journals inhibits the first concern by making published information available only to those who can pay increasingly exorbitant subscription prices. A centralized archive of preprints would open up access to that information to all. The second concern, recognition for tenure and promotion, could still be served in the traditional publishing process.[10] In a concrete effort to realize these goals, Harnad founded the E-print Archive known as CogPrints (http://cogprints.soton.ac.uk/) in 1997. CogPrints archives both preprints and reprints in all areas of the cognitive sciences, including articles from biology, computer science, linguistics, neuroscience, philosophy, and psychology.

Something remarkably close to Harnad's "subversive proposal" has come to fruition with the establishment of two biomedical archival services called PubMed Central and BioMed Central. PubMed Central is an electronic archive sponsored by the National Institutes of Health (NIH) which opened on January 1, 2000 (http://www.pubmedcentral.nih.gov). The archive grew out of a proposal made by NIH director Harold Varmus in June 1999 for a new electronic publishing library and archive to provide free access for professionals and the public to the professional biomedical literature. NIH already provides free access to the website PubMed, which is its version of Medline, the premier index to biomedical literature. The initial proposal was called E-BioMed and was designed to employ all the advantages of publishing on the Internet – wide international distribution, quick delivery to prospective readers, search engine access, multimedia capabilities, cheap archiving, open peer review, hyperlinking within documents, email announcements and table of contents distribution, and direct interaction between authors, reviewers, and readers.[11] Varmus proposed a two-tier peer review program, one with a formal peer review system established by "major players" and a second, more informal section that would open information for discussion.

Strong reactions by senior editors of *the New England Journal of Medicine and the Journal of the American Medical Association* and other major biomedical publishers caused modification of the proposal. The PubMed Central site is now an NIH repository for peer-reviewed articles that have already been published in the life sciences, which now includes plant and agricultural research as well as biomedicine. PubMed Central will organize, archive, and distribute peer-reviewed literature from journals. Individual publishers determine when the articles are submitted to PubMed Central. In the future, non-peer-reviewed reports may be screened by external independent groups and deposited in a separate preprint area if the contributing organization considers the information of value to the research community.[12]

NIH's role is to develop and maintain the website and archive, coordinate with other international initiatives along the same lines, and work to guarantee the accessibility of the information for the future.[13] A number of major journals plan to participate in PubMed Central including the *Proceedings of the National Academy of Sciences* (*PNAS*), the *British Medical Journal*, the *Canadian Medical Association Journal*, and *Nucleic Acids Research*. Soon NIH will provide direct linkage between the fulltext articles and the PubMed literature indexing database.

BioMed Central is a publisher-based Web initiative sponsored by the Current Science Group (http://www.biomedcentral.com). BioMed Central, which opened in May 2000 will function as a depository of both peer-reviewed and preprint research in all areas of biology and clinical medicine. Papers that are accepted to be published at BioMed Central will go through their peer-review process. Papers that will not undergo peer review may be deposited in a separate section and will be screened for relevance. All research distributed from BioMed Central will also be placed in full, without delay, in PubMed Central, which will archive the research. In addition to research papers, the site plans to cover a range of other services, such as commentary, analysis, reviews, collaboration tools, and information on purchasing software, materials, and equipment. BioMed Central has been an active participant in the creation of PubMed Central and is represented on PubMed Central's advisory board.[14]

Europe's response to PubMed Central has been the establishment of E-Biosci, the Electronic Publishing Initiative (http://www.embo.org/E_pub_pages.html). Groups have been meeting under the auspices of the European Molecular Biology Conference to discuss and plan a site much like, and working closely with, PubMed Central, but established and managed in Europe. E-Biosci would be a not-for-profit group providing free access whenever possible to peer-reviewed materials and secondarily to preprint materials as well. E-Biosci would coordinate the efforts of the many experts and organizations involved in the program, including government, publishing, and professional organizations.

Yet another recent initiative is PubScience, a product of the Department of Energy's Office of Scientific and Technical Information (http://pubsci.osti.gov). Opened in October 1999, this website allows researchers in the physical sciences to search for citations and abstracts from multiple publishers at no cost. It is patterned on the original PubMed database from NIH, which provides free access to citations and abstracts in biomedicine. However, PubScience does not make full text available for free to the public, and there is no plan stated to move in that direction. The cost to access a full text document is determined either by an individual or institutional subscription to the title or by a cost-per-view charge set by the publisher.

NASA Astrophysics Data System

One of the largest archives of science journal articles on the Internet is NASA's Astrophysics Data System (ADS), which includes searchable abstracts of over 2 million articles in four areas: astronomy and astrophysics, instrumentation, physics and geophysics, and the ADS/LANL physics archive. Most journals covered go back to 1975. In 1997, through purchase of data from the Institute for Scientific Information, ADS began adding references and citation information for many of the abstracted papers. In addition, ADS provides full text access to the contents of over 20 journals, some dating back to the 19th century, as well as some conference proceedings and textbooks. Mirrored worldwide, this database's U.S. site is at http://adswww.harvard.edu/.

HighWire Press

A crucial development in the electronic publication of science journals (particularly biomedical and life sciences journals) was and continues to be HighWire Press, a cooperative effort between Stanford University, professional societies, libraries, and publishers and now considered a publishing division of Stanford. By helping professional societies, most of which do not have the funding or the technical knowledge to create digitized publications, to publish their journals on the World Wide Web, HighWire has managed to accomplish a number of goals beneficial to academic libraries: provide electronic access to a number of STM journals (191 as of May 2000, or nearly 680,000 articles); provide access to a large number of back issues for free (148,000 as of May 2000); and offer its priced products at a reasonable rate. Also, HighWire allows searching across all of the journals and provides usage statistics for many of the titles.

HighWire has committed to archiving the back issues of its publications, and developed an educated and comprehensive plan to do so. "Continuing processes at HighWire include preserving publisher-supplied data and migrating data from printer formats to industry-standard SGML and HTML, along with current standard file formats such as PDF and GIF. (In addition, HighWire regularly upgrades versions of HTML over time.) HighWire also physically migrates publisher-supplied content from relatively unstable DAT tapes to robust disk arrays. HighWire also provides long-term storage of the digital source data from which subsequent delivery formats are derived; this will allow multiple options should later technology allow for superior utility and function."[15]

In addition, HighWire has partnered with societies to create new services that overcome some of the liabilities of print publications. "HighWire's approach to online publishing of scholarly journals is not simply to mount electronic images of printed pages; rather, by adding links among authors, articles and citations, advanced searching capabilities, high-resolution images and multimedia, and interactivity, the electronic versions provide added dimensions to the information provided in the printed journals."[16] It has also helped to overcome the time delay between acceptance and publication of research material. For example, in March 2000, HighWire began *JBC Papers in Press*, providing instant publication of articles accepted by the *Journal of Biological Chemistry*, a journal with one of the highest impact factors in the field.[17] These developments are a crucial part of STM publishing, and as such, all science librarians need an awareness and understanding of them.

SPARC

SPARC, the Scholarly Publishing and Academic Resources Coalition, was founded specifically to expand competition in scholarly communication, with the added goals of supporting innovative uses of technology and ensuring fair use of such communication.[18] SPARC is an initiative of the Association of Research Libraries (ARL), but membership is not restricted to ARL members. As of March 2000, 175 libraries had committed financial support to the coalition.

When ARL decided to become involved in combating the "serials crisis" in libraries and supporting alternative publishing ventures, it was a natural choice to work with science publications. This is where the highest costs are, and hence the greatest chance for making an impact. SPARC has made an impact, providing critical support for the journals *Evolutionary Ecology Research*, *Geometry and Topology*, *Organic Letters*, and its three Internet-only journals, *Internet Journal of Chemistry*, *New Journal of Physics*, and *PhysChemComm*. In 2001, SPARC will launch the second joint effort with the American Chemical Society, *Crystal Growth and Design*.

The full effects of this model of publishing, a joint effort of libraries, scientists and publishers, are at this point still unknown. Certainly, chemistry, biology, and physics journals continue to be the most expensive journals, and the percent increase for 2000 was in line with what it was over the last decade. It is still too early to tell just what impact SPARC and its partners have made.

Regardless, many science librarians feel compelled to support these efforts. Faced with cancellation decisions and shrinking collections, there seems to be little choice but to grasp the opportunity to turn things around through such ventures. As well, SPARC specifically seeks out partners who are willing to use digital technologies and the Internet to develop an electronic presence in the world of scientific communication, which is of great benefit in overcoming geographic boundaries and increasingly in demand from scientists. With their technical knowledge and the power of large subscriber bases, science libraries and librarians, through ARL and SPARC, are in a healthy position to help guide these developments. "Working through SPARC or via other avenues, libraries can play powerful roles in the metamorphosis now underway by supporting the emergence of new journals in which control is exercised by a community of scientists and users."[19]

BioOne

Unlike many other areas of science, biological research is dominated by more than 70 small professional societies such as the Soil Science Society of America and the Society for Economic Botany. Most of these societies produce important professional journals, but few can afford to digitize their publications and make them available electronically. Some societies have sold or leased their journals to commercial publishers, losing control of the pricing and profits in their bid to go electronic. The BioOne initiative was created in 1999 by a collaboration of educational, commercial, and research institutions to give these societies a better way to offer their journals on the Internet. BioOne is an online repository of fulltext society journals collected into a single aggregated database. It is planned for release in early 2001. Libraries have been instrumental in planning and funding this initiative, through SPARC, which is a division of the ARL, and through the Big 12 Plus Libraries Consortium and the University of Kansas. Allen Press and the American Institute of Biological Sciences are also founding members. Libraries support the BioOne initiative because it is an effort to keep scholarly publishing in the hands of the scientific societies and out of the commercial sector. Putting their journals on the Internet will allow the societies to continue to generate needed income from their journals in the face of declining print subscriptions. Contributing to BioOne gives libraries and their patrons access to important scholarly information through a single digital collection at a reasonable price.[20]

Open Archives Initiative

Preprint servers started within scientific disciplines, and that is where they have had the most effect and have the most promise in transforming scholarly communication. A new effort, formerly called the Universal Preprint Service and now known as the Open Archives Initiative, is under way to "establish interoperability standards supporting the search and retrieval of e-papers from all disciplines."[21] The idea is to have all preprint servers function as a single virtual library, providing uniform technical requirements for all such services and permitting retrieval of data ("harvesting") from a single interface.

The technical framework behind this effort is embodied in the *Santa Fe Convention*, a set of documents delineating appropriate standards, metadata sets, and protocols for search and retrieval functions. These standards were discussed, evaluated and selected at a meeting held in Santa Fe, New Mexico, in October 1999. Representatives from maintainers of archives ("data providers"), universities, professional societies, and government laboratories were signatories to the convention (list available at http://www.openarchives.org/ups-participants.htm).

The basic metadata set, known as the Open Archives Metadata Set (oams), required of all participating services, is largely drawn from the Dublin Core. The latter is a metadata element set intended to facilitate the discovery of electronic resources, commonly accepted both domestically and internationally.[22] Other metadata formats can then be added to "oams" in order to enhance the ability to search and harvest data. The search interface recommended in the protocol is based on the Dienst Protocol, an HTTP-based implementation, which "defines a communication procedure, as well as the syntax for the corresponding messages and responses, that will allow service providers to harvest metadata selectively from open archives that comply with the Santa Fe Convention."[23] The adoption of these standards and protocols is a pivotal change not only in the storage and retrieval of scientific (and perhaps other) research but in scholarly communication itself.

For librarians, questions arise as to whether they will help to participate in these efforts by supporting similar archives at their own institutions and how they will provide and support access to existing archives.[24] Such archives have already transformed the availability and use of information, most notably in physics, and can only be expected to grow. Certainly, support of the adopted Santa Fe Convention is of paramount importance to ensure the usability of preprint archives, and any homegrown projects need to consider adopting these standards. Science librarians in particular need to be aware, and foster awareness, of the content, scope, and interfaces of these resources. The growth of the preprint and reprint archives described above will be aided by librarians' ability to inform and instruct researchers at all levels on their use.

THE FUTURE

In reality, the impacts of the Internet on science librarianship, and all librarianship, are just beginning. New publisher and vendor agreements on cross-linking across electronic journals and databases (http://www.crossref.org/) are an indication of one certain development: the ability of scientists and students to wind their way through the published record on a given topic without leaving their office or home. Abstracting and indexing resources "have the power to become the de facto publishers of the ideal electronic journal: the one the scientist constructs for himself on the day of the search."[25] By hyperlinking from bibliographic records to fulltext, and then linking to the fulltext of cited records, researchers not only transform information services (such as those provided by librarians), but transform the concept of scholarly publication. Discrete issues or volumes under a given title cannot match the dynamic, yet focused, type of information linkage provided by electronic resources.

Another factor in the increasing remote use of library resources is the expansion in the availability of back issues of science titles. JSTOR's *General Science Collection* made available for the decade of the 1980s the *Philosophical Transactions* and the *Proceedings* of the Royal Society of London, as well as the *Proceedings of the National Academy of Sciences* and *Science*. As mentioned above, in the biomedical and life sciences, HighWire Press has also contributed to the provision of access to back issues of important titles. The availability of complete or nearly complete runs of important titles will have implications in issues of storage, library traffic, instruction, and rates of user-librarian interactions.

One of the implications for librarians is the need to educate researchers on the limitations of such convenient "fixes": the fact that many publications are and will continue to be excluded from such arrangements, the disadvantage faced by scholars in less-wired communities and countries, and the price tag. Also, generating support for librarians and libraries will likely become more difficult as more of the resources they provide are accessed remotely, and more library work is done behind the scenes.

If recent years are any indication, the future holds a continually changing marketplace for scientific research. The very structure of information dissemination in the sciences is under attack, and it is impossible to say which elements of traditional journal publishing will survive. Certainly researchers and educators will continue to produce scholarly information and will need to access the writings of their colleagues - and it is clear that the majority of that dissemination will take place electronically over the Web or its successor. In the coming maelstrom of information overload, our patrons will still need instruction and guidance on what questions to ask to find information and where to look for it. As information professionals we can offer a broad range of instructional services that will guide researchers through the multiplicity of available resources. Librarians can continue to advocate for usable products for our patrons in the unstable marketplace to come, looking beyond individual disciplines to track and influence resources on a greater scale. We can support efforts, both financially and intellectually, to change information structures that do not work for our libraries or our patrons, efforts like SPARC and BioOne and PubMed Central. We must stay in touch with the needs of our faculty and students, even if they do not come to the library as often. We must take our services outside of the library into classrooms and laboratories, wherever we are needed. Above all, we must learn to find ways to use the Internet and other technologies to facilitate access to the information our patrons depend upon.

NOTES

1. O. Gene Norman, "The Impact of Electronic Information Sources on Collection Development: A Survey of Current Practice," *Library Hi Tech* 15 (1997): 123-132.
2. Timothy Carr, Rex Buchanan, Dana Adkins-Heljeson, Thomas Mettille, and Janice Sorensen, "The Future of Scientific Communication in the Earth Sciences: The Impact of the Internet," *Computers & Geosciences* 23 (1997): 503-512.
3. "Scout Report Signpost," (URL http://www.signpost.org/signpost/).
4. Thomas E. Nisonger, "The Internet and Collection Management in Academic Libraries: Opportunities and Challenges," in *Collection Management for the 21st Century: A Handbook for Librarians*, ed. G. E. Gorman and Ruth H. Miller (Westport, CT: Greenwood Press, 1997), pp. 29-57.
5. *Issues in Science & Technology Librarianship* home page (URL http://www.library.ucsb.edu/istl/).
6. Association of Research Libraries, Association of American Universities, and the Pew Higher Education Roundtable, "To Publish or Perish," *Policy Perspectives* 7 Special Issue (March 1998) (URL http://arl.cni.org/scomm/pew/index.html).
7. Barbara Quint, "Emily Moble: Interview with a Rebel Leader," *Searcher* 7 (September 1, 1999): 41.
8. ArXiv website (URL http://arXiv.org).
9. Gary Taubes, "Electronic Preprints Point the Way to 'Author Empowerment,' " *Science* 271 (February 9, 1996): 767-768.
10. Stevan Harnad, "Learned Inquiring and the Net: the Role of Peer Review, Peer Commentary and Copyright," *Antiquity* 71 (December 1997): 1042-1048.
11. Barbara Quint, "The NIH's E-Biomed Initiative," *Information Today* 16 (September 1, 1999): 10-13.
12. "Press Release" PubMed Central (URL http://www.pubmedcentral.nih.gov/about/faq.html).
13. Ibid.
14. Robin Peet, "Two Initiatives Support PubMed Central Model," *Information Today* 17 (March 1, 2000): 3.
15. "News Extra," *BMJ* 320 (February 12, 2000): 402g (URL is http://www.bmj.com/cgi/content/full/320/7232/402/g).
16. "HighWire Press: A Brief Introduction," (URL http://highwire.stanford.edu/intro.dtl).

17. "HighWire Press Is 5 Years Old," *Journal of Biological Chemistry* 275 (April 14, 2000): pp. 107-117.
18. "SPARC Fact Sheet," (URL http://www.arl.org/sparc/factsheet.html).
19. Richard Johnson, "SPARC Whitepaper," (URL http://www.arl.org/sparc/whitepaper.html).
20. BioOne Website (URL www.BioOne.org).
21. Richard E. Luce, "The Open Archives Initiative: Forging a Path toward Interoperable Author Self-archiving Systems," *College & Research Libraries News* 61 (March 2000): 184.
22. (URL http://www. purl.org/dc).
23. Open Archive Website (URL http://www.openarchives.org/sfc/sfc.htm).
24. Luce, "The Open Archives Initiative," p. 202.
25. Tony Stankus, "Electronic Journal Concerns and Strategies for Aggregators: Subscription Services, Indexing/Abstracting Services, and Electronic Bibliographic Utilities," *Science & Technology Libraries* 18 (1999): 97-110.

CHAPTER ELEVEN

THE CHANGING ROLE OF THE ACADEMIC MEDIA CENTER IN THE AGE OF THE INTERNET

Mary Schneider Laskowski

INTRODUCTION

There may be no one defining characteristic of media librarianship, but at the top of the list would be the ability and desire to adapt. The ever-changing nature of new technologies and the problems they pose in terms of preservation, access, and collection development are nowhere more prevalent than in the realm of media librarianship. The purpose of this chapter is to provide a historic look at the way media centers have functioned in the past and how the Internet has had an impact on media center services. The Internet can provide access and up-to-date information on specialized collections such as media has greatly impacted technical services aspects of media collections and will continue to revolutionize collection development, access, and user services of media collections in the future.

THE HISTORICAL MEDIA CENTER: PROBLEMS AND PROMISE

The Emergence of the Academic Media Center

Media Centers from their inception have, out of necessity, incorporated a wide variety of formats, physical facilities, types of viewing equipment, and new technologies. The nature of media collection formats and the resulting need for very specific access controls have required the creation of media-specific collection development and circulation policies and procedures which have evolved through the years to provide academic media centers with similar missions and goals, albeit performed in differing ways. The typical academic media center has gone through a number of space changes, budget constraints, and staffing reconfigurations to arrive where they are today. As Ian Hart states in his article, "The End of an Era for the BUMC" (Big University Media Center), "A prime task of the center was to assist pedagogically ambitious faculty in setting up and operating such complicated and disaster-prone equipment as 16mm projectors, carousel slide projectors linked to open-reel tape players, and those frightening Buck Rogers video projectors that took 30 minutes to warm up."[1] As technology progressed to the stage where even children who couldn't yet read the cover of a videotape could nevertheless watch their favorite movie without adult assistance, the role of the media center had to change.

The Undergraduate Library Media Center at the University of Illinois at Urbana-Champaign serves as a fairly typical example of the evolution of a modern academic media center. Not as technologically advanced as some nor as paper-dependent as others, the media center has made great strides from its beginnings in 1932 in the cloak room of the University High School. In 1934 the small collection of educational 16mm film reels was transferred to the Division of University Extension by wheelbarrow and became the Audio-Visual Aids Service. The Audio-Visual Aids Service became at one time the world's largest educational film lending library, and much of that material has been transferred to the current location and incarnation of the media center in the Undergraduate Library. The original mission of "promoting visual education in Illinois and of building a library of visual aids for the use of schools and other educational organizations in the state"[2] has become a bit more complex. The current Media Center, created in the early 1970s in its present form, serves two major functions: (1) to support the university's curriculum by providing appropriate nonprint instructional materials to be viewed in the Media Center, as well as to be used by teaching faculty in the classroom; (2) to make available campuswide materials which are available, or are most useful only in nonprint formats (e.g., motion pictures, theatrical productions, and demonstration and tutorial tapes). These functions are supported by a collection development policy that strives to provide a collection of nonprint resources in a variety of formats for all levels of curriculum offered at the University of Illinois at Urbana-Champaign. The collection also supports research and service activities sponsored by the university and the University Library. In addition, especially given its broad interdisciplinary nature, the collection serves as a library source of emerging electronic media formats.[3]

The Instructional Media Center (IMC) at South Dakota State University has undergone a similar transformation. "From a start as a photo service in the 1940s, the IMC has evolved to provide centralized media services and operate as a regional leader in the exploration, design, and use of technology."[4] This scenario is one that is repeated over and over in the history of the academic media center. Although many academic media centers initially offered lending collections to secondary schools on a statewide level, the majority of collections were begun with the primary goal of supporting academic instruction, and that goal has become more rather than less emphasized through the years.

The average date of creation for academic media centers is 1968, and the most common format which served as the basis for a media collection was 16mm films. Over time, many of the academic media collections have grown to 10,000 titles or more in varying formats.[5] After 16mm films came capacitance electronic discs, laser discs, beta and VHS videotapes, and now digital versatile discs, or DVDs. From the initial collection of 16mm films, the media center collection at the University of Illinois at Urbana-Champaign has grown to house over 10,000 titles in a wide variety of formats, and therefore houses the requisite variety of equipment. The physical facilities and staffing have had to change in order for the media center to continue to provide adequate services to the faculty, staff, and students it strives to serve.

Issues in Media Center Collection Development

As VCRs and laser disc players replaced older, more-difficult-to-use formats, the staff at academic media centers had to overcome a new set of problems. They might no longer be needed to set up and run difficult film reels but, with the advent of each new format, the problems of access, collection development, and preservation grew. Though each new format may in and of itself be simpler to use and provide better quality, the role of the media center became more complex. It is no longer possible to provide access to many titles in their original format. Many of the necessary viewing units are no longer manufactured and marketed. Even for those units which are still available commercially, many patrons have access only to the latest one or two types of viewing units. Therefore, the usability of many formats is significantly decreased. Unlike most print materials, media titles are often offered in several different formats, and therefore purchasing decisions have to be weighed carefully.

Collection development issues in media centers are impacted greatly by changing technology. The question is not only what titles to purchase but also what format as well. Is it better to replace a worn-out copy with a replacement in the original format or to replace it in video or now in DVD? Should new titles be purchased in the newest format or in the format for which the most equipment is available? When is the appropriate time to start purchasing titles in the latest format? When does a trend stop being a trend and become the norm? Media librarians face all of these questions and more on a daily basis.

In addition to the difficulty in trying to formulate the ideal collection development policy, most media centers operate under strict budget constraints. Unlike print collections, where the physical space and staffing needs are fairly well understood, media collections require more physical space and staff that is more technologically savvy than many other units. It requires a great deal of monetary support to switch to new technologies in a timely fashion, and each time a change is made, it adds an older format to the list of possibly outdated, questionably useful, hard-to-maintain material. Media materials are hard to preserve and archive, and each time a copy is viewed, that use dramatically decreases the life span of the item. Fragile and easily outdated materials are hard to justify in a library budget.

In order for academic media centers to have the kind of budget necessary to provide adequate services, they need to be able to demonstrate their usefulness to the instructional programs of the campus to which they belong. As Kristine Brancolini states in "Video Collections in Academic Libraries," librarians cited a number of reasons it was difficult to establish a significant audiovisual collection in their libraries:

> First was the existence of well-established book collections and the fear that the purchase of expensive audiovisual materials and equipment would lead to the decline of print collections. Second, many libraries lacked the physical space needed to house a new collection that requires special equipment and handling. Third was the existence of biases on the part of faculty toward traditional instructional methods and print information sources.[6]

It took a great deal of persuasive power on the part of media librarians to overcome these obstacles. It is now generally accepted that media are here to stay as a significant component of the educational process. As the ACRL Media Resources Committee states, "Media collections are as diverse and vital as any print collection in an academic library."[7] The guidelines go on to say, "An academic library media operation may encompass a variety of activities, such as scheduling and managing the delivery of audiovisual equipment to classrooms, operating distance education television studios, offering instructional development and the production of audiovisual materials, and supporting multimedia production."[8] One advantage of new technologies such as the Internet is that it becomes easier for media collections to move into the classroom and be adequately represented in an online catalog or database, especially when facilitated by a media librarian.

Access to Media Center Collections

If media collections had not posed so many problems from the beginning, it may have been much more difficult for media librarians to embrace the Internet as a wonderful resource. However, due to the difficulties in general with access to media collections, any new resource which could be used to maximize patron access and collection visibility was readily adopted. The access to media collections within a library collection as a whole has been particularly problematic. Catalogers often do not have expertise in media formats and, even when they do, it is not always apparent early on in the process how best to catalog an emerging format. For example, many of the early records for capacitance electronic discs (CEDs) are indistinguishable from records for laser discs. Both capacitance electronic discs and laser discs were often coded as simply videorecordings and videodiscs without individual description for laser versus CED. When a collection has the title in both formats, it causes a great deal of confusion in matching the correct bibliographic record with the individual piece. As they require different machines for playback, it is much simpler if the bibliographic record specifies which format exactly is being cataloged. This is a current problem as well with the emergence of digital versatile discs. Not only are the descriptive standards not always up-to-date, but catalogers themselves are often slow to acknowledge the problems with new technologies until they are adopted en masse by a large number of institutions. Because of these cataloging problems, among other things, media are often inadequately represented in online catalogs and databases.

Most of the commercially available library systems are geared toward book collections, and don't solve the problems inherent with media collections. For example, though the catalog will most often distinguish between a book and a media format, patrons (or staff, for that matter) are not usually able to search by a specific media format for which they have available equipment. Also, the types of search fields which people like to have for media are not always available. Many times the director and/or cast is not searchable, and often even the production date is difficult to find. Typical circulation software also does not account for separate media center circulation policies. As most of the collections were built for instructional support, often faculty are the only patrons authorized to remove items from the media center for research or for classroom viewing. However, unlike book collections, many media centers need a way to circulate materials within their physical facility. It is rare for circulation software to allow for in-house charges, scheduling of viewing units, advance reservations, and equipment maintenance. In those cases where the media collection is a separate entity from the library collection as a whole, these problems were dealt with through a paper catalog or other painstakingly inefficient means. Newer technologies have led to some creative fixes for these problems.

THE IMPACT OF THE INTERNET ON MEDIA CENTERS AND COLLECTIONS TODAY

Challenges in Today's Academic Media Center

The move from a paper catalog system to a searchable Web database was not an instantaneous one, and yet the impact of the Internet was quickly felt and appreciated by media librarians and staff. To further illustrate how a typical collection is dealt with and why the Internet plays such a significant role, it is first necessary to understand what a media collection consists of. From a recent survey conducted by the author, nearly 100% of academic collections consider VHS videotapes to be the mainstay of their collection. However, many other formats are also considered major components of the media collection. Seventy-three percent of academic media collections also have audiocassettes and laser discs, 72% have CD-ROMs, 69% still have 16mm, 61% have slides, and 41% still have ¾" U-matic. Digital versatile discs are already collected in 41% of academic media centers. To a lesser degree, many of the collections still have filmstrips, PAL format tapes, SCAM, other types of computer discs, audio compact discs, ½" Beta tapes, 8mm, 35mm, DAT carts, and audio reel-to-reel. It is a matter of some importance to both patrons and staff as to what titles are available in what formats. The statistic that perhaps has the most impact is that 90% of these media centers still maintain viewing equipment for all of the formats which they have in the collection. Another 6% maintain all of the equipment for heavily used formats, which means a total of 96% of academic media centers provide viewing equipment for most of their titles.[9]

Maintaining equipment in that many formats is a difficult challenge, and represents a great commitment to patron service, access, and preservation. This challenge is one that is going to be problematic for the foreseeable future, as it does not appear that there will be one accepted technology that will replace all other older formats and then in turn not be replaced by newer technology in short order. The move to DVD, for example, has occurred at a much quicker rate than the move to VHS was accomplished. With recordable DVD now on the market, DVD technology will be firmly established. Yet, there is no guarantee that several years down the road a new technology won't replace DVD. Hopefully, as solutions are found regarding access and preservation to media collections, a change in technology will not represent a greater challenge but an opportunity for further advancement and better patron services. Some solutions have already been found.

Before most media collections were accessible through the Internet or an electronic database, they largely maintained a print list or catalog of titles. A truly paper-based catalog of available titles is costly to maintain in terms of time and, because of the huge time commitment, cannot be updated as often or as easily as an electronic version. An intermediary step to accessing media collections on the Web was the development of electronic databases that allowed for the necessary flexibility in dealing with a media collection. Unlike most circulation software that, as mentioned earlier, is not ideal for dealing with media, there are many types of electronic databases which can be designed specifically to suit the needs of a media collection. Much as customers expect a video rental store to be able to provide them with certain types of information, patrons of media centers expect that the collection will be adequately cataloged in some fashion. Though databases may or may not be made searchable to the public, even the transfer of media center processes to an electronic form was a vast improvement.

New Solutions to Old Problems: Improved Access through the Internet

Several years ago the media collection at the University of Illinois at Urbana-Champaign was entered into a modified Microsoft Access database which has become the basis of all of the circulation and access functions and is accessible through the Internet. The database allows media staff to make on-site reservations, reservations for outside loan, create course reserve notices, check on the current status of an item, view items on order and the vendor from which they are ordered, look up patron status and contact information, compile usage statistics, schedule units for on-site viewing, compile overdue/fine notices, plot equipment maintenance, archive statistical data for historical comparison, and distinguish between academic and recreational viewing. Not only do these functions improve the services offered to media center patrons, but they also help media librarians justify a media collection budget and maintenance costs which may not be obvious to those who don't work with media on a daily basis. In addition, the database allows patrons and staff to search by title, specific format, language, subject, director, cast, and date. The use of multiple access points and better indexing greatly enhances their ability to selectively search the collection and make useful choices, for example, for classroom viewings. The database tables have been loaded to the web and are searchable through a Web form. As the tables are updated daily by media center staff, patrons have access to the most current information regarding titles in the collection and their availability. The Web interface is maintained separately from the library-wide collection, which is updated through a central technical services department and is therefore not as up-to-date. Good customer service is much easier to maintain when the patrons themselves have access to basically instantaneous updates to the holdings records.

Whether the searchable Web collection started out as some other form of database or not, the evolution of searchable Web databases for media collections reduced in the end the amount of time required to provide patrons with an accurate account of the collections holdings while allowing much more flexibility. Not only can patrons do more sophisticated searching on their own, but if the collection is available through the Web they are no longer bound by media center hours. Therefore, the result is reduced patron service time and a higher emphasis on quick technical service turnaround. As Michael J. Albright states in "Internet Resources: The World-Wide Web (WWW)," "The World-Wide Web brought the 'point-and-click' technology of the desktop to the Internet, in the process greatly increasing the potential for interactivity. While such features as graphics, photographs, audio and video were possible with Gopher and other applications, the Web was the first to integrate them into a single screen."[10] Every year the incoming students at academic institutions display greater expertise with Internet technologies, and the challenge then becomes to make the most of the available technologies not only to improve access but to maintain the standards that are expected of a technologically based field.

The Impact of the Internet on Collection Development and Technical Services

It is fairly easy to determine that the Internet has had a great impact on the accessibility of media collections to media center patrons. An aspect that is a little harder to quantify is the role that the Internet has had in collection development policies and procedures for media collections. The "*Guidelines for Media Resources in Academic Libraries,*" distributed by the American College and Research Libraries section of the American Library Association, stresses the importance of balancing old and new formats and technologies.

> Technology used in teaching, learning, and research has created new challenges and opportunities for managers of college and university library media resource collections and services. Faculty and students need traditional media formats—audiocassettes, audio compact discs, videocassettes, laser discs, and so on—but librarians must also consider computer technology and emerging digital formats.[11]

The Internet serves as a useful tool for helping to make collection development decisions, both on the part of media center coordinators and faculty and staff who are interested in acquiring titles for classroom use.

The Internet, the World Wide Web in particular, has greatly facilitated the collection development process. It is not just the student body, but the faculty and staff at academic institutions, that are becoming increasingly proficient at and, in fact, increasingly reliant on, the World Wide Web for many research needs. Not only are many local collections available online and therefore speed up the process of finding materials to suit specific needs, but many collections from other institutions are accessible world-wide as well, broadening the researcher's ability to find related titles and materials. Also, there are many databases on the World Wide Web which are not tied to a specific institution's collection, but are based on commercial or purely educational information without holdings or even necessarily contact information. An enormous number of print journals and catalogs are available in electronic format, including many reviews of documentaries, and feature films. If an interested faculty member can quickly find and browse a number of online reviews regarding a specific work, the probability that that faculty member will make a recommendation, whether positive or negative, in some form or another as to the purchase of that work is much greater.

Visibility is a key issue in general with the advent of Internet technologies to the academic setting. Faculty are not only much more likely to make recommendations for specific titles without solicitation on the part of the media coordinator, but also much more familiar with new trends in technology. The multimedia collection has gained a new profile and is in higher demand than ever, based on the easy visibility of new technologies. Internet technologies have gained such prominence in business, and so many academic fields publish heavily in electronic format, that it has become the expected norm for academic media centers to provide materials, information, and instruction in the latest technological developments. The media coordinator is no longer, or at least not often, in the role of advocating the use of new technology and is often instead trying to keep up with the demands for new implementations. Luckily, Internet technologies have made it simpler in many ways for media coordinators to serve the needs of their patrons.

The available Internet tools are, of course, not only useful to teaching faculty but also invaluable to the media coordinator as well. Cumbersome print catalogs take a great deal more time to peruse than a quick search of an online database. Access to other institutions' collections online also provides a timely resource for rush requests, as many collections are available either through interlibrary loan or a fee-based rental program. Interestingly enough, as far as media collection development is concerned, perhaps the most profound change made possible by Internet technology is the development of mailing lists run through a list server, or listservs. Listservs provide a forum where interested individuals from a wide variety of backgrounds and responsibilities can exchange information in a timely manner. Many media coordinators operate in an environment where they may be the only person in that library who is working with media and new classroom/media center technologies. The opportunity to give and receive advice from peers who are solving similar problems at remote locations is a tremendous asset. Often the only way to find an obscure title is to talk to someone who has recently acquired it. It is also useful when placing orders to be able to find a current distributor for a title by looking at distributor/vendor databases and commercial movie databases online. Although 8% of media staff still prefer a traditional print catalog to searching online, 43% prefer to search a Web-based catalog. Seventy-one percent of those institutions responding to the survey state that the Internet has had at least some impact on how they make their purchasing decisions.

Technical services for media collections have also been impacted by the increasing use of Internet technologies. For example, the majority of media centers at academic institutions or their acquisitions departments are able to place orders directly through the Internet, and most report that this has significantly improved the turn-around time between placing an order and the items arrival. Also, for the majority of those media centers that are not able to order directly from the Internet, this is a capability which they would like to have.[12] Even if it is not possible to place orders directly off the Internet, finding a title through a Web-based database can help speed up the acquisitions process by providing current, accurate information regarding availability, price, and specific catalog number.

Reference Services and the Internet

Aside from collection development and technical services functions, the Internet has had a revolutionary impact on the way reference work is handled at academic media centers. Media center coordinators at academic institutions rank listservs as the Internet tool which affords them the greatest advantage in doing media reference work. The next most important are the availability of distributor/vendor pages online, access to commercial movie databases, and access to collections at other institutions, in that order. Patrons who request a title that is unfamiliar to the media center coordinator or staff can expect a much quicker response to their inquiry than they would have when largely print sources were used. The response can also be sent through email, which is often faster, and can include the latest availability information.

In addition to the general reference and information sources already listed, many respondents to the survey stated that online technical glossaries and technical support pages for specific equipment models were very useful, particularly when working with an unfamiliar technology or environment.[13] Though computer technologies have become a focus for many library science programs, many media technologies are addressed only in regard to high school media librarianship. Many of the most effective media technologies are therefore learned on the job with little or no prior experience. As Don Fallis and Marin Fricke state in their article "Not by Library School Alone," "With limited resources, the curriculum of our library school cannot reasonably be expected to cover all of the specific practical skills."[14] This problem is by no means specific to the School of Information Resources and Library Science at the University of Arizona. Without the ability to communicate effectively with peers and find up-to-date resources and news releases online, the job of the media coordinator would be much more daunting.

Organizational Change

The many capabilities of Internet technology, including the listservs, commercial databases, distributor/vendor pages, online collection catalogs, online reviews, and high visibility of media, which have already been discussed, not to mention emerging technologies which will be discussed in the next section, have changed the staffing and organizational needs of the academic media center. The largest change has come for those units which typically delivered and set up equipment in classrooms. For one thing, instead of paper forms and telephone calls, faculty can, in many instances, make their request for materials online. In addition, many academic institutions have integrated some type of digital classroom delivery of materials through the Internet or Internet-based technologies. The same title may be used as previously, but the tape, disc, and so on, no longer need to leave the media center. Rather than relying on a multitude of student assistants to hand-deliver carts of equipment and act as on-site projectionists, many media centers have had to restructure themselves to incorporate a higher number of technologically savvy permanent staff and reduce the number of student assistants. If they are lucky, this results in staff that are higher paid but fewer in number, and hopefully a balance is maintained in the types and quality of services offered.

An example of this type of organizational change is the restructuring that occurred at Kentucky State University through the successful implementation of an automated media retrieval system. Michael Rhoadarmer explains this phenomenon in his article, "Organizational Change Resulting from a Media Retrieval System." The new system has resulted in the type of change stated earlier where physical distance delivery of viewing units and titles has been replaced by a higher amount of technological work needing to be done at the media center itself. Rather than hand-delivering carts with equipment, the media center at Kentucky State University now "delivers on average about one TV/VCR unit a month, usually for an off-campus group. Deliveries through the retrieval system, however, average about 200 a month and are increasing."[15] One major advantage of using this type of Internet technology is that students can use media for presentations as easily as faculty, whereas many institutions which offer media only in its original physical form are unable or unwilling to allow this material to circulate to students, for a variety of reasons. Another advantage is that, depending on the type of delivery system used, there can be less wear and tear on the physical format.

New Issues Resulting from Internet Use

Though most of these changes are quantifiably beneficial to media patrons in terms of quick turnaround and easier integration of media into the classroom, there are some serious problems to be addressed as well. As the concept of media center one-stop-shopping continues to gain popularity, the more heavily media centers will have to invest in training and continuing education for their employees. The job description that an employee is hired for may not adequately represent the responsibilities required over a period of time. This is not always readily apparent to administration, as the constant level of change in media center technologies can be much higher than that of other library departments or units. Another effect of relying heavily on Internet technologies is the high cost of equipment purchase, maintenance, and upgrades. In an ideal world there would be a new technology that would far surpass all others, be obvious from the beginning that it was going to become the new standard, and be effective for at least 20 years, but such is never the case. Media coordinators must make as informed a decision as they can and hope that the technologies they have chosen to implement will continue to benefit their patrons for as long as possible.

There may never be a time when media centers and staff are not scrambling to incorporate the latest technology, and each change in popular format or type of delivery can be a prohibitively costly proposition. One advantage of using Internet technology to deliver media is that many of the older formats can be converted to digital and therefore preserved past their otherwise expected life span. However, there is no guarantee that the converted format is one which will survive for any length of time. Therefore, as is the case with most major shifts in technology, archiving and preservation of materials have been both improved and complicated through the advent of Internet technologies.

THE FUTURE ROLE OF THE INTERNET AND INTERNET-BASED TECHNOLOGIES IN ACADEMIC MEDIA CENTERS

The Internet within the Academic Culture

Some academic media centers are placing much more emphasis on services tied to Internet technology than others are, but this is a trend which looks as if it will continue into the foreseeable future. The majority of media centers, 79%, already offer Internet access to their patrons, and of the 21% remaining, many are part of the library structure as a whole, and therefore although there may not be Internet access physically at the media center, it would certainly be nearby. A strong indication of the fact that the Internet has been widely accepted and highly utilized by academic media centers is that 88% of those media centers responding maintain a Web presence. Also, through various means such as a distinct database for the media collection or through a library-wide Web catalog, 88% of academic media collections are searchable in some fashion through the Web.[16] This demonstrates a strong commitment to Internet resources and technology that is reflected in some of the creative ways in which academic media centers provide services. One distinct advantage of offering access to the media collection, as well as other institutions' collections and commercial databases, is that patrons can make use of this information any time, day or night. Web interfaces are becoming more and more familiar to patrons, and the amount of expertise required to satisfactorily negotiate them is decreasing. By offering media services through the Internet, media centers can greatly improve the types and number of services they offer as well as increase the number of patrons they serve.

Unfortunately, although a large majority of media centers do maintain a Web presence, a relatively small number provide information or access regarding other media resources. For example, only 55% of media center web pages contain links to collections at other institutions' media centers or distribution/production information through commercial vendors. Though this is still technically a majority, this does not adequately reflect the vast number of resources available and their possible benefit to media center patrons. This is also in direct contrast to the opinions, as stated earlier and based on a survey of academic media centers, that media center coordinators find great benefit in searching other institutions collections online, as well as other commercial databases. Apparently, though media coordinators find this useful, they have not all taken the necessary steps to provide this service to their patrons. There are a number of factors which could contribute to this, such as lack of equipment and/or systems support personnel or simply the academic library culture as a whole. Though there is a high demand for easy access to information, be it media or otherwise, the academic community still largely frowns on the use of the Internet as a viable resource. Even professors who are more than happy to attain research data from the Internet often disallow the use of Internet resources for their students. It is to be hoped that as Internet technology becomes cheaper and easier to use and gains more acceptance as a scholarly means of communication, more media centers will recognize the need to be part of a worldwide network of media resources.

The ease and availability of Internet technology will hopefully make a significant impact on the circulation policies of academic media centers as well. Most media centers were developed to support the instructional needs of the faculty and students at their particular institution. While this has led to some wonderful collections, the nature of media has placed some restraints on cooperative programs such as interlibrary loan. A media collection that is heavily based on audio cassettes or VHS videotapes, for example, is difficult to circulate to other institutions without incurring significant shipping and replacement costs due to the fragility of the items being exchanged. In fact, many academic media centers do not circulate material to anyone other than faculty members or graduate teaching assistants who need the material for instruction. Students and noninstructional staff quite often are required to make use of the materials within the media center or library at various viewing units. While these units can be a wonderful asset and are often adequate for the students' needs, there are many situations that could be greatly improved if media were not packaged in a fragile manner. For example, if one institution is just starting a particular curricular program or has not had the budget to invest in certain areas, interlibrary loan can be a valuable asset. Also, students who need media for classroom presentations are not served by many of the current arrangements. This has led to the development of many different systems of media digitization and delivery. If a digitized copy can be made for archives or, better yet, if a digital copy can be distributed through a network or over the Internet, there are many more options open regarding circulation policies. The emergence of Internet technology has made these options readily available.

New Developments in Technology

A significant event in the move toward better Internet services was the development of streaming technology in roughly 1995. Until that point, audio delivered through the Web was of inadequate quality and took a great deal of time to download, and could not be played until the file was completely downloaded. Audio and video streaming allows the material to be played as it is in the process of being downloaded, and the quality has been much improved. The process of buffering, where a small amount of the audio data is continually stored in memory before playback of the audio begins, allows for the audio to continue to play even if there is a brief interruption of the connection or slowdown of the transmission. Gloria Rohmann explains how the process of streaming audio works in her article, "Live and On-demand: Streaming Multimedia for the Academic Media Center." "As the audio plays, the play continues to put some of the file in memory. If the file has been correctly encoded for the size of the listener's connection and network traffic does not interrupt the stream, the listener experiences a smooth, broadcast quality transmission."[17] Audio-streaming is fairly simple to implement. The software is fairly cheap, and will work well on midgrade hardware components. The technology can be used in a multitude of ways, either replacing or enhancing previously offered services. For example, audio-streaming can be used for language lab materials and recorded lecture series. In some cases media centers may be able to take on responsibilities which were not theirs previously without much change in their workflow. One advantageous feature of audio-streaming is that a student who has an adequate computer at home may no longer be required to be at the same physical location as the material or lecturer. This ability has been used and will continue to be used in greater depth for numerous types of distance learning programs. Not only can print items be scanned and placed on reserve online for distance learners, but audio and video can be sent over the Internet as well, allowing distance learners much the same experiences they might find physically on campus.

Though video-streaming is still perhaps not as readily accessible or easily accomplished as audio-streaming, great breakthroughs have been made in that area as well. Not only has the technology itself become faster, cheaper and easier to use, but the available material content has significantly increased as well. The amount of video available on the Web is far greater than that of any one resource such as a media center or even a video rental store. Though some of the content that is available on the World Wide Web has questionable origins in terms of copyright issues, the fact that it exists and is so readily available puts pressure on academic media centers to provide similar types of access. One reason that such a large volume of material is so readily accessible is that broadband connections and simply faster connections in general are more easily available to large segments of the population. Granted, Champaign-Urbana is a large university town, but the advertisements for Internet connections have swiftly changed from the old modem connection that required people to go without their phone while online, to dedicated T-1 connections being offered at many of the apartment complexes across town. With the continued growth of broadband Internet connections, and with the advent of Internet2 just around the corner, the trend toward video online seems firmly entrenched and likely to achieve greater and greater acceptance and use.

The concept of broadband connections in and of itself has been around for a while, but it finally looks as though it may become a reality for more than just the techie with a lot of disposable income. There are many conflicting opinions regarding who will control broadband connections and how they will function in the future, but the prevailing opinion seems to be that they are here to stay and will quickly affect the way we view our day-to-day communications and media use. Basically, a broadband connection allows for several different channels of data to be transmitted over a single line and at a higher speed than a basic Internet connection. There is great deal of speculation, not to mention competing research, as to how broadband connections will function in the future. However, at the moment various companies are making use of the functionality in different ways. Regardless of future implementations, broadband connections today allow media coordinators, among others, a vision of things to come. Though it may be quite some time before broadband connections are a household standard, or even an academic standard, media centers and their patrons would greatly profit from increased access speed and better, standardized ways of digitizing and playing back video.

Another way in which access to media online can be improved is through the continued development of Internet2. The vision and goals of the Internet2 project can be found on the Internet2 project home page.

> Building on the tremendous success of the last ten years in generalizing and adapting research Internet technology to academic needs, the university community has joined together with government and industry partners to accelerate the next stage of Internet development in academia. The Internet2 project is bringing focus, energy and resources to the development of a new family of advanced applications to meet the emerging academic requirements in research, teaching and learning. Internet2 universities, working with industry, government and other research and education networking organizations are addressing the major challenges facing the next generation of university networks by:
>
> - First and most importantly, creating and sustaining a leading edge network capability for the national research community,
> - Second, directing network development efforts to enable a new generation of applications to fully exploit the capabilities of broadband networks, and
> - Third, working to rapidly transfer new network services and applications to all levels of educational use and to the broader Internet community, both nationally and internationally.[18]

Expectations for both media center patrons and media center coordinators can only increase due to faster, more innovative connections to the Internet. As mentioned earlier, audio and video streaming can greatly enhance services to both typical and distance education students, as well as benefit the media center directly in terms of improved circulation policies and opportunities.

BLURRED LINES: COLLABORATION BETWEEN MEDIA CENTERS AND OTHER SERVICE ORIENTED UNITS

Many of the opportunities which present themselves through the use of the Internet by media centers as a tool to facilitate services can often be best approached through collaboration with other library and/or campus units which also provide some form of media or instructional services and facilities. If the media center itself is part of the library system, there is often an instructional resources department which is not affiliated with the library. Conversely, if the media center is not affiliated with the library, there is often a library unit which is involved in the archiving and/or distribution of various forms of digitized material. In fact, there may be numerous units or service departments that are dealing with the dissemination of digitized material in one way or another, and while there may not have been collaboration in the past, the Internet has opened up ways for these differing units or departments to share resources and provide a wider range of services than might otherwise be possible. These new possibilities have gained enough notice to be mentioned in the *"Guidelines for Media Resources in Academic Libraries*" by the ACRL Media Resources Committee.

> Within the library, the boundary between media collections and services and computer software collections and services has blurred. Academic librarians are also working closely with other agencies on campus to support faculty and student information needs. In some institutions, librarians have become true partners in the delivery of instruction, working with faculty, technologists, and instructional developers to create "new learning communities."[19]

There are numerous ways in which such collaboration can be effective. One simple example already discussed would be the assumption of new responsibilities on the part of the media center such as using audio streaming to provide access to language lab or distance-learning students. However, this type of collaboration could take many forms.

Another example of the benefits of collaboration, particularly in the new highly technological environment, is illustrated in the article "Delivering Technology through Collaboration at the University of Virginia" by John Alexander, Rick Provine, Rachel Saury, and Ralph Schultz. The article explains how three separate departments or units within the University of Virginia (UVA) structure collaborate to provide more comprehensive services to the faculty and students. The three units, the Instructional Technology Group in the Department of Information Technology and Communication, the Digital Media Center and Robertson Media Center, and the Arts & Sciences Center for Instructional Technologies, all offer support in the areas of audiovisual delivery and repair, classroom technology, and faculty instructional technology development. As stated in the article, "Over the years, these three units have developed highly collegial and collaborative relationships. This has served not only to avoid duplication of services, but to also streamline the process faculty must go through in order to identify the resources they need."[20] In order to avoid duplication of services, collaboration between units is essential. Though each of the units provides some similar services, their interpretation and implementation differ, and by working closely together they are able to provide each patron with the best option and still make differing uses of modern technology such as digital delivery of media and the integration of such technology into the classroom. This type of structure, though administratively problematic at times, allows for a great deal of diversity and creativity in providing the latest technological advances with the greatest impact for daily patron use. "Between the four units or teams represented by these four authors, faculty at UVA can find in-depth support for projects varying from creating elaborate web-based digital archives to getting a diverse range of audiovisual and computer equipment for use in a single classroom."[21] A similar situation exists here at the University of Illinois, Urbana-Champaign. There are a media center in the Undergraduate Library, a Center for Educational Technologies, and an Office of Instructional Resources. Each unit reports to a different administration, and yet all three must work together to provide a wide spectrum of services to the greatest number of people possible. While these are only a few examples of how collaborative efforts can benefit both the media center patrons and the unit itself, the more technologically advanced the media center becomes, the more important such collaborative efforts will be. For one thing, if media resources are available in a digital format through the Internet, sharing resources does not create a big problem as it often does if it is the physical piece that must be shared between units. However, this creates its own problems, as sharing items, even in a strictly academic setting, causes great concern over copyright issues.

The Issue of Copyright

One of the hardest aspects about understanding copyright issues as they pertain to media is that industry standards and guidelines are constantly changing. What was considered fair use 20 years ago may no longer be fair use, and there may be more things considered fair use now than before. What makes copyright particularly difficult in the media environment is that changes in modern technology greatly affect how copyright is viewed. Unfortunately, in some respects, the greater capability we have for incorporating media into the classroom setting, the harder it can be to get copyright clearance to do so. Media distributors are rightfully leery of releasing copyright, even in terms of fair use, without strict assurances that the material will not be illegally copied or redistributed. However, with much of the technology that is currently available, such as digitally reproducing and distributing such material over the Internet, it is difficult to convince the vendors/distributors that the restrictions placed on such distribution are adequate.

Historically speaking, when a library or media center purchased a copy of a video, for example, it was understood that no copies of that video would be made and that patrons would view the material in the format in which it was purchased. The American Library Association sums up this procedure in "Video and Copyright: LARC Fact Sheet Number 7":

> When libraries purchase a videocassette, they purchase the physical object as distinct from purchasing the copyright to the content. Copyright regulations, therefore, determine what libraries can and cannot do with the videotapes they own without infringing upon the copyright they do not own. Libraries need to remember that when they want to use a videotape in such a way that would infringe upon the copyright, permission must be sought from the copyright owner or steps taken to ensure that the videotape is leased or licensed for the specific purpose of a public performance.[22]

Although there are specific provisions for fair use in copyright law which provide for the loan of videotapes to patrons for personal use, for classroom use of videotapes, and even for library use of videotapes under specific conditions, these provisions are a great deal more difficult to interpret when the library or media center wishes to make a digitized copy of the tape for any number of uses.

There are a number of reasons that a library or media center would wish to make a digitized copy of a video. The simplest is that a digitized copy can be archived, although that process also has its drawbacks in terms of changing technologies and continued availability of appropriate software for the specific format used. This does allow, however, for the media center to increase the life span of a specific item. This can be particularly useful if the item in question is in an outdated format such as capacitance electronic disc or beta, where not only might the title itself no longer be available, but even if it were the players are no longer manufactured. Many media centers face the same situation which we are encountering here at the University of Illinois, where a large portion of the collection, though the titles are still in decent condition, is in danger of rapidly becoming completely useless as the last of our CED, Beta, and U-matic machines are on their last legs. One option of course is to repurchase those items that are available in a newer format such as VHS or DVD, but not only is this cost prohibitive, but it is simply prolonging the issue. A far better solution is to find a way to digitize the material and show it through a closed network or a restricted Internet access. That way not only is the material preserved, but a wider range of services can be offered to the media center patrons.

Another reason for digitizing media materials, not only outdated formats but newer formats as well, is to provide better access. Media centers are quite often faced with the dilemma of either not being able to offer media material to distance learners or having to physically send a title which is then unavailable to on-campus students for sometimes prolonged periods of time. Not only does this complicate circulation procedures, but it can significantly decrease the life span of the material as well. By digitizing this material it can be made available to distance learners and on-campus students alike, although often through differing sources. While digitizing has its obvious advantages, this is where copyright law becomes particularly sticky. The Digital Millennium Copyright Act (H.R. 2281) made some significant changes in copyright law. For example, the summary of section 304 states that it, "expands certain rights of libraries and archives to reproduce and distribute copies or phonorecords to authorize three copies or phonorecords (currently one) to be reproduced or distributed for preservation, security, or replacement purposes."[23] While this is of great use if the format is obsolete, it does not specifically address other transmissions of digitized material. Material that is available in digital form can be manipulated much more easily than that of the original physical format. Herein lie both the beauty and the danger of transmitting digitized copies of a title. Faculty and students can integrate the material into classroom presentations more easily, but if the point of digitization is to also be able to transmit multiple copies of the material simultaneously, or adequate safeties are not employed to prevent multiple copies, then copyright permissions must be obtained. Obtaining copyright permissions can be both a time-consuming and expensive effort, however, in many cases the long-term gain of being able to provide materials in a digital form will outweigh the disadvantages of having to deal with tricky copyright issues.

CONCLUSIONS

Many formats, types of equipment, various physical facilities, and changing technologies make media librarianship and the academic media center in particular subject to ongoing change and development. Most academic media centers began with a collection of 16mm films and graduated over the years to currently collecting digital versatile discs (DVDs). The underlying mission of supporting an institutional curriculum and supplying faculty and students with timely, effective access to nonprint materials has, however, remained largely the same. The Internet has proven to be an extremely useful tool in carrying out this mission.

Many media collections are now searchable through the Internet on the World Wide Web. This is a vast improvement over the types of treatment media often received in standard online catalogs where it was difficult to search by specific format, director, cast, and so on. Also, the majority of media center coordinators make use of the Internet to make collection development decisions, and as more and more distributors/vendors have searchable Web databases, this will continue to expand. Media coordinators ranked the ability to communicate easily with their peers through listservs very highly as a benefit of Internet access as well. As more media collections and centers expand their visibility online, patrons will benefit from quick, easy access to media, and as the visibility grows, so will the demand. The Internet has allowed faculty and students to more easily integrate media into their classroom instruction and presentations as well. The continuing trend toward digitization and better access will allow for further growth in this area. Though technological changes and copyright issues can be difficult to deal with, the Internet will continue to make a major impact on the way media centers function and the types of services they offer.

The biggest drawback of the continued expansion of Internet access and tools for media collections is the inability of people without computers, or fast enough connections, to make adequate use of that information. In the long run, however, the advantages will greatly outweigh the disadvantages, especially as the cost of computers and Internet access continues to decrease. Many libraries circumvent this problem by providing computers and Internet access for patron use. If access to the Internet can be assumed, then the trend towards Web access will be a benefit to both media center staff and patrons. This is not to say that media center operations and services will finally be at a standstill, but rather that the Internet will have a great impact on further changes and be a useful tool in adapting media center services to the demands of the future.

NOTES

1. Ian Hart, "The End of an Era for the BUMC," *College & University Media Review* 4, no. 3 (Spring 1998): 87-100.
2. *Catalogs and Registers, 1935-1936* (University of Illinois, Urbana-Champaign), P. 351.
3. *Collection Development Policy Non-Print Fund, Non-Print Subcommittee of the Collection Development Committee, April 16, 1996. University Library Internal papers* (Urbana-Champaign: University of Illinois, Urbana-Champaign, 1996).
4. Gary Sheeley, "The Instructional Media Center at South Dakota State University," *College & University Media Review* 1, no. 1 (Summer 1994): 63-70.
5. Mary Laskowski, survey conducted December 1999/January 2000. Results of survey to be published in a forthcoming issue of *College & University Media Review.*
6. Gary P. Handman, ed., *Video Collection Development in Multi-type Libraries: A Handbook* (Westport, CT: Greenwood Press, 1994).
7. ACRL Media Resources Committee, *Guidelines for Media Resources in Academic Libraries* (URL http://www.ala.org/acrl/guides/medresg.html).
8. Ibid.
9. Laskowski, survey.

10. Michael J. Albright, "Internet Resources: The World-Wide Web (WWW)," *McJournal: The Journal of Academic Media Librarianship* 3, no. 2 (Fall 1995): 44-61.
11. ACRL Media Resources Committee. *Guidelines.*
12. Laskowski, survey.
13. Ibid.
14. Don Fallis and Martin Fricke, "Not by Library School Alone," *Library Journal* 124, no. 17 (October 15, 1999): 44-45.
15. Michael Rhoadarmer, "Organizational Change Resulting from a Media Retrieval System," *College & University Media Review* 5, no. 2 (Spring 1998): 93-101.
16. Laskowski, survey.
17. Gloria Rohmann, "Live and On-demand: Streaming Multimedia for the Academic Media Center," *McJournal: The Journal of Academic Media Librarianship* 6, no. 1 (Spring 1998): n.p.
18. Internet2 homepage (URL http://www.internet2.edu/).
19. ACRL Media Resources Committee, *Guidelines.*
20. John Alexander, Rick Provine, Rachel Saury, and Ralph Schultz, "Delivering Technology through Collaboration at the University of Virginia," *College & University Media Review* 5, no. 2 (Spring 1999): 49-67.
21. Ibid.
22. "Video and Copyright," *LARC (Library and Research Center) Fact Sheet Number 7* (URL http://www.ala.org/library/fact7.html).
23. Public Law 105-304 [H.R. 2281], October 28, 1998. "Digital Millennium Copyright Act," United States Public Laws, 105th Congress – 2nd Session.

CHAPTER TWELVE

ARCHIVES AND THE INTERNET

Sandra Roff and Anthony M. Cucchiara

When thinking of archives, what usually comes to mind is antiquated documents that are housed in specially designed facilities, off-limits to all but the most respected and seasoned scholar. This image was not far from the truth as recently as a decade ago. However, this has changed and will continue to change with the advances in computer technology and the Internet. What once were archival collections with limited access and finding aids accessible only with a visit to the archive are now very often available via the Web and searchable using encoded archival description. This is only the beginning of the latest information revolution, and the impact on archives is astounding.

To fully understand the effect of the Internet on the archival world, it is helpful to survey the state of archives before technology was a factor, defining its traditional mission, functions, and procedures. According to Richard J. Cox, the main mission of an archive is to enable "the researcher to use archival records effectively and efficiently."[1] The cultural heritage of civilization is housed in archival repositories around the world, and it is the function of archival administrators and curators to assure their arrangement, description, and preservation. All of these functions are the precursors to what is considered by Cox and the majority of archivists around the world to be the primary function of archives—access. Historically, archival collections were available to only a few patrons, often handpicked on the basis of the importance of their research projects or the availability of funds to travel to the repository. Hampered by these limitations, important collections and projects were often neglected.

Not quite a century ago, the National Archives defined its program in an article published in *The American Historical Review*. It emphasized the importance of archives to a nation, and the preservation of its archival documents was accepted as a function of the government. There was no disputing this, and large amounts of funds were expended to purchase historical memorabilia as well as to publish historical documents. These efforts were aimed to impact the largest possible audience. However, this was not successful and Waldo Leland in his 1912 article expressed his dismay at the situation: "No government has more signally failed in the fundamental and far more imperative duty of preserving and rendering accessible to the student the first and foremost of all the sources of the nation's history, the national archives." [2] Consequently, one of the most important functions of an archive—access—was not achieved in our nation's national repository by the beginning of the 20th century.

Access is the end result of the other functions of archival management. Arrangement and description are an early step in the process of making original materials available for study. "Throughout the history of the written word, people serving in roles equivalent to our modern concept of librarians and archivists have attempted to preserve, arrange, and describe these original documents, not only to save the ideas they contain but also to keep some sense of the process of creating those ideas."[3] Finding aids serve this function, providing a guide to what the collection consists of, its provenance, how it is organized, descriptions of the relevant subjects covered, time periods represented, and key personalities. Limitations have existed to access these guides, usually available only at the archival repository or published with small distributions, and often defined by standardized subject headings. These archival functions joined that of access in changing very little over the course of history.

Archival repositories accept collections that include a variety of types of materials. It is the responsibility of the archive to maintain the documents in the best condition possible, which often requires making the items available in other formats to reduce handling and to assure the intellectual continuation of the document. To help control newspapers from yellowing, photographs from fading, or insects from invading manuscripts, special environments have been designed to house these items. The issue of preservation is of continuing importance and although there have been considerable advances over the years, the new technology has added new dimensions as well as new considerations to the subject of preservation.

The new technology first connected with archival management in the 1960s with the development of automated descriptive systems. It was not however, until the adoption of the U.S. MARC Archives and Manuscripts Control format in 1984 that the use of these systems spread throughout the archival community.[4] The implementation of shared descriptive language standards, such as MARC, for the first time unified the profession by revealing and sharing information about the intellectual content of archival holdings. As librarians had established earlier, archivists now came to describe and share information about collections in one language with standardized nomenclature. The MICRO MARC FOR INTEGRATED FORMAT developed by Michigan State University in conjunction with the Society of American Archivists is a microcomputer software program designed to manage, describe, and access information about archival holdings utilizing the US MARC INTEGRATED

FORMAT. This PC-based, stand-alone program, not only enabled archivists for the first time to cross reference holdings across their collections with keyword indexing but enabled repositories to import and export records with other systems. RLIN and OCLC that linked archives and libraries around the world, could now add archive holdings to their list of resources. Apart from the National Union List of Manuscripts, which by comparison was primitive, the MICRO MARC system afforded archives the first opportunity to share information about its collections with a wider community of researchers and scholars.

This was a beginning, but controversy existed as to the advantages of these systems and their impact on the researcher. Some archivists felt that a researcher using these automated systems now depended less on the professional archivist, the primary intermediary between the archival documents and the scholar. The knowledge of the archivist was compromised, and the researcher would be denied his or her expertise and advice.[5] These opinions of automation did not, however, consider the increased availability of information using these new systems and the positive impact it had on researchers. Keeping the archivist as the sole transmitter of information about collections was an antiquated position often taken by those intimidated by the new technology. Information could no longer be controlled and disseminated solely by the archivist. In a discussion of librarians in the digital age Martell alludes to this same concern among librarians: "We need to remake ourselves to avoid becoming obsolete. We need to create a range of services unthinkable in the twentieth century, but mandatory in the twenty-first century."[6] Education was to become of primary importance as the profession moved into the information age.

The technological developments in the late 1980s added new concerns for archivists. Digital imaging was creating a revolution for archival collections and archivists were forced to deal with the many resulting issues. "With the advent of the 'information superhighway' and increasing worldwide access to information through the Internet, archivists have not only an opportunity, but an obligation to position themselves at the forefront of these developments and meet the issues and challenges raised by the products of digital networking and hypermedia documents."[7] Crum encourages innovation and experimentation from archivists in developing new technology, and he compares the current digital evolution to the evolution of the book—both dependent on the technological advances of the period.

Archivists employed the language of the Web, HTML (Hypertext Markup Language), to disseminate information about the content of their collections. This language was used to "mark up" the text of the standard finding aids in order to provide information about holdings through the Internet. Not a purely descriptive record, via the MARC records, finding aids transferred into HTML were made widely accessible over the Internet. For the first time, researchers could locate the resources they needed through Web search engines which provided access to specific archival finding aids created by the archival repository. This enabled them to identify portions of the collections pertinent to their research from the finding aids, as if they were doing their research in the respective institution. Consequently, it has been found that those institutions that linked their finding aids to their home pages have experienced an increased number of inquiries about their collections.

As more sophisticated computer languages emerged, such as SGML Standard Generalized Markup Language, the concept of hierarchical tag types was developed to structure the information presented in the finding aid. This resulted in the creation of EAD (Encoded Archival Description). Finding aids are marked up with tags that identify the various parts and levels of the collection; the title is tagged "title," and the scope and content note is tagged "scope note," and so on. The underlying SGML encoding and the HTML display allow finding aids to be delivered over the Internet in structured parts, permitting the user to unfold and view as much of the finding aid as is needed. This EAD record permits searching for the finding aid and its varied parts by the researcher. With the standardization of the digital finding aid there is an increasing effort to introduce a service to integrate online access by finding aids called Archival Resources, developed by the Research Libraries Group.[8] This is an initial attempt to establish a searchable union list of archival finding aids, thus furthering a greater awareness and access to the rich archival collections around the world.

The earliest digital archive projects were aimed at making finding aids available through the Web. It was, however, IBM that sponsored some of the early more ambitious digital projects, selecting beautiful and valuable manuscripts made of a variety of materials such as paper, parchment or skins. To have the capability of capturing and preserving their beauty, while maintaining their integrity, was a task requiring the best scanning, image processing, and display technology available at the time. Beginning in 1985, sponsored by the Spanish Ministry of Culture, IBM Spain, and the Ramon Areces Foundation, El Archivo General de Indias created a digital library. It is a collection of 86 million pages, which is the most complete account of the Spanish administration in the Americas, from Columbus until the close of the 19th century. It became available to the public on the Web in 1992, for the 500th anniversary of Columbus' discovery and already included approximately 9 million digital image pages, plus finding aids. This was a multifaceted project which included automating the administrative tasks, creating more than 400,000 digital descriptions, scanning the original documents, and creating software for searching, displaying, and printing.[9]

Another IBM initiative was a project to digitize the manuscripts housed in the Vatican Library. Manuscripts included early copies of works by Aristotle, Dante, Homer, and others. Access was limited to about 2,000 scholars a year—those who could incur the expense of a visit to the Vatican. The Internet would revolutionize the availability of these archival holdings for researchers around the world. The project was closely monitored by a team of scholars who helped select what was to be scanned for the Internet and defined the mission. "The committee specified that the digital library system should provide users access to catalog information describing Vatican Library contents, to high-quality image sets of entire manuscripts, to Internet delivery of this information, to representation in widely used data formats for access from diverse hardware and software platforms, and to information-finding assistance for humanities scholars with modest computer literacy."[10] This new technology brought new concerns for archivists and consequently the development of innovative solutions. They needed to devise methods of capturing the images without damaging them and protecting the materials from unauthorized reproduction. The former was accomplished by developing a protective scanning environment that avoided ultraviolet light damage and also used an easel to reduce the handling of the documents. For the latter, the Vatican Library developed hard–to-remove visible watermarks to discourage plagiarism.[11]

Archivists around the world embraced the need to digitize collections. The cost of this process meant that libraries and archives would need to seek funding sources. In the United States, a public and private partnership was formed to support a National Digital Library. The Library of Congress with the support of the U.S. Congress, the Executive Branch, and business and philanthropic leaders provided in excess of $60 million during the period 1996 to 2000 to make the National Digital Library a reality. American Memory is the online product compiled by the Library of Congress National Digital Library Program. It includes primary sources such as documents, photographs, movies and sound recordings pertaining to the history and culture of the United States. Through this project over 1 million items to date are available over the Internet to teachers, students and the public, and the digitization of more collections is planned for the future.[12]

Ameritech is a charter sponsor of the National Digital Library and since 1996 has sponsored a competition to enable academic libraries, museums, historical societies and archives to digitize their collections. Among the winners of the 1998/1999 competition was the Lee Library at Brigham Young University, Michigan State University with Central Michigan University, Mystic Seaport Museum, and the Bancroft Library at the University of California, Berkeley. Each of these institutions had distinctive archival holdings, which complemented an already existing American Memory collection. Brigham Young University joined forces with the Utah Academic Library Consortium and the Utah State Historical Society in a project called "Pioneer Trails: Overland to Utah and the Pacific, 1847-1869." It aimed to digitize 59 diaries of pioneers moving west between 1847 and 1869, 16 maps, 75 photographs and illustrations, and parts of five immigrant guides.[13] Michigan State University with Central Michigan University won the grant competition for "Shaping the Values of Youth: A Nineteenth Century American Sunday School Book Collection." The libraries involved housed the Russel B. Nye Popular Culture Collection and they selected 121 Sunday school books published between 1815 and 1865 by the American Tract Society, the American Sunday School Union and other religious publishers to add to the American Memory project.[14] The Mystic Seaport Museum, Inc. selected 7,500 archival items to digitize.

"Maritime Westward Expansion" consisted of both published and unpublished documents spanning the period from the mid-to-late 19th century. Included are logbooks, diaries, letters, business papers, images, imprints, ephemera, maps, and charts.[15] The Bancroft Library at the University of California at Berkeley, with the California Historical Society, planned "Chinese in California, 1850-1920." The number of primary documents involved is staggering, with 12,500 items documenting Chinese immigration to California and the West.[16]

This sampling of archival projects exemplifies the enormous impact that digitization can have on all of the functions of archives. Timothy Hoyer, head of technical services at the Bancroft Library of the University of California at Berkeley, was quoted in the *San Diego Union-Tribune* as saying: "It really is going to change the whole organization of knowledge."[17] The change in access is inevitably the most dramatic. The sheer numbers are dazzling. The Library of Congress, which houses 117 million items in its archives wants to digitize 4 million of them and provide access via the Internet by 2000; the Denver Public Library wants to place 95,000 photographs online, and the 35 universities and museums in California are in the process of also producing an online archive.[18] These few examples illustrate what John Throop called the "democratization of collections."[19] What can be placed on the Web is not limited to only large universities, research institutions, or museums, but small historical collections worldwide now have an opportunity to provide Internet access to their treasures.[20]

On the website for the Digital Scriptorium project at Duke University the archivists outline the advantages of digital access. "By providing scholars with digital versions of library materials (full text, images, and bibliographic information) as well as tools to browse, search, and analyze these materials remotely via the Internet, they will be able to do their research more quickly and from a location that may be more convenient to them."[21] All documents that are made accessible through the Web are available to students of all ages as well as scholars. The excitement of using original sources for study and research is possible for everyone and the teaching implications are tremendous. Such is the case with the development of national standards for the study of history, affecting the educational experience of elementary through secondary school students. One of the guiding principles of the new standards calls for the introduction of a wide variety of historical artifacts and records to be used by students in understanding the nation's past. According to these standards: "Real historical understanding requires that students engage in historic reasoning; listen to and read historical storie; interview old-timers in their communities; analyze documents, photos, historical newspapers, and the records of the past in local museums and historical sites; and construct timelines and historical narratives of their own...these skills are also the processes of active learning."[22] Historically, such a youthful constituency would be extremely problematic for most archival collections due to the fragile nature of the materials and the lack of adequate finding aids. However, with the digitization of collections and of original source materials, as developed by the Library of Congress with its

American Memory site and the National Archives, an innovative attempt has been made to introduce primary source materials into the social studies curriculum. The "digital classroom" of the National Archives and Records Administration provides numerous primary sources and lessons and activities that teachers can incorporate into their classroom instruction. Included among their offerings are records relating to numerous historical events including the Amistad case, Zimmermann telegram, and woman's suffrage movement, and the Nineteenth Amendment. These electronic "kits" enable students to examine these documents and help evaluate them in the context of the historical period.

Although we are using 21st century technology, in actuality we might be accused of being 19th century "armchair scholars." These were educated people, content to sit at home and theorize about the world, eliminating fieldwork and other methods of active research. In defense of technology, although much work can be done from a computer terminal, the scholar now has the advantages of often viewing facsimile copies of documents through the Web. Consequently, not only is the information transmitted electronically, but the document itself comes alive. The aesthetics which make primary documents exciting is perhaps lost, but it is replaced by often enhanced, easier to read, always available digitized sources. However, Graham argues that "there is no concept of origin, in the sense of one document being the more authoritative source for another. One copy is just as good as any other identical copy, or as the original."[23]

Digitization of archival documents and artifacts has recently become the subject of an exhibit at the Smithsonian's National Museum of American History. The exhibit is called "DigiLab" and presents how the Smithsonian produces digital reproductions of two and three-dimensional objects. The museum owns 140 million items and can display only about 1% of the collection. About 20 million people visit the Smithsonian each year, but its website has in excess of 200 million visits. Consequently, the DigiLab, in addition to other digitizing projects at the Smithsonian museums, will allow researchers to use online many of its archival collections. This project was funded privately by Hewlett-Packard Company, Intel Corporation, Fuji Photo Film U.S.A. Inc., Polaroid Corporation, and other high-tech companies. "The DigiLab is the first significant enhancement to the history museum's Graphic Arts Hall in 28 years, says Stan Nelson, a museum specialist in printing arts."[24]

The arrangement and description of archival collections were already presented as one of the functions of an archive. The question is now whether electronic documents need special consideration when they are organized or described. "The standard archival methods of arrangement and description of documents and records can apply to electronic archives. There is an added advantage of keyword searching through a database that can take a researcher more quickly to the information she or he is seeking."[25] Using tools such as controlled vocabulary, keyword indexes, citation indexes, published bibliographies, and other sources is argued by Thomas Mann to be additional avenues of information on archival holdings. If these are neglected, he argues, the researcher can miss important information, which may otherwise enhance his or her research.[26] This, however, can be overcome if archivists work closely with scholars. Links can be maintained to already existing websites to provide the researcher with added information on the subject. It is also possible to scan bibliographies or citation indexes for easy access for Internet users. Many colleges and universities have successfully taken this course when considering scholarly researchers using their Internet resources. It is essential that the archivist think in the broadest possible terms when arranging and describing electronic records.

The important consideration of the physical preservation of archival collections and the Internet warrants attention. Traditionally archivists have always needed to be on guard against vandalism of valuable documents. Each time an item is retrieved for a researcher, the possibility of damage, whether intentional or not, exists. It is necessary to encourage special handling and supervision of the researcher. Archivists must ban pens, scissors or other potential enemies of archival collections from reading rooms. Obviously once a document is available through the Internet, handling of archival materials can be greatly reduced, and consequently the physical life of documents extended. Zeidberg considers measures to prevent similar damage to electronic archival materials. An offensive passage can be deleted and not detected for some time, or texts can be replaced with the censor's own views, destroying the original meaning. He mentions the possibility of "read-only" access, or the previously mentioned electronic watermarking.[27]

In addition to the preservation of the actual document on the Internet, consideration must be given to preservation of the hardware or software used to deliver the electronic sources. Changes occur so quickly in technology that the equipment used today will be obsolete in a few years. There are already examples of lost data because of the obsolescence of equipment. The 1960 census was written on the Univac I, which has been out of date for many years, and unfortunately much of the census data has been lost. Even if outdated terminals or software survive, no one will know how to use them.[28] Research is presently going on to remedy this problem, and possible solutions include "bundling electronic records," which would make the archive self-contained electronically and retrievable with the hardware of the future.[29] Another possible solution proposed by computer scientists is metadata, data about data. This means that information will have metadata attached to it which will identify the way it was created, what system it was stored on, who owns it, and what privileges the owners granted. This might mean that a program could periodically scan archives to see if they are in danger and automatically take action that might include copying the data to a new format. Cornell University has received a $2.2 million, four-year grant from the National Science Foundation, the National Endowment for the Humanities, and other agencies to develop a prototype digital library system which has built-in mechanisms to preserve documents, as well as to protect their intellectual property rights and allow for connections with other library systems around the world. This work will expand on the research already done by the Digital Library Research Group in the Cornell University Department of Computer Science.[30]

The Internet not only presents problems of preservation for the archivist to resolve, but also presents websites that attempt to offer solutions for preserving digital materials, as well as traditional collections housed in archives around the world. There are multitudes of websites now available with advice on the physical preservation of archival materials. As early as 1987 conservator Walter Henry began the Conservation DistList, it quickly drew subscribers from around the world. Participants discuss a wide variety of preservation issues ranging from standard concerns of treating mold and mildew, to preserving artifacts uncovered during an archaeological dig.[31]

Several other Internet sites are worthy of mention. The best of them include the Library of Congress Directorate which is on the Library of Congress website; Stanford University's Conservation OnLine; the Cornell University's Department of Preservation and Conservations' site; and finally the State of Library of Victoria, Australia's Preservation and Storage Division site.[32] The Library of Congress is involved with preservation issues through its Preservation Directorate, which is administered by the director for preservation. It is organized into five program areas including the binding and collections care division, the conservation division, the preservation research and testing division, the preservation reformatting division, and photo duplication services. The divisions offer information on caring for collections, announcements on fellowships in conservation, preservation awareness workshops, and frequently asked questions. The Preservation Directorate also has publications on topics such as care, handling, and storage of books; care, handling and storage of motion picture film; caring for photographic collections; emergency drying procedures for water-damaged collections; leather dressing, and so on. Of special interest is the guide to other preservation sources where there are links to organizations, institutions, and research centers.[33]

Another excellent online resource is the Conservation OnLine site. CoOl describes itself as "a project of the Preservation Department of Stanford University Libraries, [which] is a full text library of conservation information, covering a wide spectrum of topics of interest to those involved with the conservation of library, archives and museum materials."[34] The site is divided into several sections, including news, finding people, author index, conservation topics, organizations, mailing list archives and miscellaneous information. Each of the conservation topics links to a listing of selected professional sources which are available full-text. Landmark articles and reports are included, providing patrons with authoritative sources of information available instantly.

Cornell University also has a preservation and conservation website which is especially good for informing the profession about preservation programs and workshops on digital imaging. Since educating the 21st century archivist in the new technology is of primary importance, the Department of Preservation and Conservation at Cornell University is performing a needed service to the archive community.[35] Also of note is the State Library of

Victoria, Melbourne, Victoria, Australia preservation site. The Preservation and Storage Division of the library offers the viewer information on the programs of the division as well as access to fulltext conservation Information Sheets on a variety of topics. The sheets provide easy-to-understand guidelines for preservation issues such as storing newspapers, controlling insects, and dealing with mold.[36]

Mounting exhibits using archival materials is one way the public has of experiencing primary sources usually reserved for view only by research scholars. Most major archive repositories curate special exhibitions, often open to the public for a limited time. Preparing exhibits is a time-consuming task, and a limited engagement is disappointing for those who are unable to visit the archive, museum, or library while the exhibit is still showing. In addition, when deciding on exhibiting archival materials, administrators must consider security and preservation. Insurance issues might prevent a smaller repository from allowing priceless artifacts to be placed in a public area where there is little or no security. Also, preservation concerns are always paramount in importance. Exposure to light might restrict viewing time, and temperature and humidity considerations can prevent the display of artifacts in poorly controlled environments. Consequently, what actually is displayed might not be determined by the educational value of the items, but by external factors.

The educational value of archival exhibitions cannot be overestimated. Having access to an exhibit can provide pleasure as well as stimulate intellectual interests. This experience, however, is limited not only by travel issues or finite exhibit schedules, but also in many cases by the age or affiliation of the patron. Many archival libraries restrict their collections as well as their exhibits to college-age students or in some cases even graduate students. Some even add the requirement of affiliation with the particular institution. An exhibit originally designed to educate the public can in reality be extremely restrictive and not have a significant educational impact.

The digital revolution has dramatically penetrated the exhibit world, with digital images accessed online as a virtual exhibit. Many of the obstacles of access to exhibits are overcome on the Web. The online exhibit can be viewed anytime and by anyone with Internet access. Also, the problems previously discussed of security and preservation when exhibiting archival documents are removed. The original materials, after they are handled in the scanning process can then be returned to their protective environment and not exposed to environmental and security hazards. The educational advantages are numerous. Teachers can use these online exhibits without scheduling class trips to museums or libraries. Often virtual exhibits are prepared with materials linked to the site for teachers, so that they can use the exhibit to its best advantage. Bibliographies and other websites with supportive materials can make the online exhibit especially useful as an educational tool.

One of the early efforts to mount an online exhibit was in 1992, when the Library of Congress released "Revelations from the Russian Archives" on America Online, Internet, and Sovset, an international computer network. There were 20,000 visitors to this exhibit in its first month of operation, when viewers could contrast the new Russia with the old brutality of the past. Through the Library of Congress Web address, users had the opportunity to find internal records of the Soviet communist rule, which included documents from the presidential archive and the KGB. This exhibit went further than making available historical records; it held an online conference monitored by the chief archivist of the Russian Federation, Rudolph Pikhoia and librarian of Congress James H. Billington. "This is the first time any institution anywhere will offer direct electronic access to the contents of an exhibit," said James H. Billington when the exhibit first opened. "It is a dramatic example of how new information technologies enable us to offer the American people a 'library without walls.'"[37]

The March/April issue of *Museum News* had the theme "The Virtual Visitor in the Internet Century." From a museum standpoint, virtual exhibits can have the same impact for viewers to a museum site as they have for those visiting a library or archival Web address. George F. MacDonald, a long time advocate of technology in museums, has been hired by the Melborne Museum to attract visitors to the museum via the World Wide Web. "In an increasingly technology and information-rich society, he says, the museum can serve as a source of experience and learning that is accessible to all who are interested, whether they choose to walk through the doors or use a modem."[38] As in archival collections, museums have always had large databanks of information under the supervision of curators who would add documents, artifacts, and research findings to their collections. With museum holdings being placed online, museum administrators and museum boards question the value of large curatorial staffs, similar to concerns in the archival world. This article points out that often these virtual exhibits are linked to Internet sites, allowing the viewer to obtain more information. The Melbourne Museum in March 1999 began using "Ed-online," which placed tens of thousands of museum records with visuals online. In addition there are search engines that permit users to manipulate the data on the site.[39] What can be done with museum collections can also be done to make archival collections exciting and interactive when viewed on the Internet. Librarian James H. Billington, uses the term "library without walls" for praising the advantages of virtual exhibits, while George F. MacDonald, a museum administrator, designates the "museum without walls" as the mark of the future.

This chapter has made a strong case for the numerous advantages of digitization and Internet access. However, in addition to the disadvantages previously mentioned there are still other concerns for archivists. "Electronic archiving, as simultaneously godsend and curse, is plaguing and will continue to plague preservation interest groups worldwide with more questions than solutions. It also demands that archivists face serious decisions, choices, and challenges as they consider which content, which media, and which political or ideological biases will combine to constitute the historical record—a global time capsule of sorts—of yesterday and today."[40] Information is already considered power, and governments as well as the media are realizing that what is preserved in our archives and digitized can color our historical memory. "More ideas, more histories, and more personal experiences from more and varied types of people have a chance, if not a right, to be heard."[41] Arguments for or against selecting items for digitization also touch upon the issue of evolving research interests. Research needs are unpredictable, and subjects for attention by scholars are constantly changing.[42] The archivist of the 21st century will take on the role of partner to the scholarly community. Joint decisions will be made to prioritize the importance of digital projects. Adrian Berry in his book, *The Next 500 Years: Life in the Coming Millenium,* predicts "the death of history." He considers diaries and manuscript correspondence the most important sources to tell the real history while political speeches he feels reveal very little about the speaker.[43]

To make any digital project viable the most necessary element is funding sources. This means that archives worldwide need to take a good look at their holdings and make major decisions about what should be digitized and what should not. This is often a time-consuming process which involves making certain that there are adequate finding aids to collections so that justification can be made to Boards of Trustees, administrators, and funding agencies as to the importance of selected collections. As Hamid pointed out, there are political implications of what is preserved through digitization, and archivists need to take a strong stand when making decisions. Finding funding sources and writing grants involve matching projects to funding agencies, doing the research to write the grant, meeting guidelines and deadlines, and being persistent. Smaller institutions can be at a disadvantage in this process because often there are fewer staff members and the time to devote to these efforts can be minimal. However, there are an increasing number of foundations both public and private that are interested in the possibilities of Internet access and its educational implications. It is important that archivists become aggressive in their search for funds and that they explore the many options available.

Archivists face the issue of whether to preserve the paper copy if the digital version is available. Institutions are cost-conscious and administrators and Boards of Trustees can argue that a digital version is enough. The professional must defend the integrity of the original document and take a stand on the need for its preservation. There is no assurance that a digitized version will remain untouched. Electronically, it can be manipulated and its historical meaning compromised. Hamid contends that the process can be likened to oral tradition where as the story passes to different people it continues to change. Over the course of time the story might bear very little likeness to the original. Some archivists and rare book librarians have offered an alternative to this dilemma. By advocating the creation of both the master and derivatives, the master would capture the entire document whereas the derivative images would be made available for online viewing by the public. The latter image could be manipulated to enhance or sharpen for greater usability, whereas the master would be held close to the original. There are companies such as Octavo, Inc. in conjunction with such major institutions as the Library of Congress and the New

York Public Library, which strive to capture the original, untouched image.[44] Although cost can become an issue, this is one area where there must not be a compromise, and the original archival document must be preserved.

The profession is also concerned with intellectual property considerations. This goes further than just copyright privileges and making sure that the home institution gets service fees. Protection is also needed for values, which are often not thought about, such as the right of readers to privacy, the right of authors to be given credit for their work, and the right of enterprises to confidentiality.[45] Visible markings and resolution adjustment are ways previously mentioned to maintain intellectual property protection. However, these areas need further exploration, and archivists need to work closely with technical staff to develop feasible solutions to the problems.

The job of an archivist is rapidly changing, and archivists must make certain that they keep abreast of the latest developments in the field. Many archival and conservation organizations provide educational tools over the Internet, whether it is conservation or preservation guidelines, workshops, or information about educational programs. Solinet is one organization that has a link via its website to Preservation Services Leaflets. They list preservation resources on the Internet on various subjects, including copyright and imaging. There are copyright and imaging and electronic information links, which summarize what each site provides.[46] The variety of sources gives the archivist a vast amount of information, and the many different organizations and institutions available on these websites help answer questions quickly and efficiently. Often state or local agencies hold workshops to train professional and technical staff in digital imaging. This is especially important for local historical societies, since their collections are deteriorating at an alarming rate. Paper used in the last quarter of the 19th century contained a high acidic content, and unless specially treated, it will fall apart. Training staff to digitize these collections can be time-consuming and costly, but when dealing with fragile and unique materials, digitization can be the last resort. Institutions must prioritize and consider the long-range impact of digitization.

The New York Public Library has made use of funds appropriated by the governor and the New York state legislature during the fiscal years 1997 and 1998 for the development of a virtual exhibit, "Travels along the Hudson." Part of the project was preparing a document which was then placed on their website called "Planning Digital Projects for Historical Collections." This has proved to be an excellent educational tool, which institutions as well as individuals can use when considering a digital project. They answer questions such as, what a digital project involves, why undertake a digital project, how to plan for digital projects, how to select collections and materials for a digital project, how to organize information and how to deliver materials effectively. In giving the background of their projects, they say: "Library staff have participated in the promulgation of standards and guidelines for this rapidly evolving technology, and borrowed from the guidelines developed elsewhere, in particular those developed in the National Digital Library Program at the Library of Congress."[47]

This document is a model of education through the Web. In the future there will certainly be many more examples of providing the information via the Web necessary for archivists to begin electronic projects.

The Internet has altered the physical concept of an archive. Library literature has already considered the implications for the traditional library setting of bricks, mortar, and shelves. The library is a highly formalized physical operation. Discontinuities of time and space have rarely been allowed to intrude on the library environment. Things are fixed in space in a linear pattern. Time is carefully structured in order to optimize the use of the library's resources. Library and unit hours and a wide array of policies and procedures impose limits on the user. Some of these limits will be irrelevant in cyberspace; remote users can access the Internet 24 hours a day.[48] Irrelevant, too, is the consideration of time and space to an archive and its constituency. Perhaps the very concept of a face-to-face archival interview with an archivist will become an interchange with a "distant archivist." Providing reference and access assistance to holdings electronically could become the norm. Archivists will still be required to perform the traditional processing functions for both paper and electronic records. However, access will be in a virtual setting, eliminating the physical access barriers.

We definitely have come a long way since Waldo Leland wrote the article, "The National Archives: A Programme," in 1912. He complained that the government had failed in preserving and making accessible the national archives. Today when we explore the National Archives and Records Administration Website we see that much of the materials which were once unavailable to researchers are now digitized, or else a detailed finding aid is available which can be searched, identifying archival holdings. Leland wrote "the records of the Freedmen's Bureau, as well as much else which until within a few months has been wholly inaccessible to students."[49] Now the "Records of the Bureau of Refugees, Freedmen, and Abandoned Lands" is record group 105 and includes a detailed table of contents, an administrative history, and histories of all the offices and locations of the documents. [50] From this Web address there are links to an alphabetical list of agencies and record group numbers. The resources are available to everyone with Internet access. This is a far cry from the stipulations that Congress set forth in its Act of March 3, 1901:

> That facilities for study and research in the Government Departments, the Library of Congress, the National Museum, the Zoological Park, the Bureau of Ethnology, the Fish Commission, the Botanical Gardens, and similar institutions hereafter established, shall be afforded to scientific investigators and to duly qualified individuals, students, and graduates of institutions of learning in the several States and Territories, as well as in the District of Columbia, under such rules and restrictions as the heads of the Departments and Bureaus mentioned may prescribe.[51]

The subject of archives and the Internet is complex, and the advantages of the Internet in the areas of preservation and access are impressive. However, there are problems, some of which were addressed in this chapter, and others, which probably have not as yet even come to light. The future is exciting for the archival profession, and instead of the prediction that the Internet would put an end to history, the contrary is true. The archival materials that tell our story can be sent via the Web across the world in seconds and bring events of the past to life. There can be an integration of visual and written materials, and archives holding complementing documents can be linked together. The possibilities are astounding, and the archival profession eagerly awaits future developments.

NOTES

1. Richard J. Cox, "Researching Archival Reference as an Information Function: Observations on Needs and Opportunities," *RQ* 31, no. 3 (Spring 1992): 387.
2. Waldo Gifford Leland, "The National Archives: A Programme," *The American Historical Review* 18, no. 1 (October 1912): 1.
3. David S. Zeidberg, "The Archival View of Technology: Resources for the Scholar of the Future," *Library Trends* 47 no. 4 (Spring 1999): 796.
4. Cox, "Researching Archival Reference," 391.
5. Ibid., P. 392.
6. Charles Martell, "The Disembodied Librarian in the Digital Age," *College and Research Libraries* 61, no. 1 (January 2000): 13.
7. Laurie B. Crum, "Digital Evolution: Changing Roles and Challenges for Archivists in the Age of Global Networking," *Archival Issues* 20, no. 1 (1995): 51.
8. "RLG's Archival Resources," (URL http://www.rlg.org/arr/arrfaq.html).
9. Henry M. Gladney, Fred Mintzer et al., "Digital Access to Antiquities," *Communications of the AMC*, (April 1998): 50-51.
10. Ibid., 52.
11. Ibid., 54.
12. "American Memory,"(URL http://rs6.loc.gov/).
13. "1998-1999 Award Winners—Lee Library at Brigham Young University," (URL http://memory.loc.gov/ammem/99award/byu.html)
14. "1998-1999 Award Winners—Michigan State University," (URL http://memory.loc.gov/ammem/award/99award/msu.html).
15. "1998-1999 Award Winners—Mystic Seaport," (URL http://memory.loc.gov/ ammem/award/99award/mystic.html).
16. "1998-1999 Award Winners—Berkeley," (URL http://memory.loc.gov/ ammem /award/99award/berkeley.html).
17. Jo Thomas, "Worldwide Research Revolution: Libraries, Museums Are Putting Archives, Rare Collections Online," *The San Diego Union-Tribune* (January 5, 1999): p. 6.

18. Ibid.
19. John Throop, "Archival Treasures Readied for the Web $101,000 Grant to Help Library Consortium Display Diaries, Photos on Internet," *Peoria Journal Star* (March 1 1999):B1
20. Hillary Theyer, "Planning the Future of History: Making a Digital Historical Resource," *Computers in Libraries* (October 1, 1999): p. 16.
21. "About the Digital Scriptorium," (URL http://scriptorium.lib.duke. edu/ scriptorium/about.html).
22. "National Standards for History K-4," (URL http://www.sscnet. ucla.edu/ nchs/ usla-b.html).
23. Peter S.Graham, "New Roles for Special Collections on the Network," *College and Research Libraries* (1998): p. 234.
24. Florence Olsen, "Smithsonian's Museum of American History puts Digitization on Display," *Chronicle of Higher Education,* January 7, 2000, p. A58.
25. Zeidberg, "The Archival View of Technology," 801.
26. Thomas Mann, *Library Research Models: A Guide to Classification, Cataloguing, and Computers (*New York: Oxford University Press, 1993) as cited in Zeidberg, "The Archival View of Technology," 801.
27. Zeidberg, "The Archival View of Technology: Resources for the Scholar of the Future," 803.
28. Sarah Hamid, "Constructing a Global Time Capsule: Challenges in the Digital Preservation of Society's Cultural Memory Archive," *Information Technology and Libraries* (December 1, 1998): P. 209.
29. J. Rothenberg, "Ensuring the Longevity of Digital Information," *Scientific America* 272, no. 1. Revised presentation version, January 1998, p. 15 as cited by Zeidberg, "Archival View," 804.
30. "Cornell Receives Grant for System to Manage Digital Collections," *Information Today* (October 10, 1999), p.36.
31. Steve Fisher, "Preservation via the Internet," *Colorado Libraries* 20 (Fall 1994): 52.
32. Janet Balas, "Preservation: A Special Concern," *Computers in Libraries* 17, no. 6 (June 1997): 49.
33. "The Library of Congress Preservation," (URL http://lcweb.loc.gov/ preserv/).
34. "COOL Conservation Online: Resources for Conservation professionals," (URL http://palimpsest.stanford.edu/).
35. "Preservation at Cornell," (http://www.library.cornell.edu/preservation/).
36. "Preservation and Storage/State Library of Victoria," (URL http://www. slv. vic. gov.au/slv/conservation/).
37. Llyse J. Vernon. "The Electronic Exhibit," *Congressional Quarterly Weekly Report* (March 15, 1993): 1203.
38. "Digital Visionary: George F. MacDonald and the Melbourne Museum—the World's First Museum of the Internet Century," *Museum News* 79, no.2 (March/April 2000): 35.

39. Ibid., p. 37.
40. Hamid, "Constructing a Global Time Capsule," p. 207.
41. Ibid., p. 210.
42. Henry M. Gladney, Fred Mintzer, Fabio Schiattarella, Julian Bescos, and Martin Treu, "Digital Access to Antiquities," *Communications of the AMC* 41, no. 4 (April 1998): 56.
43. Hamid, "Constructing a Global Time Capsule," p. 208.
44. Roy Tennant, "The Purpose of Digital Capture: Artifact or Intellectual Content?" *Library Journal* 124, no. 9 (May 15 1999): 28.
45. Gladney et al. "Digital Access to Antiquities," p. 57.
46. "COOL—Conservation Online" (URL http://palimpsest.stanford.edu/solinet/ electres.htm).
47. "Planning Digital Projects for Historical Collections" (URL http://digital.nypl.org/brochure/nypl.htm).
48. Charles Martell. "The Diembodied Librarian in the Digital Age, Part II," *College & Research Libraries* 61, no. 1 (January 2000): 105.
49. Leland, "The National Archives," p. 4.
50. "Guide to Federal Records in the National Archives of the U.S.—Records of the Bureau of Refugees, Freedmen, and Abandoned Lands" (URL http://www.nara.gov/guide/rg105.html).
51. As quoted in Leland, "The National Archive," p. 7.

PART IV

INTERNET TRAINING IN LIBRARIES

CHAPTER THIRTEEN

INTERNET TRAINING

D. Scott Brandt

What is "Internet training"? By any other name it is information technology skill development, Web training, technology teaching, or end-user online training. Often called many things, Internet training seems to sometimes overlap with end-user searching and online instruction and other times sets itself apart by focusing heavily on software and hardware (such as File Transfer Protocol, telnet, accessing by modem, saving records to floppy, etc.). Typically, it can cover a wide range of topics including Internet history, Web browsers, email, search engines, and from finding web pages, to evaluating them, to creating them (HTML or authoring software).

A traditional definition of training states that it deals mostly with the mechanics of a tool or system and places an emphasis on measuring performance change or assessing outcomes. In business and industry, such practical and applied distinctions can be found discussed among many members of the American Society of Training Development (the leading group for training) in a variety of discussion lists at its website (www.astd.org). In education, the focus of training is on either practical and applied on-the-job training or continuing education and development. Training can be used synonymously with teaching or instruction which emphasizes when and where to use skills to eventually act like or become an expert.

A quick scan of the library-related literature reveals the term "training" was used differently depending on whether there were computers available and who was using them. Before computers, training seems to have been used primarily to distinguish on-the-job learning from formal education. In the early to mid-1980s there were several discussions in the literature about end-user and staff training related to the proliferation of computers—for the most part they involved attempts to familiarize users and staff with new, computerized versions of old tools.[1] Just before the Web began to explode (1992-1993), training was set in the context of "information technology training," which meant enhancing the expertise of the members of a profession (primarily library and information science) in using computer-based or online resources to better help and sometimes train end-users with a specific interface of a computer-based system. Other than a few articles which discussed using computers connected to networks, the earliest collection of writing on Internet training appeared in a 1994 issue of the Bulletin of the American Society for Information Science.[2]

This discussion will focus on Internet training for either staff (members of the library and information science profession) or users (of information technology systems) which emphasizes building both skills and understanding to achieve proficiency and comfort in using the system. Specifically, training will refer to building both skills and knowledge for the outcome of using the Internet to facilitate information retrieval. As part of that definition, it will emphasize that "teaching for an understanding of technologies changes the nature of training. It requires that the student push beyond the normal boundaries of merely learning narrow skills. It requires that the trainer look beyond what the tools can be used to do, to identify and demonstrate where conceptual understanding will help in anticipating problems and solving them."[3]

MENTAL MODELS OF USING TECHNOLOGY

How do people understand the Internet? Some will argue that the Internet is simply a delivery means. They suggest that the Web is merely a graphical user interface for online access to resources. This is a view which interprets the Internet as a technological converter of what was once printed material into digital material. For some, the Internet might as well be a digital reader similar to a microform viewer—a type of technology which allows one to access and read information in a format different from printed text. For them, the technology is something like a distributed electronic page reader. For some, the Internet is like a telephone answering tree—a communication to a series of choices that reveal some information. For them, the technology is similar to the telephone.

In a general studies course which the author teaches at Purdue, he asks students to fill out a survey on which question asks what their "personal view" of a computer is. Given a range of responses from "electronic file cabinet" to "communications device," students have more often chosen the response "a maze of rooms." This seems to be based partly on an interface promulgated by AOL that sections of a website are like rooms and partly on their experience in playing computer games with various levels and rooms.

A person's generalized understanding of how things work is called a mental model. For instance, having a generalized understanding of how streets are laid out, how traffic lights work, and the rules of driving allows us to get safely by car from one place to another. A mental model is both a conceptual understanding of a system—how it works and relates to other systems—and the tools by which we understand other similar systems. Our general understanding of street addresses allows us to find a house in the country, the suburbs, or downtown, even if we've never been there. A mental model is not simply knowledge but a collection of learning which has been built and strengthened by experience and helps us solve problems. A look at mental models can give us insight into what works when it comes to Internet training.

One example from teaching of a conceptual model which serves as a mental model is that atoms behave similarly to the solar system—there is a central object (the sun or electron) around which other objects orbit (planets or electrons). Another is that electricity is like flowing water.[4] In actuality, the electrons do not literally move like drops of water in a flow, but the model provides a foundation of knowledge upon which to develop principles, such as that electricity must have a complete circuit to work just like water—if there is a gap or break or leak, neither the electricity nor water will flow completely. In both of these examples, an analogy is used to convey the conceptual understanding and becomes the basis of the mental model until it is later reshaped or altered. The analogy need not be accurate (and in fact rarely is) but must be useful in that it supplies a basis of understanding to learn further and upon which to solve problem. In the latter example, pipes and valves can be used as further analogies to circuits and switches and diodes.

A specific example of a mental model related to computers and understanding the Internet might be the knowledge needed to understand how an icon works. At face value, an icon is some kind of image that starts an application or opens a folder or file when clicked. A mental model of an icon might be that it is a remote control switch. In reality it is a shortcut, a visual representation of a command that allows you to start an application from anywhere within a system. But understanding it as a remote device can help explain how it works. For instance, it can be used from a distance, and removing it does not remove the application it is used on (though you do have to find another way to start it). With such a mental model, someone should be able to understand how a URL hyperlink works. The link is simply a remote pointer to an application or folder or file or web page. A URL is a shortcut and in fact is sometimes represented as an image, like an icon. A broader mental model might be that the Internet is a like a local-area network and that URLs are like icons.

The importance of a mental model is twofold. First, conceptual understanding promotes problem solving. By having this "big picture view" of things, it is easier to see when something is wrong and to generate ideas on how to fix it or work around it. Second, research shows that giving someone a conceptual understanding prior to teaching a procedure or explaining steps enhances training. Instructions make more sense when they are placed in a larger context.[5] In the case of teaching about icons, for instance, simply training someone in the steps of making or using an icon presents a limited view of the process. However, using analogy to shape or alter a learner's mental model is more likely to make the learning deeper.

If learners can gain insight into why it works, it is likely they can better understand how it works. From the examples above, it might be useful to help users build mental models which view the Internet as similar to other networks (telephone or television) which convert information (images, voice, etc.) into signals which are subject to many of the same problems and benefits as other systems. This mental model could help demystify how pages are found, bookmarks work, and errors happen when combined with effective Internet training.

WHY INTERNET TRAINING IS NEEDED

In the March 2000 issue of American Libraries, basic information technology skills are listed as one of several "bread and butter" issues. These skills range from understanding application software programs (database management, email, etc.) to troubleshooting hardware and software problems. It is noted for libraries that fundamental computer competence relates directly to providing high-quality service. It is argued that these skills amount to technical literacy which should be looked upon as a "survival skill."[6] At this time it has become difficult to find computers which are not attached to an intranet or the Internet. It almost goes without saying that if someone is talking about computer literacy, he or she is also talking about Internet literacy.

With the successful combination of easy-to-use Web browsers, prolific Web servers, and broader bandwidth, the Internet has helped to fulfill the prophecy that we are living in the information age. The first decade of the third millennium will see that television, telephone, and other applications allow us to reach a tremendous amount of information from almost anywhere. Pick up any computer magazine from a year ago and notice how much technology continues to change. HTML is barely a decade old and has already gone through four major iterations. Web browsers are now in their fifth or sixth generation in a little over five years.

Internet training is needed for a variety of reasons, for both users and those in the information profession. Many users don't have good mental models, or they lack in-depth experience using information technology. Even for users who have a cursory understanding, technology is undergoing ongoing change, continually introducing new programs and applications or constantly updating old ones. There are multiple browser platforms (PC, Mac, Unix), multiple applications within those platforms (e.g., IE vs. Netscape), and a lack of standards among them (e.g., only IE supports ActiveX). New search engines are popping up on the Internet all the time, as tracked by Greg Notess' Search Engine (notess.com), and each has different features, interfaces, advantages and disadvantages.

Users are constantly impacted by technology. More and more people have Internet access at home. Increasingly, schools as well as colleges use the Internet both in class and to find assignments or send homework. Increasingly students have to be able to post discussion lists, download class notes, and submit homework by email. Some teachers acknowledge that they are requiring students to use the Internet, even though they lack the skills to do so effectively.[7] Researchers know that students can use trial-and-error skills learned by playing computer games to muddle their way to success, but in doing so they are not really learning how to use information technology and are likely not to learn the content of lessons.[8]

And yet, at the same time, librarians understand that because anyone can put information on the Internet, it is essential to address critical thinking processes and evaluation skills as they apply to a networked environment.[9] These higher-level skills are not new, but they are changed a little in this new arena. For instance, librarians cannot simply teach the Internet as an "add-on" resource and treat it separately from catalogs or indexes. In fact, if anything, the Internet causes us to think differently about information resources on the whole. The similarities between these three—each has a scope of information from a source, an internal structure in the way that the information is contained, and an interface for searching that information—make catalogs, indexes, and search engines all subcategories of the larger category, resources. By comparing their similarities and dissimilarities, one not only teaches how to use them but helps shape or alter mental models about information resources in general.

INTERNET TRAINING AND INFORMATION LITERACY

Sometimes a distinction is made between the kind of skills and competence needed for using a computer for information retrieval and the intellectual capabilities needed for critical thinking as part of information literacy. While some experts may argue that there are distinctions between the Internet and the Web, teaching and training, and bibliographic instruction and information literacy, others note that they are merging and becoming dependent on each other. An important way to look at it is to say that if technology supports learning, then gaining skills in using information technology to pursue critical thinking exemplifies "good practice."[10]

The distinction between Internet training and teaching technology is based on a traditional theoretical construct which says training refers to specific skills but teaching refers to building knowledge. Training people to use a tool, like a mouse or operating system, involves different levels of skills and outcomes than teaching people how to search using natural language processing or interpret relevance ranking. This is similar to the distinction between traditional bibliographic goals of instructing users on when, where, or how to navigate through the content of sources as opposed to teaching them how to apply critical thinking or evaluation. All of them require objectives and outcomes and rely on mental models and experiences, but how do they fit together?

In the past, bibliographic instruction focused more on where to get information and what to do with it once it is found and not as much on the tools themselves. But computers changed everything. Look at what happens when a print tool is computerized, such as *The Reader's Guide to Periodic Literature,* which many students are required to use in high school or early in their college careers. In the past this guide was called an index, a description of the bibliographic information which was sorted by author or title into a catalog through which one browsed. When it became computerized, the entries were hidden away in a table of data, and a computer interface for searching required users to understand a little about the technology of the computer as well as information technology of how the bibliography data are contained and manipulated by the system. The user needed to do more than just browsing, and thus needed to understand how information retrieval works and apply critical thinking to creating and revising searches as well as evaluating information.

To break this down further, we could identify areas of skills needed for overall information literacy. Though they build on one another, it would be incorrect to imply that they are levels of skills for which the preceding is a prerequisite for the next. As noted, users must know something about technology (operating system features such as moving between windows or using commands), as well as information technology (marking records and sorting them to email), information retrieval (the difference between a keyword and subject and keyword subject search) and critical thinking. Some argue that literacy is at one end of a set of skills placed along a continuum from more behavioristic (moving a mouse) to more cognitive (articulating need and selecting tools).[11] Within such a spectrum, Internet training would be somewhere in the middle.

As bibliographic instruction has developed into something which is larger than just showing people how to use resources, so too, is Internet training more than just showing people how to use the Web. Granted, sometimes a simple, step-by-step recipe will suffice when time is of the essence, but providing underlying concepts to help build or shape mental models is important. For instance, when someone clicks on a link given as a result of a search in a search engine and gets a "404 Not Found" error message, it may suffice to tell the person simply to try another link. However, provided with a rudimentary knowledge of client server actions, users can do a little problem solving if the link was important to them. If told that using the Internet is like using a phone, then they could relate the message to a busy signal and try again later. Or they could relate it to a jammed network where no calls are going through because of heavy traffic or weather. Or they could relate it to a business which has changed numbers and for which they need to find the new one. An analogy, taught as part of Internet training, would give them a mental model upon which they could further build.

In addition to the need for end-user Internet training, there is a growing movement incorporating the use of the Web as a delivery means for training and instruction. The ACRL (Association of College and Research Libraries) Internet Education Project reviews materials designed for user education, and instructional programs and materials for teaching in the networked environment and serves as a clearinghouse for these projects. In order to take advantage of the Web as a delivery medium it requires that librarians become better adept at designing online training.[12] To use the Internet effectively, designers have to know what works and how it works. They have to use tools to build learning communities. While a little more specialized than average, learning these tools requires Internet training as a prerequisite and integral part of designing and developing online.

APPROACHES TO INTERNET TRAINING

All too often, especially in academic settings, people look at two singular and different "approaches" to Internet training, focusing on either methodology of training or selection of content to be taught. In other words, they know they want to do it, or what they want to do, but they rarely connect the two into a larger process. Looking at methodology means reviewing how to train and all the aspects which that entails. Selecting content means deciding what to teach. Several ways to train exist, from lectures to demos to exercises, to online tutorials, and more. The list of what things to teach is nearly endless.

For the most part, methodologies can be broken down into a three categories: one-way versus two-way or interactive participation, hands-on versus hands-off, and in-class versus out-of-class. One-way communication can include guides, recipes, exercises, manuals, web pages and links to those pages—basically anything that is read by individuals on their own time. Two-way interaction obviously involves communication between people either face-to- face or via some medium such as phone, email, or video. Hands-on indicates that the participant will get to practice the learning to reinforce it, usually by working through some activity or exercise. In-class not only takes advantage of having an expert on-hand to answer questions and give advice, but also allows group participation and sharing of experiences. It seems that quite often people choose a methodology with which they are comfortable or experiment with something because it is new and trendy.

However, methodology is really only a piece of a larger process for creating training. As noted above, the ASTD (American Society of Training & Development) is a professional training organization which looks at training as a science. For them, training often focuses on aspects which often seem "too corporate" to noncommercial information professionals (benchmarking, accountability of performance, return on investment). Some of the tools which they use should be of interest to anyone involved in doing training, in particular, a structured approach, such as use of the ADDIE model can ensure applicability, reliability, and sustainability. Each of the letters of the model represents a series of steps which can be taken: analyzing needs, outcomes, environment; designing structure and content; developing system, objectives, tasks; implementing managing, training; evaluating reviewing, revising. The process can be fairly simple, or quite complex.[13] No matter how simple or detailed the content, a trainer should use some process to structure the training.

Analyze the "learners" (staff, clients, patrons, etc.) to find out what they want or need and what they already know. They can be surveyed formally or informally, directly or indirectly (through observation or experience). Too many trainers base what they teach on what they think might be important, or in reaction to one or two very vocal complainers. Find out what your constituents want, what their setting is like, and how they are going to use the Internet and Web. Identify their skill levels, their preferences for learning, and their availability. Be prepared to offer a variety of types of training methodologies to meet varying needs.

Based on learner analysis, design the structural blueprint for what you want to (or can) do. Identify primary areas of content—sometimes based on software ("How to use X browser") and sometimes based on function or application ("12 places to find health information"). Determine whether you will have introductory, intermediate or advanced courses. Estimate who might be doing the training and what kinds of training are needed for your constituents.

Development differs from design because it is the production phase. Using the blueprint you've designed, you need to put the training together. It starts with identifying the training objectives, which should be as specific as you can make them ("After saving several bookmarks, learner will be able to open the bookmark manager in Netscape and delete unwanted bookmarks, rename unclear ones and create a folder and move similar ones together in it"). Once objectives have been determined, handouts, exercises, and supplemental materials will follow.

Implementation includes both the training itself and any other activities involved in setting up and maintaining the training. As noted, many people jump directly into this step and bypass the others. However, in addition to doing the training, it includes things like scheduling rooms, registering people, reproducing materials, setting up computers, and even providing refreshments before or after (not during, please!). Implementation includes the trainer's presentation style (slow, humorous, reflective, etc.) as well as how she or he takes into account the participants' learning styles. Visual learners want to see diagrams and models and demonstrations; auditory learners want to hear the instructor and others and themselves articulate the learning; tactile learners, whether deductive ("tell me the rule, and I'll figure out the particulars") or inductive ("let me practice several examples so I can understand the rule"), want to try hands-on to reinforce learning.

Evaluation, while often a step that is overlooked, is an important way to review a particular class content, an instructor's methodology, and the overall program. Class content can be evaluated to ensure that what was covered meets the participants' needs. The instructor's teaching style can be reviewed to assess how the participants' needs were met—asking questions like "Was the instructor loud enough?" or "Did the instructor go slowly enough?" can help identify participants' preferences for learning. Questions about the variety or level of classes can give input to shape future courses.

All of these steps are iterative, meaning that one may go through them several times. And all of them overlap, an idea which is started at one point may be further developed at another. Take, for example, the idea of using analogy. Analogies are considered strong training and teaching devices. They work on several levels by comparing known things to unknown things, by representing concepts, by helping to build mental models, and thus helping to transfer knowledge which can later be used in problem solving. In the analysis part of designing training, it will be necessary to gain insight into users' currently held views related to technology. During the design phase, an analogy might be created--perhaps making an analogy between regular postal mail and email. During the development phase, this analogy might be drawn using pictures of a post office to represent a mail hub. During implementation, it might be decided that participants can role-play the process by having a person act as a letter which gets routed from sender through routers, to recipient. Evaluation would test to see if the analogy was successful, perhaps by posing questions to see if participants can solve problems ("What happens if you send your mail to the wrong person, but the address is correct?").

Applying this brief model to teaching the Internet points out some areas of concern for trainers. In analyzing the potential learners, be sure to find out what their setting is like and with what things they are having problems. A variable such as having a slow Internet connection (operating out of the house) should make the trainer think twice about showing sites that are graphic-intensive, require the very latest browser plug-ins, or require a specific browser to use. Inquire as to their interests and try to match examples to what will appeal to them—not everyone is interested in e-trading or pasta recipes.

Story-boarding is one way to design the blueprint for teaching the Internet. Some people literally draw squares (or use Post-it-notes) for various steps and ideas in the process, moving or rearranging them to show relationships as needed. One should always start by describing what participants should be able to do before coming to the training. As part of learner analysis, the process should start by pointing to resources for help if participants are not quite up to that level yet. It should continue on to the learning outcomes of the training. Each outcome should be broken down into separate objectives. For example, "manage browser bookmarks" might be divided into several story-board squares such as save bookmarks, locate and open bookmark manager, highlight a bookmark, and right-click to open its properties. For each one on the story-board, the trainer might jot down how this will be accomplished—what will be demonstrated (fun or serious sites), what will be practiced (save, delete, rename, move, copy), what examples will be used (a web page which has a cryptic title which could be better named), and so on.

Development will include refining objectives and materials. For example, an objective might be worded, "Having highlighted a bookmark in the bookmark manager, learner can move it between two others by dragging." These objectives could be distributed ahead of class to familiarize the learners (and if staff, their supervisors) with what they will be learning. Likewise they could be used after the class as a class test item ("How do you move a bookmark between two others?") or as survey item ("On a scale of 1 to 5, how comfortable do you feel about creating bookmark folders?") or as an evaluation item ("The objective of renaming bookmarks was met—Strongly Agree, Agree, Undecided, Disagree, Strongly Disagree"). Materials could then be produced which directly relate to the objectives. A handout might repeat the steps needed (1. Save a bookmark, 2. Open bookmark manager, 3. Highlight the bookmark, 4. Right-click, 5. Change name in the properties box) and include graphics demonstrating this. The materials could be used in class by visual learners or used after class for review.[14]

Implementation includes setup as well as training. If possible, register users—some people see registration, especially if there is even a nominal fee involved, as more of a commitment than if it is a drop-in class. Be sure to have all materials and facilities prepared, including having printed or online handout available, making computers and overhead viewing accessible (can you enlarge the font or lower resolution to make it easier to see?), making bookmarking sites accessible or creating a web page with selected links for easy access. During the training try to get the class to speak, answer questions, and share experiences. Remember to go slowly—often someone will glance down and get lost, even though the trainer has simply clicked on the OK button.

As far as content goes, two listservs of note (NETTRAIN and web4lib) repeatedly address questions regarding core areas of content. Most notably, people seem to be primarily teaching about, and interested in emailing and etiquette, using search engines and directory pages, creating web pages, customizing Web browsers, and specific applications such as indexes, and catalogs. Secondarily, some people teach how to download (can be as simple as saving images to the more complicated use of FTP) and program (JavaScript, perl, Unix script, etc.).

Above all, ask your constituents what they want, but observe and dig beneath the surface of their requests. I was surprised recently when someone who I thought was an experienced Net surfer quizzed me about how I got a page into her favorites folder. It turns out that I had started a page, and announced it, and she bookmarked it. Immediately, but unknown to her, I updated the page. When she clicked on the bookmark/favorite later that day, she was astounded to see that it had changed and later asked how I updated it on her machine. This tells me that her mental model of a bookmark/favorite is of storing a file, not storing the link to a page. But it surprised me that I had over-estimated her knowledge. Don't take anything for granted—find out.

As part of any class a trainer should be able to articulate what a participant needs to know before taking a given course. This is often called prerequisite knowledge or entry-level behaviors. By articulating the prerequisites, the trainer provides the learner with a list of things to check against (ever had learners who walked out because they "already knew all this"?) and can review these quickly at the beginning of the class as a kind of refresher.

A technology trainer tends to work more closely with the end of the spectrum that deals with computer technology and information technology. Things for which concepts may be emphasized include the importance of using right-click menu options for features and preferences; how linking works (including icons, mapped drives, shortcuts, URLs); and client-server interaction (as noted above).

Teaching email is important because it is the basis of communication over the Internet. In its simplest form it may include simply how to send and receive messages or how to send or open attachments. It may involve registering for free accounts, setting preferences for POP clients, or configuring IMAP to allow multiple access to accounts. It might include a piece on managing folders and filters and archives. It should include a section on etiquette—how to improve clarity and conciseness in an otherwise expressionless one-way communication medium. Building on email one may branch into other means for communicating online, such as chat rooms, discussion list, ICQ or AOL Instant Messenger (personal pager systems) or online video conference calling.

Teaching how to use search engines is essential because while everything one needs is not likely on the Internet (yet!), a lot of information is there, and finding it can be troublesome with the current generation of tools available. It is important to give users a conceptual understanding of how search engines work—many think they are literally going out to search the contents of each server on the Internet rather than a database of select pages and files found on the servers by a "spider" or "information robot." The emphasis on selectivity is very important because unlike indexes, they rarely provide scope notes or list how comprehensive they are. It is estimated that any given search engine cannot contact all servers and index all pages; thus there is a small amount of overlap between even the largest. And it is never emphasized that the engines index pages indiscriminately—unless humans are reviewing the pages, there is absolutely no filtering for quality (which makes critical thinking all the more important).

Teaching how to create and develop web pages and sites can involve many skills. Some people insist on first story-boarding how the site will look and work—layout, navigation, type of information, and so on. Design of pages might include attention to building pages which can be better indexed by search engines for maximum "hit rates." This includes using hidden metatags for keyword descriptors, a title which accurately reflects the content, organizing information with section headings and using well thoughtout alternative tags for naming images. Actually developing the pages could involve coding HTML tags or using authoring programs (such as FrontPage, Dreamweaver, etc.). People have strong feelings about both. Hand-coding enthusiasts argue that web pages should be developed using sparse, readable programming which conforms to the latest W3 Consortium standard, HTML 4.0. Authoring program advocates aver that outcomes are more important than what can't be seen under the surface, and sophisticated results can be accomplished easily and quickly because users transfer skills from using word processors.

THE FUTURE OF INTERNET TRAINING

When talking about trends and the future of Internet training, it is important to distinguish between training delivered on or by the Internet (CBT/WBT) and training on using the Internet. Training on using the Internet is likely to increase with the complexity and continued introduction of new software and applications. How that training is delivered is also likely to change as bandwidth increases and tools to facilitate delivery are developed.

Currently, there are a number of different variations on how to deliver training over the Internet. These include course-based tools such as WebCT, Web-based instructional CDs, step-by-step tutorials via web pages or PowerPoint slides, animated tutorials using Flash et al., manuals which can be downloaded as documents in PDF, and so on. A 1998 survey available at the ASTD site investigated the growth of information technology (IT) training. The results showed that provision of training was increasing, that almost a third of those surveyed were spending over 10% of their training budget on IT topics such as desktop applications and the Internet, and that everyone admits to keeping up with the fast pace of change in technology and systems. Increased availability, wider bandwidth within which to deliver, and the economic appeal of remote asynchronous access are opening the door for doing more online. Yet there still seems to be a lot of room for improvement.

Elliot Masie, head of the think tank Learning Center (masie.com), notes that while the pieces may be in place (infrastructure, needs assessment tools, software), there are still some barriers to making online training easy, easily accessible, and free. He notes that there are no standards (a tutorial can be anything from a web page, to a manual, to an animated program of instruction) and no national drive for experimenting and sharing results in these areas of training. Technology is in place to do some things, but not to make all learning online effortless and seamless. Society still hasn't studied online learning well enough to create new metaphors (rather than try to reapply old ones) and trainers haven't learned the skills for managing and deploying online learning. He adds that we all need to be a little more patient—streaming video has been around for a couple of years, but if it still sounds or looks bad, we shouldn't use it until it gets better. Companies as diverse as Oracle, KnowledgeSoft, Simon & Schuster, Lotus, and the Gardner Group are pulling together online delivery systems and content, but it has yet to be seen if they will make splash in the marketplace.

The variety of things to be taught as part of Internet training is bound to grow. For instance, as reference librarians experiment with email paging like ICQ (web.icq.com) and online reference using something like LivePerson (liveperson.com), more training will be needed in how to manage and manipulate the tools to use them for desired outcomes. Likewise, as more systems become connected to the Internet (from shopping, to banking, to monitoring the home), information technologies to facilitate these developments will need to be mastered. Training is also likely to be needed for personal consumer systems which are beginning to proliferate, from handheld devices (palm computers and telephones) which connect to the Internet, to customizable, scaled-down versions of Web servers or search engines.

The future looks good for Internet trainers. While technology continues to grow at a blistering pace, it is not likely that they will be replaced by robots or independent online learning assistants anytime soon. Given the large population of users, training is going to continue to be a commodity in need. If anything, the future of Internet training is that it will continue to get better. As more and more trainers apply instructional design practices to assess and analyze needs, they will be able to develop friendly and helpful systems of training, regardless if they are presented online or off-line.

Internet training will be needed until using the technology becomes second nature. Back when libraries had card catalogs, trainers didn't have to show people how to use the technology for opening a drawer or thumbing through cards because people had previous experiences doing those things (opening clothes drawers, thumbing through telephone books). Eventually, computers will become second nature for the majority of people instead of the small minority who use them only when they have to (at work) or when they can (for play). For now, professionals in the library and information business will continue to be faced with user complaints of "How can I find information if I don't know what these buttons do?" And as long as technology, especially the Internet, continues to be of an ephemeral and elusive nature, training will be needed. Imagine if you will, the following scenario:

> Trainer smiles into the camera and scans participants compiled in a grid on a monitor. "Good morning or afternoon to everyone, " she starts. "We're here to talk about using our ultra-search engine tool to search for out-of-print book collections. Go ahead and put your virtual reality glove and goggles on, be sure to put the glove on the hand you use for the mouse. Adjust the microphone. And when you're ready, view the first resource screen."

NOTES

1. Arja Riitta Haarala, "Training for Online Information: Automation, Libraries, Users And The Future," in *International Association of Technological University Libraries Conference Proceedings*, ed. Sinikka Kosiala and Nancy Fjallbrant (Goteborg, Sweden: IATUL, 1985).
2. Margret G. Lippert, "Continuing Computer Competence: A Training Program for the '90s," *Bulletin of the American Society for Information Science* 20 (1994): 18-19.
3. D. Scott Brandt, "What (How, Where, When, Why) Is Training?" *Computers in Libraries* 19 (1999): 32-34.

4. Dedre Gentner and D. R. Gentner, "Flowing Waters or Teeming Crowds: Mental Models of Electricity," in *Mental Models*, ed. D. Gentner and A. L. Stevens (Hillsdale, NJ: 1983).
5. Nancy Staggers and A. F. Norcio, "Mental Models: Concepts for Human-Computer Interaction Research," *International Journal of Man-Machine Studies* 38 (1993): 587-605.
6. Joyce Latham, "The World Online: IT Skills for the Practical Professional," *American Libraries* 31 (2000): 40-42.
7. D. Rothenberg, "How the Web Destroys the Quality of Student's Research Papers," *Chronicle of Higher Education.* August 15, 1997.
8. Sherry Turkle, "Seeing through Computers: Education in a Culture of Simulation," *The American Prospect* 31 (1997): 76-82.
9. Kari McBride and R. Dickstein, "The Web Demands Critical Reading by Students," *Chronicle of Higher Education*, March 20, 1998.
10. Avril Loveless and David Longman, "Information Literacy: Innuendo or Insight?" *Education and Information Technologies* 3 (1998): 27-40.
11. Elizabeth Dupuis, "The Information Literacy Challenge: Addressing the Changing Needs of Our Students," *Internet Reference Services Quarterly* 2 (1997): 93-111.
12. Nancy Dewald, Ann Scholz-Crane, Austin Booth, and Cynthia Levine, "Information Literacy at a Distance: Instructional Design Issues," *The Journal of Academic Librarianship* 26 (2000): 33-44.
13. For detailed models of instructional design: Walter Dick and Lou Carey, *The Systematic Design of Instruction* (HarperCollins College, 1996); Don Clark. *Big Dog's ISD Page* (June 5, 1999) (URL http://www.nwlink.com/~donclark/hrd/sat.html).
14. For other examples of Internet training development, see William D. Hollands, *Teaching the Internet to Library Staff and Users* (New York: Neal-Schuman, 1999); Tara Calishain and Jill Nystrom, *Official NetScape Guide to Internet Research* (Research Triangle Park, NC: Ventana Communications Group, 1998).

AUTHOR INDEX

SUBJECT INDEX

ABOUT THE EDITOR AND CONTRIBUTORS

Bryce Allen is Associate Professor in the School of Information Science and Learning Technologies of the University of Missouri at Columbia. His research interests focus on how individual users interact with information. He teaches in the areas of reference, managing collections and access, and research methods. His current research includes projects to customize information systems for users who are accomplishing specific information and learning tasks, and who have specific cognitive and learning abilities. He comes to Library and Information Science education from a background of twelve years of experience in public and academic libraries. He obtained his Ph.D. from the University of Western Ontario, and taught at the University of Illinois for eight years before coming to Missouri in 1996. Allen's research has resulted in more than 35 articles in LIS journals, and his book *Information Tasks* (1996) was recognized as Best Information Science Book of the Year (1996-1997) by the American Society for Information Science. He is currently the book review editor for the *Journal of Education for Library and Information Science.*

Gillian Allen received an H. B. Comm. from Lakehead University, Thunder Bay, Canada, a Master's in Library Science and in Labor Relations and a Ph.D. in Labor Relations (Human Resource Management) from University of Illinois at Urbana-Champaign. She teaches Management and Instruction at the University of Missouri School of Information Science and Learning Technologies. She has published a number of articles in the business and library science literatures.

Mathew Beacom has been a cataloger for 10 years and is currently catalog librarian for networked information resources for Yale University Library. He is a member of ALCTS CC:DA (1996-2000) and a member of the PCC Standing Committee on Automation (1999-2001) and was once chair of the LITA/ALCTS Interest Group on Technical Services Workstations (1998). Beacom is currently specific tasks he has worked on for professional committees are the ALCTS CC:DA Task Force on Harmonization of ISBD(ER) and AACR2 [1998-99] and the PCC SCA Task Group on Journals in Aggregator Databases.

D. Scott Brandt is Associate Professor of Library and Information Science at Purdue University. His Master's degree in Library and Information Science is from Indiana University (1983). As Technology Training Librarian he is responsible for the design, development and implementation of a progressive training program for a staff of 200. He has been involved with training since 1991 when he won an award for Internet training while at the MIT Libraries, where he also wrote a book *Unix and Libraries* (1991). He is an editorial reviewer for *Online Information Review*, sits on several conference program committees and currently writes a column for *Computers in Libraries*, "Techman's Techpage." Major publications include: With Hal Kirkwood, "A Web page is Not a Page." In *All That Glitters: Prospecting for Information in the Changing Library World.* Steven R. Vincent & Sue K. Norman, eds. (Stamford, CT: Jai Press Inc., 1999); "The PLACES Game: Integrating Technology Concepts." *Research Strategies*, 15, no. 4 (Sept. 1997): 287-292; and "Constructivism: Teaching for Understanding of the Internet." *Communications of the ACM* (Association for Computing Machinery) 40, no.10 (October 1997): 112-117.

Vinton G. Cerf holds a Bachelor of Science degree in Mathematics from Stanford University and Master of Science and Ph.D. degrees in Computer Science from UCLA. Cerf is senior vice president of Internet Architecture and Technology for WorldCom. Cerf's team of architects and engineers design advanced Internet frameworks for delivering a combination of data, information, voice and video services for business and consumer use. Widely known as a "Father of the Internet," Cerf is the co-designer of the TCP/IP protocols and the architecture of the Internet. In December 1997, President Clinton presented the U.S. National Medal of Technology to Cerf and his partner, Robert E. Kahn, for founding and developing the Internet. During his tenure from 1976-1982 with the U.S. Department of Defense's Advanced Research Projects Agency (DARPA), Cerf played a key role in leading the development of Internet and Internet-related data packet and security technologies. Cerf served as founding president of the Internet Society from 1992-1995 and recently completed his term as chairman of the Board. He also is chairman of the newly created Internet Societal Task Force that will focus on making the Internet accessible to everyone and analyzing international, national and local policies surrounding Internet use. In addition, Cerf is honorary chairman of the newly formed IPv6 Forum, dedicated to raising awareness and speeding introduction of the new Internet protocol. Cerf is a member of the U.S. Presidential Information Technology Advisory Committee (PITAC). Cerf is a fellow of the IEEE, ACM, and American Association for the Advancement of Science, the American Academy of Arts and Sciences, the International Engineering Consortium and the National Academy of Engineering. Cerf is a recipient of numerous awards and commendations in connection with his work on the Internet. Among them are the Marconi Fellowship, the Alexander Graham Bell Award presented by the Alexander Graham Bell Association for the Deaf, the NEC Computer and Communications Prize, the Silver Medal of the International Telecommunications Union, the IEEE Alexander Graham Bell Medal, the IEEE Koji Kobayashi Award, the ACM Software and Systems Award, the ACM SIGCOMM Award, and the Computer and Communications Industries Association Industry Legend Award. In December, 1994, People magazine identified Cerf as one of that year's "25 Most Intriguing People."

Anthony M. Cucchiara is Associate Professor, Archivist and Associate Librarian for Information Services and Distinctive Collections at Brooklyn College Library, CUNY. Since coming to Brooklyn College in 1987, he has developed a very active archival program including the design of an undergraduate archival course, an internship program and the first minor in archival management to be offered at CUNY. In addition to his teaching assignment at Brooklyn, Professor Cucchiara is a visiting professor at the School of Library and Information Science at Pratt Institute since 1996. He has held positions at the Brooklyn Historical Society, the Museum of American Immigration, Newsday, Inc., and the William Cullen Bryant Manuscript and Rare Book Collection at the Bryant Library in Roslyn, New York. Professor Cucchiara received his MLS from Pratt Institute, MBA from Long Island University and attended the Cooperstown Museum Studies Program. He has published several articles and is the co-author of *From the Free Academy to CUNY* (2000).

Arthur Downing received an MLS from Rutgers University, an MA in Linguistics from New York University, and a Ph.D. Cand. at Rutgers Univeristy. He is Professor and Chief Librarian at Baruch College of the City University of New York. He was previously an Academy Librarian and Director of Information Resources, New York Academy of Medicine and Director of Middle Atlantic Region, National Network of Libraries of Medicine, and Public Services Librarian of Kilmer Area Library of Rutgers University.

Sherry Engle is Assistant Professor and Government Documents Librarian at Ohio State University. She received an M.S.L.S. from Clarion University of Pennsylvania and an M.S. from Mankato State University. Her publications include "Reference Services and Issues in Resource Sharing via NREN," *Current Studies in Librarianship* and "The Academic Library in Higher Education: A Selective Annotated Bibliography," in Gerald McCabe and Ruth J. Person, eds. *Academic Libraries: Their Rationale and Role in American Higher Education* (Greenwood Press, 1995).

Robert E. Kahn received a B.E.E. from the City College of New York in 1960. Dr. Kahn earned M.A. and Ph.D. degrees from Princeton University in 1962 and 1964 respectively. He is Chairman, CEO and President of the Corporation for National Research Initiatives (CNRI), which he founded in 1986. In 1972 he moved to DARPA and subsequently became Director of DARPA's Information Processing Techniques Office (IPTO) for thirteen years. Dr. Kahn conceived the idea of open-architecture networking. He is a co-inventor of the TCP/IP protocols and was responsible for originating DARPA's Internet Program which he led for the first three years. Dr. Kahn also coined the term National Information Infrastructure (NII) in the mid 1980s which later became more widely known as the Information Super Highway. In his recent work, Dr. Kahn has been developing the concept of a digital object infrastructure as a key middleware component of the NII. This notion is providing a framework for interoperability of heterogeneous information systems and is being used in several applications such as the electronic copyright registration system at the Library of Congress and its National Digital Library Program. He is a co-inventor of Knowbot programs, mobile software agents in the network environment. Dr. Kahn is a member of the National Academy of Engineering and a former member of its Computer Science and Technology Board, a Fellow of the IEEE, a Fellow of AAAI, and a former member of both the Board of Regents of the National Library of Medicine and the Presidents Advisory Council on the National Information Infrastructure. He is currently a member of the President's Information Technology Advisory Committee. He is a recipient of the AFIPS Harry Goode Memorial Award, the Marconi Award, the ACM SIGCOMM Award, the President's Award from ACM, the IEEE Koji Kobayashi Computer and Communications Award, the IEEE Alexander Graham Bell Medal, the ACM Software Systems Award, the Computerworld/Smithsonian Award, the ASIS Special Award and the Public Service Award from the Computing Research Board. He was twice the recipient of the Secretary of Defense Meritorious Civilian Service Award, and most recently a recipient of the 1997 National Medal of Technology awarded by President Clinton.

Leonard Kleinrock received his BEE degree from the City College of New York in 1957, and MSEE and Ph.D. degrees from MIT in 1959 and 1963, respectively, all in Electrical Engineering. In 1997, he received an Honorary Doctor of Science degree from the City University of New York and in 2000 he received an Honorary Doctor of Science degree from the University of Massachusetts. For his Ph.D. research, he was the first to develop the mathematical theory of data networks and the underlying principles of packet switching (the technology underpinning the Internet). These principles included (i) demand access (packet switching is one example); (ii) large shared systems (a high-speed channel is one example); and (iii) distributed control (distributed routing is one example). His 1962 thesis was later published as the first book on computer networks. He has been a UCLA faculty member since 1963 where he has graduated 43 Ph.D. as well as many MS students, serving as the Chairman of the Computer Science Department from 1991-1995. He (co)founded (and was the first President of) Linkabit Corporation, the Computer Channel, and Technology Transfer Institute. Recently he founded Nomadix, Inc, a California high-tech startup that is developing advanced nomadic computing technology. Dr. Kleinrock is referred to as one of the Fathers of the Internet for his pioneering work on packet switching; in 1961 he published the first paper on the subject. His laboratory at UCLA became the first node of the Internet on September 2, 1969 and from that laboratory he supervised the first Internet message transmission on October 29, 1969. His research focus has not only been on developing the basic principles of data networks, but also on packet radio, satellite packet switching, time-shared systems (he was the first to introduce and analyze processor-sharing systems), distributed systems, gigabit networks and nomadic computing (a field he launched in the early 1990's). Dr. Kleinrock is a member of the National Academy of Engineering, a Fellow of the IEEE, an ACM Fellow and an IEC Fellow. He has published six books and well over 200 papers. Among his many honors, he is the recipient of the L.M. Ericsson Prize, the Marconi Award, the C.C.N.Y. Townsend Harris Medal, the CCNY Electrical Engineering Award, the UCLA Outstanding Teacher Award, the Lanchester Prize, the ACM SIGCOMM Award, a Guggenheim Fellowship, the Sigma Xi Monie Ferst Award, the INFORMS Presidents Award, the IEEE Communications Society Leonard G. Abraham Prize Paper Award, the IEEE ICC 1978 Prize Winning Paper Award, the IEEE Harry Goode Award and the Millennium IEEE Internet Award.

Cindy Kristof is Assistant Professor and Document Delivery Librarian at Kent State University Libraries and Media Services. She supervises interlibrary loan, campus document delivery, and periodical information services. She initiated the Libraries' electronic reserves pilot project. She has a B.A. in English from The Ohio State University and an M.L.S. from Kent State University. She has published an article for *American Entomologist* entitled "Accuracy of Reference Citations in Five Entomology Journals" and complied SPEC Kit no. 245 for the Association of Research Libraries, "Electronic Reserves Operations in ARL Libraries." An article about Kent State University's experience with the ERes system for electronic reserves is currently in press. It is a citation accuracy study of business and economics journals.

Mary Schneider Laskowski is the Assistant Undergraduate Librarian, Coordinator of Media Services and Cataloging, and Assistant Professor of Library Administration at the Undergraduate Library, University of Illinois, Urbana-Champaign. She has a Bachelor's degree in English and a Master's degree in Library and Information Science, both from the University of Illinois at Urbana-Champaign. She has also worked as an Instructional Media Specialist at the high school level. Current publications include "The impact of electronic access to government information: What users and documents specialists think," *Journal of Government Information* 27, no.2 (Spring 2000).

Barry M. Leiner is a graduate of Rensselaer Polytechnic Institute (B.E.E.E. 1967) and Stanford University (M.S.E.E. 1969, Ph.D. 1973). He is a member of Eta Kappa Nu, Tau Beta Pi, ACM, and the Internet Society and a senior member of the IEEE. He is Director of the Research Institute for Advanced Computer Science (RIACS) at NASA Ames Research Center. RIACS, an institute of the Universities Space Research Association, conducts research collaboratively with NASA scientists. Dr. Leiner has spent the last 20 years working in the area of packet switched networking technology and its applications. He has held several research management positions, including two positions at DARPA (1980-1985 and 1994-1996) where he was Assistant Director of the Information Processing Techniques and Information Technology Offices respectively. He was responsible for the area of Networked Systems, developing the information technologies required to support widely distributed operation, including management of the Internet research program.

Lewis-Guodo Liu holds an MS from the University of Illinois at Urbana-Champaign and a Ph.D. from the State University of New York at Buffalo. He is currently Associate Professor at the Newman Library of Baruch College of the City University of New York, where he teaches credit courses in business information research, provides reference service, and is responsible for collection development in finance. He authored and co-authored the following books: *Internet Resources and Services for International Finance and Investment: A Global Guide* (2001); *Global Economic Growth: Theories, Research, and Studies* (Greenwood Press, 2000); *Internet Resources and Services for International Business* (1998); and *The Internet and Library and Information Services: Issues, Trends, and Annotated Bibliography* (Greenwood Press, 1996). His articles have appeared in *Library Collections, Acquisitions, and Technical Services* and *Online Information Review: The International Journal of Digital Information Research and Use*. He is the series editor of Oryx Press's *Internet Resources and Services for International Business, Real Estates, Finance and Investment, Marketing,* and *Entrepreneurship.*

Daniel C. Lynch received undergraduate training in mathematics and philosophy from Loyola Marymount University and obtained a Master's Degree in mathematics from UCLA. He is a private investor, a founder of CyberCash, Inc. (CYCH), and currently is on its Board of Directors. He also founded Interop Company, which is now a division of Ziff Davis. As a member of the ACM and ISOC, Lynch is active in computer networking with a primary focus in promoting the spread of the Internet. Lynch is also a member of the Board of Trustees of the Santa Fe Institute, the Bionomics Institute, and CommerceNet. Dan is a private investor in a number of startup companies in the Internet arena. He formerly served as manager of the computing laboratory for the Artificial Intelligence Center at SRI, which conducts research in robotics, vision, speech understanding, automatic theorem proving and distributed databases. While at SRI he performed initial debugging of the TCP/IP protocols in conjunction with

Bolt, Beranek and Newman (BBN). Dan's latest book is *Digital Money: The New Era of Internet Commerce*.

Carolyn Mills is the biology librarian at the University of Connecticut at Storrs. Previously she was the assistant science librarian at the College of the Holy Cross in Worcester, MA, and later the medical librarian for Memorial Hospital, a teaching hospital for Brown University in Pawtucket, RI. She received a B.S. in Environmental Science from Allegheny College in Meadville, PA, and an M.S.L.I.S. from the University of Rhode Island in 1993. She has published articles in *Science & Technology Libraries, RQ, Library Journal,* and *Connecticut Libraries.*

Jonathan Nabe is Manager of the Gerstenzang Science Library at Brandeis University. He assumed this position after having served as Head of the Biology and Chemistry Libraries at SUNY at Stony Brook. He earned a B.S. in Zoology from SIU-Carbondale, and has worked as a wildlife researcher and marine biologist. He earned an M.S.L.I.S. from the University of Illinois in 1994. Recent publications include a collection development guide to evolution in Science and Technology Libraries and numerous book reviews.

Thomas E. Nisonger is Associate Professor at Indiana University's School of Library and Information Science, where he teaches collection development/collection management and revaluation of library resources and services. He has a B.A. from the College of Wooster, an MLS from the University of Pittsburgh, and a Ph.D. in political science from Columbia University. He is the author of *Collection Evaluation in Academic Libraries: A Literature Guide and Annotated Bibliography* (1992) and *Management of Serials in Libraries* (1998). He serves on the Editorial Boards of *Library Collections, Acquisitions, and Technical Services*, *Collection Building*, and *Serials Librarian.*

Jon Postel (Deceased) was the Director of ISI's Computer Networks Division. The division has 70 staff members working on about 10 projects, including the NSF sponsored Routing Arbiter, and DARPA sponsored projects in the areas of Active Networks, Middleware, Security, Distributed Systems, and High Speed Networking. He received his B.S. and M.S. in Engineering, and his Ph.D. in Computer Science from UCLA, in 1966, 1968, and 1974 respectively. Jon was a member of the ACM and the Internet Society. At UCLA he was involved in the beginnings of the ARPANET and the development of the Network Measurement Center. He worked in the areas of computer communication protocols, especially at the operating system level and the application level. His research interests included multi-machine internetwork applications, multimedia conferencing and electronic mail, very large networks, and very high speed communications. Jon was also involved in several Internet infrastructure activities including the Internet Assigned Numbers Authority, the RFC Editor, the US Domain, and the Los Nettos network (a regional network for the greater Los Angeles area).

Sandra Roff received her A.B. degree in History from Hunter College, an M.A. degree in American Folk Culture and Museum Training from the Cooperstown Graduate Program of the State University of New York at Oneonta, an M.A. degree in Folklore/American Studies from the University of Pennsylvania and an M.L.S. in Library and Information Science from Pratt Institute. She is an Associate Professor in the Library Department of Baruch College of the City University of New York and is the College Archivist and a Reference Librarian. She has curated many exhibits, using archival materials, for both public and private institutions. Her latest exhibit, co-curated with Anthony Cucchiara and Barbara Dunlap, celebrated the 150 year anniversary of the founding of the Free Academy, forerunner of the City University of New York. The exhibit traveled to many CUNY college campuses, and is now the subject of the book, *From the Free Academy to CUNY* (2000) co-authored with Anthony Cucchiara and Barbara Dunlap. She is the author of 24 articles on topics ranging from primary archival resources, genealogy, local history, women's history, and African American history.

William J. Wheeler is Coordinator of Collection Development for the Social Science Libraries & Information Services at Yale University. He holds a Ph.D. from Indiana University and an MLS from the University of Illinois where he has taught as an adjunct professor. He has written on table of contents enhancement to cataloging records, presented at ASIS and ALA on catalog access issues, and recently edited a work on subject access entitled *Saving the User's Time Through Subject Access Innovation.*